The Coventry Corpus Christi Plays

The Coventry Corpus Christi Plays

Edited by Pamela M. King
and Clifford Davidson

Early Drama, Art, and Music
Monograph Series 27

Medieval Institute Publications

WESTERN MICHIGAN UNIVERSITY

2000

ISBN: 1-58044-055-X (casebound)
ISBN: 1-58044-056-8 (paperbound)

Library of Congress Cataloging-in-Publication Data

The Coventry Corpus Christi plays / edited by Pamela M. King and Clifford Davidson.
p. cm. -- (Early drama, art, and music monograph series ; 27)
Includes bibliographical references (p.).
ISBN 1-58044-055-X (casebound : alk. paper) -- ISBN 1-58044-056-8 (pbk. : alk. paper)
1. Mysteries and miracle plays, English--England--Coventry. 2. Coventry Corpus Christi plays--History and criticism. 3. Mysteries and miracle-plays, English--History and criticism. 4. Performing arts--England--Coventry--History--To 1500. 5. Christian drama, English (Middle)--History and criticism. 6. English drama--To 1500--History and criticism. 7. Christian drama, English--England--Coventry. 8. Jesus Christ--In literature. 9. English drama--To 1500. 10. Jesus Christ--Drama. I. King, Pamela M. II. Davidson, Clifford. III. Series.

PR1261.C59 2000
822'.05120802--dc21 99-047962

Cover Illustration:
Angel Musician (c.1460); painted glass from Fotheringhay Collegiate Church.
Drawing by Marianne Cappelletti.

Cover Design by Linda K. Judy

Printed in the United States of America

Contents

Illustrations

Preface

A new edition of the Coventry plays—that is, the Shearmen and Taylors' and Weavers' plays, not the East Anglian N-Town plays, which have sometimes been (mistakenly) known as the *Ludus Coventriae*—has long been needed. Hardin Craig's Early English Text Society edition, though reissued in 1957, is essentially a work prepared early in the twentieth century and reflecting the editorial standards of that time. Our attempt here has been to provide an edition with full apparatus and as complete a survey as possible of the Coventry plays, including those for which texts no longer exist. In doing this we have been dependent on the Coventry dramatic records collected by the late Reg Ingram for Records of Early English Drama and studied by him in a number of important scholarly articles.

Editing the Weavers' pageant and fragments from the manuscripts has been facilitated by Pamela King's access to electronic scans of those manuscripts, made for the purpose of a forthcoming digital facsimile which she is preparing. The scans were made under the British Library's "Initiatives for Access" program with the permission of the Coventry Company of Broadweavers and Clothiers and the collaboration of Andrew Prescott, David French, and Joanna Lomax of the Department of Manuscripts in the British Library. We are grateful to the Company of Broadweavers and Clothiers for permission to publish these texts in the present edition.

Our survey of the Coventry plays in our introduction is in part adapted, in revised form, from a previously published monograph (Pamela King's *Coventry Mystery Plays*) and articles (Clifford Davidson's discussions of the lost Drapers' and Mercers' pageants) in *Leeds Studies in English* and *The Stage as Mirror*, the latter edited by Alan Knight; for permission to use these segments we are indebted to the Coventry Branch of the Historical Association, the School of English of the University of Leeds, and Boydell and Brewer. Joanna Dutka kindly agreed to allow us to use her transcriptions of the music of the songs accompanying the Shearmen and Taylors' pageant as the basis for Appendix III, and we must thank Jeremy Ribando for his work in setting up the musical notation and inserting the underlay in which the old spelling has been retained. Permission to use the accounts of royal entries from the Coventry Leet Book has kindly been granted by the Coventry City Record Office. Richard Beadle and the University of Leeds School of English have allowed us to use relevant passages from the York, Towneley, and Chester plays which appear in Appendix IV.

We especially need to acknowledge the Coventry City Archivist, Mr. Roger Vaughan, and his staff; Mr. R. Browne of the Department of Printed Books in the British Library; the librarians of All Souls College (Oxford), Glasgow University Library, the National Library of Wales, the Bodleian Library, the University of Michigan Libraries, Michigan State University Library, and Western Michigan University Library; the staff of the National Monuments Record; and the staff of Records of Early English Drama, especially Alexandra F. Johnston and Sally-Beth MacLean. Elizabeth Baldwin provided access to her unpublished Ph.D. thesis and also read portions of our manuscript. Additional individuals who assisted and encouraged us in various ways included, among others, Meg Twycross, Peter Meredith, Richard Rastall, Timothy Graham, Richard Beadle, Jennifer Alexander, Margaret Rogerson, Deborah McGrady, Mary Hulton, and Anne F. Sutton of the London Mercers' Company. Marianne Cappelletti provided assistance with graphics. We also acknowledge Nigel Alexander's drawing of a portion of the Coventry tapestry relevant to the discussion in our survey of the plays, and for the map of Coventry we are grateful for permission from Records of Early English Drama and the University of Toronto Press.

Support was provided for the editors by the Research Committee of St. Martin's College (Lancaster), and by Dean Elise Jorgens through the Dean's Appreciation Fund of the College of Arts and Sciences, Western Michigan University. Juleen Eichinger, production editor of Medieval Institute Publications, provided essential technical support.

Pamela M. King
Clifford Davidson

In memoriam
Reg Ingram

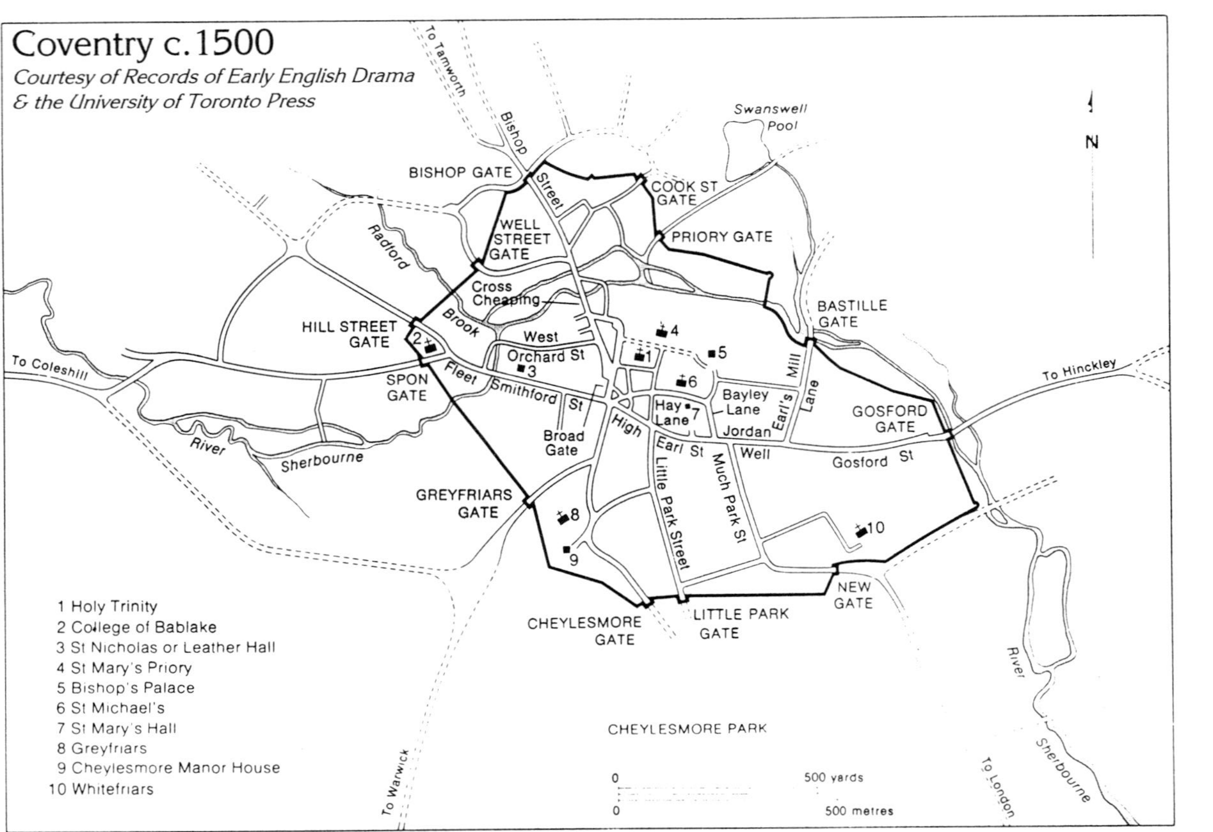
Coventry c.1500
Courtesy of Records of Early English Drama
& the University of Toronto Press
N
To Tamworth
Bishop
Street
BISHOP GATE
COOK ST GATE
Swanswell Pool
PRIORY GATE
WELL STREET GATE
Radford
Cross Cheaping
BASTILLE GATE
HILL STREET GATE
Brook
West
Orchard St
To Coleshill
SPON GATE
Fleet
Smithford
St
Mill
Lane
Bayley Lane
Earl's
Hay Lane
Jordan
High
Earl St
Well
GOSFORD GATE
To Hinckley
Gosford St
Broad Gate
River
Sherbourne
GREYFRIARS GATE
Little Park Street
Much Park St
CHEYLESMORE GATE
LITTLE PARK GATE
NEW GATE
CHEYLESMORE PARK
To Warwick
To London
River
Sherbourne
0
500 yards
0
500 metres
1 Holy Trinity
2 College of Bablake
3 St Nicholas or Leather Hall
4 St Mary's Priory
5 Bishop's Palace
6 St Michael's
7 St Mary's Hall
8 Greyfriars
9 Cheylesmore Manor House
10 Whitefriars

The Coventry Corpus Christi Plays

The Coventry mystery plays, staged by the town guilds at Corpus Christi, seem to have been well known throughout all of England. Held in conjunction with Coventry's annual Corpus Christi fair, these religious plays were presented in the streets both for local audiences and for visitors to the city. In 1656 Sir William Dugdale reported that "some old people, who in their younger years were eye-witnesses of these *Pageants*," had told him that "the yearly confluence of people to see that shew was extraordinary great, and yeilded no small advantage to this city."[1] Though Dugdale published this report more than seventy-five years after the suppression of the Coventry plays, we have no reason to doubt that the plays were believed to be a great spiritual and economic asset to the city. The Coventry *Leet Book* refers to "the goode name *and* fame" brought to the city by the plays,[2] while the will of former mayor William Pysford, who gave garments to the Tanners and Mercers in 1518 for use in their plays, affirmed that the pageants were "laudable customes of the Citie."[3]

Because of their reputation, the Coventry plays could serve as a reference point in dialogue and narrative. The pardoner who appears as one of the characters in John Heywood's *The Playe Called the Foure PP* describes meeting "the devyll that kept the gate" of hell and boasts:

> Thys devyll and I were of olde acqueyntaunce,
> For oft in the play of Corpus Cristi
> He hath played the devyll at Coventry.[4]

The Playe Called the Foure PP was published by Heywood's father-in-law, John Rastell, who also was the printer of a jestbook in 1526 that includes a rare and credible reference to the Coventry plays. In this instance an unlearned Warwickshire village priest, preaching on the articles of the Creed, advised: "Yf you beleue not me, then for a more suerte *and* suffycyent auctoryte, go your way to Couentre and there ye shall se them all played in Corpus Cristi playe."[5] Rastell, a dramatist himself, was entered by his father, who was Coventry's coroner, into the town's Corpus Christi guild in 1489, and between 1506 and 1509 he succeeded his father as coroner before resigning, after which he moved in humanist court circles in London and was married to the sister of Sir Thomas More.[6] While these citations of the Coventry plays do not themselves argue for a high quality of theatrical production, they do suggest their great popularity and their ability to attract large crowds.

The central location of Coventry in the Midlands in relation to the principal roads leading to other parts of the country was, of course, also a factor, and then too the town was only five miles from Kenilworth, ten from Warwick, and next door to Caluden Castle, the seat of the Mowbrays and Berkeleys. Unsurprisingly, therefore, the plays attracted not only large numbers of commoners but also aristocratic and royal visitors. Royal visits to the cycle were not without difficulty, however, because of the special arrangements that had to be made. When Margaret of Anjou "came p*re*uely to se the play" in 1457, the route that the pageants took through the city was arranged to pass her lodgings before being played elsewhere in the city. The unspecified delays encountered on this occasion caused the Drapers' Doomsday play not to be played "for lak of day."[7] In 1485, less than three months before he was killed at Bosworth Field, Richard III came to see the Corpus Christi plays "*and* gaue þ*e*m great co*m*mendacions,"[8] and his successor Henry VII became an honorary member of the Corpus Christi and Trinity guilds of the city. Henry came to see the plays at Corpus Christi in 1493 and likewise, according to the city annals, "gaue þ*e*m great co*m*mendacions."[9]

Unfortunately, in contrast to the great cycles of York and Chester which exist in reasonably complete manuscripts, the texts of the Coventry plays are lost except for late two plays, the Shearmen and Taylors' pageant and the Weavers' pageant. Only the latter is extant in manuscript since the Shearmen and Taylors' playscript, along with almost all other related guild records, was burned in the fire which destroyed the Birmingham Free Library in 1879. More records were lost in 1940 in the air raid which destroyed the Church of St. Michael, latterly Coventry Cathedral. For the Shearmen and Taylors' pageant, therefore, we have only the transcriptions by Thomas Sharp that were first published in 1817 and thereafter included in his *Dissertation on the Pageants or Dramatic Mysteries*

Anciently Performed at Coventry (1825). In spite of the loss of play texts and many other documents, the dramatic records, edited for Records of Early English Drama by the late R. W. Ingram in 1981, are surprisingly rich for the Coventry Corpus Christi plays, which collectively may well have been the most spectacular dramatic performances among those presented annually or at least on a regular basis in England in the fifteenth and sixteenth centuries even in periods of severe economic decline.

At the close of the fourteenth century Coventry, along with Bristol, ranked only below London in the size of its population, but by 1520 had shrunk severely both demographically and economically, as Charles Phythian-Adams has shown.[10] The precise nature of the Coventry cycle in the earlier fifteenth century cannot now be determined, though its inception antedates the *Leet Book*, which began to be kept in 1420. The central management supervising the performance of the cycle was controlled by the Leet, and the *Leet Book* contains a great many injunctions to lesser guilds which, though they lacked direct responsibility for pageant production, were ordered to provide financial assistance to plays that were brought forth by other companies. A history of redactions, at least after 1491, may be largely explained as efforts at accommodation to changing guild resources. Especially with the decline of many of the guilds responsible for individual pageants, the cycle itself could hardly be expected to remain stable in its organization or in financial support from contributory guilds. In the 1530s, no more than ten pageants seem to have been included at Coventry in contrast to the forty-seven in York's surviving text from the 1460s.[11] During the economic depression of this period, a reformist Coventry mayor, William Coton, petitioned Cromwell to request permission to abandon the Corpus Christi plays since, on account of the "decay *and* pou*er*tie" of the city, "the poore Co*mm*ene*r*s be at suche charges w*ith* ther playes *and* pagyont*es* / that thei fare the worse all the yeire after."[12] However, nothing more is heard of this petition, and the cycle would continue, probably with little diminution of its popularity, until 1579. With the coming of Protestantism the cycle was not at first suppressed, and actually may have had substantial support from those who normally opposed everything connected with the "old religion." There is the well-known story told by John Foxe in his *Acts and Monuments* of the Coventry weaver John Careles who was jailed for his Protestantism under Queen Mary but was temporarily "let out to play in the Pageant about the City w*ith* his other companions."[13]

The Coventry Corpus Christi cycle thus was an integral part of the ritual life of the city which encompassed those religious and civic activities by which the municipality defined itself.[14] Its history cannot be separated from the religious context in which it developed. The craft and trading guilds which sponsored the plays were quasi-religious confraternities, usually with special devotion to a saint, to the Virgin Mary, or to a particular episode in the life of Christ, as in the case of the Shearman and Taylors' devotion to the Epiphany.[15] These guilds maintained chapels both as independent foundations and within the parish churches, and their members sat together as a group during services. Individually they contributed generously to charitable causes, both for the relief of the poor and for the spiritual wellbeing of the people of the city. Thus, for example, in c.1465–66, a time of plague, the Drapers founded a Jesus altar in St. Michael's Church "to the end that Almighty God, appeased by the prayers of the faithful, might deliver the said city" and endowed a Mass which was to be celebrated "at the same altar every Friday."[16] As at York and other cities, parish churches before the Reformation were the recipients of wealth even in times of plague and economic decline, and they were hence richly decorated with wall paintings, painted glass, and images, most of which were swept away by Reformation iconoclasm and subsequent neglect.[17]

Moreover, the trade and craft guilds were not the only civic organizations: late medieval Coventry had religious confraternities which were social and religious in character and whose membership encompassed clergy and laity alike. Until they were dissolved at the Reformation, the local Holy Trinity and Corpus Christi guilds, which have been mentioned above, conferred status on the citizens and functioned as further instruments of social stability in addition to fulfilling the complex collective religious purposes indicated by their respective dedications.[18] The Corpus Christi guild was the less prestigious of the two, but its members, dressed in livery provided "at their own cost," had responsibility for the procession on the feast of Corpus Christi and were appointed to "carry viij. torches around the body of Christ, when it is borne through the town of Coventry"—a considerable honor.[19]

Protestant sympathies were already finding their way to Coventry, a city known for its toleration of Lollardy,[20] by the time that

Robert Croo undertook to make the copies of the Shearmen and Taylors' and Weavers' pageants in the form that survives. In order to outlast the other trappings of Roman Catholicism (including the religious confraternities) by a further half-century, the entire cycle would need to have been tailored to remove the most overtly Roman Catholic matter. There probably would have been considerable effort toward the Protestantizing of the pageants, and Croo may have had a hand in this process. The theological discussion in the prophets section in the Shearmen and Taylors' pageant (ll. 313–424)—a section bridging two segments of the action that give every appearance of having been two separate plays at some time in the past—includes some assertions that are less consistent with Rome than with Wittenberg.[21] The play of the Shearmen and Taylors and the pageant of the Weavers, which Croo also copied, must both be understood to have existed in a very different religious atmosphere after the mid-1530s than in previous times. Thus while the Coventry plays had their roots in the traditional religion of Catholic England, they had to adapt to the various shades of Protestantism—as well as to the reversion to Rome under Queen Mary that was so unpopular in Coventry—which followed in the sixteenth century.

Close attention also needs to be given to the relationship between the Coventry cycle and economic developments as well as to relevant alterations in the civic organization that supported the late medieval and early modern community. Coventry was a single product economy, the hub of a rural network, based on the manufacture of textiles, particularly the famous "Coventry blue," a thread dyed with woad which had been fixed with alum[22] and used for weaving broadcloth. Leland reported in the 1530s that "[t]he towne rose by makynge of clothe and capps, that now decayenge the glory of the city decayethe."[23] From an economic standpoint, therefore, the city was much more vulnerable than York with its greater diversity of guilds. The shifting wealth and population loss which Coventry sustained in the late fifteenth and early sixteenth centuries—changes that were exacerbated by religious upheaval—guaranteed that neither financial support for plays nor their make-up could remain static.

The guilds were essentially independent but related monopolies, all of which had a common interest in protecting themselves from the operation of drastic market forces by maintaining prices at artificially high levels when food was inexpensive in order to sustain themselves in periods of sluggish trading. This was done by regulation of the labor supply through levies, extended apprenticeship periods, and strict control of trade and manufacturing.[24] An organizational system such as this does not reduce prices at times of prolonged hardship; it limits expenditure. When the city went into economic decline, popular festivals were not canceled since they had a very important role to play in validating and sanctifying the economic activity of the city, but they were required to adapt to changed circumstances.

In spite of the impoverishment of the city, certain costs of the pageants and other festive events remained fiscally viable only because expenditures were on the whole retained locally: the members of one guild would be buying the goods of other guilds—e.g., cloth, wood, ironwork, leather, nails, etc.—and services from the other companies. Maneuvering in such changed circumstances might have involved the combining and rationalizing of pageants, and this could be the significance of the creation of a "new reygenale" for the Smiths in 1491 or the entry in the city annals reporting "New Plays at Corpus chr*ist*i tyde" in 1519.[25] It seems possible, then, that Coventry's long composite plays of the 1530s are evidence of a direct response to the hard economic conditions that have been influentially charted by Phythian-Adams.[26] The general problem from the middle of the fifteenth century was a decline in the textile industry, a significant element of which was the collapse of the supplies of woad, vital for Coventry's distinctive product. The surviving guilds which had the economic power to carry what may have been a radically remodeled cycle were those more capable, at least to a degree, of protecting themselves by diversifying and by operating cartels, illustrated by, for example, the Drapers' successful attack on the Dyers' monopoly.[27] The records relating to early sixteenth-century York illustrate similar but less extreme patterns with sponsorship there too going through a period of flux in order to continue to produce individual pageants.[28]

A significant moment in the history of the Coventry cycle is captured in an entry in the *Leet Book* on 10 April 1494:

> ffor asmoche as þe vnyte, concorde, *and* amyte of all citeez *and* com*in*alteez is p*r*incipally atteyned *and* contynued be due Ministrac*i*on of Iustice *and* pollytyk guydyng of þe same forseyng þ*at* no p*er*sone be opp*re*ssed nor put to ferther charge then he conuenyently may ber*e* and þ*at* eue*r*y p*er*sone withoute fauo*ur* be cont*r*ibutory aft*er* his substance

> *and* faculteez þ*at* he vseth to eu*er*y charge had *and* growyng for the welth *and* worship of the hole body and wher*e* so it is in þis Cite of Couentr*e* that dyu*er*s charg*es* haue be contin*ue*d tyme oute of mynde for the worship of the same as pagantes *and* such other whech haue be born be dyu*er*s Craft*es* whech craft*es* at þe begynnyng of such charg*es* wer*e* mor*e* welthy, rich, *and* moo in nomb*re* then nowe be as openly appereth for whech causez they nowe be not of powier to contin*ue* þe seid Charg*es* w*ith*out relief *and* comfort be shewed to them in þ*at* partie. . . .[29]

The crafts that had borne charges of "pagant*es and* such other" were now in need of relief and were to be assisted by the Dyers, Skinners, Fishmongers, Cappers, Corvisers, and Butchers, who were enjoined to support those guilds overburdened by their pageants. At this time Coventry's population, which also had suffered severely in the plague of 1479, was already much reduced from what it had been earlier in the century. While in 1434 its population has been estimated to have been nearly 10,000 persons, by the middle of the sixteenth century it was probably fewer than 5,000.[30]

Regrettably, evidence about Coventry's cycle in the affluent years before its decline toward the end of the fifteenth century is not detailed enough to allow us to extrapolate a performance analogous with either York's in the same period or Coventry's at the much later date of the surviving play texts. The tabulation of guilds participating in the 1445 Corpus Christi procession gives a list of the available companies which might support or contribute to the plays,[31] but the available documentation for drama is disappointing. Our access to the sixteenth-century records does not indicate how many of these guilds actively staged pageants which, as decline and even dissolution of the guilds set in, may plausibly have been absorbed into longer plays.

After 1494, the next entry in the *Leet Book* to consider is a memorandum of the next year that enjoins the Butchers to contribute to the "ov*er*charged" Whittawers because of "olde acqueyntaunce *and* amyty þ*at* of long tyme hath be" between the crafts, unsurprising in view of the symbiosis of the leather and meat trades.[32] The Skinners and Barbers were to contribute to the Cardmakers, the Tilers and Pinners to the Wrights (an old association, though usually the Pinners or Tilers had collected the funds for the play), the Cappers and Fullers to the Girdlers.[33] Then in 1506 the Tanners' ordinances report that the Corvisers had been ordered to contribute to their Corpus Christi day expenses.[34] When this alliance was confirmed in 1552, the Tanners were said to be "not of such substance as they haue bin in tymes past to mentayne the padiant."[35] The Fishmongers and some other guilds were unassigned in 1533, when the mayor's intention to appoint affiliations for them was noted, though not what they were.[36]

The documentation for Coventy's pageants throughout the whole period of written record suggests that the retrievable history of the cycle is one of rearrangement, rationalization, and probably contraction. The craft organizations which we know to have been able to maintain pageants on known subjects up to and through the catastrophic decline of the early sixteenth century all have certain economic characteristics in common that give them an advantage over others.[37] In the context of what was essentially a single-product economy, certain of the textile guilds, such as the Shearmen and Taylors and the Weavers, managed to maintain sufficient numbers to continue to mount a pageant. The Cappers' complex history is, in addition, characteristic of a specialist craft whose fortunes followed fashion and reputation, sometimes going against general economic trends but ultimately falling on hard times when wool caps lost favor with the general public. The Drapers in Coventry were a monopoly which had obtained the right to buy and sell textiles across the industry. The Mercers too, in common with the same guild elsewhere, were insulated for a time by their trade practices, which included the control of imports into the city and diversifying to include, for example, vintners, grocers, hatters, and, eventually, haberdashers and other kinds of merchandizing.[38] An exception may seem at first sight to be the Smiths, not conventionally thought of as an elite trading guild. This guild included ironmongers as well as workers in iron. Hence when the price of iron rose after 1450 the ironmongers' buying and selling activities would have become increasingly profitable, while worked iron goods tolerated commensurately high profit margins.[39] The Smiths' guild of Coventry also included goldsmiths.[40] Goldsmithing was an area of quality cartel, and in a city which had its own mint, goldsmiths acted as wholesale merchants in products which tolerated very high profit margins. In times of economic depression, the guilds noted here therefore represent those which survived both in trade and in sponsoring Corpus Christi pageants; other associations of occupations less well insulated by cartel or monopoly potential, by skill, specialty, or fashion, or by trade in high-profit luxury goods were relegated to the role of being contributors to the pageantry.

Recently Margaret Rogerson, citing the description of the Coventry Corpus Christi play as a Creed play in *A Hundred Merry Tales*,[41] has advanced an intriguing argument that it may have been organized not as a regular chronological biblical cycle similar to York and Chester but rather as a series of plays with a credal arrangement.[42] Such a structure would require that this Corpus Christi play would differ even more than previously suspected from the Corpus Christi and Whitsun plays at York and Chester,[43] but at this point her theory must remain speculation. The presence of apostles in the Corpus Christi procession[44] is not by itself indicative of a credal format of the plays, though this detail and the other suggestions which are put forth by Rogerson provide a persuasive argument for not assuming that the Corpus Christi cycle at Coventry can be understood simply by means of the evidence from other locations.

Ignoring for the moment those crafts maintaining pageant houses to store their pageant wagons but lacking record of the subject of their plays, and concentrating only on the known plays, we will see that these by themselves present a nearly coherent series from the Annunciation to Doomsday. Unless there once had been Old Testament plays at Coventry (there is no extant evidence for this, though Rogerson suggests that they not impossibly could have been present[45]), it can be argued that local resources were stretched to allow the staging of the complete narrative that had existed originally at the peak of economic prosperity. In short, what is now recognized as the Coventry cycle could plausibly be the result of an intelligent, if piecemeal, exercise in rearranging the biblical material. This is the historical context in which our reconstruction of what Coventry's mystery cycle evokes for the mid-sixteenth century—the only period for which we have enough information to attempt the exercise—must be placed.

PAGEANT ROUTE, WAGONS, AND PAGEANT HOUSES

The cycle was performed processionally in that the "pageants" (a term used in Coventry and elsewhere in England to designate both the plays and the vehicles on which they were performed[46]) were taken in sequence around the city and presented at "stations" along the route. Coventry's route (see Map) has never been indisputably established, nor has the number of stations, and, over a period which amounts to almost two centuries, both probably changed. Although ten stations are mentioned at various times, this does not mean that all the plays were played at all stations every year.[47] Perhaps no more than three performances of each pageant were normally mounted in the day, a view corroborated by accounts of expendable props such as the three worlds burned by the Drapers in their Doomsday beginning at some time after 1550,[48] presumably one at each stop.

Gosford Street was the traditional starting point for the wagons, as indicated by the request from the inhabitants there in 1494 "that þe pageant*es* ȝerely frohensfurth be sette *and* stande at þe place ther*e* of olde tyme vsed."[49] This is not to assume that plays were actually performed at this location: in York though the pageants assembled at Toft Green, the first station definitely was not there but at Holy Trinity Priory.[50] Elizabeth Baldwin has suggested that in Coventry there might have been a pattern of "request stops," which would explain inconsistencies in the records. By tabulating all of the stops in the available records, she has provided the most definitive, if inconclusive guide to the route.[51]

Baldwin argues that the wagons must have moved toward the center of the city from Gosford Street, and the junction of Much Park Street and Jordan Well is therefore a probable station. The players received refreshments at the Swan Tavern in 1534 and other years.[52] The location of this tavern is not definitely known, but one possibility is that it was in Jordan Well; however, other accounts mention ale bought at "mickelparke strete ende," and the tavern could be at the junction. Earl Street (fig. 6) is the next point for which there is an accumulation of evidence; Margaret of Anjou lodged at the grocer Richard Wood's house there in 1457, and in 1471 the Smiths paid "for ale to þe pleyers" at Wood's door.[53] Unless their refreshment stops were very frequent, it is likely that the house was at the Little Park Street end of Earl Street where Queen Elizabeth saw the Smiths' play in 1566.[54] Broad Gate is another likely location, since Prince Edward in 1474, Henry VIII in 1511, and possibly Prince Arthur in 1498 saw pageants there.[55] Thereafter there are two possible routes. Records of Margaret of Anjou's visit mention the conduit in Smithford Street, the east end of St. John Bablake Church, Bablake Gate (i.e., Spon Gate), and Cross Cheaping, while Bablake Gate and Cross Cheaping are also mentioned at

Prince Edward's visit (see Appendix II). There are, however, only irregular Corpus Christi records of stops on Smithford Street, and a more likely route would lead to Cross Cheaping, where Prince Edward in 1474 saw three prophets and the children of Israel "syngyng and castyng out whete obles *and* ffloures." Isolated references also name New Gate, Whitefriars, Greyfriars, and Cook Street Gate, which seem out of the way of any route.[56]

If the pageant route began in Gosford Street, continued to Broad Gate, turned back and crossed to Cross Cheaping, and continued as far as Bishop Street, there could have been stations in Jordan Well, Earl Street, Broad Gate, and Cross Cheaping. Further, more than one stop could technically have been possible in these locations. That the Coventry play had only three performances need not be incompatible with such a hypothesis if different guilds performed at different stations, or if they identified their stations by different names. Like everything else, arrangements probably changed over the years.

Processional production as described here of course used pageant wagons as the basic unit of staging, as in the Chester Whitsun plays and the York Corpus Christi cycle. Dugdale's *Antiquities of Warwickshire* described the Coventry wagons as "Theaters for the severall Scenes, very large and high, placed upon wheels, and drawn to all the eminent parts of the City, for the better advantage of Spectators."[57] This description is frustratingly vague, but no English illustrations of such vehicles have been found to provide more specific information about their appearance. It would appear that they were not uniform in design from wagon to wagon, since the plays required different features to accommodate their differing productions. The Drapers' Doomsday pageant, for example, would have required an upper level for heaven and a lower space to which the Judge would have been lowered by some sort of mechanical device. The righteous also needed to enter heaven somehow, while the damned must have been rounded up and forced into a hell mouth, also operated mechanically. Other pageants would not have had the same requirements, but all apparently were elaborate and impressive in design.[58]

There has been a temptation to imagine the wagon as a boxed-in stage with its long side open to the audience, as in the famous drawing by David Gee in Sharp's *Dissertation on the Pageants or Dramatic Mysteries*.[59] In spite of being the first reconstruction of a pageant wagon based on the evidence of dramatic records, Gee's drawing shows the influence of the nineteenth-century proscenium-arch stage, which necessarily introduces an anachronistic element into the way the wagons were imagined. In the absence of contemporary drawings, more recent reconstructions have tended to favor using wagons oriented end-on.[60] This has the immediate advantage of allowing the scene to be observed by an audience on three sides, like a thrust stage, and, because of its greater depth, makes the stepping of different levels of staging easier to achieve. Illustrations of Continental triumph cars, such as those shown in Denis van Alsloot's *Triumph of Isabella* or William Boonen's illustrations of the Leuven Ommegang,[61] also substantiate this orientation, and further the Corpus Christi wagons still used in the Corpus Christi procession at Valencia in Spain are oriented in this way.[62]

If the description of the Norwich Grocers' pageant is representative, the vehicles at Coventry would have involved heavy structures made of wainscot or high quality oak planks, painted, and placed on a four-wheeled "Carte."[63] An overhead covering or roof, specified at Coventry as well as Norwich, would have been useful for both acoustical reasons and as protection against the weather.[64] Meg Twycross has aptly described such wagons as "custom-built theatrical machines."[65] Though the wagons may have possessed moveable front axles to facilitate steering, as at Valencia, the usual way of moving them through the streets was by men appointed for the task. According to Sharp's and Halliwell-Phillips' transcriptions of guild records now lost, the Coventry Smiths differed in apparently having used horses to draw their wagon.[66] However, the references to "horssyng" are not necessarily unambiguous, as Ingram notes, and it is not entirely impossible that the term was merely applied to men doing the task of pulling the wagon —a task normally in other circumstances given to horses.[67] The Smiths nevertheless were closely associated with horses since they provided and attached horseshoes,[68] and they did hire a horse for Herod to ride in their pageant.[69]

Neither of the surviving Coventry pageants, however, could be performed in their entirety on a single wagon alone, since both the Shearmen and Taylors' pageant and the Weavers' play call for multiple locations of action. The stage directions offer clues. In the Shearmen and Taylors' pageant, the Magi, when they enter, speak "*in þe strete*," and Herod "*ragis in þe pagond* and *in the strete also*" (ll. 490 *s.d.*, 729 *s.d.*). But even with the use of the street for some of the action, and a given space representing more than one location, it is difficult to conceive of an arrangement whereby the Bethlehem stable, the shepherds' hillside, and Herod's court could have been all staged on a single vehicle. It seems, as we will see below, that the Coventry Shearmen and Taylors had more than merely a single wagon, and stage directions in the Weavers' pageant also suggest a complex acting area—something more than a single wagon with upper and lower playing levels.

Where we have no surviving playscripts, speculation about scenic arrangement becomes even more complicated. The Smiths' wagon had the usual wheels but in 1470 also had two "legges," most likely to compensate for the inherent instability created by a steering mechanism.[70] Cappers' records between 1543 and 1578 indicate that their wagon had—in addition to the hell mouth and windlass like the Drapers' pageant—a "forep*ar*te," a sidepart, a "skaffolde" with wheels, and a sepulcher.[71] Also, their records noted trestles and a ladder.[72] Scaffolds suggest fixed place-and-scaffold staging, but here the term must mean some kind of platform on a wagon. In this case it appears that an absolute distinction between place-and-scaffold staging and processional performance is misleading, and what was set up at each station was a moveable place-and-scaffold arrangement. Further, in 1552 the Cappers added a "Castell of emavs" scene, which would seem to indicate yet another demand on the staging requirements as the Cappers tried to absorb a *Peregrinus* play into their pageant.[73] However, in this case there is no payment for the necessary characters for the episode, so it may in fact never have been played.

The lengths and expenses to which the companies were prepared to go to house their pageant vehicles says much about the prestige value of the cycle in corporate municipal life. The Coventry records indicate that pageant wagons were designed to be dismantled and stored in pageant houses. The records of these storage buildings supply the earliest references to civic drama in the city: the Cartulary of St. Mary's Priory mentioned the Drapers' pageant house ("dom*um* p*ro* le pagent") in 1392.[74] The Whittawers were apparently involved in a land dispute over their Hill Street pageant house in 1402.[75] The records of pageant houses also help to trace guilds which produced plays but are otherwise lacking in documentation for their role in civic drama.

The Weavers' pageant house was transferred in 1434 by an indenture which tells us that it was situated in Mill Lane and was flanked by the Tailors' pageant house.[76] The first mention of the Smiths' pageant house, also located on Mill Lane, appeared in 1499 in the accounts of Cheylesmore Manor which record payments for rent and for its repair; it was situated on a plot that was at least twelve feet square.[77] An entry in the *Leet Book* for 1531 reports that the Cardmakers and Saddlers were "now but a fewe p*er*sones in nomber" and without sufficient assistance from other crafts; thus their pageant and pageant house, along with their chapel in St. Michael's Church, were to be held jointly with the more prosperous Cappers.[78] A city rental roll of 1574 makes reference to fourpence received for the rent of the Girdlers' pageant house.[79] The Mercers' pageant house, which was located on Gosford Street, first appeared in the records in 1576 when the municipal Payments Out Book reported £6 for "rep*ar*acions" to it; this wealthy guild did not own it but rather rented it from the city, which provided for more extensive work on it when required but not for minor repairs.[80] In 1590, after the suppression of the plays, the Shearmen and Taylors' deed of conveyance which transferred their pageant house to other hands indicated that it had been situated next to the pageant house of the Tilers and Coopers.[81] As will be recognized, these surviving references to pageant houses should not be thought to be at all complete. Nevertheless, examination of the pageant house records provides essential evidence of dramatic activity by specific guilds even though we are not able to ascertain the content of all the plays that were staged in the streets of Coventry.

THE PARTICIPATING GUILDS AND THEIR PAGEANTS

The Shearmen and Tailors. The subject matter of the pageant of the Shearmen and Taylors, which covers the Infancy story from the Annunciation to the killing of the Innocents, is perhaps best known for the poignant *Coventry Carol*, which was sung by the mothers of the children slain by Herod's soldiers. The play, as indicated above, is available only in the edition published by Sharp under the title *The Pageant of the Company of Sheremen and Taylors, in Coventry, as Performed by Them on the Festival of Corpus Christi* and then in the diplomatic text included in his *Dissertation on the Pageants or Dramatic Mysteries*. Sharp, as an antiquarian, appears to have been a careful copyist, and his text seems reasonably reliable. Because he also copied the Weavers' pageant for which his manuscript is extant, we can see that he is remarkably accurate when compared with other nineteenth-century antiquarians. The oddities of Croo's text, including eccentric spelling and word division, are retained by Sharp in his *Dissertation*.

Except for the deed of conveyance, noted above, by which they disposed of their pageant house to John Wilks, none of the dramatic records of the guild were transcribed by Coventry antiquarians. Dugdale reported that the company was founded in the time of King Richard II "to the honour of *Christs Nativity*."[82] The company's seal illustrated their devotion to the Epiphany—that is, the Virgin and Child, adored by the Three Kings.[83] The Shearmen and Taylors were linked with each other and with the Fullers through the religious Confraternity of St. George from the mid-fifteenth century, but by the end of the century the Fullers were contributing to the Girdlers' unidentified pageant.[84] The muster of the guilds, ordered by the Leet in 1450, shows that there were then sixty-four participating tailors and shearmen, a higher number than that recorded for any other guild at that time, but few if any of them, unlike the fifty-nine Drapers, had held civic office.[85] The pageant, surviving only because of Sharp's fortuitous copying, must therefore stand as the sole testimonial of the company's impact on the ritual life of medieval Coventry.[86]

The pageant itself is a collage of contemporary written styles. As poetry, the elements that appear to be later additions to the play are over-ornate and rather banal, but the drama nevertheless is a sound script for the theater. Shifts of tone between the solemn and the burlesque are well handled, as are shifts of pace from narrative to action to instruction and back again, while managing a giddying number of location changes. The "lude de taylars and scharmen" is quite readable, but it remains eminently playable.

The prologue, presenting the prophecy of Isaiah, which opens the play is written in the seven-line rhyme royal stanza favored for all linking and non-narrative elements. It may be conjectured that Isaiah's speech was delivered from the street while stage hands were setting up the wagon and whatever further staging elements were needed. So too the dialogue of the two prophets at the center of the play may have covered the entry of Herod's court, perhaps on a second vehicle or scaffold. Isaiah is here ultimately derived from the traditional *Ordo Prophetarum* or Prophets play that linked Old Testament and New Testament events. As the first of the known plays of the Coventry cycle, the Shearman and Taylors' play is thus appropriately introduced by a prophet, whose role here is to alert the audience to the significance of coming events in salvation history.

Thereafter, the first "scene," the Annunciation, follows St. Luke's Gospel and is written in simple quatrains which suit the intimacy and solemnity of the subject. The verse form is most likely derived from an earlier Annunciation play and illustrates the way that these pageants are made up of apparent layers of composition attributable to multiple authors who copied, re-copied, and made changes to the pageants over the years. The iconography is very familiar, and presents a speaking picture that focuses on Mary's acceptance of her role as the Mother of God. The representation of the Incarnation event imaginatively visualizes the pivotal point in the history of the world—a point which is also a crucial moment in the salvation story. In contrast to the expository prologue of Isaiah, this speaking tableau serves a mnemonic function, bringing to mind a typical devotional scene as a way of imaginatively placing viewers before the historical event.

The same affectingly simple stanza form that has been used in the Annunciation will reappear in all the momentous events of the play: the angel communicating with the shepherds, the coming of the Magi, the angel's warning to take the Child into Egypt, and the laments of the mothers whose infants are killed by Herod's soldiers. In addition, an eight-line stanza similar to that of the Chester cycle is employed for humorous and burlesque elements in the play. The same three stanza forms will be favored for equivalent material in the Weavers' pageant. The biblical scenes seem, then, to represent an earlier stratum, to which later writers apparently composed amplifications in what was felt to be a more sophisticated and modern style.[87]

More than a change of meter marks the transition from the Annunciation to Joseph's return. The conventional intervening episode of the Visitation, which introduced Mary's visit to Elizabeth, pregnant with John the Baptist, is not dramatized but is only reported in Gabriel's parting lines. Then an abrupt change in tone occurs when Joseph addresses the audience directly, as if he were the elderly cuckold with a young wife of the medieval comic fabliau tradition as in Chaucer's *Miller's Tale*. His position is highly ironic, and he is enlightened in his despair by a visiting angel. The author or reviser is by no means innovative in introducing this burlesque episode into the play: the picture he gives us of Joseph as the natural man, with whom the members of the audience must sympathize and then with whom they will be corrected, derives from apocryphal accounts of events surrounding the Nativity. Introducing ridicule into religious plays was common and accepted in the late medieval tradition since laughter was used to assert a superior spiritual vision. It was commonplace to see jesting as a source of illumination: *ridendo dicere verum.*[88] In the play, the episode of Joseph's doubts is well handled as the laughter never touches Mary herself.

A long composite play such as this has a distinct advantage with regard to the presentation of the Nativity itself. Elsewhere, as in the York cycle, the appearance to the shepherds and the Nativity of Christ must be treated as sequential actions although they are in fact simultaneous. Then too the dramatist must confront the difficulty of having the Virgin give birth on stage. In the Coventry play the focus of the action moves from Joseph settling Mary in the stable and setting out to obtain help, to the shepherds on their hillside, and back to the stable where the Infant has already been born. How the two locations were staged, and how the audience's attention was moved between them is unclear, but the composite nature of this play suggests that the members of the audience were directed by the action to look elsewhere when the central event of the play occurred, or that the area representing the stable was temporarily obscured from view.

The shepherds at Christ's Nativity are probably the best known figures in the mystery plays because of their appearance in the Wakefield Master's *Prima Pastorum* and *Secunda Pastorum.* Presented as contemporaries of the audience and wearing coarse garments appropriate to their social status,[89] they are like local men with local names and a common occupation, yet they are direct witnesses of divine revelation. Either surprised by the angelic greeting or worshipping the holy Child, they appear in painted glass, manuscript illuminations, and woodcuts,[90] where by the date of the Coventry Shearmen and Taylors' play we would expect them to possess hats, as in the *Kalender of Shepeherdes.*[91] As in all the other extant cycles and play collections, the Coventry shepherds are comic, but laughter directed at them is controlled and sympathetic. They are discovered on the hillside where one has lost the others, who creep up and give him a fright. All then complain about the weather and loss of sheep. This is not light comic relief, since it sets them up as unredeemed men in need of a comforting Savior, the Good Shepherd. Another traditional element that Croo's text employs is the shepherds' feast, a piece of comic business with a serious symbolic meaning that relates to the ritual year at Coventry —the breaking of the Advent fast at midnight on the first day of Christmas. When they have sung in joyous response to the angels' song, the shepherds go to Bethlehem to present their humble gifts to the Child. There is no consistent tradition of what these gifts are, and they vary in the various plays in which they appear, but in all cases they are everyday objects needed by their owners and charitably given. Here the second shepherd gives the baby a hat to protect him from the bad weather. Christ will later repay physical comfort with spiritual, as the teaching on the Corporal Acts of Mercy proclaims in the context of Doomsday. It was a teaching on the necessity of charity that was taken very seriously in the years leading up to the Reformation.[92]

After the shepherds have gone out of the place, two rather prolix "profettis" replace them on the scene and provide analysis of the story up to this point. This section functions to fulfill both the theatrical exigencies of this moment in the action and the playwright's apparent need to introduce explicatory material into the play. But these characters are not really prophets at all, for they are rather more teacher and pupil than mystic dignitaries. The dialogue form here borders on the catechetical. Inserting this type of material into mystery plays is not unique to Coventry, of course; the Expositor who appears in the sixteenth-century cycle from Chester likewise has the role of telling the audience what to think. Quite possibly such a character type is a sign of the intellectual climate of the times which left playwrights less willing to leave their material stand without overt explanation; thus they seem to have been less inclined than in times past to leave their meaning to visual and verbal *figurae*. At least the dramatist or reviser makes the effort to render this didactic material—on the relation between doubt and belief—dramatic by creating two characters in Socratic dialogue. But the audience is wrenched from the essentially emotional world of the star, and the scene at the stable, back into the medieval schoolroom.[93]

After the prophets' dialogue another abrupt change is brought about by the entry of Herod's messenger, who makes an extended speech in French which is a satiric attack on courtly affectations that is an invitation to the audience to engage in cat calls. The contrast with the ideals of chivalry is continued later when Herod's soldiers, sent out to kill babies, are confronted with resistance by their mothers. The general impression, however, is of the exotic, and Herod, supplied as he was in the Smiths' pageant with elaborate headwear, a painted face and robe, a scepter, and falchion, is certainly made to seem very foreign.[94] Herod, the worshipper of Mahownd rather than of Christ, is the stereotype of the angry, ranting tyrant whom Hamlet invokes in Shakespeare's play.[95] David Staines has complained that in the Coventry play Herod's behavior lacks subtlety of presentation and is more likely to have inspired laughter than any sense of menace.[96] While we must beware of imposing modern theatrical tastes and judgments on medieval characterizations, it seems that Robert Croo devised the Shearmen and Taylors' Herod according to what were by then well-established audience expectations of a virtuoso role.

But Herod may also be seen as a direct contrast to the three Kings, the Magi, who combine the pomp which Herod abuses with quiet faith. They are also associated with learning and hence become another vehicle for providing intellectual explanations of the events of which they are a part. They apply right reason and rescue the action from what might otherwise have descended into cruel farce. They fulfill a formal and processional role, and their manner of presenting their gifts is reminiscent of the scene in innumerable examples of painted glass, wall painting, alabaster carvings, and manuscript illuminations.[97] As noted above, this is precisely the scene depicted in the seal of the Shearmen and Taylors. In the practice of traditional religion, the Magi's devotion to the Virgin and Child is a model to be replicated by contemporary Christians.

The scene of the killing of the Innocents pits the boys' mothers against Herod's knights. This treatment of the bereaved mothers departs from the pattern set in the twelfth-century *Ordo Rachelis* from the *Fleury Playbook*, which movingly dramatizes Rachel lamenting for her children, and the later York play in which the laments of the mothers anticipate the Virgin's *planctus* at the base of the cross.[98] The Coventry play keeps the women's laments for their famous carol and also gives us another tonal shift into the burlesque as the women angrily set upon the murdering soldiers.

The dramatic effect very likely was affected by the dolls that apparently would have been used to represent the infants.[99] Once more, therefore, the play succumbs to popular tradition. For the modern audience the play will seem to end on a downbeat since it lacks a final glimpse of the holy family's escape to Egypt. But it must be remembered that the cycle was a continuum and the emotional unity of an individual episode not a priority.

The Weavers. Much more is known about the Weavers than about the Shearmen and Taylors. Their pageant survives in manuscript and in two earlier fragments, and theirs is the best set of documentary records overall. Though weaving may have been an activity with only moderate prestige at Coventry, this guild, in common with the Shearmen and Taylors, had the strength of numbers and furthermore was associated with a crucial process in the textile industry, which produced an expensive and highly profitable product.[100] They also had a stable work force, since weaving is a skill requiring long training and then is practiced for one's lifetime. In 1530, when the economy of Coventry was in recession, the Leet ruled that the Weavers were to relinquish their Corpus Christi pageant to the parvenu Cappers' company, but in the next year the decision was reversed. Contributions to the Weavers' pageant were to be provided from other less prosperous companies, and the Skinners and Walkers were enjoined to give them assistance. The Weavers continued to sponsor their pageant until the cycle itself ceased production.

The company's business, the protected production of high quality woolen broadcloth, was a product of fourteenth-century technological advance.[102] The sale of broadcloth was restricted to Drapery Hall, where each cloth was sealed with the civic seal, making the guild vulnerable to the cartel practices of the Drapers. In 1510, the Weavers extended their right to seal cloths to all members of their company—a move endorsed by the Leet in 1535.[103] This successful assumption of responsibility for protecting the trade in quality cloth, and also for having control of the trade in it, contributed significantly to the Weavers' ability to survive the economic depression, though because of the severe decline in the cloth trade they could hardly have maintained their former prosperity as the sixteenth century progressed.

The Weavers were not only a group of people drawn together

by coincidental economic imperatives but a true fraternity that lived together in the wards of Bishop Street, Gosford Street, Spon Street, and Jordan Well.[104] They operated as landlords of substantial property, and above all worshipped together, accepting to their number "love brothers" who did not practice the craft of weaving but who wished to ensure a respectable funeral as well as other benefits available to the members in good standing.

From the Weavers' ordinances we gain a unique insight into the basic funding mechanism for a pageant. The Master of the guild made an annual visit to the members of the fellowship to collect pageant money. In addition to the pageant money collected from the masters, he demanded 4*d* from each journeyman of the craft—an amount for which the journeyman's master was held liable. It was the responsibility of the journeymen of the guild to take the pageant wagon out of storage, to "dryve it from place to place ther as it schalbe pleyd," and to put it away again "w*ith*out ony hurte in ther defawte." For this they were to be paid 6*s* 8*d*, although in practice they never received as much. Responsibility for seeing that the annual production went ahead fell to "the masters felow," who had to pay five shillings to the craft if he failed to produce the play; he was also to be personally responsible for financing one of the rehearsals.[105]

In most years the accounts for Corpus Christi are not broken down but are presented as a simple total that fluctuates up and down. In the second accounting year (1524), expenses were £1 10*s* 8½*d*, but dropped to a low of £1 4*s* 2*d* in 1531.[106] Income dedicated to the pageant does seem to change radically when in 1530 and 1531 the Walkers begin to contribute at the rate of 10*s* per annum, lowered to 6*s* 8*d* in the following year when the Skinners' contribution of 5*s* was added. Certain expenses remain the same, such as the annual 3*s* paid to William Blackburn the minstrel for playing at Midsummer and Corpus Christi, until he began to pay 1*s* for guild membership in 1535, after which his pay was reduced to 2*s*. In 1538 the guild received 10*d* for burying Blackburn's wife.[107] Occasional expenses intervene, such as the 2*s* for repair of the pageant house window in 1531 and 5*s* to Robert Croo for making the new playbook in 1535. The next year in which the accounts are broken down is 1541, when expenses rose to £1 14*s*, though how much of this is attributable to the rewritten play is unclear since repair work on the wagon accounts for much of the increase. The following year saw a further rise, as major construction work was undertaken at the pageant house. Expenses for the year then reverted to a more normal £1 8*s* 4*d* in 1543. In spite of confusion in the ordering of the Weavers' accounts, expenditures for the play were remarkably consistent thereafter until the last performance in 1579.

In 1586, 2*s* 6*d* was "spent at Iames ileges when we met a bovt the pagone," and in the next year the Weavers received £2 when they sold their pageant wagon to John Showell, while its ironwork brought them an additional 10*s* 6*d*. The pageant house was dismantled at a cost of 2*s* 10*d* and another building erected on the site. These expenditures brought the total cost to £11 17*s* 10*d*.[108] With the sale of the pageant wagon, the Weavers did not cease to be involved in civic festive and dramatic activity, but their part in Coventry's cycle of mystery plays had drawn to a close.

There is little in these records to help us to visualize the presentation of the pageant. Beyond odd bits of ecclesiastical vestment, there is a passing reference, for instance, to Jesus' costume, in 1564, when the "payntyng of Iesus heade" is also noted.[109] The hiring of two false beards enters the accounts in 1570, perhaps rendered necessary by changing contemporary fashions in facial hair, and two angels' crowns were mended in 1577.[110] Had the inventory of the craft's goods compiled in 1547 survived, no doubt more information of this kind would have been available.

The Weavers' records have nevertheless yielded important information about who performed in the pageants and to what standard. From an early date it seems that there was competition for good actors, and it was accepted practice that actors did not necessarily or even normally act in the pageant produced by their own company. In 1444, an order of the Leet required members of the Cardmakers, Saddlers, Masons, and Painters to seek the mayor's permission to perform in any pageant other than that of their own guild, and, as Ingram has noted, the Weavers made some of those who acted in their pageant members of their company rather than utilize only the existing membership of the guild.[111] But the evidence of the Weavers' records points further to a more complex picture.

Guild records show that some performers were unpaid, others were paid but also paid membership fees to the company, and a third group received payment apparently without joining the company. All of this has led Margaret Rogerson to deduce that some of the performers could have had nothing to do with the guild but simply were brought in and hired for their services.[112] Certainly the musicians hired for the play were not guild members. Then other well-to-do citizens were also paid, but in return paid the guild membership dues for the privilege of being allowed to take roles—for example, Jesus, Anna, and Simeon's clerk, and also Joseph and Mary in the 1523 performance[113]—which allowed them to make a show of public piety. This leaves the remaining unpaid parts, in Ingram's view, as either evidence of doubling or of playing by ordinary members of the Weavers' guild. It may be, then, as Rogerson suggests, that some major roles were customarily given to paid men, quality actors and total outsiders. Thus the weaver John Careles, when he was let out of jail to play in the Corpus Christi cycle, did not necessarily play in the pageant of his own craft.[114] And Japheth Borsley, who joined the Weavers and paid to play in 1524, was a member of a family of prominent cappers with a house on the pageant route substantial enough to entertain the cast and helpers "be twene ye plays" and during rehearsals.[115] He seems a plausible candidate for someone prepared to pay for the social privilege of playing a particular type of role in the pageants.

The pageant of the Weavers, the Purification, or Presentation in the Temple, and the episode of Christ before the Doctors, survives in Croo's manuscript (CRO Acc. 11/2), written on parchment and dated 2 March 1535. The Weavers' payment to Croo for this playbook was recorded on fol. 16ʳ of the Weavers' account book for the years 1523–1634,[116] and internal evidence of the marginalia and the Weavers' accounts suggest that this version of the play was in production for more than forty years. In spite of some damage and a missing folio (following fol. 10 in the present numbering) which was lost before the nineteenth century, the playbook is in good condition.

In addition to Croo's text, there are two earlier fragments comprising two paper leaves; both were written in the same fifteenth-century hand in brown ink (CRO 11/1) and correspond to portions of the Purification segment in MS. 11/2. The fragments are unadorned, and the speakers' names are indicated in the same way as in Croo's manuscript—that is, in the right-hand margin—though without the use of colored ink. There is no evidence of any extra-textual apparatus, and it may from this be fairly safely assumed that Croo was responsible for stage directions in MS. 11/2. The pages in the fragments have been numbered 1–4 in a modern hand.

The earlier fragments, bound in modern binding in 1969 and rebound in 1987, are severely defaced and show signs that they were to be thrown away after being crumpled and used to wipe and blot ink. It would seem that they had been rendered obsolete after the new playtext had been prepared. The general wear and tear suffered by these pages would be consistent with heavy use, probably as a single working copy, an "original," from which the performers learned their lines. The fragments' functional appearance suits this designation, as does the small and easily handled page size (115 mm. x 215 mm.) and the use of paper, lighter and cheaper than parchment. Craig believed that these fragments were used by Croo in the preparation of his 1535 text of the Purification, and that, by comparing his work with the earlier texts, one might "form an idea of what Croo did." According to Craig, Croo "spoiled a great deal of the verse, mixed up the stanza forms, and used many large words; but he devoted himself mainly to homiletic passages and let the stories alone."[117] The segment concerning the Doctors may never have been included in MS. 11/1 in its current form, but may have come from an entirely different manuscript, given that it draws on material common to more than one of the other extant cycles. What is beyond doubt is that Croo was responsible for MS. 11/2; its relationship with the fragments is circumstantial.

Croo's copy is described in a colophon, written in red ink on the penultimate page of the manuscript, as "nevly translate" by him—meaning that he had performed some revisions and changes rather than serving as merely a copyist. His manuscript remained in the ownership of the Weavers' guild (latterly called the Company of Broadweavers and Clothiers) until it was placed on permanent loan to the Coventry Record Office in 1916. At the time when Sharp wrote his *Dissertation* it had not been available but was "unexpectedly" discovered only in 1832 and did not appear in print until 1836 when it was published by the Abbotsford Club in Sharp's transcription under the title *The Presentation in the Temple, A Pageant, as Originally Represented by the Corporation of Weavers in Coventry*. This title, however, was an editorial insertion since the manuscript opens with the name of the first character to speak, designated as "p*rim*u*s* p*ro*feta" in the left-hand margin in red ink. The manuscript, lacking one folio as noted above, is currently thirty-two pages in length with the pageant taking up thirty-one pages. The original collation was $A^4B^4C^2D^5E^2$, with the missing leaf removed at a later date from signature C. The evidence of the parchment and handwriting demonstrates that otherwise the quires were in order from the start.

This copy also seems to have been used as a prompt copy: the attribution of speeches to the Doctors has been altered in the second half of the play—the kind of alteration that takes place to meet the needs of individual performances—and "cantant" was inserted by a later hand in the margin of folio 16^v in reference to the songs that were added subsequently. The casual graffiti scribbled as marginalia prove that it remained in the custody of members of the guild.

The various names that appear on the flyleaves include some that are familiar from other sources for the cycle, but others are not: "William Umpton," written in heavy ink among other casual doodles on the first flyleaf; "Tho<ma>s norys," also in heavy ink, among other faint doodles, on flyleaf iv. The name Umpton appears nowhere else, but James Norres received 4*d* from the Cappers in 1550, and another "norrisse" hung pageant house windows for the Mercers in 1579.[118] On the first page of the raised paste-downs at the back of the manuscript is written "Richard pyxleye is my nam." Ingram notes that Richard Pixley was a member of the Weavers' guild "by 1591 when he paid for his man's indentures."[119] In addition on the flyleaf are written "Thomas" and "Righte Reuerente father and mother." Finally, on the last flyleaf are written "John," "William," and, much more informatively, "Allin Pyxley the day of Aprill." Alan Pixley was Master of the Weavers in 1567 and 1570.[120] Another Pixley receives notice as Master of the Weavers in Croo's colophon; there is a space left for the forename, but it is omitted. He may be Harry Pixley, who is mentioned as a Master of the guild in the relevant account book.[121] The guild accounts relating to the play in the later sixteenth century abound in persons called Pixley, and in the expenses of the play on Corpus Christi in 1574 there is one intrusion, the sum of 8*d*, paid at the funeral of a "Mistress Pixley."[122]

Throughout the text of Croo's manuscript there are further casual marks which appear to belong to the period when the book was in active use as a performance script. Particularly there are little crosses in the margins on fols. 13^r, 13^v, 14^r, 14^v, and 17^r opposite the speeches of the second Doctor. The same mark appears earlier, on fol. 5^{r}, opposite “clarecus,” and on the torn stub of fol. 10^{r}. The marks by the Doctor’s speeches may have been inserted when the sequence of Doctors’ speeches was adjusted, or they may simply have been provided to assist the person who played that part at some stage. These marginal marks are not to be confused with the series of double *t*’s or *c*’s which were inserted on fol. 3^{r}–3^{v}, apparently as paragraph markers—a practice soon abandoned, probably in view of the complicated apparatus of rhyme-linking which makes them unnecessary. There are also some marks and odd words and letters that are now illegible and of no obvious significance on fols. 6^{r}, 7^{v}, 8^{r}, 9^{r}, 14^{r}, and 14^{v}. The most interesting piece of the marginalia, however, is an interpolated stage direction written in careful secretary hand along the top of fol. 11^{r}, immediately after the missing leaf: “Jhesus in geare of scarlete ys put in.” This obviously has the status of a stage manager’s note.

The other stage directions in the Weavers’ pageant are likewise of considerable interest. Sixteen explicit directions are written in Croo’s hand. These are written in red ink, usually within boxes drawn in the same red ink. We can attribute them to Croo, who also, since he was involved in the practical aspects of production of other plays, may be expected to have had a particular creative interest in this element of the text. His stage directions, however, would have given little help to the actors in the play, though they do direct positioning and movement on the elaborate set.

Croo’s playbook, measuring 170 mm. x 275 mm., is bound in polished tanned calf, with a stamped pattern. The binding has been heavily repaired, including being restitched and given a new spine in 1969. At this time the original paste-downs were removed for repair and guarded in as flyleaves. These are made from three pages of an edition of the *Expositio hymnorum secu*n*dum vsum Saru*m. The setting of a woodcut here is identical to that in a copy printed by Richard Pynson in 1498 at All Souls College, Oxford (*STC* 16,113) except that the woodcut ought to carry the heading “Expositio hymnorum vsum Sarum.”[123]

Beyond the evidence of the playbook itself, the survival of the Weavers’ dramatic records embedded in their account book provides interesting additional information. The dramatic records from 1541–79 are quite detailed. Players are occasionally identified, including “rychard ye capp*er* borsleys man that playth ane” in the Purification and “Iohan heynnys broder that playt Ih*es*u” in 1544.[124]

In 1550 and 1551 these roles were taken by Christopher Dale and Hugh Heyns, the latter not necessarily the same member of the Heyns family since a twelve-year-old Jesus is required by the script, and Simeon's clerk was played by the weaver Harry Bowater.[125]

Moreover, the extensive use of music in the pageant is corroborated by records in the accounts of the retaining of singing men and a minstrel, who was named as John Cooper in 1543 and 1544.[126] In 1554 James Hewet, leader of the waits and described as an "organpleier" in the Council Book,[127] began his long association with the Weavers' pageant which lasted until at least 1573. He played the regals, for which he was paid 8*d*, increased to as much as 1*s* 8*d* in 1569 but later reduced to 4*d*.[128] The payments for music in the extant Weavers' records thus suggest variations between one year and another, but they nevertheless point to this element as vital to the spectacle that was presented in the pageant and probably affecting both the Purification and Doctors episodes.

The Purification or Presentation in the Temple, which has its source in Luke 2:22–40, was associated in the liturgical year with Candlemas, celebrated on 2 February and regarded as a major Marian feast before the Reformation. This episode dramatizes the answering of Simeon's prayer that he might see the Messiah before his death. Forty days after his birth, the infant Jesus is brought to the Temple for the ritual which, according to Leviticus 12:1–4, is demanded for Jewish children. There Simeon greets the Virgin and Child, and he is able to proclaim the fulfillment of the prophecy concerning Jesus' birth. As in the visual arts, Simeon will take the Child in his arms as he stands behind an altar,[129] and he will also present him to the audience like an infant who has just received baptism. A little child is specified for the role in the Weavers' accounts, which in 1553 involved payment to his mother of 4*d*,[130] an amount that remains constant thereafter.

Joseph is again presented as a burlesque character, though, as V. A. Kolve has noted, here he "is given larger independent life . . . than anywhere else in the medieval drama."[131] While the pageant account follows Luke 2:24 in describing how Joseph took two doves as an offering in the Temple, he is nevertheless presented as a crotchety old man who complains tetchily about his age and his willful young wife, and the Virgin Mary is a trifle indecorously tart with him. Yet the hunting of the doves is treated seriously enough. The more "real" Joseph becomes, the more the Virgin's marriage becomes plausible and domestic, and hence the family in which Jesus will be reared takes shape for the audience.[132] The effect is not unlike the lost wall painting in the Carpenters' Hall in London in which Joseph was depicted very much like a member of the guild at work in his shop while the Child, now a few years older, picks up chips; the domestic scene is completed with Mary seated and spinning.[133] Mystery plays may appear to the modern audience or reader to take liberties with time, as Old and New Testament time are conflated through typological figures, then collapsed with the audience's present. All the events depicted thus belong not only to a distant biblical past but also more immediately to a recurrent liturgical present whereby Christ is born every Christmas and rises from the dead every Easter. The effect when realized dramatically is to render the events of the past simultaneously marvelous and accessible.

When the Weavers' play makes its transition to the later episode in which Jesus is now twelve years of age, the way in which his earthly parents marvel at how he has grown is touching and successful. In this episode, which dramatizes the story of Christ with the Doctors in the Temple, Mary's fretting and Joseph's relieved anger acquire a topical edge when the play is put back into its original context. The performance coincided with Coventry's great Corpus Christi fair when one might imagine a number of children of visiting families provoking similar anxiety by becoming separated from their parents in the throng.

As in the case of the Shearmen and Taylors' pageant, the principal expansions are designed to explain the biblical stories; it would be tempting to date these from the sixteenth century except that the opening prophets' scene also appears in one of the fifteenth-century fragments. The Weavers' prophets, indistinguishable from those in the middle of the Shearmen and Taylors' pageant, are not listed in the Weavers' accounts, but their presence may be connected with the two beards that were rented from Harry Bennet in 1570 and 1571.[134] The second prophet's credulous questions in this case cause his companion to lead the audience through a giddying catalogue of all the Old Testament prophecies of the birth of Christ and also to provide an account of the events of the previous pageant, ending with a call for penitence.

The Doctors episode, following Luke 2:41–51, has the twelve-year-old Jesus presiding like a teacher among the learned men of the

Temple. Like the prophets in the preceding scene, the men playing the Doctors were apparently working *pro bono*, since the Weavers' accounts do not list payments to them. In the play Jesus, as the bringer of the New Law, focuses on the Ten Commandments—the Law of Moses—as the knowledge, unspecified in the biblical account, which impresses the Jewish doctors (the Vulgate had used the word *stupebant* to express their reaction to his teaching). It is widely accepted that four of the five Doctors pageants from the extant English cycles draw on a common source, possibly the York play.[135] As Daniel Kline has noted, however, the conclusion of the Weavers' pageant "presents a more expansive dialogue where the three doctors discuss their encounter with Jesus among themselves. . . . Rather than retaining different views of Jesus as in York, the doctors at Coventry uniformly accept Jesus' special status."[136]

However, a picture of early Tudor urban taste in religious plays as well as of the intellectual stance of its redactor begins to emerge when the Coventry Weavers' play is compared with its close analogues. The Coventry play is doctrinally conservative and does not tamper with the liturgical wording and traditional iconography of most of the biblical scenes. The revisions and changes in these scenes, however, also demonstrate that the revisers, including Croo, were not simply provincial hacks, since the major concern with the exposition of ideas reflects contemporary preoccupations about education in the vernacular. In many cases changes were made for linguistic reasons because the vocabulary in the original was either too archaic, too Northern, or both. On other occasions, however, Croo or a reviser who preceded him seems to have been working to create a different dramatic effect, leavening the sober metrically regular evenness of the earlier version with the verbal idiosyncrasies that characterize Joseph as a grumbling old man and creating a cameo role for at least one of the Doctors as a rather crusty elderly gentleman with a strong distaste for precocious children.

The Smiths. A patchwork survives of the Smiths' records, preserved in antiquarian transcriptions, incomplete but comparatively early. These demonstrate that from the early fifteenth century the Smiths were responsible for the Passion, to which they seem to have had a special devotion. Their occupation was one which had a special connection with the Crucifixion through the nails, which were products of the metal crafts, and it will be recalled that the nails comprised one of the important signs of the Passion. Thus in the Coventry tapestry (c.1510) in St. Mary's Hall one of the angels holding the implements used in the Crucifixion prominently grasps three nails in his right hand and balances the cross with his right.[137] And in Coventry's Holy Trinity Church, the spandrels in the nave roof were painted in the fifteenth century with angels supporting the emblems of the Passion, including one with a hammer and three nails.[138] Of course, devotion to the Passion was extremely widespread,[139] and we can see why a play on this segment of the biblical story would have been jealously guarded by the sponsoring guild.

Considerable information in the antiquarian transcriptions of the Smiths' accounts concerns various aspects of their play's organization and production. These accounts, by distinguishing between work done on the pageant "amonge the feliship" and that which was contracted out (e.g., the work done by a joiner in 1471),[140] draw attention to the way in which the guilds traded expertise with one another in the production of their pageants. In addition, the employment from 1450 of a skinner named Thomas Colclow to organize the performance for the guild is the first instance in the Coventry records of an identified individual being heavily involved in pageant organization without necessarily being a member of the guild or of a craft directly related to the job in hand. In that year and subsequently Colclow received £2 3*s* 4*d* for "the playe."[141] Then in 1453 there appears a contract which sets out his precise duties as pageant master:

> Thom*as* Colclow, skyn*n*er ffro this day forth shull have þe Rewle of þe pajaunt unto þe end of xij yers next folowing he for to find þe pleyers and all þ*at* longeth þerto all þe seide t*er*me save þe kep*er* of the craft shall let bring forth þe pajant *and* find Cloþes þ*at* gon abowte þe pajant and find Russhes þerto and ev*ery* wytson-weke who þ*at* be kep*ers* of þe crafte shall dyne w*ith* Colchow *and* ev*ery* mast*er* ley down iiij d and Colclow shall ȝerely ffor his labor xlvj s viij d *and* he to bring in to þe mast*er* on sonday next aft*er* corp*us* chr*ist*i day þe originall *and* ffech his vij nobulleȝ and Colclow must bring in at þe lat*er* end of þe t*er*meȝ all þe garme*n*ts þ*at* longen to þe pajant as good as þey wer delyv*er*ed to hym.[142]

In 1491 the Smiths obtained a "new rygenale," which may have meant merely copying the text rather than full-scale revision, and in 1495 John Harryes was paid 6*d* at Corpus Christi for "beryng of þe Orygynall," apparently acting as prompter.[143] In the next year payments were made "for copyying of the ij knyghts p*ar*tes *and* demons," and in 1506 the amount of 2*s* 9*d* was collected for the "original" again.[144] Two leaves "of ore pley boke" were also recopied in 1563 by Robert Croo, whose name had been earlier connected, as we have seen, with copying both the Shearmen and Taylors' and the Weavers' plays.[145] Though nothing survives of the Smiths' playtexts, their annual accounts give a fairly detailed picture of the dimensions of their play. In 1477 the accounts include a cast list, itemizing payments to Jesus, Herod, Pilate, Pilate's wife, Caiaphas, Annas, the Beadle (called Dycar in 1489), two knights, Peter, Pilate's son, and Malchus.[146] There are expenditures for arsedine (a metallic substance that is gold in color), gold paper, gold foil, silver paper and "grene ffoyl" (perhaps copper), all of which would have been within the range of materials that could have been provided by a goldsmith. A painter painted Herod's falchion and his face, probably a sign that he appeared with dark complexion, and the devil's leather garment was mended though he was not paid for playing until the next year.[147] There was a payment for sewing Procula's sleeves, which were possibly white,[148] though later, in 1488, women's clothing is hired for this character from a Mistress Grimsby.[149] In 1496 Procula was played by "Ryngolds man Thomas."[150] In 1452 Jesus had a suit of leather that had been sewn from six skins of "whitled*er*" to simulate nudity during the Crucifixion.[151] A loincloth may be indicated in 1565 in a record of payment "for a gyrdyll for God."[152]

A presumably full set of accounts for 1490 is recorded in Sharp's *Dissertation*.[153] In this year the first rehearsal took place in Easter week and the second in Whitsun week. Previously rehearsal dates had been specified in the accounts for 1479: "Blak Monday" (Easter Monday); Sunday, 16 May; Sunday after Holy Thursday (Ascension Day); and Tuesday in Whitsun week. In this year Easter fell on 11 April, Ascension Day on 20 May, Whitsunday on 30 May, and Corpus Christi on 10 June. Payments for the cast in 1490 are recorded as before, followed by a listing of the garments and stage properties that were refurbished at this time. These included four jackets of black buckram "w*ith* nayles *and* dysse upon þem" for tormentors, another four with "damaske fflowers" for another four tormentors, two jackets of buckram with "hamers crowned," two particolored jackets of red and black, a cloak for Pilate, a gown for Pilate's son, a gown and hood for the Beadle, and two further hoods. Mitres, later decorated with gold and silver foil,[154] for Annas and Caiaphas are noted, along with hats for tormentors, Pilate, Pilate's son, and two princes, who have not otherwise been identified. Properties include a "poll ax" and scepter for Pilate's son, a mask for the devil, four scourges and a pillar for the Scourging, and gilt wigs for Jesus and Peter, the latter appearing in the scene in which he denied his Lord.[155] In 1480 Pilate was also provided with a quart of red wine, which may have been a prop and may explain the reference to "a quarte of wyne" in the 1490 accounts.[156] In the York cycle Pilate certainly drinks on stage.

The 1490 listing notes some of the elaborate costume items and accouterments given to Herod: a falchion, a scepter, a mace, and a gilt-colored crest, which in 1495 is described as made of three pieces of iron.[157] The latter could have been a devil crest, as in some examples in the visual arts (e.g., in the fifteenth-century painted glass in the church of St. Michael Spurriergate, York).[158] The 1476 accounts indicate that he also had a horse hired for him,[159] and in 1480 he received a slop, or loose outer garment; in the latter year his "stuf" also required painting.[160] Herod's finery was in fact a constant expense: in 1501 another new gown was made for him from satin and blue buckram.[161] In the latter days of the Coventry cycle, Herod's gown was hired rather than replaced.[162] That he had been fitted with a mask is suggested by an entry in 1516: "It*em* payd to a peynter for peyntyng *and* mendyng of herodes heed."[163]

The accounts not only provide insight into the construction and likely iconography of the costumes, however, but also reveal that, as in the case of the Weavers, there were more characters to be clothed than were paid for performing. It may well be that the Smiths were paying non-guild members to play the leading speaking parts in their pageant, while using their own members as supernumeraries and tormentors. The paid knights, of which there were always two, probably wore one of the sets of two jackets and perhaps acted as escort officers both for Annas and Caiaphas and for Pilate. The four jackets with dice and nails on them seem obviously for those who tortured and executed Christ, but these characters are not mentioned among the paid cast. Certainty is impossible here, but it may be noted that the problematic jackets with "damaske fflowers" find a parallel in painted glass of the late fourteenth century from St. Michael's Church where a man grasping Jesus' arm at the Betrayal wears just such a garment.[164]

Other extracts from guild records indicate that the Smiths' wagon had to be taken out of their pageant house by the journeymen, washed, and brought down to Gosford Street along with, by 1565, the scaffold which needed new "trulles" (small wheels).[165] In 1574, four men are paid to "bryng yn herod," perhaps on the scaffold.[166] One further set of technical details survives which suggests modifications to their play in the 1570s. In 1572, a costume and props required for hanging Judas were acquired: a coat of canvas, a pulley, an iron hook, and a "lase" (noose).[167] In the following year, Fawston is paid "for hangyng Judas."[168] Problems with the mechanism seem to have occurred since in 1578 the Coventry theater enthusiast Thomas Massey was paid to make a truss for Judas, and the guild bought a new hook.[169]

There is no doubt that the Smiths' pageant, made new and painted in 1565,[170] represented the core of the Coventry cycle, its most essential segment, for the remembrance of the work of salvation on the cross. Since the twelfth century the Crucifixion had been regarded as the essential event of salvation history, for emphasis had shifted from Easter to the Passion, which increasingly stirred the emotions of believers. The highly emotional piety of the fifteenth century stressed the role of Christ's death in atoning for humankind's fallen condition. That the Passion could continue to be played through much of the sixteenth century, although probably with some changes in text and *mise en scène*, is witness to the unchanged emphasis on the atonement in spite of the imposition of revisionist sacramental theology.[171]

The Cappers. In the declining economy of sixteenth-century Coventry, the Cappers emerged for a time as one of the most prominent guilds. Individual Cappers' names had appeared in the Leet from 1434, but only in the 1490s did they form their own separate guild.[172] The Cappers' affluence, which lasted until the fashion for caps gave way to hats, was based not only on hard work but also on their ability to put out work to cheap labor.[173] The process of capmaking required many processes, involving subsidiary specialties, most notably the employment of spinners and knitters who were exclusively female and were often the wives of the journeymen of the guild. The most successful master cappers were engaged as much in trade as in manufacture.

The Cappers aggressively pursued the right to present a play of their own, and in 1529 attempted to take over the Weavers' pageant.[174] In 1531, as we have seen, they were successful in assuming not only the pageant but also the chapel formerly possessed by the Cardmakers and Saddlers in St. Michael's Church. The Cardmakers, with contributions from the Saddlers and Painters, were connected with an unspecified play from 1435,[175] but during the depressed 1520s had become impoverished.[176] The Cappers stood ready to capitalize on their poverty. The document affirming the Cappers' acquisition of the play and chapel is contained in the *Leet Book*, which reports:

> the Company feliship *and* Craft of Cardemakers *and* Sadelers of this Citie meny yeires *and* of longe continuaunce haue hadd *and* yet haue the cheif rule gou*er*n*au*nce rep*ar*yng *and* meyntena*u*nce as well of a Chappell w*ith*in the p*ar*ishe Churche of seynt Michell*es* in the seid Citie named seynt Thomas Chappell *and* of the ornament*es* Iuell*es and* light*es* of the same/ As also of a pagiaunt with the pagiaunt house *and* pleyng geire w*ith* other app*ur*tena*u*nces *and* app*ar*ell*es* belongyng to the same pagiaunt.[177]

However, only in 1537 did the legal surrender of the chapel, pageant, and pageant house occur. The indentured conveyance of this property is unfortunately not specific in its account of the pageant, which, like the chapel, the Cardmakers and Saddlers are said to have maintained "in good order *and* rep*ar*ac*io*n to the Honor of God *and* worshipp of the said Citie to ther great cost*es and* charges."[178]

In 1531 the play began with the Harrowing of Hell and not, as has been suggested, with the Deposition and Burial of Christ,[179] which would have required further characters in the cast. On the other hand, the "sprett [spirit] of God" or Anima Christi and a "demon," each of whom was given 16*d* as a standard fee for his services, were certainly part of a Harrowing segment.[180] But volunteer actors playing minor non-speaking roles and whose presence in the play would not have been recorded in the accounts must also have been present, for a mere confrontation between Anima Christi and the Devil would not have been sufficient to make up the scene. There is fortunately an inventory of 1567 which lists a spade, Adam's usual emblem in representations in the visual arts, and a distaff, Eve's symbol; the costumes required for these characters probably come under the rubric of "solles hedes" (Sharp's reading, "folles hedes," seems to be a mistake[181]) of which there are three, thus allowing for one further soul to be rescued along with Adam and Eve.[182] The spade of Adam and Eve's distaff will again appear in an inventory of 1591 more than a decade after the suppression of the Coventry cycle.[183] In the visual arts, Anima Christi normally reaches forth and grasps Adam by the forearm to pull him forth from the darkness of hell to which he has been consigned for thousands of years. The Cappers' inventories of 1567 and 1591 reveal that Anima Christi in their production was provided with a mask ("the spyryts hede") and a coat,[184] which was described as of buckram in the 1576 accounts.[185] One of the crosses listed in the inventory of 1567 was reserved for Anima Christi for use in this scene;[186] in illustrations in the visual arts, a banner, not impossibly like one of the "v small stremers" likewise noted in the same inventory,[187] was normally attached to the cross as a sign of the Savior's victory over death, hell, and the devil.

The conventional depiction of the Anima Christi's arrival at the mouth of hell draws upon apocryphal writings, liturgical practices, and typology to establish the scene. Anima Christi comes as a light-giver to those who sit in darkness (see Isaiah 9:2). When he intones the words of Psalm 23 (*AV*: Psalm 24)—"Open up, ye gates, that the king of glory might come in" ("Atollite portas, principes . . .")—the gates of the locale of darkness, placed within the opening of the mouth of hell, miraculously collapse before him to let him pass.[188] The devil is overcome, and the souls of Adam, Eve, and the other souls (perhaps at Coventry only one other soul) are extracted from the mouth of hell. More problematic is the character ambiguously designated as the "mother of deth,"[189] appearing up to 1554 and thereafter discontinued, and the "dede man" who was included in the cast in 1576–79.[190] Sharp suggested that the latter might be a Patriarch, "a person delivered from hell by the descent of our Saviour."[191]

As for the "demon" who consistently appeared in the Cappers' accounts from 1534 to 1579, a suggestion advanced in 1823 by William Hone in his pioneering but rather confused account of the mysteries[192] connected him with the figure to which reference is made in Heywood's *The Playe Called the Foure PP*, as cited above. We will recall that in Heywood's play the Pardoner encounters "the devyll that kept the gate" of hell. Hence the "demon" in the Cappers' play would also be the porter of hell, a familiar figure in the visual arts. He appeared wearing a mask—described as "his hed" in the inventory of 1567[193]—as well as a coat[194] and carrying a "mall" made from "a yard of canvas" in 1544 (listed as a "clvbbe" in 1576),[195] perhaps not unlike the club or mall still visible in the faded wall painting over the chancel arch of the Guild Chapel in nearby Stratford-upon-Avon.[196] In the Cappers' pageant, then, the devil is literally guardian of a hell mouth,[197] listed as one of the properties of the Cappers' play. Hell mouth was repaired and painted for a total of 5*d* in 1543, again painted in 1544, made new for 1*s* 9*d* (a surprisingly small amount, not suggesting an elaborate structure) in 1568, and inventoried in 1591.[198]

Usefully, a local example of fifteenth-century painted glass containing the Harrowing was present in the Church of St. Michael.[199] This fragmentary glass may be seen as an analogue to the lost scene of the Harrowing in the Cappers' play. Adam, who is bearded and nude with his right hand raised, was very likely being grasped (probably by the forearm, hidden behind the leading) by the figure of Anima Christi, who is lost. Eve, also nude and with long blond hair, stands immediately behind him; other figures follow. Most of the hell mouth itself is now lost, but the glass retains a vertical band of sharp teeth at the right of the fragment. In the original panel of painted glass, the shape of the hell mouth, as determined by this fragment, would easily have allowed for gates within the opening that might have appeared broken by Anima Christi.

The Cappers' "hellmowthe," perhaps like the fifteenth-century theatrical example at Rouen ("made like a great mouth opening and closing as is needful"), seems to have involved a mechanical device that was manipulated by the "wynde" (windlass) cited in the records.[200] It is not specified what the "wynde" was designed to do at Coventry; however, the person "keeping the wind" most likely was called upon to open the mouth of hell when Anima Christi demands that the gates to the underworld be loosened, and then to close them again at the appropriate time. The windlass was supplied with a rope or cord,[201] which could have been attached to the mouth mechanism.[202] On the other hand, though smoke and an evil odor were often associated with hell and hell mouth,[203] no such effects can be determined from the Cappers' records.

The second part of the Cappers' play staged the Resurrection, in which Pilate was played by the highest paid actor (3*s* 8*d* in 1534, but later raised to 4*s* 4*d*)—a sign that this character, who was accompanied by two "bishops" (Caiaphas and Annas) dressed in

1. Assumption of the Virgin Mary. Above, detail of Coventry Tapestry, in St. Mary's Hall. ©Crown copyright, NMR. The drawing below, by N. J. Alexander, provides an outline of the figures.

3. Above. Thomas Sharp. Drawing by Marianne Cappelletti, after an engraving dated 1823 reproduced in Sharp's *Illustrative Papers on the History and Antiquities of the City of Coventry* (1871).

2. Left. The Guild Chair, St. Mary's Hall, Coventry, showing carved figure of Virgin and Child. Photograph: Courtauld Institute, Conway Library; by permission of Canon M. H. Ridgway.

4. The tomb of Julian Nethermyl, Draper, with his wife and family. Formerly in St. Michael's Church (later Cathedral), Coventry; destroyed by bombing in World War II. Photograph: Conway Library, Coutauld Institute; by permission of Canon M. H. Ridgway.

5. Last Judgment, showing Christ seated on rainbow, angel trumpeters, and souls rising out of tombs. Misericord (c. 1465; destroyed in World War II), formerly in St. Michael's Church (later Cathedral), Coventry. ©Crown copyright, NMR.

6. Earl Street (south side) in the early nineteenth century. Drawing by Marianne Cappelletti, after a sketch by Dr. Nathaniel Troughton.

colored hoods and garments with fur as well as mitres, was the character with the largest role.[204] Pilate's post-Crucifixion function, as in other vernacular plays on the Resurrection from medieval England, would have been to send soldiers to guard the tomb against those who might wish to rob it of the body of Christ. The inventories of 1567 and 1591 designate for him a mask ("hede," "heade") and a doublet, which elsewhere is identified as made of canvas.[205] He wore a green cloak or gown of silk that appears in the dramatic records in the last decade of the performance of the play.[206] The inventory of 1567 indicates that he wore gloves and carried a mall or club, which is verified also in a number of other years.[207] In 1579 a payment was recorded to Richard Hall "ffor makinge pylates clvbbe," which contained "ij pounde and halffe off woole."[208] The club was seen by Sharp, who reported its length (without the handle, which was missing) as seventeen inches and provided an illustration of it in his *Dissertation*.[209] Such an implement would argue for visualizing Pilate in terms of a stereotypical comic tyrant who, like the fool in illustrations in the visual arts,[210] held a non-rigid club, and this depiction likely also had something to do with the numerous balls that were supplied to the actor playing this role.[211] That the balls were leather is verified by the accounts of 1555 ("p*ai*d for a skyn for ball*es* for makyng *and* sowyng").[212] The balls were also seen by Sharp.

Four knights also had a substantial role in the play. These are the soldiers who, on the orders of Pilate, were sent forth to guard the sepulcher, which was made of wood.[213] Armor that was rented for the knights would easily have been supplemented by the swords and other weapons available from the property owned by the guild. Their role in guarding the tomb and their fall into a trance involved a well-known iconography. Fifteenth-century painted glass formerly in a clerestory window of St. Michael's and now in the new Coventry Cathedral shows the soldiers, appearing to be asleep, in contemporary plate armor.[214] The restored glass contains a figure of Christ, stepping onto the body of one of the soldiers—a sign of his victory over the weaknesses to which the flesh is heir. This is a common iconographic feature that is to be seen in alabasters illustrating the scene of the Resurrection,[215] and it is also reported in the Chester play in which Primus Miles says, "He sett his foote upon my backe/ that everye lythe beganne to cracke."[216]

The actor who played the Resurrected Christ, identified as

"God," was paid 1*s* 4*d* annually. His garment or "coat" was described in the 1567 inventory as "apparell of red say."[217] His costume also included a mask, hose, presumably gloves painted with wounds, and certainly a cross, which, when fitted with a banner,[218] was the conventional sign of the Resurrected Christ. The common iconography of the scene shows him holding the vexillum in his left hand and with his right hand in the gesture of blessing but also making visible the wound created by the nails in the palm, sometimes extending his arm. A piece of cloth is draped over his shoulders (the wound in his side is visible), and he wears a loincloth. In alabaster carvings, he steps forth more often with his right foot (also wounded) than with his left, which remains still inside the sepulcher.

The sight of the wounds of Christ as he rises from the tomb is joined elsewhere in drama with lyric expression normally associated with the crucified Christ to reflect the scene identified as the Christ of Pity.[219] In the Towneley play, Jesus' speech thus calls attention to his "woundys . . . weytt and all blody."[220] Such a tableau seems to have been present in the much damaged fifteenth-century Resurrection presented in sculpture on a door frame in the chancel of Holy Trinity Church in Stratford-upon-Avon, a market town with close commercial connections with Coventry.[221] Here the remains of three soldiers are present in seated posture before the coffer tomb, and above it the torso of a much mutilated Christ rises. At each side of him there are angels holding scourges and a spear, the instruments of the Passion. Evidence for the presence of a tableau of this sort rather than one in which the actor playing Christ merely rises up and quickly steps out of the tomb may be found at Coventry in the use of music, which was provided by the singers who were paid 1*s* 4*d* in 1534 and increased amounts in other years for which records were kept, except in 1549 when they apparently were excluded.[222]

Pamela Sheingorn has given a tentative description of the iconic center of the Resurrection play in England:

> Evidence from the texts themselves and from art suggests that the audience may have seen . . . two sides of Christ's nature sequentially, not simultaneously. First they may have seen a *Christus triumphans* and heard his victory sung by the angels; then, perhaps with a simple motion of pulling aside his cloak and opening out his hands, Christ revealed his wounds and became the *Christus patiens* who suffered and continues to

> suffer for mankind. This break in the narrative thread, not without precedent in the cycle plays, could have had an especially deep and dramatic impact on the medieval audience.[223]

While some details in Sheingorn's reconstruction may be questioned (how could a hand grasping a cross-staff be opened to show the wounds, for example?), her conclusion that the scene would easily have involved a dramatically and devotionally effective "break" in the action rings true. Meg Twycross's report of her experience in staging the York Resurrection play, which has no speech for Christ as he silently rises from the tomb, reveals that the moment of the resurrection in her production "took some three minutes of extreme tension to play through, heralded by the thundering of the earthquake, and acted in silence, while the Angel chanted its Easter Sepulchre anthem *Christus resurgens*."[224] That the earthquake was a likely effect also in the Cappers' pageant is perhaps suggested by the mention in 1544 of a "Rattell," which was painted,[225] though this item does not appear in either of the extended inventories of 1567 and 1591.

At Coventry angelic singing was actually provided by professional musicians, who may, as at York and Chester[226] as well as in the Towneley play,[227] have sung the Easter antiphon *Christus resurgens*: "Christ having risen from the dead dies now no more: death shall have no more dominion over him. For the life he lives, he lives with God. Alleluia, alleluia."[228] However, there may have been a change in the music at the Reformation since the guild records note payments for "makynge the songe" (1563, when 1*s* was apparently paid for this service) or for "prikynge the songes" on several occasions (1*s* 4*d* in 1566; 1*s* in 1568; 1*s* in 1569, to the wait Thomas Nyclys or Nicolas, who also had been rewarded "for settyng a songe" for the Drapers guild three years before[229]). On the other hand, these expenditures may only have paid for music copying. The minstrel entered in the lists of roles in the Cappers' pageant most likely was an instrumentalist attached to Pilate's entourage rather than an accompanist for the singers.

The next segment of the Cappers' pageant, dramatizing the arrival of the three Marys at the tomb with their boxes of ointments, is a scene familiar from the liturgical *Visitatio Sepulchri*. It presents the procession of the three women, who wonder, as the second Mary in the York play says, what person "schall nowe here of vs thre/ Remove þe stone?"[230] Shortly thereafter will be staged the exchange with Angelus, who asks: "Ȝe mournand women in youre þought,/ Here in þis place whome haue ȝe sought?" And their response is: "Jesu, þat to dede is brought,/ Oure lorde so free."[231] At Coventry payments of 12*d* to Mary Magdalene and 6*d* to each of the two "side Marys" are consistently recorded from 1534 to 1579. Sculpture on the Balsall tomb (c.1491) in the chancel of the parish church at nearby Stratford-upon-Avon shows a single angel seated on the coffer tomb as the Marys approach,[232] but in the Cappers' pageant two angels were present. Mary Magdalene, outfitted with a wig (or mask), kirtle, coif, and crown, clearly had a more extensive role than the other Marys in the play, though they also held boxes of ointments and wore costumes which included crowns, wigs, rolls, and coifs.

The larger role of Mary Magdalene suggests the inclusion of the *hortulanus* scene in which she meets the risen Christ, whom she mistakes for the gardener. The *hortulanus* scene, which had been introduced into the liturgical *Visitatio* in the twelfth century,[233] was apparently a popular one. It found illustration in the visual arts in two Warwickshire examples, one in painted glass of c.1530 at Merevale and the other in a fourteenth-century carved chest formerly at Snitterfield. In the Merevale glass, Christ's body, which is bare under his cloak, is partly hidden by a bush, while Mary Magdalene, who is kneeling, is typically pictured with long blond hair.[234] In the carving, which appeared on the front of the chest, Jesus was shown in a loose garment that left his upper torso exposed; he held a staff in his left hand and raised his right hand. At his feet was the kneeling Mary Magdalene.[235] Often, as in alabaster carvings in the Victoria and Albert Museum, he holds a spade in his right hand.[236] The spade listed as a stage prop in the Cappers' pageant could have been used for this scene as well.

Preceding the appearance to Mary Magdalene in the Cappers' play, however, would have been Christ's appearance to his mother, the Virgin Mary, who is listed in the guild's records from 1534 to 1547 as receiving payment identical to that of Mary Magdalene. Tradition asserted that she was the first to see her Son after his resurrection,[237] but this was a point that the Reformation theologians with their anti-Marian bias were quite vociferous in denying.[238] Marian devotion at Coventry was apparently very active prior to the Reformation, but once the municipal leadership had become staunchly Protestant, the effect on the drama cycle was inevitable.

In the case of the Virgin Mary's role the change came at the end of the troubled 1540s, for she was dropped in 1548 and apparently thereafter not returned to the play.[239] After 1546 even the representation of Mary in the Corpus Christi procession was also no longer recorded.[240]

Ideological developments very likely also dictated the preparation of an entirely new playbook at the cost of 5*s* in 1552, the same year that payment was made for the "matt*er* of ye Castell of emavs,"[241] which, as noted above, may never have been played. A prologue was added by 1567 and remained in use until 1579.[242] The playbook remained in the hands of the Cappers at least until the inventory of 1591, but unfortunately was not seen thereafter.[243] Further references show that the clerk was paid as keeper of the book ("for bereng the boke").[244]

The Mercers. The 1450 muster reveals that the thirty-eight Mercers available for bearing arms included two mayors, six bailiffs, and five chamberlains and wardens.[245] They resided in the most fashionable parts of the city and indeed were second only to the Drapers in their influence in late medieval Coventry.[246] Except for the temporary ascendancy of the Cappers, who vastly outnumbered them in 1522,[247] there is no other reason to suppose that their relative position was weakened until the poverty of the city overtook them in the latter part of the sixteenth century,[248] and there is no evidence that they required or received assistance from any other guild for their pageant. But, except for William Pysford's will of 1518 and one reference to the pageant when Princess Mary came to Coventry in 1526, the dramatic records only begin with the surviving accounts in 1579, on the very eve of the abandonment of Coventry's cycle, so we know a great deal less about their participation than we might wish.

Pysford's will, which has been mentioned above in connection with his bequests of costumes to the Tanners' and Mercers' guilds, commences with a special appeal to the "intercession and prayer of that most blessed Virgyn Mary the moder of our blessed Savyor."[249] In spite of his apparent sympathy for Lollardy, he thus nevertheless seems to have had a special devotion to the Virgin—a devotion which may shed light on the subject of the Mercers' pageant if his piety in this regard was shared with other members of his guild. Hardin Craig believed that the Mercers' arms included a representation of the Assumption of Mary into heaven: "gules, a demy Virgin Mary with her hair disheveled crowned, rising out and within an orb of clouds, all proper; motto, *Honor Deo*."[250] Recent research has called this attribution into question and has suggested that the figure depicted was probably the secular Maid of the Mercers, dressed in the guild's fashionable products, as was the case where the London guild was concerned.[251] Nevertheless, a number of other pieces of evidence survive which demonstrate the guild's Marian devotion. The guild's fourteenth-century ordinances specify the date for the annual meetings as 15 August, at the feast of the Assumption, which is to be celebrated by the "Warden, bretheren, and sisteren," who are to be "clad, some of them in livery suits at their own cost, and others in hoods at the common cost of the guild."[252] The Mercers also had a connection with the Coventry tapestry (fig. 1) which is still displayed in St. Mary's Hall and which retains the Assumption, though the Trinity that formerly appeared above it was removed by Protestant iconoclasts,[253] probably in the 1560s when the city's Puritan council engaged in "an orgy of iconoclasm."[254] The dedication of St. Mary's Hall itself, the long-established meeting place of the Coventry merchants, likewise shows the strength of local affiliation, and the guild chair from the fifteenth century has a relief carving of the Virgin, seated and holding her Son (fig. 2). Quite appropriately a roof boss on the exterior of the gatehouse of the hall also depicted the Coronation of the Virgin,[255] a scene which likewise appears on a chest from St. Michael's Church, the parish church where the Mercers had their chapel of St. Mary.[256] A misericord in this church with a carving of the Assumption, destroyed in an air raid in 1940, is also worth noticing.[257]

The enlistment of the Mercers' pageant for Princess Mary in 1526 provides further circumstantial evidence for its content. Record of this visit is contained in the city annals which report that, when "the Lady Mary Came to Coventry *and* Lay at the Priory, the Mercers Pageant Gallantly trimed stood in the Cross Cheaping."[258] The staging of a pageant of the Assumption, we can surmise, should have been a very acceptable display for the eleven-year-old princess, for her mother was especially devoted to the Virgin in general and to the image of the Assumption in particular. Queen Catherine, whose emblem was the pomegranate, a symbol of the virgin birth, is said to have been responsible for embroidering the design showing the Assumption on a chasuble now at Coughton Court in Warwickshire as a sign of her devotion.[259]

Evidence for a Mercers' pageant of the Death, Assumption, and Coronation of the Virgin is, then, circumstantial but reasonably convincing. Nevertheless, with Protestant antagonism toward the cult of the Virgin gaining in strength both before and after the reign of Queen Mary, it is logical that the religious change would have brought about alterations in the Mercers' play. Other guilds' plays appear to have been affected, if we can judge from the revisions and new playbooks that were produced between 1519 and the 1570s. The Mercers for a time may have held onto their play with some tenacity, however. There is a stray early entry from 1551 in the Mercers' account book that states: "This ys to Rememb*er* of certayne pwint*es* Which longen to o*ur* crafte Ordened of olde tyme for mendyng of Dyuers fawtes Which ar founden W*ith*in oure said crafte Wherby our said crafte ys noysed *and* slanderd a monge the co*m*myn pepull as Well a monge Strangers knowen *and* that to grett Dysworschipp to vs all *and* no p*ro*fett to the Said crafte. . . ."[260] The craft then guarantees that its members will attend upon the mayor at watches, weddings, and funerals. This year, during the Protestant Protectorate, is certainly one in which any adherence to traditional guild devotions to the Virgin would have been particularly prone to bring slander and disworship upon the company, but the lacuna in the accounts which follows leaves the reference cryptic.

Although an Assumption play survives in the earlier York cycle, a Protestant iconoclast tore the Assumption and Coronation play out of the Towneley manuscript (a West Riding anthology formerly thought to be the Wakefield Corpus Christi cycle[261]) and the extant Chester plays lack these episodes (they were present in the cycle before the Reformation, but have been lost),[262] so it is probable that the Mercers' play did not go unscathed if it indeed staged these scenes. At one time the Mercers' play was probably comparable with the East Anglian N-Town play of the Assumption, which appears to have been written originally for large-scale performance, and with Continental analogues. At Elche in Spain the Assumption play continues to be performed and uses elaborate aerial machinery for flying angels, the Virgin, and even the Trinity.[263] Moreover, the late Mercers' accounts show them spending £3 7*s* 8*d*—a comparatively large sum, especially for a guild no longer at the peak of affluence—on the "ordinarye charge*es*" for their pageant in 1579.[264] When nine years later they sold their "pagant stufe," including "a copper chayne" which may have been used as a lifting device, they received £2 19*s* 8*d*.[265] Mary Dormer Harris speculated that the chain might have indicated the presence of a "Binding of Satan," suggested by local devotion to St. Michael, but this action may already have taken place in the Cappers' pageant.[266] Other possibilities, sharing with the Assumption the need for a similar cast and some lifting gear, would be the Ascension and Pentecost, but for neither of these is there a shred of evidence whatsoever. All we can say is that the Mercers' play was very elaborate indeed and that we should perhaps beware of being too conservative in imagining how it may have been performed or how it may have been adapted or displaced in Protestant times.[267]

The Drapers. The power and wealth of the Drapers, Coventry's foremost entrepreneurial trading company whose members lived in Gosford Street, Earl Street, and Bayley Lane, grew dramatically over time in relation to the other guilds. The 1445 list in the *Leet Book* specified that the place of greatest honor at the end of the Corpus Christi procession was to be taken by the Mercers, who were to follow the Drapers.[268] But in the sixteenth century the status of these two guilds was reversed. By 1578 the Drapers were collecting nearly triple the amount of rent that was being taken in by the Mercers, and only fourteen years later they were taking in almost five times as much.[269] The Drapers were a monopoly with their own Drapery from which they controlled buying and selling.[270] While concerning the Drapers' first pageant house we only know that it was in Little Park Street, their new pageant house in Gosford Street was a substantial edifice two bays wide, but it was just one item in the impressive list of properties owned by them throughout the city.[271]

The Drapers' chapel was located on the north side of the chancel in St. Michael's Church where until destroyed by a German bomb in 1940 stood the tomb of a prominent member of this guild, Julian Nethermyl, with its relief portraiture of the rich citizen in a long gown, his wife Johanna in a gown with square-cut neck over a kirtle, and their five sons and five daughters, all kneeling (fig. 4).[272] Nethermyl, whose tomb has been dated 1539, was mayor of the city in 1523–24. His arms appeared on his tomb along with the arms of the Drapers, "azure three clouds proper radiated in base, or, each surmounted with a triple crown or, caps gules."[273] The Drapers' arms also appeared on their pageant, as their accounts indicate: "Item for

. . . Crest ffor the boxxe of the padgen."[274] Later members of the Nethermyl family are reported to have stored an organ utilized by the guild and noted in dramatic records.[275]

Before its destruction the Drapers' chapel also retained iconography which connected it with the subject of the guild's play. As Mary Dormer Harris notes in her edition of the *Leet Book*, "Doomesday is the subject of one of the misere seats in the drapers' chapel in S. Michael's."[276] The misericord, dated c.1465, illustrated Christ seated on a rainbow supported by clouds and with his feet on the world, while two angels blew trumpets (fig. 5). On the supporters, resurrected figures rose from their graves or emerged from coffins.[277]

The first reference to the Drapers' Doomsday play as the concluding segment of the Coventry cycle appears in the Coventry *Leet Book* in 1457, the year that Margaret of Anjou "came p*re*uely to se the play." From her vantage point at Richard Wode's house, "She sygh then alle the Pagentes pleyde saue domes day which myght not be pleyde for lak of day."[278]

The Drapers' accounts, however, tell us nothing about their play prior to the sixteenth century. Further, we are dependent for these accounts on the efforts of Thomas Daffern (?1795–1869), a shopkeeper with neither the broad knowledge of the period nor the illustrious antiquarian connections of Thomas Sharp, though he had a bookkeeper's eye for detail. Ironically, what Daffern's transcriptions reveal is the utter chaos of the Drapers' accounting methods, contributing to the late R. W. Ingram's outburst that "Coventry accounts are an anthology of bad book-keeping practice"[279] and leaving him no choice but to print the mid-sixteenth-century material as an appendix to his chronological collection of Coventry's drama records. Nonetheless, Ingram was able to see a picture of change and development emerging from the chaos:

> [W]hatever their numbers in the 1530s, they were more than twice as wealthy as the Weavers and could easily support so demanding a play as Doomsday with its burning worlds, earthquakes, and hell-mouth spouting real flames—yet most of these wonders belong to their last production, which dates only from 1555. Until 1554, I think that the accounting is for another version of the play. What Margaret of Anjou missed in 1457 because of "lak of day" may well have been yet an earlier version. Each awesome, but its own play.[280]

We must, in the light of the confusion in the records, proceed cautiously. If there was a 1519 revision of the Drapers' play,[281] the pageant that emerged may already have included the following: angels sitting on seats and holding trumpets, three white (i.e., good) and three black souls dressed in body garments made of white leather or colored canvas, devils who wore masks, and a hell mouth. Four angels were noted, and these required wings that were painted. A windlass with a long attached rope was utilized, probably for raising and lowering Christ who returns in majesty at the Judgment.[282] It seems perfectly safe to assume that at this time the scene in the drama was derived mainly from the popular account of the Last Judgment in chapter 25 of St. Matthew's Gospel rather than from the Apocalypse, and hence its iconography might be expected to be similar on the whole to that of the four extant Doomsday plays in other late medieval English cycles and collections, all of which also draw on the Gospel account.[283]

The St. Michael's misericord to which reference has been made above provides a further angle for exploration of the connection with the Doomsday play since it is related to other misericords in the same series that depict not only the Dance of Death but also the Seven Corporal Acts of Mercy. The Dance of Death, by depicting the leveling power of death over all estates in medieval society, invites one to consider his or her likely end; the Corporal Acts of Mercy fulfill a related function by reminding the viewer of his or her particular contribution to those things which will guarantee the right outcome at the general resurrection.[284] They derive from Matthew 25, the Gospel account of the Last Judgment, frequently supplemented with a seventh work, the Burial of the Dead, taken from the book of Tobit. The Works of Mercy are not visualized in any dramas, but they nevertheless provide a framework in the York, Chester, N-Town, and Towneley plays for understanding the division of souls to take place on the Last Day and are recited by Jesus in his role as Judge. The Corporal Acts were regarded as tremendously important in the period immediately prior to the Reformation, for charity was held to be a strict demand rather than an abstract ideal; failure to perform them would place one in Purgatory or worse, as a strict reading of Jesus' words in the Gospel would demonstrate. At St. Martin's, Bullring, Birmingham, an undated fragment of a wall painting on a beam reported at the time of the nineteenth-century restoration of the church illustrated the upper portion of a Last Judgment scene with the head of Christ, his hands, and angels at each side. Scrolls at Christ's right and left contained the words "Venite bene*dicti* p*at*ris me*i*" and "Ite male*dicti* in igne*m* et*ernam*" —the words of the Judge to the good and evil souls his right side or his left in St. Matthew's Gospel.[285] There is no good reason to suppose that the disposition of the good and bad souls in the Coventry play would have been any different from this. The division of souls thus would not have required the weighing of souls, a motif that appears occasionally in the visual arts but not in drama.[286] This does not mean that one of the angels specified in the play might not have been designated as St. Michael, who was patron of the Drapers' parish church and also of the city itself (he appeared on the reverse of the municipal seal from the fourteenth century[287]).

Perhaps a slight correction is in order here with regard to the designation 'souls,' sincc thc Last Judgmcnt as depicted in drama and art implied also the resurrection of the body. Further, the color coding that has been noted—white for the good, black for the evil—should not be understood to have racial connotations: medieval theologians accepted the view that everyone would be restored to physical perfection at the general resurrection, and the way that the worthy should be distinguished from the damned would be by their *claritas*, by which they would shine.[288]

Before the 1560s the accounts are at their most chaotic, and this is unfortunate since better records would show more clearly what changes were made in deviating from previous productions when Robert Croo wrote out a new playtext for the guild in 1555. The accounts for 1561 give a full list of characters, including God, two devils, the "iij whyte Sowles and iij blank [sic] Sowles," four angels, two "wormes of Conscyence," three patriarchs, and a prologue which is here identified as "the protestacyon." Additionally, music was provided by "Syngyng men," a "trompeter," and a musician who played the regals.[289] Payments were made for the technical crew to man the windlass and hell mouth ("for kepyng of the wynd and of hell mowthe xvj d") as well as for the usual charges of getting the wagon out of storage and outfitting it, though it seems that the new pageant was more expensive to produce than the older version that had existed before Croo's text in spite of the consistency in payments to actors. Separate payments were made for "blankyng [sic] of the Sowles facys" and for expenses associated with the three rehearsals, perhaps including payment for "the players Sowper" on one of these occasions. Finally, the accounts list payment of 2*s* 8*d* "for iij worldes" made by "Robert Bro," apparently an error for

Robert Croo, whose name not only is associated with the rewriting of the playtext but also appears frequently in the dramatic records during this period, most prominently in the role of God, who presumably was shown initially on an upper level (identified as his "welke" in 1563) of the Drapers' pageant wagon before descending to act as Judge.[290]

The Drapers' accounts for 1561–73 reveal why three worlds were required and how these devices were utilized to create a spectacular effect. Each was set on fire, as the 1565 accounts are the first to indicate ("It*em* Settynge the worldes on fyre iiij d"), presumably one at each of three stations where the Doomsday play was being presented in the city.[291] Further, in this year there was also a payment for "a lynke to Sette the worlds on fyre" for which the amount of 6*d* was paid.[292]

The "worlds" to be burned were thus items of disposable stage property, needed at each station, and they surely were separate from the world as Christ's footstool—a familiar iconographic detail that was, for example, present in the misericord formerly in St. Michael's. A similar world also appeared beneath the Judge's feet in another Coventry representation of the Doom, the wall painting, now totally blackened and in need of restoration, over the chancel arch of Holy Trinity Church.[293] A drawing made from this wall painting in the nineteenth century shows the world which is Christ's footstool as a small globe beneath his feet, while above it he is seated on a rainbow (though none is visible in the drawing) and with his hands raised to show the wounds in them.[294] Such display of Christ's wounds is consistent with the emphasis on the Corporal Acts of Mercy, for the wounds are emblems of Christ's mercy to those who believe and do the deeds of love.

The burning of the world in the Drapers' play, however, was apparently an initial effect that served as a preliminary to the main subject matter of the pageant. It would indeed have been a spectacular theatrical display and would have served as a signal, a warning that the time of mercy has expired and that the world itself will now conclude its history. As such, this fireworks display, coming within the last play of the cycle, reflects an expectation of the total destruction of this earthly sphere by fire, as foretold in 2 Peter 3:10: "But the day of the Lord shall come as a thief, in which the heavens shall pass away with great violence, and the elements shall be melted with heat, and the earth and the works that are in it, shall be burnt up"

(Douay-Rheims translation). In the fourteenth-century *Holkham Bible Picture Book*, the burning of the world in a fiery holocaust is shown immediately prior to the return of the divine Judge as one of the signs in the Fifteen Signs of Doomsday series.[295] There is, however, an example of the world in flames closer to the Drapers' play in time and location; this occurs in the sixteenth-century wall painting of the apocalyptic Whore of Babylon in the nave of the Guild Chapel at Stratford-upon-Avon, where the earth is represented as flat rather than as a round.[296] It should be noted that Doomsday and Apocalypse often appear as alternate versions of the end of the world, drawn from different parts of the New Testament, but in sequences such as the York Minster's Great East Window (1405–08) Doomsday is integrated into the larger apocalypse narrative.[297]

In addition to the flames, the Drapers' Doomsday had an "Earth quake," an effect that was worked by means of a barrel.[298] No extant English Doomsday play has such a fiery and noisy introduction. But again this effect was one of those that appeared in the Fifteen Signs of Doomsday which the popular *Golden Legend* of Jacobus de Voragine and other writers predicted would come on one of the last days before the end of history. According to Jacobus, this sign was to happen on the eighth day, when "there will come a worldwide earthquake, which will . . . be so great that neither man nor beast will be able to stand, and all will fall prostrate on the ground."[299] In contrast, the finale is likely to have been harmonious, an ending supplied by the singing men, accompanied by the regals, retained for the play.

In his descent to do judgment, God, wearing a garment of "Redde Sendall," may have utilized the windlass and rope which are recorded in the dramatic records.[300] The Chester stage directions for the descent may have relevance here: "quasi in nube, si fieri poterit, quia, secundum doctoris opiniones, in aere propre terram judicabit Filius Dei" ("as if in a cloud, if it can be contrived, because, according to the opinions of scholars, the Son of God shall give judgement in the air close to the Earth").[301] Another Chester stage direction, following Christ's words announcing "see my blood freshe owt flee/ That I bleede on roode-tree/ for your salvatyon," reads: "Tunc emittet sanguinem de latere eius" ("Then he shall send forth blood from out of his side").[302] Christ's bleeding often appeared in the visual arts, as in the now fragmentary wall painting of the Crucifixion in the Charterhouse at Coventry in which angels caught the blood from Christ's wounds in chalices.[303]

The blowing of the angel trumpets is verified in the Drapers' accounts, which mention the repair of such instruments, but the actual trumpet playing would necessarily have been done by a professional trumpeter, who appears listed regularly for his services and who logically would have been outfitted like an angel.[304] The angel trumpeters were probably placed in the "pullpytts for angells" noted in the accounts for 1565.[305] The angels may also have shown off the Instruments of the Passion, since one of the undated accounts notes the making and painting of a cross.[306] The holding of these implements by angels was common in depictions of the Last Judgment, as in the Stratford-upon-Avon Guild Chapel wall painting,[307] and also occurred in the Chester and York plays.[308] The Coventry angels are also known to have had gold skins, and probably the four "dyadynnes" (diadems) listed in c.1567 and possibly the surplices in 1572 were for them, though their more common garment in pre-Reformation England was the alb.[309]

In contrast to the angelic orders and to the saved were of course the damned, doomed to enter hell by way of hell mouth in the Drapers' play. This stage property, sometimes referred to as "hell hed," appears prominently in the dramatic records of the Drapers' company. It was frequently repaired, repainted, and re-made, suggesting that its fabric construction, presumably over a wood frame, was not particularly durable.[310] The design would undoubtedly be similar to the hell mouth previously encountered in the Cappers' play, but, as noted above, their records lack notice of smoke or stench. Not so the Drapers, who after 1556 paid a man to attend the flames and smoke at the hell mouth.[311] The traditional location of hell mouth, as in the wall painting in Coventry's Holy Trinity Church, is at Christ's left in the lower portion of the scene.

Attending the damned were devils, for whom masks, described as "the demones heed," "a demons face," etc., were reported by Sharp in accounts from as early as 1536 which are no longer extant,[312] and frequent mention is made in the records of coats and hose for them. The most interesting of the latter references is the notice of 1572 of payment "for mendyng ye demens cotts *and* hose" and "for ij pound of heare for ye Same."[313] Traditionally, as in yet another misericord in St. Michael's, devils had hair over their entire bodies, and also they had hideous faces or masks as well as grotesque masks.[314] Their weapons were normally clubs and flesh hooks, the latter a standard implement used by butchers.[315] The

Drapers' play does not present persons being condemned to hell in a sympathetic light, but the drama is notwithstanding a commentary on the anxiety of human life faced with its uncertainties.

Other Guilds. While the Pinners and Needlers' ordinance of 1414 refers to a "pagent callyd the takyng down of god fro þe cros" and later accounts indicate that they maintained some sort of responsibility for a pageant which may later, after 1547, have been surrendered to the Coopers,[316] other guilds' documents are silent concerning pageant sponsorship. Other possible pageants are easily enumerated: the Baptism of Christ, Ministry episodes, Palm Sunday, and the Last Supper. The records of the Corpus Christi plays of Coventry are incomplete to the point of frustrating our desire to discover more. The companies that are named in the records were not only the contributory guilds which merely assisted with the financial burden but also those fully responsible for plays. For example, the Coventry *Leet Book* reports in 1428 that the Smiths—subsequently responsible, as we have seen, for the Passion—requested to be discharged from responsibility for contributing to the Cutlers' pageant.[317] Between 1495 and 1522 the Girdlers' pageant received contributions from various guilds, including the Painters, who had their own play in 1526 with the Carvers as contributors.[318]

The Tanners' pageant has already been mentioned above in connection with a bequest—a "lyned Crymsyn gowne not furred"—by William Pysford.[319] This play was identified, but without indication of subject matter, in the Tanners' ordinances of 1497.[320] In 1552 the guild pleaded poverty and asked for help from other guilds, though this is curious since the leather trades were among the more prosperous in the middle of the sixteenth century.[321] The guild maintained its chapel in the south aisle of Holy Trinity Church, but again no special devotions have been identified with this company.[322] As noted above, the pageant house of the Whittawers, another leather guild, was recorded in 1407 as being in Hill Street, outside Hill Street Gate, a location convenient to where its members lived and worked.[323] The Butchers were contributors to the Whittawers' pageant in 1495, while in 1548 their wagon was rented by the Cappers.[324] In 1526 the Painters also had a pageant, to which the Carvers were to contribute, but this play was no longer being performed for some time before 1532.[325]

It should not, of course, be assumed that guilds not directly responsible for pageants might only be involved to the extent of handing over their contributions of cash to the sponsoring guild, as in the case of the Carpenters as early as 1449 when they paid out 10*s* to the Pinners.[326] The Carpenters were not only contributors to the pageants, we need to remember, but they were also indispensable to them, for without their skills none of the plays could have been staged on the wagon stages for which this guild was largely responsible. They were indeed as crucial to the plays as the Painters, who were required for painting not only the wagons but also costumes and even, at times, the faces of the actors.[327]

Robert Croo

Robert Croo is named more frequently and significantly than any other person associated with Coventry pageants, and yet we cannot even be absolutely sure whether he is one man or more than one person by the same name.[328] In 1510 a Robert Croo was admitted brother of the Cappers and thereafter paid 1*s* 8*d* for his fees annually until 1515–16 when his membership dues were paid off. In 1513–14 a Robert Croo was also involved in a lawsuit with the Cappers. He paid quarterage in 1517–18, and in 1520 was the Master of the Cappers[329] and was himself engaged in creating new brothers.[330] In 1522 he took his only apprentice, paid 1*s* in the Grand Subsidy on goods worth £2, and appears to have lived in Bailey Lane ward. Baldwin suggests the possibility that he could have been the same Robert Croo who married Joyce Botiler in 1532–33 and, since she was an heiress, that he may have given up his craft.[331] In any case, the Cappers' records cease to refer to Croo from about this date forward.

But prior to this time Robert Croo appears already to have embarked on a theatrical career, first directing in 1525 an extravagant Candlemas celebration, called "the Goldenflecc" in the Cappers' records. The accounts refer to the provision of painted subtleties, to cresset lights, torches, two gallons of wine, singers, and, most significantly, players, who were paid 3*s* 4*d*. John Crooe and William Lynes were also paid "for the same."[332] What happened at this performance cannot be reconstructed and was not repeated. The name John Croo (a separate person, presumably) appears twice more in the records: he was paid 8*d* by the Cappers under their Corpus Christi day expenses in 1540 for something unspecified, and 2*s* by the Smiths in 1547 "for menddyng of Herrode hed and a mytor and other thynges."[333]

Robert Croo hereafter became associated with many different companies, but now he has otherwise no recorded existence outside of the theatrical context. As indicated above, he wrote out and made some changes in the Shearmen and Taylors' and Weavers' pageants in 1535. He then enters the record playing God for the Drapers in 1562 and 1566, making the worlds that they burned in 1561, 1563, and 1566, and also creating a hat for a Pharisee in 1562.[334] In 1563 he was paid by the Smiths "for ij leves of ore pley boke."[335] In 1568 the Drapers paid him £1 "for makyng of the boke for the paggen," and gloves were provided for him, probably a sign he was once again playing God in their pageant.[336] In 1567 he also made the two giants for the Drapers' Midsummer Show but had disappeared from their Corpus Christi pageant.[337] The activity looks sporadic, but this is the nature of the records rather than a probable indication of Croo's level of engagement.

Unfortunately, in 1535 when Croo was writing for the Shearmen and Taylors and the Weavers, the Cappers, who had recently taken over their pageant, presented only summary accounts, and no Cappers' accounts survive for the decade in which Croo was most active for the Drapers. Robert Croo, if indeed he was one single man (he must have been in his seventies by the time he played the Drapers' God), remains elusive.[338] Our most tangible access to the man remains the two scripts which he left behind, one of them an extant holograph copy.

Other than Croo, one other person appears in the dramatic records as having provided a play text. Francis Pinning, Master of the Cappers on several occasions in the second half of the sixteenth century, was paid 5*s* by the Drapers "for a playe" in 1568.[339] The sum is identical to the amount paid by the Weavers to Robert Croo, who was, however, paid four times as much by the Drapers for a seemingly similar service in c.1567. As Ingram notes, it is possible that all Pinning did was to copy out the play from a worn-out book.[340]

The Songs

The manuscript containing Croo's text of the Weavers' pageant also contains texts on its final page for a set of two songs, both written in iambic tetrameter. They are datable to the middle decades of the sixteenth century and are by two different hands, neither of which is the main scribe's. The first has the name "Richard" (without indication of surname) written below it, and the other is signed "Iamis hewyt," whose association with the Weavers' pageant has been noted above. As an organist and the leader of the waits, Hewet also during the 1560s played for the Drapers pageant as well.[341] At the top of the page is written the name of "Thomas Maudycke," whose name is also printed by Sharp across the top of the songs at the end of the Shearmen and Taylors' pageant.

The first song in the Weavers' pageant is *Rejoyce, rejoyce, all that here be*, which is a suitable Candlemas carol. Neither this nor the second song, *Beholde, now hit ys come to pase*, appears elsewhere in any form. The latter is, however, the more problematic piece at first glance. The song seems to be unsuitable for the play since it fits dramatically between the Crucifixion and Resurrection. But, as Richard Rastall indicates, the text is related to "Simeon's rehearsal of messianic prophecy" in the Weavers' pageant, "and there are resonances in the language that suggest a connection."[342] On the other hand, Rastall also has raised the possibility that the latter song may have been written by Hewet for another pageant that did in fact stage the Crucifixion or Resurrection.[343] Nevertheless, the Weavers hired singers regularly, and since the three other waits —Richard Styff, Thomas Nicholas, and Richard Sadler—were also employed along with Hewet as singing men at Holy Trinity Church, these three could have been the singers paid to sing the songs, while Hewet accompanied them on the regals.[344] If so, and keeping in mind that Nicholas was recorded as copying songs for the Drapers (in 1566) and the Cappers (in 1569),[345] then the "Richard" whose name appears with *Rejoice, rejoice, all that here be* could be either Styff or Sadler.[346] The name, however, may not after all have anything to do with the text or music, and on the basis of the handwriting a more likely "Richard" may be the Richard Pixley who wrote his name elsewhere in the manuscript.

In the Shearmen and Taylors' pageant, cues for music call for singing by the angels, the shepherds, and the mothers of the Innocents. The angels' music is an antiphon with the familiar Latin text, and was taken from a standard liturgical source.[347] The songs of the shepherds and the mothers, however, are in English and are provided by Sharp from the now lost manuscript where, as in the case of the Weavers' songs, they were written out at the end. The first and third (actually two sections of the same song) were to be sung by the shepherds,[348] the second by the mothers. These were notated for three voices, though they have often been edited in modern times inauthentically with the addition of a fourth part. They appear, as noted above, with Mawdycke's name as a heading, and provide a date of 13 May 1591, only six days before the city council decided against a revival of the Coventry plays and instead authorized a choice of other plays, out of which Stephen K. Wright has speculated that *King Edward the Fourth* may have been the one picked.[349] Rastall suggests that Mawdycke may have "collected up in 1591 whatever materials he could find" in the expectation that the Shearmen and Taylors' pageant could be staged once again after a twelve year hiatus.[350] The songs are, according to Rastall, from the first half of sixteenth century—in other words, contemporary with Croo's text for the Shearmen and Taylors.[351]

PLAYTEXTS AND RECORDS PRESERVED

Credit for the preservation not only of the text of one of the two extant Coventry pageants but also of a substantial portion of the city's dramatic records must go to Thomas Sharp (1770–1841), whose antiquarian interests were especially focused on the religious plays that had been staged there prior to 1579, the date of their suppression (see fig. 3).[352] The first edition of his transcription of the Coventry Shearmen and Taylors' pageant, printed by William Reader in 1817, was limited to only twelve copies. His *Dissertation on the Pageants or Dramatic Mysteries Anciently Performed at Coventry* included the Shearmen and Taylors' play and also a substantial amount of documentary material selected from the even more substantial quantity of records then available, much of it since lost. His edition of the Weavers' play, which, as noted above, came to light after the completion of his *Dissertation*, is less crucial only because of the preservation of the manuscripts.

Sharp's interest in the early drama was unusual for his time. When he suggested to J. H. Maitland that the Chester pageants be published in full, he received the following response: "Few readers are to be found who enjoy even specimens of ancient relics like these, *and* still fewer would peruse a copious collection—besides, tho' not intended by the compilers, or so considered in former days, there are unquestionably in these compositions both speeches and incidents that combine so much obscenity and profanity as could disgust the taste of the present eye."[353] Elsewhere Sharp's attention to the details of early theatrical production was subjected to severe ridicule. The reviewer for *The Monthly Review* complained:

> Whatever certain antiquarians may delight to believe, the useful end of investigation does not consist in the laborious trifling with which attention is frittered away upon minute certainties and petty doubts. The scholar of enlarged mind and philosophical reflection will view such enquiries as those before us with reference only to the light which they can shed upon the progress of the intellect, manners, and literature: he will take care to examine only the great operations of the machinery of society, not to count every nail and peg in its rude and original structure. We cannot choose but smile—without offence to Mr. Sharp be it spoken —at the solemnity with which he dwells on the uses of iron pins and clamps, "tenter-hooks, rings, wire, thread, and small cord." Neither can we sympathise in his grievous lamentation over the loss of some "drapers' book of accounts," (p. 68.) which could only have accumulated his sufficient catalogue of such important articles. . . .[354]

According to this anonymous writer, "almost all that was worth knowing on the characteristics of the [medieval] religious plays" had already been published by Malone in his *Historical Account of the English Stage*. Remembering the loss of the Shearmen and Taylors' play in the fire at the Birmingham Free Library only a little more than a half century later, we may find it even more amazing to read his condemnation of the value of this play: "There is no intrinsic merit in this wretched and doggerel piece to render its publication at all necessary. . . ."[355]

As a critic, Sharp did not hold an exaggerated opinion of Robert Croo, and indeed he found him "so illiterate and confused, as not to exhibit the language of the time in a fair and appropriate dress. . . ."[356] Our modern opinion of Croo is much less damning, for we see him as a man of the theater who was well conversant with the demands of the pageant stages of his time, but we must nevertheless give due respect to Sharp for the integrity with which he approached the plays and records of Coventry's past. Francis Douce, with whom he corresponded concerning the early drama of his city, found Sharp a "kind," "candid," and "liberal" critic.[357]

The Shearmen and Taylors' pageant was later edited by J. M. Manly and appeared in his *Specimens of Pre-Shaksperean Drama* (1897). It was re-edited, from Sharp's transcription but following

Manly in most details, by Hardin Craig in 1902, whose Early English Text Society edition of *Two Coventry Corpus Christi Plays* also includes the Weavers' pageant. Craig in the latter based his edition on Croo's manuscript but nevertheless relied heavily on Sharp's Abbotsford Club edition. Another edition of the play was published in the same year by F. Holthausen ("Das Spiel der Weber von Coventry," *Anglia* 25 [1902]: 209–50), but this was based entirely on Sharp since he incorrectly believed that the original had been burned in 1879. Craig's text and commentary were reissued in a second EETS edition with few substantial improvements in 1957.

THE COVENTRY PLAYS IN MODERN PERFORMANCE

After a final performance of the Coventry pageants in 1579, the plays were laid aside.[358] That many in the guilds hoped for a resurrection of the plays is demonstrated by their failure to sell off their pageant wagons and gear or to dispose of their pageant houses for some time. The Weavers, for example, still retained their costumes in 1606 when they rented their "playres aparell" to Thomas Massey, the contentious booster of playing; it is not known how the costumes were used.[359] And the Cappers finally "gaue posession" of their pageant house to a Mr. Jesson only in 1630, more than sixty years after the last performance of their play.[360] As noted above, in 1591 there had been an attempt to bring back the mysteries, but in this year a different play was substituted. Authorization was given on 19 May, only five weeks before the performance date. This play was to be "plaid on the pagents on Midsomer daye *and* St Peters daye next in this Cittie *and* non other playes./ And that all the mey poles that nowe are standing in this Cittie shalbe taken downe before whitsonday next [i.e., on 23 May], non hereafter to be sett vpp in this Citte."[361] Attempts by men such as Massey, who was deeply involved on behalf of the Cappers, Drapers, and Mercers in the 1591 play and previously in the *Destruction of Jerusalem*, to keep civic drama and pageantry alive were ultimately doomed.[362]

While the suppression of the mysteries was the result of rising Protestant hostility to the plays—a hostility that was related to the rejection of depictions of God and of visible depictions of religious scenes generally[363]—other factors also contributed to their demise. The structures which had supported the religious drama had been severely damaged by the Reformation. The dissolution of the religious confraternities, which had overlapping membership and complex relationships with the trade guilds, was a blow to the social network that fostered traditional pageantry. The suppression of chantries and of the belief in Purgatory, joined to an attack on the concept of merit and on the doctrine concerning works of supererogation,[364] changed the tone of civic life to the point where the energy and money involved in such things as plays may have seemed ill spent. Radical Puritanism, as is well known, tended to object to playing, and playing with religious themes would be severely rejected by many. When James I came to the throne, he agreed to an act of Parliament "For the Preventing and avoyding of the greate Abuse of the Holy Name of God in Stageplayes, Interludes, Maygames, Shewes, and such like" which legislated against any persons who "in any Stage play, Interlude, Shew, Maygame, or Pageant jestingly or prophanely speake or use the holy Name of God or of Christ Jesus, or of the Holy Ghoste or of the Trinitie, which are not to be spoken but with feare and reverence."[365] Added to this antitheatricalism were severe economic decline, increased poverty, and indifference bred of the religious conflicts of the past century.[366] Theatrical tastes also changed, and the dissemination by traveling troupes of professional drama, necessarily secular in nature on account of the authorities' nervousness about things religious, meant that the new fashions in stage plays were shared not only by Londoners but also by people in provincial cities such as Coventry.

Protestantism would join with Enlightenment ideas in subsequent years to prevent any serious interest in reviving the medieval drama. Writing of the Chester plays in 1609, David Rogers would see in them "nothinge profitable to anye vse excepte it be to showe the Ignorance of oure forefathers."[367] With the changes wrought by Romanticism, however, the plays could inspire antiquarian interest of a fairly serious sort, though very often a level of prejudice would be simultaneously present. Sharp did not edit the two extant Coventry plays in order to provide texts for performance, and nowhere was there any enthusiasm whatsoever for the early theater that might lead to the staging of such dramas. A surprising indifference with regard to such plays generally is revealed in the case of the first edition of the Towneley plays, issued in 1836 by the Surtees Society; revealingly, the edition was only accepted for publication since "next to the Continuation of Wills and Inventories it received the greatest number of votes."[368]

Nevertheless, since the middle of the twentieth century the discovery has been made that the medieval drama is much better theater than previously suspected, and the legal barriers against the depiction of God on stage that were believed to prevent its production have been overcome. E. Martin Browne's presentation of the York plays in the ruins of St. Mary's Abbey in 1951 succeeded in leading the way, while thereafter subsequent productions have often resulted in a far less reverential style of acting and eventually have come down to the staging of *The Mysteries* at the National Theatre —a staging that Darryll Grantley has categorized as "parody of medieval drama" for its unconcern with the conceptual integrity of the original plays.[369] On the other hand, experiments with wagon staging in recent years at Toronto, Wakefield, Leeds, and York have been not only illuminating but also good theater in spite of frequent limitations, especially the lack of the substantial funding that underpinned the plays in medieval and Tudor times.[370]

The Coventry Shearmen and Taylors' play had been staged, however, well before the 1950s as a pageant for the Christmas season. An adaptation of the play was reported at the Old Vic in December 1918 (repeated in January 1919), while a version arranged from the Coventry and York Nativity plays by E. K. Chambers was staged at the Everyman Theatre in Hampstead on Christmas eve in 1920.[371] E. Martin Browne staged the Coventry play in the mid-1920s "in a church so hidebound that the vicar would not let Henzie [Browne's wife] to play in it because she was a professional actress" and thereafter at the chapel at Wakefield Prison, where the prisoners broke into a "great gale of laughter, full-throated, that went on for several minutes" in response to Browne's Herod.[372] Browne also organized a production in Pittsburgh at Carnegie Tech (now Carnegie-Mellon University) in Christmas week of 1929.[373] By 1945 the play had been taken up by the Players of St. Peter-upon-Cornhill as a Christmas pageant.[374] The first performance at Coventry in the ruins of St. Michael's Cathedral took place in 1951,[375] the same year as the York Festival production of the York plays; the production, which also included the Weavers' pageant, was by the Religious Drama Society and the Coventry Cappers under the direction of Carina Robins.

In 1978 the Coventry Weavers' and Shearmen and Taylors' pageants, augmented by scenes from other plays, were given their first "annual" staging by the Belgrade Theatre Company in the cathedral ruins, and in the next year the second performance was reviewed by Peter Happé, who commented: "It is clear that the form in which these Coventry plays have survived, the long sequence of short episodes running without a break, has a peculiar force, and that this sequence is held together by a fascinating mixture of humour, reverence, and powerful dramatic characterisation."[376] The production was again staged in 1980, and in keeping with fashion in the performance of early drama, the 1981 production brought innovation: the devil in a bowler hat, Herod in an aviator costume, etc.[377] Further stagings by the Belgrade Theatre Company took place in 1984, in 1987 (the twenty-fifth anniversary of the new Coventry Cathedral), in 1990 (the fiftieth anniversary of the destruction of St. Michael's Cathedral in 1940), and in 1997. In 1993 the Shearmen and Taylors' pageant (without prophets) and plays from other cycles were presented, again in the ruins of St. Michael's, by the Rev. John F. Blackman. At the time of going to press, the next performance, by the Belgrade Theatre Company, is scheduled for 2000.

Editorial Principles

The edition of the Weavers' pageant in the present volume follows Croo's manuscript, now in the Coventry Record Office (CRO Acc. 11/2), with the text as it appears in the fifteenth-century fragments (CRO Acc. 11/1) included below in Appendix I. Folio numbers for the Weavers' play refer to those which have been assigned in the manuscript in modern times. For the Shearmen and Taylors' pageant it has of course been necessary to rely on Sharp's transcription, here followed from the diplomatic edition included in his *Dissertation* of 1825. Both pageants have been edited according to conservative principles, but adding punctuation and capitalization conforming to modern conventions, and normalizing Robert Croo's eccentric word divisions. Abbreviations have been expanded, and are so indicated by italics in our texts. The Glossary provides glosses for words which persons inexperienced in Middle English might find difficult. The folio numbers in the Shearmen and Taylors' play refer to Croo's manuscript, now lost, and are supplied from Sharp's *Dissertation*.

Finally, an explanation may be necessary for uninitiated readers with regard to the monetary designations in the accounts cited in this edition. One pound (£1) was equal to twenty shillings (20*s*), and each shilling was equal to twelve pence (12*d*).

NOTES

[1] William Dugdale, *The Antiquities of Warwickshire* (London, 1656), 116. Dugdale, however, inaccurately says that the plays were acted by the Franciscan friars of Coventry.

[2] *Records of Early English Drama: Coventry*, ed. R. W. Ingram (Toronto: University of Toronto Press, 1981), 80 (hereafter *REED: Coventry*); *The Coventry Leet Book, or Mayor's Register*, ed. Mary Dormer Harris, EETS, o.s. 134–35, 138, 146 (London: Kegan Paul, Trench, Tübner, 1907–13), 2:558 (hereafter *Leet Book*).

[3] Public Record Office, Prob. 11/19; quoted in *REED: Coventry*, 112–13.

[4] John Heywood, *The Plays*, ed. Richard Axton and Peter Happé (Cambridge: Boydell and Brewer, 1991), 132.

[5] *A C Mery Tales* (London, 1526), sig. Dii (*STC* 23,663–64).

[6] Richard Axton, ed., *Three Rastell Plays* (Cambridge: D. S. Brewer, 1979), 2–4.

[7] *REED: Coventry*, 37.

[8] *REED: Coventry*, 77. Corpus Christi was on 2 June in 1485, and the battle of Bosworth Field occurred on 22 August.

[9] *REED: Coventry*, 77.

[10] Charles Phythian-Adams, *Desolation of a City: Coventry and the Urban Crisis of the Late Middle Ages* (Cambridge: Cambridge University Press, 1979), passim.

[11] See Pamela King, "The York and Coventry Mystery Cycles: A Comparative Model of Civic Response to Growth and Recession," *REED Newsletter* 22 (1997): 20–26.

[12] For Coton's letter, in the Public Record Office, see *REED: Coventry*, 148–49.

[13] John Foxe, *Acts and Monvments of Martyrs*, enlarged ed., 2 vols. (London: John Day, 1583), 2:1920; quoted in *REED: Coventry*, 207–08. After his return to prison, Careles was said to have been transferred to London, where he died.

[14] See Charles Phythian-Adams, "Ceremony and the Citizen: The Communal Year at Coventry, 1450–1550," in *Crisis and Order in English Towns, 1500–1700*, ed. Peter Clark and Paul Slack (Toronto: University of Toronto Press, 1972), 57–85, and for further discussion Mervyn James, "Ritual, Drama and Social Body in the Late Medieval English Town," *Past and Present* 98 (1983): 3–29.

[15] The coming of the Three Magi to Bethlehem was illustrated on the seal of the Shearmen and Taylors; see p. 241, below.

[16] *Calendar of the Papal Registers Relating to Great Britain and Ireland: Papal Letters*, XII: *1458–1471*, ed. J. A. Tremlow (London: HMSO, 1933), 644; cited by Phythian-Adams, *Desolation of a City*, 118n. Coventry annals report that the Jesus Mass was suspended in 1491–92; see Bliss Burbidge, *Old Coventry and Lady Godiva, Being Some Flowers of Coventry History Gathered and Arranged* (Birmingham, 1952), 223.

[17] The remaining art of Coventry as well as records of lost art are listed in Clifford

Davidson and Jennifer Alexander, *The Early Art of Coventry, Stratford-upon-Avon, Warwick, and Lesser Sites in Warwickshire*, Early Drama, Art, and Music, Reference Series, 4 (Kalamazoo: Medieval Institute Publications, 1985), 13–58. For some relevant studies of iconoclasm, see John Phillips, *The Reformation of Images: Destruction of Art in England, 1535–1660* (Berkeley and Los Angeles: University of California Press, 1973); *Iconoclasm vs. Art and Drama*, ed. Clifford Davidson and Ann Eljenholm Nichols, Early Drama, Art, and Music, Monograph Series, 11 (Kalamazoo: Medieval Institute Publications, 1988); Margaret Aston, *England's Iconoclasts*, vol. 1 (Oxford: Clarendon Press, 1988); and Eamon Duffy, *The Stripping of the Altars: Traditional Religion in England, c.1400–c.1580* (New Haven: Yale University Press, 1992), 377–593.

[18] See Phythian-Adams, *Desolation of a City*, 118–22, 138.

[19] *English Gilds*, ed. Toulmin Smith, EETS, o.s 40 (London: N. Trübner, 1870), 232.

[20] See Ingram's note in *REED: Coventry*, 576–77, and also John Fines, "Heresy Trials in the Diocese of Coventry and Lichfield, 1511–12," *Journal of Ecclesiastical History* 14 (1963): 162–63, as well as Imogen Luxton, "The Lichfield Court Book: A Postscript," *Bulletin of the Institute of Historical Research* 44 (1971): 122–23.

[21] See Pamela M. King, "Faith, Reason and the Prophets' Dialogue in the Coventry Pageant of the Shearmen and Taylors," in *Philosophy and History*, ed. James Redmond, Themes in Drama, 12 (Cambridge: Cambridge University Press, 1990), 37–46.

[22] Phythian-Adams, *Desolation of a City*, 41; King, "The York and Coventry Mystery Cycles," 22; Ronald M. Berger, *The Most Necessary Luxuries: The Mercers' Company of Coventry, 1550–1680* (University Park: Pennsylvania State University Press, 1993), 67. For a reference to "*Coventrie blue*" by Ben Jonson, see his *Masque of Owls*, in *The Workes of Benjamin Jonson: The Second Volume* (London, 1640), 127–28, as quoted in *REED: Coventry*, 517.

[23] John Leland, *The Itinerary*, ed. Lucy Toulmin Smith, 5 vols. (1907; reprint Carbondale: Southern Illinois University Press, 1964), 2:108.

[24] For debate on the effects of recession on English towns, see especially J. N. Bartlett, "The Expansion and Decline of York in the Late Middle Ages," *English Historical Review* 12, no. 2 (1959–60): 17–33; D. M. Palliser, "A Crisis in English Towns? The Case of York, 1460–1640," *Northern History* 14 (1 978): 108–25; S. H. Rigby, "Urban Decline in the Later Middle Ages," *Urban History Yearbook* (1979): 4–59; Susan Reynolds, "Decline and Decay in Late Medieval Towns," *Urban History Yearbook* (1980): 76–79; A. R. Bridbury, "English Provincial Towns in the Later Middle Ages," *English Historical Review* 34, no. 1 (1981): 1–24; Jennifer Kermode, "Urban Decline? The Flight from Office in Late Medieval York," *English Historical Review* 35, no. 2 (1982): 138–47; and Berger, *The Most Necessary Luxuries*, passim.

[25] *REED: Coventry*, 75, 114.

[26] See Phythian-Adams, *Desolation of a City*, passim.

[27] See ibid., 42, 213.

[28] See King, "The York and Coventry Mystery Plays," 20–26, and Alexandra F. Johnston and Margaret Rogerson, *Records of Early English Drama: York*, 2 vols. (Toronto: University of Toronto Press, 1979), 2:212 and passim (hereafter *REED: York*). Economic

decline at York is studied by D. M. Palliser, *Tudor York* (Oxford: Oxford University Press, 1979), esp. chap. 8. The extent to which the dissolution of monasteries, chantries, and religious guilds affected the poverty of Coventry is more difficult to ascertain than in the case of York, since the latter was a more important ecclesiastical center with more concentration of Church wealth.

[29] *REED: Coventry*, 79; see also *Leet Book*, 2:555–56.

[30] Phythian-Adams, *Desolation of a City*, 33–35, 281; see also J. L. Bolton, *the Medieval English Economy, 1150–1500* (London: J. M. Dent, 1980), 258–59.

[31] *REED: Coventry*, 16–17.

[32] *REED: Coventry*, 82; *Leet Book*, 2:559.

[33] *REED: Coventry*, 83–84; *Leet Book*, 2:564–65. Rather surprisingly, persons not in compliance with the ordinance were threatened with imprisonment. It will need to be remembered that at this time economic decline had set in severely. Reluctance of other guilds to contribute to guilds with plays suggests further that the contributing guilds lacked control over the pageants and hence felt less obligation to support them.

[34] *REED: Coventry*, 103; see also ibid., 104.

[35] Ibid., 192–93.

[36] *REED: Coventry*, 136. The bow makers, fletchers, "*and* suche other" were also named here as not "charged w*ith* eny pagiant."

[37] See Sylvia Thrupp, "The Gilds," in *Cambridge Economic History of Europe*, 8 vols. (Cambridge: Cambridge University Press, 1944–89), 3:230–80.

[38] Phythian-Adams, *Desolation of a City*, 100: Berger, *The Most Necessary Luxuries*, passim.

[39] See H. R. Schubert, *History of the British Iron and Steel Industry from 450 B.C. to A.D. 1775* (London: Routledge and Kegan Paul, 1957), 14–45.

[40] See R. F. Tylecote, "The Medieval Smith and His Methods," in *Medieval Industry*, ed. D. W. Crossley, Research Report no. 40 (British Council for Archaeology, 1981), 42, and Clifford Davidson, *Technology, Guilds, and Early English Drama*, Early Drama, Art, and Music, Monograph Series, 23 (Kalamazoo: Medieval Institute Publications, 1996), 36–40.

[41] *A C Mery Tales*, sig. Dii; see above.

[42] Margaret Rogerson, "The Coventry Corpus Christi Play: A 'Lost' Middle English Creed Play?" *Research Opportunities in Renaissance Drama* 36 (1997): 143–77.

[43] See, however, Peter Travis's argument, in his *Dramatic Design in the Chester Cycle* (Chicago: University of Chicago Press, 1982), 192–222, for seeing a Creed arrangement in the Chester plays.

[44] See *REED: Coventry*, 152, 154–55, 157, 162, 166, 170, 172–74, covering the years 1539 to 1546.

[45] Rogerson, "The Coventry Corpus Christi Play," 171. However, the addition of a reference to Old Testament plays in the revised edition of Dugdale's *Antiquities of Warwickshire*, 2 vols. (London, 1730), 116, was probably not based on solid evidence.

[46] The term 'pageant' is ambiguous, as is the Latin term (*pagina*) from which it derives in medieval usage; for discussion of the meaning of the term as synonymous with "picture," see A. S. G. Edwards, "Middle English Pageant 'Picture'," *Notes and Queries* 237 (1992): 25–26. At Chester, however, 'pageant' did not signify the pageant wagon or carriage until the seventeenth century; see David Mills, *Recycling the Cycle: The City of Chester and Its Whitsun Plays* (Toronto: University of Toronto Press, 1998), 117.

[47] See Reg Ingram, "The Coventry Pageant Wagon," *Medieval English Theatre* 2 (1980): 11.

[48] *REED: Coventry*, 217, 221, 224, 230, 237, etc.

[49] *REED: Coventry*, 79; *Leet Book*, 2:558.

[50] *REED: York*, passim.

[51] Elizabeth Baldwin, "'The Worship of the Cyte and the Welthe of the Craft': The Cappers of Coventry and Their Involvement in Civic Drama, 1494–1591," unpublished Ph.D. diss. (University of Leeds, 1991), 174–82.

[52] *REED: Coventry*, 140, 223, 253, 264, 284, 573–74.

[53] *REED: Coventry*, 37, 50.

[54] Ibid., 234.

[55] See Appendix II, below, and also *REED: Coventry*, 54, 88, 107.

[56] Ibid., 54, 67, 77, 106, 234.

[57] Dugdale, *Antiquities of Warwickshire* (1656), 116.

[58] See the discussion of pageant wagons in Davidson, *Technology, Guilds, and Early English Drama*, 17–31.

[59] Sharp, *Dissertation on the Mysteries*, frontispiece.

[60] See, for example, Meg Twycross, "The Theatricality of Medieval English Plays," in *The Cambridge Companion to Medieval English Theatre*, ed. Richard Beadle (Cambridge: Cambridge University Press, 1994), 47.

[61] See Davidson, *Technology, Guilds, and Early English Drama*, figs. 24–27; Leuven, Stedelyk Museum, MS. Boonen, esp. fols. 455^v–456^r, 447^v–449^r, 459^v–460^r, 465^v–469^r; and Meg Twycross, "The Flemish *Ommegang* and Its Pageant Cars," *Medieval English Theatre* 2 (1980): 15–41. We are grateful to Alexandra Johnston and Records of Early English Drama for permitting access to a microfilm of the Boonen Manuscript.

[62] See Pamela King, "Corpus Christi, Valencia," *Medieval English Theatre* 15 (1993):103–10.

[63] *Records of Early English Drama: Norwich 1540–1642*, ed. David Galloway

(Toronto: University of Toronto Press, 1984), 52–53. For important discussion of the Coventry wagons, see especially the discussion in Ingram, "The Coventry Pageant Waggon," 3–14.

[64] *REED: Coventry*, 63, 200.

[65] Twycross, "The Theatricality of Medieval English Plays," 46.

[66] See Sharp, *Dissertation on the Mysteries*, 20n (for 1497), and J. O. Halliwell-Phillips, *Illustrations of the Life of Shakespeare*, 9th ed. (London: Longmans, Green, 1890), 339; both cited in *REED: Coventry*, 88, 91, 254. Horses were commonly used to draw pageants on the Continent, but seem not to have been much used in England. The Coventry Drapers paid for "horssyng the pagen" in 1591 (ibid., 335), but this play was of course not part of the cycle though the wagons were used. At Canterbury, the wagon carrying the St. Thomas Becket pageant was horse-drawn in 1514–15 and perhaps also subsequently; see *Records of Plays and Players in Kent*, ed. Giles Dawson (Oxford: Malone Society, 1965), 192ff.

[67] *REED: Coventry*, 559.

[68] See the Smiths' ordinances, in *The Coventry Leet Book*, 3:744–45, which state that "no smyth w*ith*in this Cetie [shall] shoo no horse w*ith* forest shoyes nor forest nailles in deceyvyng the kyng*es* subiect*es*." Iron from the Forest of Dean smithies was apparently regarded as inferior.

[69] See *REED: Coventry*, 58.

[70] Ibid., 49.

[71] *REED: Coventry*, 162–287. With regard to the scaffold, see, for example, Glynne Wickham, *Early English Stages, 1300 to 1660*, 3 vols. (London: Routledge and Kegan Paul, 1959–81), 1:171–73; and, more recently, Peter Meredith, "The Iconography of Hell in the English Cycles," in *The Iconography of Hell*, ed. Clifford Davidson and Thomas Seiler, Early Drama, Art, and Music, Monograph Series, 17 (Kalamazoo: Medieval Institute Publications, 1992), 166–68. The wheels on the scaffold were smaller than on the main pageant.

[72] *REED: Coventry*, 193, 278.

[73] Ibid., 191.

[74] Ibid., 3. The location of the Drapers' pageant house at this time was in Little Park Street.

[75] *Calendar of the Close Rolls: Henry IV*, 5 vols. (1927–38), 2:290; this reference is indebted to the Ingram papers, Records of Early English Drama, University of Toronto, and represents a citation received by Ingram from Peter Meredith after *REED: Coventry* had gone to press.

[76] *REED: Coventry*, 528.

[77] *REED: Coventry*, 93; Halliwell-Phillips, *Illustrations of the Life of Shakespeare*, 51.

[78] *REED: Coventry*, 131–32.

[79] Ibid., 266.

[80] Ibid., 276.

[81] Ibid., 329–30. Sharp's citation of a 1503 deed giving this location for the Shearmen and Taylors' pageant house (*Dissertation*, 66) is either an earlier record, now lost, from this date or an error.

[82] Dugdale, *The Antiquities of Warwickshire* (1656), 125.

[83] Davidson and Alexander, *The Early Art*, 23–24, fig. 6; Davidson, *Technology, Guilds, and Early English Drama*, 65–66, fig. 65.

[84] *REED: Coventry*, 83.

[85] Joan C. Lancaster, "Trades and Industries," in *A History of the County of Warwickshire*, ed. W. B. Stephens *et al.*, 8 vols., Victoria County History (London: Oxford University Press, 1904–49), 8:155 (hereafter *VCH*).

[86] For illustrations of shearmen and their tools, see Davidson, *Technology, Guilds, and Early English Drama*, figs. 75–76.

[87] W. W. Greg, "Bibliographical and Textual Problems of the English Miracle Cycles: III. Christ and the Doctors: Interrelations of the Cycles," *The Library*, 3rd ser. 5 (1914): 280–319, supported the view that the major revisions were made in 1520 (that is, 1519) when new plays were reported.

[88] See Ernst Robert Curtius, *European Literature and the Latin Middle Ages*, trans. Willard R. Trask (1953; reprint New York: Harper and Row, 1963), 417–35.

[89] Davidson, *Technology, Guilds, and Early English Drama*, 67–69; L. F. Salzman, *English Industries of the Middle Ages*, 2nd ed. (Oxford: Clarendon Press, 1923), 242–43.

[90] See, for example, the glass at East Harling, discussed and illustrated in Christopher Woodforde, *The Norwich School of Glass-Painting in the Fifteenth Century* (Oxford: Oxford University Press, 1950), 46–47, pl. XI; Kathleen L. Scott, *Later Gothic Manuscripts, 1390–1490*, 2 vols. (London: Harvey Miller, 1996), 1: fig. 60; and Roger S. Wieck, *Time Sanctified: The Book of Hours in Medieval Art and Life* (New York: George Braziller, 1988), 61, fig. 34d, pl. 21.

[91] See *The Kalender of Shepeherdes* (Wynkyn de Worde, 1528), sigs. A7^r, A8^v, and *The Kalender of Shephardes* (Julian Notary, c.1518), sigs. A5^v, F3^v, I5^v; these English editions are based on the French edition published by Antoine Vérard at Paris in 1499.

[92] See Clifford Davidson, *From Creation to Doom: The York Cycle of Mystery Plays* (New York: AMS Press, 1984), 179–81.

[93] For a more extended discussion, see King, "Faith, Reason and the Prophets' Dialogue," 29–53.

[94] *REED: Coventry*, 73–74. Herod the Great was very often conflated with the Herod who reigned at the time of the execution of John the Baptist: see David Staines, "To Out-Herod Herod: The Development of a Dramatic Character," *Comparative Drama* 10 (1976): 30–32.

[95] Hamlet's reference to Herod (*Hamlet* 3.2.13–14) is presumably a sign of Shakespeare's familiarity as a boy with the plays at Coventry, a town which was only a short

distance from his native Stratford-upon-Avon. For further discussion concerning his knowledge of the Coventry mystery plays, see Clifford Davidson, *On Tradition: Essays on the Use and Valuation of the Past* (New York: AMS Press, 1992), 56–69.

[96] Staines, "To Out-Herod Herod," 48.

[97] Except for the seal of the Shearmen and Taylors, the Magi appear nowhere in the extant art of Coventry. At nearby locations in Warwickshire there are, however, two fragmentary examples. One is a wall painting at Burton Dassett of a crowned head with a hand that is holding a gift, and the other is a set of three headless figures under niches at Chesterton who carry gifts in their hands. In the latter example, the figure on the right is kneeling, while the others stand (Davidson and Alexander, *The Early Art*, 118).

[98] See Karl Young, *The Drama of the Medieval Church*, 2 vols. (Oxford: Clarendon Press, 1933), 2:110–17; *The York Plays*, ed. Richard Beadle (London: Edward Arnold, 1982), Play XIX.

[99] See Sophie Oosterwijk, "Of Mops and Puppets: The Ambiguous Use of the Word 'Mop' in the Towneley Plays," *Notes and Queries* 242 (1997): 169–71.

[100] The Weavers were the third most numerous company in the mid-fifteenth-century muster with fifty-seven members having sufficient resources to bear arms, but only one chamberlain and one bailiff were drawn from its ranks; see *REED: Coventry*, 545; Lancaster, "Trades and Industries," in *VCH*, 8:155. Cf. Davidson, *Technology, Guilds, and Early English Drama*, 63, 65. On the general status of cloth makers, see ibid., 57–61.

[101] *REED: Coventry*, 128, 133; *Leet Book*, 3:697, 710.

[102] See Mary H. M. Hulton, *"Company and Fellowship": The Medieval Weavers of Coventry*, Dugdale Society, 31 (Oxford, 1987), 10–11.

[103] CR0 34/I Weavers 2a, fol. 9ᵛ, as cited by Hulton, *"Company and Fellowship,"* 12; *Leet Book*, 3:722.

[104] Hulton, *"Company and Fellowship,"* 24, n. 21.

[105] CR0 34/I; REED: Coventry, 26–27.

[106] *REED: Coventry*, 122, 134. For other accounts cited below, see ibid., passim.

[107] Ibid., 148.

[108] Ibid., 315, 318–19.

[109] Ibid., 226.

[110] Ibid., 252, 285.

[111] Ibid., 16; Reg Ingram, "'Pleyng geire accustomed belongyng & necessarie': Guild Records and Pageant Production at Coventry," in *Records of Early English Drama: Proceedings of the First Colloquium*, ed. JoAnna Dutka (Toronto: Records of Early English Drama, 1979), 70–72.

[112] Margaret Rogerson, "Casting the Coventry Weavers' Pageant," *Theatre Notebook* 48 (1994):138–47.

[113] *REED: Coventry*, 121.

[114] See Foxe, *Acts and Monvments*, 569; *REED: Coventry*, 563.

[115] *REED: Coventry*, 122, 169, 178, 180, 563.

[116] *REED: Coventry*, 142.

[117] Hardin Craig, *English Religious Drama* (Oxford: Clarendon Press, 1955), 295. Craig, however, valued most the passages which retained the most reverent tone; Croo's final version displeased him clearly for the wrong reasons as being too theatrical!

[118] *REED: Coventry*, 185, 292.

[119] Ibid., 566.

[120] Ibid. 566.

[121] CRO Acc. 100/17/1, fol. 15ᵛ.

[122] CRO Acc. 100/17/1, fol. 66; Ingram omits this line from the records in *REED: Coventry*.

[123] The shelfmark of the All Souls Library copy is LR 4b 21.

[124] *REED: Coventry*, 168. Borsley also entertained the Weavers' players "betwen ye plays" at his house (ibid., 169). John Heyns, who like Borsley was a capper and would later be Master of this company, was also one of those who agreed in 1566 to play in this guild's pageant for the expected visit of the queen (ibid., 235, 563).

[125] Ibid., 186, 188. Bowater would be Master of the Weavers' company in 1558 (ibid., 563). Christopher Dale's will of 9 May 1559 is printed in Hulton, "*Company and Fellowship,*" 20–23.

[126] *REED: Coventry*, 165–68.

[127] Ibid., 211.

[128] Ibid., 248, 262.

[129] See Davidson, *From Creation to Doom*, 73–74.

[130] *REED: Coventry*, 196.

[131] V. A. Kolve, *The Play Called Corpus Christi* (Stanford: Stanford University Press, 1966), 249.

[132] See C. Philip Deasy, *St. Joseph in the English Mystery Plays* (Washington, D.C.: Catholic University of America, 1937), 104; Rosemary Woolf, *The English Mystery Plays* (Berkeley and Los Angeles: University of California Press, 1972), 200; Kolve, *The Play Called Corpus Christi*; and Mikiko Ishii, "Joseph's Proverbs in the Coventry Plays," *Folk-Lore* 92, no.1 (1982): 47–60.

[133] Davidson, *Technology, Guilds, and Early English Drama*, 67, 69, fig. 68.

[134] *REED: Coventry*, 252, 255, 573.

[135] Greg, "Bibliographical and Textual Problems of the English Miracle Cycles, III—Christ and the Doctors," 297–319. See also Woolf, *The English Mystery Plays*, 212–15; and Daniel T. Kline, "Structure, Characterization, and the New Community in Four Plays of Jesus and the Doctors," *Comparative Drama* 26 (1992–93), 344–57.

[136] Kline, "Structure, Characterization, and the New Community in Four Plays of Jesus and the Doctors," 352–53.

[137] A. F. Kendrick, "The Coventry Tapestry," *Burlington Magazine* 44 (1924): 84, fig. 1.

[138] Davidson and Alexander, *The Early Art*, 29–30, fig. 10.

[139] See, for example, Duffy, *The Stripping of the Altars*, 234–38. For an interesting "Measure of the Nails," depicted below Jesus' Wounds, on a prayer roll owned by King Henry VIII in his youth and now at Ushaw College, see ibid., fig. 110. The nails as depicted here were held to have miraculous powers.

[140] *REED: Coventry*, 50.

[141] Ibid., 20, 24.

[142] Sharp, *Dissertation*, 15; *REED: Coventry*, 27.

[143] *REED: Coventry*, 75, 85.

[144] Ibid., 86, 101–02.

[145] Ibid., 225.

[146] For a table comparing payments in 1477 with those to actors in 1489–90, 1499, and 1573–74, see Davidson, *Technology, Guilds, and Early English Drama*, 41.

[147] *REED: Coventry*, 59–61.

[148] See *REED: Coventry*, Glossary, *s.v.* 'wyff shevys.'

[149] *REED: Coventry*, 69.

[150] Ibid., 86.

[151] Ibid., 25.

[152] Ibid., 231.

[153] Sharp, *Dissertation*, 15–17; *REED: Coventry*, 72–74.

[154] *REED: Coventry*, 95.

[155] In 1573 the Smiths paid 4*d* to Fawston "for Coc-croyng," obviously for the scene of Peter's denial; this payment was repeated in 1574 (*REED: Coventry*, 265, 269).

[156] Ibid., 63.

[157] Ibid., 73, 85. For the use of gold foil for Herod's crest, see ibid., 95; see also the discussion of Herod and the Smiths' pageant in Davidson, *Technology, Guilds, and Early English Drama*, 34–47.

[158] See Miriam Skey, "Herod's Demon Crown," *Journal of the Courtauld and Warburg Institutes* 40 (1977): 274–76; for a different suggestion concerning Herod's crest, see Meg Twycross and Sarah Carpenter, "Masks in Medieval Mystery Plays," *Medieval English Theatre* 3 (1981): 9.

[159] *REED: Coventry*, 58.

[160] Ibid., 63.

[161] Ibid., 97.

[162] Ibid., 243, 265, 579.

[163] Ibid., 111.

[164] See Davidson, *Technology, Guilds, and Early English Drama*, 61, fig. 61; Davidson and Alexander, *The Early Art*, 27, fig. 8.

[165] *REED: Coventry*, 231 and Glossary, *s.v.* 'trulles.'

[166] Ibid., 265.

[167] Ibid., 260.

[168] Ibid., 265.

[169] Ibid., 289. For Thomas Massey, see ibid., 495–502 (Appendix 6).

[170] Ibid., 231.

[171] See *Certain Sermons or Homilies (1547) and A Homily Against Wilful Rebellion and Disobedience*, ed. Ronald B. Bond (Toronto: University of Toronto Press, 1987), 79–81. For Luther's influential views on the atonement, see for convenience *What Luther Says*, ed. Ewald M. Plass, 3 vols. (St. Louis: Concordia, 1959), 3:1418–27.

[172] Baldwin, "The Worship of the Cyte," 9–10; *Leet Book*, 1:153.

[173] Baldwin, "The Worship of the Cyte," 17.

[174] See *REED: Coventry*, 128.

[175] Ibid., 11.

[176] Phythian-Adams, *Desolation of a City*, 44, 214, and passim.

[177] *REED: Coventry*, 131; see also R. W. Ingram, "'To find the players and all that longeth therto': Notes on the Production of Medieval Drama at Coventry," in *The Elizabethan Theatre V*, ed. G. R. Hibbard (Hamden, Conn.: Archon Books, 1975), 20.

[178] *REED: Coventry*, 145, 486–87.

[179] See Ian Lancashire, *Dramatic Texts and Records of Britain: A Chronological Topography* (Toronto: University of Toronto Press, 1984), 115.

[180] British Library, MS. Add. 43645, fol. 57; *REED: Coventry*, 139–40.

[181] See Ingram, "To find the players and all that longeth therto," 37.

[182] *REED: Coventry*, 240, 567. The 1567 inventory was prepared at the death of the pageant master Thomas Linacers, who had held the pageant properties and costumes in his possession.

[183] Ibid., 334; on the spade, see Steven May, "A Medieval Stage Property: The Spade," *Medieval English Theatre* 4 (1982): 77–92.

[184] *REED: Coventry*, 240, 334.

[185] Ibid., 277.

[186] Ibid., 240.

[187] Ibid., 241.

[188] On the iconography, see Davidson, *From Creation to Doom*, 142–43.

[189] *REED: Coventry*, 139, 202. See especially Elizabeth Baldwin, "Who was the Mother of Death?" *Notes and Queries* 237 (1992): 157–58. Cf. Jacqueline Joan Underhill, "The Staging of Biblical Drama in Coventry 1390–1579," unpublished diss. (University of Toronto, 1995), 162–64.

[190] *REED: Coventry*, 278, 291.

[191] Sharp, *Dissertation*, 63.

[192] William Hone, *Ancient Mysteries Described, Especially the English Miracle Plays* (London: William Hone, 1823), 139; see also Sharp, *Dissertation on the Mysteries*, 57–58.

[193] *REED: Coventry*, 240; see also ibid., 278.

[194] Ibid., 278.

[195] Ibid., 167, 278.

[196] See Clifford Davidson, *The Guild Chapel Wall Paintings at Stratford-upon-Avon* (New York: AMS Press, 1988), pl. 17; and Davidson and Alexander, *The Early Art*, fig. 28.

[197] For the iconography, see especially Pamela Sheingorn, "'Who can open the doors of his face?': The Iconography of Hell Mouth," in *The Iconography of Hell*, ed. Davidson and Seiler, 1–19.

[198] *REED: Coventry*, 163, 167, 245, 334.

[199] Bernard Rackham, "The Glass-Paintings of Coventry and Its Neighbourhood," *Walpole Society* 19 (1930–31): 99, pl. XVI: see also Davidson and Alexander, *The Early Art*, 32.

[200] See *REED: Coventry*, 185; *The Staging of Religious Drama in Europe in the Later Middle Ages*, ed. Peter Meredith and John E. Tailby, Early Drama, Art, and Music, Monograph Series, 4 (Kalamazoo: Medieval Institute Publications, 1983), 90.

[201] *REED: Coventry*, 182, 240.

[202] See Meredith, "The Iconography of Hell in the English Cycles," 175–76, and also Davidson, *Technology, Guilds, and Early English Drama*, 85–86, fig. 86.

[203] See Thomas H. Seiler, "Filth and Stench as Aspects of the Iconography of Hell," in *The Iconography of Hell*, ed. Davidson and Seiler, 132–40.

[204] *REED: Coventry*, 167, 185–86, 228, 240, 277–78, 334. The mitres were painted.

[205] Ibid., 182, 240, 334.

[206] In 1573, 1576, 1578–79; see ibid., 261, 278, 288, 291.

[207] *REED: Coventry*, 240. On this entry, see also Elizabeth Baldwin, "Some Suggested Emendations to *REED: Coventry*," *REED Newsletter* 16, no. 2 (1991): 8.

[208] *REED: Coventry*, 291.

[209] Sharp, *Dissertation*, pl. 9, and Sharp's annotated proof copy of this work, British Library Add. MS. 43645, fols. 53–54.

[210] See Clifford Davidson, *Illustrations of the Stage and Acting in England to 1580*, Early Drama, Art, and Music, Monograph Ser., 16 (Kalamazoo: Medieval Institute Publications, 1982), 67ff.

[211] The first record appears in 1539; see Baldwin, "Some Suggested Emendations," 8–9.

[212] *REED: Coventry*, 202.

[213] See ibid., 163.

[214] Philip B. Chatwin, "Medieval Stained Glass from the Cathedral, Coventry," *Transactions of the Birmingham Archaeological Association* 66 (1950): pl. V.

[215] See Francis Cheetham, *English Medieval Alabasters, with a Catalogue of the Collection in the Victoria and Albert Museum* (Oxford: Phaidon-Christie's, 1984), nos. 199–208; W. L. Hildburgh, "Iconographic Peculiarities," *Folk-Lore* 44 (1933): 44, pl. XX, and "Note on Medieval English Representations of 'The Resurrection of Our Lord'," *Folk-Lore* 48 (1937): 95–98; Davidson, *From Creation to Doom*, 150. A Warwickshire alabaster of the Resurrection was very likely the item (large, and painted) noted in an inventory at Warwick in 1454, but this carving disappeared, like so much medieval church art, without a trace at the Reformation; see Davidson and Alexander, *The Early Art*, 72.

[216] *The Chester Mystery Cycle*, ed. R. M. Lumiansky and David Mills, EETS, s.s. 3, 9 (London: Oxford University Press, 1974–86), 1:349 (XVIII.274–75).

[217] *REED: Coventry*, 240–41.

[218] The cross ("Godes crose") is noted in the inventory of 1567 (*REED: Coventry*, 240) which also lists several "stremers" and "pensells" (ibid., 240–41).

[219] See the half-figure of Christ crucified rising out of a tomb on an alabaster formerly at Coughton Court, Warwickshire; Davidson and Alexander, *The Early Art*, fig. 41. For important discussion of the iconography, see J. W. Robinson, "The Late Medieval Cult of Jesus and the Mystery Plays," *PMLA* 80 (1965): 508–14.

[220] *The Towneley Plays*, ed. Martin Stevens and A. C. Cawley, EETS, s.s. 13–14 (Oxford: Oxford University Press, 1994), 1:342 (26.237).

[221] Davidson and Alexander, *The Early Art*, 66, fig. 26.

[222] *REED: Coventry*, 139 and passim. The minstrel was not excluded in 1549, however.

[223] Pamela Sheingorn, "The Moment of the Resurrection in the Corpus Christi Plays," *Medievalia et Humanistica* n.s. 11 (1982): 122.

[224] Meg Twycross, "Playing the Resurrection," 289.

[225] *REED: Coventry*, 167.

[226] JoAnna Dutka, *Music in the English Mystery Plays*, Early Drama, Art, and Music, Reference Series, 2 (Kalamazoo: Medieval Institute Publications, 1980), 23–24, and Richard Rastall, *Heaven Singing*, 2 vols. (Cambridge: D. S. Brewer, 1996–), 1:189; *York Plays*, *s.d.* at XXXVIII.187 (added in hand of John Clerke); *Chester*, *s.d.* at XVIII.153.

[227] *Towneley Plays*, *s.d.* at 26.230.

[228] Trans. in Dutka, *Music in the English Mystery Plays*, 115. The text in abbreviated form may also have appeared as a respond or *communio*; see ibid., 23–24. For the use of the antiphon in the Easter *Elevatio* ceremony, see Pamela Sheingorn, *The Easter Sepulchre in England*, Early Drama, Art, and Music, Reference Series, 5 (Kalamazoo: Medieval Institute Publications, 1987), 116, 134, 249, 349–50, 352, 365.

[229] *REED: Coventry*, 223, 236–37, 245, 249, 573; similar post-Reformation payments "for pryckyng songes for ye churche" were recorded in 1560 at Holy Trinity Church (Thomas Sharp, *Illustrative Papers on the History and Antiquities of the City of Coventry*, ed. W. G. Fretton [1871], 120).

[230] *York Plays*, XXXVIII.221–22.

[231] Ibid., XXXVIII.235–38.

[232] Davidson and Alexander, *The Early Art*, 66–67, fig. 27.

[233] See especially the *Visitatio Sepulchri* in the *Fleury Playbook*; for the *Fleury Playbook* text of the *Hortulanus* scene, see Young, *The Drama of the Medieval Church*, 1:395–97.

[234] Davidson and Alexander, *The Early Art*, 135.

[235] Charles J. Hart, "Old Chests," *Transactions of the Birmingham Archaeological Society* 20 (1895): 80.

[236] Cheetham, *English Medieval Alabasters*, nos. 211–12.

[237] The appearance of Mary to her Son is dramatized in *The N-Town Play*, ed. Stephen Spector, EETS, s.s. 11–12 (Oxford: Oxford University Press, 1991), 1:353–54 (35.89–136);

see also the discussion in Woolf, *The English Mystery Plays*, 279–80.

[238] For an example of early Protestant iconoclasm directed against Marian iconography, see the discussion of the defacing of the sculptures in the Lady Chapel at Ely in Clifford Davidson, "The Devil's Guts: Allegations of Superstition and Fraud in Religious Drama and Art during the Reformation," in *Iconoclasm vs. Art and Drama*, ed. Davidson and Nichols, 122–27.

[239] For the final reference (in 1547) to the Virgin Mary in the Cappers' play, see *REED: Coventry*, 175.

[240] Ibid., 173.

[241] Ibid., 191.

[242] Ibid., 241, 291.

[243] Ibid., 334.

[244] See ibid., 150, 153, 163.

[245] Joan Lancaster, "Crafts and Industries," in *VCH*, 8:155.

[246] See Mary Dormer Harris, "The Craft Guilds of Coventry," *Proceedings of the Society of Antiquaries*, 2nd ser. 16 (1895): 5; Phythian-Adams, *Desolation of a City*, 100, 160.

[247] In 1522 there were twenty-six Mercers and twenty-eight Drapers, while the Cappers' numbers had risen to eighty-three; see Hoskins, "English Provincial Towns in the Early Sixteenth Century," *Transactions of the Royal Historical Society*, 5th ser. 6 (1956): 13.

[248] Berger, *The Most Necessary Luxuries*, 98–99, 110–11.

[249] Public Record Office Prob. 11/19, fols. 67^{r}–68^{v}. Ingram quotes only the passage from the will that directly seemed to him to be relevant to the Coventry plays (*REED: Coventry*, 112). The formulaic nature of Pysford's will might invite some scepticism concerning his views except that he also founded a chantry chapel and an obit for himself on the anniversary of his death. See also Sharp, *Illustrative Papers*, 38, 44.

[250] Hardin Craig, ed., *Two Coventry Corpus Christi Plays*, xvi, and *English Religious Drama*, 289.

[251] See Anne F. Sutton, *I Sing of a Maiden: The Story of the Maiden of the Mercers' Company* (London: Mercers' Company, 1998), esp. 35.

[252] Smith, *English Guilds*, 229–31.

[253] Davidson and Alexander, *The Early Art*, 13, 35, frontispiece. The principal guild association, of course, was with the Holy Trinity Guild.

[254] Diana K. Bolton, "Social History to 1700," in *VCH*, 8:218.

[255] Davidson and Alexander, *The Early Art*, 35; John Carter, *Specimens of the Ancient Sculpture and Painting Now Remaining in the Kingdom*, 2 vols. (London, 1780), 1: pl. following 15. The present gatehouse boss is a modern replacement of 1878–79.

[256] See the plan of St. Michael's Church in Davidson, *Technology, Guilds, and Early English Drama*, fig. 33.

[257] Davidson and Alexander, *The Early Art*, 35; for an illustration of the misericord in St. Michael's, see Mary Dormer Harris, "The Misericords of Coventry," *Transactions of the Birmingham Archaeological Society* 52 (1927): pl. XXXI.

[258] *REED: Coventry*, 125, 564; cf. Sharp, *Dissertation*, 77.

[259] Davidson and Alexander, *The Early Art*, 136.

[260] Mercers' Account Book, CR0 Acc. 15, fol. 2; as quoted in *REED: Coventry*, 188.

[261] Martin Stevens, "The Missing Parts of the Towneley Cycle," *Speculum* 45 (1970): 258–59; Barbara D. Palmer, "'Towneley Plays' or 'Wakefield Cycle' Revisited," *Comparative Drama* 21 (1987–88): 318–48.

[262] See *Records of Early English Drama: Chester*, ed. Lawrence M. Clopper (Toronto: University of Toronto Press, 1979), 20–21, 23, 37.

[263] See Pamela M. King and Asunción Salvador-Rabaza, "*La Festa d'Elx*: The Festival of the Assumption of the Virgin, Elche (Alicante)," *Medieval English Theatre* 8 (1986): 21–60; Pamela M. King, "The *Festa d'Elx*: Civic Devotion, Display and Identity," in *Festive Drama*, ed. Meg Twycross (Woodbridge: D. S. Brewer, 1996), 95–109; Francesc Massip, "The Cloud: A Medieval Aerial Device, Its Origins, and Its Use Today," *Early Drama, Art, and Music Review* 16 (1994): 65–77; Davidson, *Technology, Guilds, and Early English Drama*, 97–98.

[264] *REED: Coventry*, 292.

[265] Ibid., 321–22.

[266] Harris, ed., *Leet Book*, 4:857, and, for the Cappers' pageant, Baldwin, "The Worship of the Cyte," 103–04.

[267] See, for example, Sally-Beth MacLean, "Marian Devotion in Post-Reformation Chester: Implications of the Smiths' 'Purification' Play," in *The Middle Ages and the North-West*, ed. Tom Scott and Pat Starkey (Oxford: Leopard's Head Press, 1995), 237–55, for comment on the retention of Catholic pageantry in the Chester cycle.

[268] *REED: Coventry*, 16–17; *Leet Book*, 1:220.

[269] Berger, *The Most Necessary Luxuries*, 113–14.

[270] Lancaster, "Craft Organisation to the Sixteenth Century," in *VCH*, 8:159–60.

[271] *REED: Coventry*, 280–81, citing Drapers' Ordinance (eighteenth-century copy), CRO Acc. 99/6/1, fol. 4^v; CR0 154 Drapers 12, Ic 1950/33, fol. 5.

[272] Philip B. Chatwin, "Monumental Effigies in the County of Warwick," *Transactions of the Birmingham Archaeological Association* 48 (1925): 148–49, pl. XXI. On the Drapers' chapel, see also Sharp, *Illustrations of the History*, 20–23, and, for the location of the Drapers' chapel, Davidson, *Technology, Guilds, and Early English Drama*, fig. 33.

[273] Chatwin, "Monumental Effigies," 148–49; *Coventry Leet Book*, 3:684; see also

Phythian-Adams, *Desolation of a City*, 265–66.

[274] *REED: Coventry*, 242.

[275] Ibid., 599–600.

[276] *Coventry Leet Book*, 2:300; *REED: Coventry*, 549; see also Mary Dormer Harris, *The History of the Drapers Company* (n.p., n.d.), 14–15.

[277] Harris, "The Misericords of Coventry," 264; Davidson and Alexander, *The Early Art*, 36; there are also some fragments of painted glass from St. Michael's which are from a Last Judgment scene; see Chatwin, "Medieval Stained Glass from the Cathedral Coventry," pls. VI–VII.

[278] *REED: Coventry*, 37, 549; *Leet Book*, 2:300.

[279] Ingram Papers, Records of Early English Drama, Toronto; see also Ingram, "Pleying geire accustomed belongyng & necessarie," 62–63.

[280] Ingram, "Pleying geire accustomed belongyng & necessarie," 74.

[281] Suggested by the Coventry annals; see *REED: Coventry*, 114.

[282] *REED: Coventry*, 465–69; Sharp, *Dissertation*, 69–71.

[283] See the discussion in Woolf, *The English Mystery Plays*, 297–98, and, for the York Doomsday play, *REED: York*, 1:55–56; Alexandra Johnston and Margaret Rogerson, "The Doomsday Pageant of the York Mercers, 1433," *Leeds Studies in English*, n.s. 5 (1971): 29–34; Davidson, *From Creation to Doom*, 177–92.

[284] Harris, "Misericords of Coventry," 262–63, pl. XXXII: Davidson and Alexander, *The Early Art*, 52. A scene which combines giving food and drink to the hungry and thirsty also appeared in a painted glass roundel from Coventry that is now lost; see Herbert Read, *English Stained Glass* (New York: Putnam's, 1926), pl. 42. Also lost is the Warwickshire example in the church at Coughton where a Corporal Acts of Mercy window along with a Last Judgment window were purchased through a bequest by Robert Throckmorton in 1518; see Dugdale, *Antiquities of Warwickshire* (1656), 560.

[285] "Come, ye blessed of my father," and "Depart from me, you cursed, into everlasting fire" (Matt. 25:34, 41; Douay translation). See J. R. Holliday, "St. Martin's Church, and the Discoveries Made During Its Restoration," *Birmingham and Midland Institute* 5 (1874): 56–57.

[286] See Mary Phillips Perry, "On the Psychostasis in Christian Art," *Burlington Magazine* 22 (1912–13): 94–105, 108–18, and Pamela Sheingorn, "'For God is such a doomsman': Origins and Development of the Theme of Last Judgment," in *Homo, Memento Finis: The Iconography of Just Judgment in Medieval Art and Drama*, ed. David Bevington, Early Drama, Art, and Music, Monograph Series, 6 (Kalamazoo: Medieval Institute Publications, 1985), 15–58. A Warwickshire example of St. Michael weighing souls appears on a fourteenth-century font at Tysoe; see Davidson and Alexander, *The Early Art*, 141.

[287] R. B. Pugh, "Seals, Arms, Insignia, Plate, and Officers," in *VCH*, 8:415; "Coventry Corporation Seals," *The Old Cross* 1 (1878–79): 93, fig. 8.

[288] See Meg Twycross, "'With what body shall they come?' Black and White Souls in

English Mystery Plays," in *Langland, the Mystics, and the Medieval Religious Tradition: Essays in Honour of S. S. Hussey*, ed. Helen Phillips (Cambridge: D. S. Brewer, 1990), 271–86. For further discussion concerning those denied salvation, see Clifford Davidson, "The Fate of the Damned," in *The Iconography of Hell*, ed. Davidson and Seiler, 41–46.

[289] *REED: Coventry*, 217. Ingram, "To find the players and all that longeth therto," 33, implies, if I understand him correctly, that the "wormes of Conscyence" were added in 1561, which might seem to indicate that they were possibly Protestantizing additions to the play; see Underhill, "The Staging of Biblical Drama in Coventry," 164, who suggests the influence of a gloss to Isaiah 66:24 in the Geneva Bible. Worms of conscience are not specifically Protestant, however, as Underhill admits (165–66).

[290] *REED: Coventry*, 217, 224.

[291] Ibid., 230.

[292] Ibid., 230. Rosin was probably used to set the fire; see Philip Butterworth, *Theatre of Fire: Special Effects in Early English and Scottish Theatre* (London: Society for Theatre Research, 1998), passim.

[293] See Benjamin Poole, *The History of Coventry* (Coventry, 1852), 76–77, and, for its present condition, Jennifer Alexander, "Coventry Holy Trinity Wall Painting," *EDAM Newsletter* 11 (1989): 37.

[294] George Scharf, Jr., "Observations on a Picture in Gloucester Cathedral and Some Other Representations of the Last Judgment," *Archaeologia* 36 (1855), pl. XXXII; see also Davidson, *Technology, Guilds, and Early English Drama*, 87–88, fig. 89.

[295] W. O. Hassall, *The Holkham Bible Picture Book* (London: Dropmore Press, 1954), fol. 42. The Fifteen Signs of Doomsday are reported, however, in the Chester cycle. For general discussion, see especially William W. Heist, *The Fifteen Signs Before Doomsday* (East Lansing: Michigan State College Press, 1952).

[296] Davidson, *The Guild Chapel Wall Paintings*, 31, fig. 16.

[297] See Thomas French, *York Minster: The Great East Window*, CVMA Summary Catalog 2 (Oxford: Oxford University Press, 1995).

[298] *REED: Coventry*, 230, 474; see also Sharp, *Dissertation*, 73.

[299] Jacobus de Voragine, *The Golden Legend*, trans. William Granger Ryan, 2 vols. (Princeton: Princeton University Press, 1993), 1:8. It is possible that these signs in the Coventry Doomsday pageant were accompanied by an Antichrist scene. Antichrist was also predicted in the last days in Jacobus's account (1:8–9), and there is a reference to an Antichrist play in the Wycliffite *Tretise of Miraclis Pleyinge*, an antitheatrical document written in English that is linguistically characteristic of counties near to Coventry. For further discussion, see Clifford Davidson, "The Signs of Doomsday in Drama and Art," *Historical Representations*, forthcoming.

[300] *REED: Coventry*, 230; Sharp, *Dissertation*, 72.

[301] *The Chester Mystery Cycle*, ed. Lumiansky and Mills, 1:450 (XXIV.46 *s.d.*); trans. David Mills, in *The Chester Mystery Cycle: A New Edition with Modernized Spelling* (East Lansing: Colleagues Press, 1992), 426.

[302] *The Chester Mystery Cycle*, ed. Lumiansky and Mills, 1:453 (XXIV.429 *s.d.*); trans. Mills, 429.

[303] See Pierre Turpin, "Ancient Wall Paintings in the Charterhouse, Coventry," *Burlington Magazine* 35 (1919): pl. facing 252.

[304] See, for example, *REED: Coventry*, 217, 224, 229, and Ingram, "Pleyng geire accustomed belongyng & necessarie," 77. Trumpet playing was a jealously guarded skill, as the Coventry *Leet Book* implies (1:189); see also *REED: Coventry*, 12.

[305] *REED: Coventry*, 229–30, 466.

[306] Ibid., 465, 479. There are further listings for a ladder and a pillar, but it is not certain that these represented Instruments of the Passion since they may have had other uses; see ibid., 237, 474.

[307] Davidson, *The Guild Chapel Wall Paintings*, fig. 17; these angels were fragmentary in 1804 when the wall paintings were discovered and Thomas Fisher made his drawings of them.

[308] *Chester Mystery Cycle*, ed. Lumiansky and Mills, 1:439; *REED: York*, 1:55.

[309] *REED: Coventry*, 259, 474; Sharp, *Dissertation*, 71.

[310] *REED: Coventry*, 242, 259, 465,472; Sharp, *Dissertation*, 71.

[311] *REED: Coventry*, 217, 237; Sharp, *Dissertation*, 61, 73.

[312] Sharp, *Dissertation*, 69; for discussion of devil masks, see Twycross and Carpenter, "Masks in Medieval English Theatre: The Mystery Plays, II," *Medieval English Theatre* 3 (1981): 71–90.

[313] *REED: Coventry*, 259.

[314] Harris, "Misericords of Coventry," pl. XXXII.

[315] See especially Barbara D. Palmer, "The Inhabitants of Hell: Devils," in *The Iconography of Hell*, ed. Davidson and Seiler, 25.

[316] Sharp, *Dissertation*, 78–79; *REED: Coventry*, 11, 83, 174.

[317] *REED: Coventry*, 9, 543; *Leet Book*, 1:115–16.

[318] *REED: Coventry*, 83, 125, 133–34, 190, 449–50.

[319] Ibid., 112–13.

[320] Ibid., 87.

[321] *REED: Coventry*, 192–93; Phythian-Adams, *Desolation of a City*, 216.

[322] Sharp, *Illustrative Papers*, 85.

[323] *REED: Coventry*, 6, 526, 541; Phythian-Adams, *Desolation of a City*, 161.

[324] *REED: Coventry*, 82, 102, 542.

[325] Ibid., 125, 563–64.

[326] Ibid., 17.

[327] For the importance of the guilds' technical skills for mounting the pageants, see Davidson, *Technology, Guilds, and Early English Drama*, passim.

[328] Ingram, "To find the players and all that longeth therto," 25–29, came to the conclusion that at least two men named Robert Croo were involved. Ingram searched Coventry wills and inventories both in the Public Record Office and in the Lichfield diocesan records, but he found no new material on Croo (Ingram papers, Records of Early English Drama, Toronto). Baldwin, "The worship of the Cyte," 199–205, has argued that there may have been as many as three men of the same name.

[329] Cappers' Accounts, cited from the transcription in Baldwin, "The worship of the Cyte," 199.

[330] There has been confusion over this record with the result that a "ghost" Croo has been created. Baldwin has pointed out that "Robart Crow made breder" in this year refers to his creation of other brothers rather than to his being made a brother himself ("Some Suggested Emendations," 8–10).

[331] Baldwin, "The worship of the Cyte," 200.

[332] *REED: Coventry*, 123; Ingram, "To find the players and all that longeth therto," 25–26.

[333] *REED: Coventry*, 154, 177.

[334] Ibid., 217, 221, 224, 237. The reference in 1561 to "Robert Bro" (ibid., 217) is almost certainly a mistake.

[335] Ibid., 225.

[336] Ibid., 476.

[337] Ibid., 474.

[338] Demographers have verified that although life expectancy was much lower in the sixteenth century than today, the strong and fortunate could live to a great age. The appearance of a very old man as God would be quite consistent with the usual iconography. On the question of longevity, see also Creighton Gilbert, "When Did a Man in the Renaissance Grow Old," *Renaissance Studies* 14 (1967): 7–32.

[339] REED: Coventry, 247.

[340] Ibid., 476, 576.

[341] On the feasibility of playing the regals for both the Weavers' and Drapers' pageants, see Rastall, *Heaven Singing*, 1:64, 341–43.

[342] Ibid., 1:63–64.

[343] Ibid., 1:64. Both the Smiths and the Cappers would be candidates for the original sponsorship of the pageant which included this song.

[344] Rastall, *Heaven Singing*, 1:64–65; Holy Trinity Churchwardens' Accounts, as cited in *REED: Coventry*, 491, and see also listings for these four waits together in the Chamberlains' Account Book, as quoted in ibid., 231, 243, 251.

[345] *REED: Coventry*, 237, 249.

[346] See ibid., 566.

[347] See Dutka, *Music in the English Mystery Plays*, 28–29.

[348] See John Stevens, "Music in Medieval Drama," *Proceedings of the Royal Musical Association* 84 (1958): 91; Rastall, *Heaven Singing*, 1:67. An appropriate song for the return of the shepherds from their visit to the Christ Child is not provided, though one is required by the playtext.

[349] *REED: Coventry*, 332; Stephen K. Wright, "'The Historie of King Edward the fourth': A Chronicle Play on the Coventry Pageant Wagons," *Medieval and Renaissance Drama in England* 3 (1986), 69–81. It is often assumed that the play chosen was the *Destruction of Jerusalem*, which had been previously played in 1584.

[350] Rastall, *Heaven Singing*, 1:138.

[351] Ibid., 1:66–67, 137–38.

[352] Thomas Sharp, the son of a Coventry hatter, was a respected member of a coterie of antiquarians who were attempting to bring to light and were publishing whole texts and detailed records of early dramatic performance. His correspondence about his project includes letters from Sir Walter Scott, Francis Palgrave, Dawson Turner, and Robert Pitcairn, among others, as well as lengthy sets from J. H. Maitland, who was researching and publishing the Chester pageants and documents at the same period, and from Francis Douce, to whom the *Dissertation* is dedicated. Douce and Sharp concurred that the so-called *Ludus Coventriae*, now known more generally as the N-Town plays, in MS. Cotton Vespasian D VIII had nothing to do with Coventry, though the confusion has persisted into the twentieth century; see, for Douce, MS. Add. 43645, fol. 240^r, and for Sharp's opinion, *Dissertation*, 7.

[353] British Library MS. Add. 43645, fol. 224.

[354] *The Monthly Review* 110 (May 1826): 2–3.

[355] Ibid., 12. For a listing of potentially useful manuscripts destroyed in the Birmingham Free Library fire, see *REED: Coventry*, lxv– lxvi.

[356] MS. Add. 43645, fol. 93^r.

[357] Ibid., fol. 239^r.

[358] See especially R. W. Ingram, "Fifteen Seventy-Nine and the Decline of Civic Religious Drama in Coventry," in *The Elizabethan Theatre VIII*, ed. G. R. Hibbard (Port Credit, Ontario: P. D. Meany, 1982), 114–28.

[359] *REED: Coventry*, 370, 502.

[360] Ibid., 430.

[361] Ibid., 332.

[362] See *REED: Coventry*, 333–35, 495–502. The classic study of the suppression of the mysteries is Harold Gardiner, *Mysteries' End* (New Haven: Yale University Press, 1946). Father Gardiner's views have been modified by recent scholarship.

[363] See especially Clifford Davidson, "The Anti-Visual Prejudice," in *Iconoclasm vs. Art and Drama*, ed. Davidson and Nichols, 33–46, and Michael O'Connell, "The Idolatrous Eye: Iconoclasm, Anti-Theatricalism, and the Image of the Elizabethan Theater," *ELH* 52 (1985): 279–310. There was clearly a broad spectrum of opinion about images in the sixteenth century from those who wished to retain them, including those who actively sought to hide them from the authorities, to the radicals who would destroy all traces of them. Similar attitudes toward scenes in religious drama were common.

[364] See Articles of Religion, art. XIV.

[365] 3 James I, c 21, as quoted in E. K. Chambers, *The Elizabethan Stage*, 4 vols. (Oxford: Clarendon Press, 1923), 4:338–39.

[366] It is to the point to note the adoption of the alehouse as the center of the community in the course of the sixteenth century as opposed to the previous choice of the parish church; see Peter Clark, *The English Alehouse: A Social History, 1200–1830* (London: Longman, 1983), 151–56, and also, for a general discussion of the effects of the Reformation, Duffy, *The Stripping of the Altars*.

[367] *REED: Chester*, 248. However, cf. Mills, *Recycling the Cycle*, 145.

[368] *The Towneley Mysteries*, 2 vols. (London: J. B. Nichols, 1836), 1:xviii.

[369] John R. Elliott, Jr., *Playing God: Medieval Mysteries on the Modern Stage* (Toronto: University of Toronto Press, 1989), 71–100; Darryll Grantley, "The National Theatre's Production of *The Mysteries*: Some Observations," *Theatre Notebook* 40 (1986): 73.

[370] See especially John Marshall, "Modern Productions of Medieval English Plays," in *The Cambridge Companion to Medieval English Theatre*, ed. Beadle, 290–311.

[371] Harold Child, "Revivals of English Dramatic Works 1919–1925," *Review of English Studies* 2 (1926): 179–80.

[372] E. Martin Browne with Henzie Browne, *Two in One* (Cambridge: Cambridge University Press, 1981). 35–36.

[373] Ibid., 54; see also Elliott, *Playing God*, 58–70, esp. 58.

[374] John R. Elliott, Jr., "Modern Productions of Medieval Mystery Cycles," *Research Opportunities in Renaissance Drama* 13–14 (1970–71): 263–64.

[375] Ibid., 263.

[376] *Research Opportunities in Renaissance Drama* 22 (1979): 140.

[377] David Mills, "Coventry Plays, 4th–22nd August 1981," *Medieval English Theatre* 3 (1981): 135.

The Pageant of the Company of Shearmen and Taylors in Coventry

ISAYE.

THE Sofferent thatt seithe ev*er*e seycrette,
He saue you all and make you p*er*fett *and* stronge,
And geven*us* g*r*ace w*ith* his marce forto mete.
For now in grett mesere mankynd ys bownd,
The sarpent hathe gevin vs soo mortall a wonde
That no creature ys abull vs for to reyles
Tyll thye right vncion of Jvda dothe seyse.

Then schall moche myrthe and joie incresse,
And the right rote in Isaraell sprynge
Thatt schall bryng forthe the greyne off whollenes;
And owt of danger he schall vs bryng
Into thatt reygeon where he ys kyng
Wyche abowe all othur far dothe abownde,
And thatt cruell Sathan he schall confownde.

Wherefore I cu*m* here apon this grownde
To comforde eyu*er*e creature off birthe,
For I, Isaye the p*ro*fet, hathe fownde
Many swete matt*er*s whereof we ma make myrth
On this same wyse,
For thogh that Adam be demid to deythe
W*ith* all his childur asse Abell *and* Seythe,
Yett "Ecce v*ir*go consepeet,"
Loo, where a reymede schall ryse.

Beholde, a mayde schall conseyve a childe
And gett vs more g*r*ace then eyu*er* men had,

And hir meydin<h>od nothing defylid.
Sche ys deputyd to beare the sun, almyghte God.
Loo, suffern*n*tis, now ma you be glad,
For of this meydin all we ma be fayne;
For Adam þ*a*t now lyis in sorrois full sade
Hir gloreose birth schall reydeme hym ageyn
From bondage and thrall. [fol. 1v
Now be myrre, eyu*ere* mon*n*,
For this dede bryffly in Isaraell schal be done
And before the Fathur in trone
Thatt schall glade vs all.

More of this matt*er* fayne wolde I meve,
But lengur tyme I haue not here for to dwell.
That Lorde þ*a*t ys m*ar*cefull his m*ar*ce soo in vs ma p*re*ve
For to sawe owre sollis from the darknes of hell,
And to his blys he vs bryng asse he ys bothe Lord *and* Kyng
And schal be eyu*er*lastyng in secula seculor*um*. Amen.

GABERELL. Hayle, Mare, full of g*r*ace: owre Lord God ys w*ith* the;
Aboue all wemen*n* þ*a*t eyu*er* wasse,
Lade, blesside mote thow be.

MARE. Allmyght Fathur *and* Kyng of blys,
From all dysses þ*o*u saue me now,
For inwardely my spretis trubbuld ys
Thatt I am amacid *and* kno nott how.

GABERELL. Dred the nothyng, meydin, of this.
From heyvin abowe hyddur am I sent
Of ambassage from that Kyng of blys,
Unto the, lade *and* v*ir*gin reyu*er*ent,
Salutyng the here asse most exselent
Whose v*er*tu aboue all othur dothe abownde;
Wherefore in the g*r*ace schal be fownde,
For thow schalt conseyve apon þ*is* grownd
The Second P*er*sone of God in trone.
He wyl be borne of the alone; w*ith*owt sin þ*o*u schalt hy*m* see.
Thy g*r*ace *and* thi goodnes wyl neyu*er* be gone
But eyu*er* to lyve in v*ir*genete. [fol. 2r

MARE. I marvell soore how thatt ma be.
Man*is* cu*m*pany knev I neyu*er* yett,
Nor neyu*er* to do kast I me,
Whyle thatt owre Lord sendith me my wytt.

GABERELL. The Wholle Gost in the schall lyght
And schado thy soll soo w*ith* v*er*tu
From the Fathur thatt ys on hyght.
These wordis, turtill, the be full tru.
This chylde that of the schal be borne
Ys the Second P*er*sone in Trenete.
He schall saue that wase forlorne,
And the fyndis powar dystroie schall he.
These wordis, lade, full tru the bene,
And furthur, lade, here in thy noone lenage
Beholde Eylesabeth thy cosyn clene,
The wyche wasse barren *and* past all age,
And now w*ith* chyld sche hath bene
Syx monethis and more asse schal be sene,
Wherefor discomforde þe not, Mare,
For to God onpossibull nothyng ma be.

MARE. Now and yt be thatt Lordis wyll
Of my bodde to be borne *and* for to be,
Hys hy pleysuris for to fullfyll
Asse his one handemayde I submyt me.

GABERELL. Now blessid be þe tyme sett
That þ*o*u wast borne in thy degre,
For now ys the knott surely knytt,
And God conseyvide in Trenete.
Now farewell, lade off myghtis most;
Vnto the Godhed I the beteyche.

MARE. Thatt Lorde the gyde in eyu*er*e cost,
And looly he leyde me *and* be my leyche. [fol. 2v

*Here the angell dep*ar*tyth,* and *Joseff cu*m*yth in* and *seyth:*

JOSOFF. Mare, my wyff soo dere,

How doo ye, dame, and whatt chere
Ys w*ith* you this tyde?

MARE. Truly, husebonde, I am here,
Owre Lordis wyll for to abyde.

JOSOFF. Whatt, I troo thatt we be all schent.
Sey, womon*n*, who hath byn here sith I went
To rage wyth thee?

MARE. Syr, here wase nothur man*n* nor mans eyvin
But only the sond of owre Lorde God in heyvin.

JOSOFF. Sey not soo, womon*n*, for schame ley be.
Ye be w*ith* chyld soo wondurs grett,
Ye nede no more þ*e*rof to tret
Agense all right.
For sothe this chylde, dame, ys not myne.
Alas that eyu*er* w*ith* my nynee
I suld see þ*is* syght.
Tell me, womon*n*, whose ys this chyld?

MARE. Non but youris, husebond soo myld,
And thatt schal be seyne.

JOSOFF. But myne, allas, alas, why sey ye soo?
Wele awey, womon, now may I goo
Begyld as many anothur ys.

MARE. Na, truly, sir, ye be not begylde,
Nor yet w*ith* spott of syn I am not defylde.
Trust yt well, husebonde.

JOSOFF. Husebond in feythe, *and* þ*a*t acold.
A, weylle awey, Josoff, as thow ar olde;
Lyke a fole now ma I stand *and* truse.
But, in feyth, Mare, þ*o*u art in syn.
Soo moche ase I haue cheyrischyd þe, dame, *and* all þi kyn,
Behynd my bake to s*er*ve me thus.

All olde men insampull take be me;
How I am begylid here may you see [fol. 3r
To wed soo yong a chyld.

Now farewell, Mare, I leyve the here alone.
<Wo> worthe the dam and thy warkis yche one,
For I woll noo more begylid be for frynd nor fooe.
Now of this ded I am soo dull,
And off my lyff I am soo full no farthur ma I goo.

ANGELL I. Aryse up, Josoff, *and* goo whom ageyne
Vnto Mare thy wyff that ys soo fre.
To comford hir loke þ*at* thow be fayne,
For, Josoff, a cleyne meydin ys schee.
Sche hath conseyvid w*ith*owt any trayne
The Seycond P*er*son in Trenete.
Jh*es*u schal be hys name sarten,
And all thys world sawe schall he; — be not agast.

JOSOFF. Now, Lorde, I thanke the w*ith* hart full sad;
For of these tythyngis I am soo glad
Thatt all my care awey ys cast,
Wherefore to Mare I woll in hast.

A, Mare, Mare, I knele full loo;
Forgeve me, swete wyff, here in þ*is* lond.
Marce, Mare, for now I kno
Of youre good gou*er*nance and how yt doth stond
Thogh thatt I dyd the mysname,
Marce, Mare, whyle I leve.
Wyll I neyu*er*, swet wyff, the greve in ernyst nor in game.

MARE. Now thatt Lord in heyvin, sir, he you forgyve,
And I do forgeve yow in hys name foreu*er*more.

JOSOFF. Now truly, swete wyff, to you I sey the same.
But now to Bedlem must I wynde
And scho myself soo full of care,
And I to leyve you this grett behynd.
God wott the whyle, dame, how you schuld fare.

MARE. Na, hardely husebond, dred ye nothyng, [fol. 3v
For I woll walke w*ith* you on the wey.
I trust in God, allmyghte Kyng,
To spede right well in owre jurney.

JOSOFF. Now I thanke you, Mare, of youre goodnes
Thatt ye my wordis woll nott blame.
And syth þ*at* to Bedlem we schall vs dresse,
Goo we togedur in Goddis wholle name.

Now to Bedlem haue we leygis three.
The day ys ny spent: yt drawyth toward nyght.
Fayne at your es, dame, I wold þ*at* ye schulde be,
For you groue all werely, yt semyth, in my syght.

MARE. God haue marcy, Josoffe, my spowse soo dere.
All p*ro*fettis herto dothe beyre wyttnes:
The were tyme now draith nere
Thatt my chyld wol be borne wyche ys Kyng of blis.
Vnto su*m* place, Josoff, hyndly me leyde
Thatt I moght rest me w*ith* g*r*ace in þ*is* tyde.
The lyght of the Fathur ou*er* hus both spreyde,
And the g*r*ace of my sun w*ith* vs here abyde.

JOSOFF. Loo, blessid Mare, here schall ye lend,
Cheff chosyn of owre Lorde *and* cleynist in degre,
And I for help to towne woll I wende.
Ys nott this the best, dame, whatt sey ye?

MARE. God haue marce, Josoff, my husebond soo meke,
And hartely I p*r*a you, goo now fro me.

JOSOFF. Thatt schal be done in hast, Mare soo swete,
The comford of the Wholle Gost leyve I w*ith* the.
Now to Bedlem streyght woll I wynd
To gett som helpe for Mare soo free.
Su*m* helpe of wemen*n* God ma me send
Thatt Mare, full off g*r*ace, pleysid ma be.

PASTOR I. Now, God that art in Trenete, [fol. 4r,

Thow sawe my fellois and me,
For I kno nott wheyre my scheepe nor the be
Thys nyght, yt ys soo colde.
Now ys yt nygh the myddis of the nyght.
These wedurs ar darke and dym of lyght
Thatt of them can hy haue noo syght,
Standyng here on this wold.
But now to make there hartis lyght,
Now wyll I full right stand apon this looe
And to them cry w*ith* all my myght—
Full well my voise the kno—
W*ith* hoo, fellois, hoo, hooe, hoo!

PASTOR II. Hark, Sym, harke; I here owre brothur on the looe.
This ys hys woise right well, I knoo;
Therefore toward hym lett vs goo
And follo his woise aright.
See, Sym, se where he doth stond.
I am ryght glad we haue hym fond.
Brothur, where hast thow byn soo long,
And this nyght hit ys soo cold?

PASTOR I. E, fryndis, þ*er* cam a pyrie of wynd w*ith* a myst sudden*n*ly
Thatt forth off my weyis went I;
And grett heyvenes made I,
And wase full sore afrayde.
Then for to goo wyst I nott whyddur,
But trawellid on this loo hyddur *and* thyddur.
I wasse so were of this cold weddur
Thatt nere past wasse my might.

PASTOR III. Brethur, now we be past þ*a*t fryght,
And hit ys far w*ith*in the nyght; [fol. 4v
Full sone woll spryng the day lyght,
Hit drawith full nere the tyde.
Here awhyle lett vs rest
And repast owreself of the best.
Tyll thatt the sun ryse in the est
Let vs all here abyde.

There the scheppardis drawys furth there meyte and *doth eyte* and *drynk; and asse the drynk the fynd the star,* and *sey thus:*

PASTOR III. Brethur, loke vp and behold
Whatt thyng ys yondur thatt schynith soo bryght;
Asse long ase eyu*er* I haue wachid my fold
Yett sawe I neyu*er* soche a syght in fyld.
A, ha, now ys cu*m* the tyme þ*at* old fathurs hath told
Thatt in the wynturs nyght soo cold
A chyld of meydyn*n* borne be he wold
In whom all p*ro*feciys schal be fullfyld.

PASTOR I. Truth yt ys w*ith*owt naye,
Soo seyd the p*ro*fett Isaye,
Thatt a chylde schuld be borne of a made soo bryght
In wentur ny the schortist dey
Or elis in the myddis of the nyght.

PASTOR II. Loovid be God, most off myght,
That owre g*r*ace ys to see thatt syght.
Pray we to hym ase hit ys right,
Yff thatt his wyll yt be,
Thatt we ma haue knoleyge of this syngnefocacion
And why hit aperith on this fassion,
And eyu*er* to hym lett vs geve lawdacion
In yerthe whyle thatt we be. [fol. 5r

There the angelis syng "Glorea in exselsis Deo."

PASTOR III. Harke, the syng abowe in the clowdis clere.
Hard I neyuer of soo myrre a quere.
Now, gentyll brethur, draw we nere
To here there armony.

PASTOR I. Brothur, myrth and solas ys cu*m* hus among,
For be the swettnes of þ*er* songe
Goddis sun ys cu*m* whom we haue lokid for long,
Asse syngnefyith thys star þ*at* we do see.

PASTOR II. "Glore glorea in exselsis"—þ*at* wase þ*er* songe;

How sey ye, fellois, seyd the not thus?

PASTOR I. Thatt ys wel seyd; now goo we hence
To worschipe thatt chyld of hy manyffecence
And that we ma syng in his p*re*sence
"Et in tarra pax omynibus."

*There the scheppar*dis *syngis "Ase I Owt Rodde,"* and *Josoff seyth:*

JOSOFF. Now, Lorde, this noise þ*a*t I do here
W*ith* this grett solemnete,
Gretly amendid hath my chere.
I trust hy nevis schortly wol be.

There the angellis syng "Gloria in exsellsis" ageyne.

MARE. A, Josoff, husebond, cu*m* heddur anon;
My chylde ys borne þ*a*t ys Kyng of blys.

JOSOFFE. Now welcu*m* to me, the Makar of mon;
W*ith* all the omage thatt I con
Thy swete mothe here woll I kys.

MARE. A, Josoff, husebond, my chyld waxith cold,
And we haue noo fyre to warme hym w*ith*.

JOSOFF. Now in my narmys I schall hym fold.
Kyng of all kyngis be fyld *and* be fryth,
He myght haue had bettur *and* hymselfe wold [fol. 5v
Then the breythyng of these bestis to warme hy*m* w*ith*.

MARE. Now, Josoff, my husbond, fet heddur my chyld,
The Maker off man and hy Kyng of blys.

JOSOFF. That schal be done anon, Mare soo myld,
For the brethyng of these bestis hath warmyd well, I wys.

ANGELL I. Hyrd men*n* hynd, drede ye nothyng
Off thys star thatt ye do se,

For thys same morne Godis sun ys borne
In Bedlem of a meydin fre.

ANGELL II. Hy you thyddur in hast.
Yt ys hys wyll ye schall hym see
Lyinge in a crybbe of pore reypaste,
Yett of Davithis lyne cu*m*on*n* ys hee.

PASTOR I. Hayle, mayde, modur, *and* wyff soo myld.
Asse the angell seyd soo haue we fonde.
I haue nothyng to present w*ith* þi chylde
But my pype—hold, hold, take yt in thy hond—
Wherein moche pleysure þ*a*t I haue fond;
And now to oonowre thy gloreose byrthe
Thow schallt yt haue to make the myrthe.

PASTOR II. Now hayle be thow, chyld, *and* thy dame,
For in a pore loggyn here art thow leyde;
Soe the angell seyde *and* tolde vs thy name.
Holde, take thow here my hat on thy hedde,
And now off won thyng thow art well sped,
For weddur thow hast noo nede to complayne,
For wynde ne sun, hayle, snoo, and rayne.

PASTOR III. Hayle be thow, Lorde, ou*er* watur *and* landis,
For thy cu*m*yng all we ma make myrthe.
Haue here my myttens to pytt on þi hondis;
Othur treysure haue I non to present the w*ith*.

MARE. Now, herdmen*n* hynd, for youre comyng
To my chylde schall I p*r*ae,
Asse he ys heyvin Kyng, to grant you his blessyng [fol. 6r
And to hys blys þ*a*t ye may wynd at your last day.

*There the scheppardis syngith ageyne and goth forthe of þe place; and the ij p*ro*fettis cumyth in, and seyth thus:*

P*RO*FETA I. Novellis, novellis of wondrfull m*ar*vellys,
Were hy *and* defuce vnto the heryng.
Asse scripture tellis, these strange novellis to you I bryng.

P*RO*FETA II. Now hartely, sir, I desyre to knoo
Yff hytt wolde pleyse you for to schoo
Of whatt maner a thyng.

P*RO*FETA I. Were mystecall vnto youre heryng:
Of the natevete off a Kyng.

P*RO*FETA II. Of a Kyng, whence schuld he cu*m*?

P*RO*FETA I. From thatt reygend ryall *and* mighty mancion,
The sede seylesteall and heyvinly vysedome,
The Seycond P*er*son *and* Godis one sun
For owre sake now ys man becum*m*.
This godly spere desendid here
Into a v*ir*gin clere, sche ondefyld,
Be whose warke obskevre
Owre frayle nature ys now begilde.

P*RO*FETA II. Why, hathe sche a chyld?

P*RO*FETA I. E, trust hyt well *and* neu*er* the las,
Yet ys sche a mayde evin asse sche wasse,
And hir sun the Kyng of Isaraell.

P*RO*FETA II. A wondurfull marvell, how thatt ma be,
And far dothe exsell all owre capasete
How thatt the Trenete of soo hy regallete
Schuld be jonyd vnto owre mortallete.

P*RO*FETA I. Of his one grett marce, as ye shall se þe exposyssion,
Throgh whose vmanyte all Adam*is* p*ro*gene
Reydemyd schal be owt of p*er*dyssion.
Syth man*n* did offend, who schuld amend
But the seyd mon*n* and no nothur, [fol. 6v
For the wyche cawse he incarnate wold be
And lyve in mesere asse man*is* one brothur.

P*RO*FETA II. Syr, vnto the deyite, I beleve p*er*fettle,
Onpossibull to be there ys nothyng:
How be yt this warke vnto me ys darke

In the opp*er*acion or wyrkyng?

P*RO*FETA I. Whatt more reypriff ys vnto belyff then*n* to be dowtyng?

P*RO*FETA II. Yet dowtis oftym*is* hathe derevacion.

P*RO*FETA I. Thatt ys be þe meynes of comenecacion*n*
Of trawthis to haue a dev p*ro*bacion
Be þe same dowts reysoning.

P*RO*FETA II. Then to you thys won thyng:
Of whatt nobull *and* hy lenage ys schee
Thatt myght þ*is* v*er*abull p*r*incis modur be?

P*RO*FETA I. Ondowtid sche ys cu*m* of hy parrage,
Of the howse of Davith *and* Salamon the sage,
And won off the same lyne joynid to hir be mareage
Of whose trybe we do subscryve this chy<l>dis lenage.

P*RO*FETA II. And why in thatt wysse?

P*RO*FETA I. For yt wasse the gysse
To conte the parant on the manys lyne
And nott on the feymyne
Amonst vs here in Isaraell.

P*RO*FETA II. Yett can I nott aspy be noo wysse
How thys chylde borne schuld be w*itho*w<t> naturis p*re*judyse.

P*RO*FETA I. Nay, no prejvdyse vnto nature I dare well sey,
For the Kyng of nature may hawe all at his one wyll.
Dyd not þe powar of God make Aronis rod beyre frute in on day?

P*RO*FETA II. Truth yt ys, inded.

P*RO*FETA I. Then loke you and rede.

P*RO*FETA II. A, I p*er*seyve the sede where apon thatt you spake.
Yt wasse for owre nede þ*at* he frayle nature did take,
And his blod he schuld schede amens for to make [fol. 7^{r}

For owre transegression.
Ase yt ys seyd in p*ro*fece þ*a*t of the lyne of Jude
Schuld spryng a right Messe
Be whom all wee schall haue reydemcion.

P*RO*FETA I. S*ir*, now ys the tyme cu*m*,
And the date thereof run*n*
Off his natevete.

P*RO*FETA II. Yett, I beseke you hartele, þ*a*t ye wold schoo me how
Thatt this strange nowelte were broght vnto you.

P*RO*FETA I. This othur nyght soo cold
Hereby apon a wolde,
Schepp*ar*dis wachyng there fold
In the nyght soo far
To them aperid a star,
And eyu*er* yt drev them nar,
Wyche star the did behold
Bryght*er*, þe sey, M folde
Then the sun so clere
In his mydday spere;
And the these tythyngis tolde.

P*RO*FETA II. Whatt, seycretly?

P*RO*FETA I. Na, na, hardely;
The made thereof no conseil,
For the song ase lowde
Ase eyu*er* the cowde,
Presyng the Kyng of Isaraell.

P*RO*FETA II. Yett do I marvell
In what pyle or castell
These herdmen*n* dyd hym see.

P*RO*FETA I. Nothur in hallis nor yett in bowris
Borne wold he not be,
Nothur in castellis nor yet in towris
Þ*a*t semly were to se,

But att hys Fathurs wyll
The p*ro*feci to fullfyll
Betwyxt an ox and an as
Ih*esum* þ*is* Kyng borne he was.
Heyvin he bryng us tyll.

P*RO*FETA II. S*ir*, a, but when these schepp*ar*dis had seyne hym there,
Into whatt place did the repeyre?

P*RO*FETA I. Forthe the went and glad þe were,
Going þe did syng;
W*ith* myrthe *and* solas þe made good chere
For joie of þ*a*t new tything,
And aftur, asse I hard the<m> tell,
He reywardid them full well:
He graunt them hevyn þerin to dwell.
In ar the gon w*ith* joie and myrthe,
And there songe hit ys neowell.

[fol. 7v

*There the pro*fettis *gothe furthe,* and *Erod cu*myth *in and þe messenger.*

NONCEOSE. Faytes pais, dn*n*yis, baronys de grande reynowme,
Payis, seneoris, schevaleris de nooble posance.
Pays, gentis homos, co*m*paneonys petis egrance.
Je vos com*m*and dugard treytus sylance,
Payis, tanque vottur nooble Roie syre ese p*re*sance.
Que nollis p*er*sone ese non fawis p*er*wynt dedfferance,
Nese harde de frappas; mayis gardus to to paceance:
Mayis gardus voter seneor to cor reyu*er*ance,
Car elat vottur Roie to to puysance.
Anon*n* de leo pase tos; je vose cum*m*ande;
E lay Roie Erott la grandeaboly vos vmport.

ERODE. *Qui statis* in Jude et Rex Iseraell
And the myghttyst conquerowre þ*a*t eyu*er* walkid on grownd:
For I am evyn he thatt made bothe hevin *and* hell,
And of my myghte powar holdith vp þ*is* world rownd.
Magog *and* Madroke bothe þe did I confownde,
And w*ith* this bryght bronde there bonis I brak onsundr

Thatt all the wyde worlde on those rappis did wondr.

I am the cawse of this grett lyght and thundr.
Ytt ys throgh my fure þ*a*t the soche noyse dothe make;
My feyrefull contenance þe clowdis so doth incu*m*bur
Þ*a*t oftym*is* for drede þ*e*rof the verre yerth doth quake.
Loke when I w*ith* males this bryght brond doth schake:
All the whole world from the north to þe sowthe,
I ma them dystroie w*ith* won worde of my mowthe.

To reycownt vnto you myn innevmerabull substance,
Thatt were to moche for any tong to tell,
For all the whole Orent ys vndr myn obbeydeance
And prynce am I of purgatorre *and* cheff capten of hell.
And those tyraneos trayturs be force ma I com*m*pell
Myne en*n*myis to vanquese *and* evyn to dust them dryve,
And w*ith* a twynke of myn iee not won to be lafte alyve.

Behold my contenance and my colur,
Bryghtur then the sun in the meddis of þe dey.
Where can you haue a more grettur succur
Then to behold my p*er*son that ys soo gaye?
My fawcun *and* my fassion w*t*t*h* my gorgis araye:
He thatt had the g*r*ace allwey þ*e*ron to thynke,
Lyve the myght allwey w*ith*owt othur meyte or drynke.

And thys my tryomfande fame most hylist dothe abownde
Throghowt this world in all reygeons abrod,
Reysemelyng the fau*er* of thatt most myght Mahownd,
From Jubytor be desent *and* cosyn to the grett God
And namyd the most reydowndid Kyng Eyrodde,
Wyche thatt all pryncis hath vnd*er* subjeccion
And all there whole powar vndur my p*ro*teccion.

And therefore my hareode here, callid Calcas,
Warne thow eyu*er* porte thatt noo schyppis aryve,
Nor also aleond strang*er* throg my realme pas
But the for there truage do pay markis fyve.
Now spede the forth hastele,
For the thatt wyll the contrare

Apon a galowse hangid schal be,
And, be Mahownde, of me the gett noo g*r*ace.

NONCIOS. Now lord and mastur, in all the hast,
Thy worethe wyll ytt schall be wroght,
And thy ryall cuntreyis schal be past
In asse schort tyme ase can be thoght.

ERODE. Now schall owre regeons throghowt be soght
In eyu*er* place bothe est *and* west.
Yff any katyffis to me be broght,
Yt schal be nothyng for there best.
And the whyle thatt I do resst,
Trompettis, viallis, and othur armone
Schall bles the wakyng of my mai*e*ste.

Here Erod goth awey, and *the iij kyngis speykyth in þe strete.*

REX I. Now blessid be God of his swet sonde,
For yondur a feyre bryght star I do see.
Now ys he com*m*on vs amonge
Asse the p*ro*fettis seyd thatt yt schuld be,
A seyd there schuld a babe be borne, [fol. 8v
Comyng of the rote of Jesse
To sawe mankynd that wasse forlorne,
And truly come*n* now ys he.

Reyu*er*ence and worschip to hym woll I do
Asse God and man thatt all made of noght.
All the p*ro*fettis acordid and seyd evyn soo
That w*ith* hys p*r*esseos blod mankynd schuld be boght;
He grant me g*r*ace be yond*er* star þ*at* I see,
And into thatt place bryng me
Thatt I ma hym worschipe w*ith* umellete
And se hys gloreose face.

REX II. Owt off my wey I deme thatt I am,
For toocuns of thys cuntrey can I non see.
Now God thatt on yorth madist man,
Send me su*m* knoleyge where thatt I be.

Yondur methynke a feyre bryght star I see,
The wyche betocunyth the byrth of a chyld
Thatt hedur ys cu*m* to make man fre,
He borne of a mayde *and* sche nothyng defyld.

To worschip thatt chyld ys myn intent;
Forth now wyll I take my wey.
I trust su*m* cu*m*pany God hathe me sent,
For yond*er* I se a kyng labur on the wey.
Towarde hym now woll I ryde.
Harke, cu*m*ly kyng, I you pray:
Into whatt cost wyll ye thys tyde,
Or weddur lyis youre jurney.

REX I. To seke a chylde ys myne intent
Of whom the p*ro*fetis hathe ment.
The tyme ys cu*m*: now ys he sent;
Be yondur star here ma <you> see.

REX II. S*ir*, I prey you w*ith* your lysence
To ryde w*i*th you vnto his presence.
To hym wyll I offur frankinsence,
For the hed of all Whole Churche schall he be. [fol. 9r

REX III. I ryde wanderyng in veyis wyde
Ou*er* montens and dalis; I wot not where I am.
Now Kyng off all kyngis, send me soche gyde
Thatt I myght haue knoleyge of thys cuntreys name.
A, yondur I se a syght besemyng all afar
The wyche betocuns sum nevis, ase I troo,
Asse methynke a chyld peryng in a stare:
I trust he be cu*m* þ*a*t schall defend vs from woo.
To kyngis yondur I see and to them woll I ryde,
For to haue there cu*m*pane I trust þe wyll me abyde.

Hayle, cu*m*ly kyngis augent,
Good surs, I pray you whedd*er* ar ye ment?

REX I. To seke a chylde ys owre intent,
Wyche betocuns yond*er* star, asse ye ma see.

Rex II. To hym I purpose thys present.

Rex III. Surs, I pray you and thatt ryght vmblee
W*ith* you thatt I ma ryde in cu*m*pane.
To Allmyghte God now prey we
Thatt hys pressiose pe*r*sone we ma se.

*Here Erode cu*m*yth in ageyne,* and *the messengere seyth:*

Nuncios. Hayle, lorde most off myght,
Thy com*m*andement ys right;
Into thy land ys comyn þ*is* nyght
iij kyngis and w*ith* them a grett cu*m*pany.

Erod. Whatt make those kyngis in this cuntrey?

Noncios. To seke a kyng and a chyld, the sey.

Erode. Of whatt age schuld he bee?

Noncios. Skant twellve deyis old fulle.

Erod. And wasse he soo late borne?

Noncios. E, syr, soo the schode me thys same dey in the morne.

Erod. Now in payne of deyth bryng them me beforne,
And therefore, harrode, now hy the in hast [fol. 9[v]
In all spede thatt thow were dyght,
Or thatt those kyngis the cuntrey be past.
Loke thow bryng them all iij before my syght,
And in Jerusalen inquere more of that chyld.
But I warne the that thy wordis be mylde,
For there mast thow hede and crafte wey<lde>
How to fordo his powere, and those iij kyngis shal be begild.

Noncios. Lorde, I am redde att youre byddyng
To sarve the ase my lord and kyng.
For joye thereof, loo, how I spryng
W*ith* lyght hart *and* fresche gamboldyng

Alofte here on this molde.

ERODE. Then sped the forthe hastely,
And loke þ*at* thow beyre the eyvinly.
And also I pray the hartely that thow doo
Comand me bothe to yong and olde.

NONCIOS. Hayle, syr kyngis, in youre degre.
Erood, kyng of these cuntreyis wyde,
Desyrith to speyke w*ith* you all thre,
And for youre comyng he dothe abyde.

REX I. Syr, att his wyll we be ryght bayne.
Hy us, brethur, vnto thatt lordis place;
To speyke w*ith* hym we wold be fayne,
Thatt chyld thatt we seke he grant us of his g*r*ace.

NONCIS. Hayle, lorde w*ith*owt pere,
These iij kyngis here have we broght.

ERODE. Now welcu*m*, syr kyngis, all in fere,
But of my bryght ble, surs, bassche ye noght.
S*ir* kyngis, ase I vndurstand,
A star hathe gydid you into my land
Wherein grett harie ye haue fonde
Be reysun of hir beym*is* bryght,
Wherefore I pray you hartely
The vere truthe thatt ye wold s*er*tefy: [fol. 10^{r}
How long yt ys surely
Syn of that star you had furst syght?

REX I. S*ir* kynge, the vere truthe to sey,
And for to schoo you ase hit ys best,
This same ys evin the xijth dey
Syth yt aperid to vs be west.

ERODE. Brethur, then ys there no more to sey
But w*ith* hart and wyll kepe ye your jurney,
And cu*m* whom by me this same wey,
Of your nevis thatt I myght knoo.

You schall tryomfe in this cuntre,
And w*ith* grett conquorde bankett w*ith* me;
And thatt chyld myself then woll I see
And honor hym also.

REX II. S*ir*, youre com*m*andement we woll fullfyll
And humbly abaye owreself there tyll.
He thatt weldith all thyng at wyll
The redde way hus teyche,
S*ir* kyng, thatt we ma passe your land in pes.

ERODE. Yes, and walke softely eyvin at your one es,
Youre paseporte for a C deyis
Here schall you haue of clere cum*m*and;
Owre reme to labur any weyis
Here schall you haue be spesschall grante.

REX III. Now farewell, kyng of hy degre;
Humbly of you owre leyve we take.

ERODE. Then adev, s*ir* kyngis, all thre,
And whyle I lyve be bold of me;
There ys nothyng in this cuntre
But for youre one ye schall yt take.

Now these iij kyngis ar gon on þ*er* wey,
Onwysely *and* onwyttely haue the all wroghte.
When the cu*m* ageyne the schall dy þ*a*t same dey: [fol. 10v
And thus these vyle wreychis to deyth þe schal be broght.
Soche ys my lykyng:
He that agenst my lawis wyll hold,
Be he kyng or keysar neyu*er* soo bold,
I schall them cast into caris cold
And to deyth I schall them bryng.

There Erode goth his weyis, and *the iij kyngis* cum *in ageyne.*

REX I. O blessid God, moche ys thy myght,
Where ys this star thatt gawe vs lyght?

REX II. Now knele we downe here in this presence,
Besekyng that Lord of hy maugnefecens
That we ma see his hy exsellence
Yff thatt his swet wyl be.

REX III. Yondur, brothur, I see the star
Whereby I kno he ys nott far;
Therefore, lordis, goo we nar
Into þ*is* pore place.

There the iij kyngis gois into the jesen to Mare and *hir child.*

REX I. Hayle, Lorde, thatt all this worlde hath wroght.
Hale, God and man togedur in fere,
For thow hast made all thyng of noght,
Albeyt thatt thow lyist porely here.
A cupe full <of> golde here I haue the broght
In toconyng thow art w*ith*owt pere.

REX II. Hayle be thow, Lorde of hy maugnyffecens,
In toconyng of p*re*ste<h>od *and* dyngnete of offece
To the I offur a cupe full off insence,
For yt behovith the to haue soche sacrefyce.

REX III. Hayle be thow, Lorde longe lokid fore,
I haue broght the myre for mortalete
In tocunyng thow schalt mankynd restore
To lyff be thy deyth apon*n* a tre.

MARE. God haue m*ar*ce, kyngis, of yowre goodnes.
Be the gydyng of the Godhed hidd*er* ar ye sent;
The p*ro*vyssion off my swete sun your weyis whom*m* reydres,
And gostely reywarde you for youre present.

REX I. Syr kyngis, aftur owre p*ro*mes [fol. 11r
Whome be Erode I mvst nedis goo.

REX II. Now truly, berthur, we can noo las,
But I am soo farwachid I wott not wat to do.

REX III. Ryght soo am I; wherefore I you pray,
Lett all vs rest vs awhyle upon þ*is* grownd.

REX I. Brethur, you*r* seying ys right well vnto my pay;
The g*r*ace of thatt swet chylde saue vs all sownde.

ANGELL*US*. Kyng of Tawrus, S*ir* Jesp*ar*;
Kyng of Arraby, S*ir* Balthasar;
Melchor, kyng of Aginare;
To you now am I sent:
For drede of Eyrode goo you west whom
Into those p*ar*ties when ye cu*m* downe;
Ye schal be byrrid w*ith* gret reynowne.
The Wholle Gost thus knoleyge hath sent.

REX I. Awake, s*ir* kyngis, I you praye,
For the voise of an angell I hard in my dreyme.

REX II. Thatt ys full tru thatt ye do sey,
For he reyherssid owre names playne.

REX III. He bad thatt we schuld goo downe be west
For drede of Eyrodis fawls betraye.

REX I. Soo for to do yt ys the best;
The child that we haue soght gyde vs the wey.
Now farewell, the feyrist of schapp soo swete,
And thankid be Jh*esum* of his sonde
Thatt we iij toged*er* soo suddenly schuld mete
Thatt dwell soo wyde *and* in straunge lond,
And here make owre presentacion
Vnto this kyngis son clensid so cleyne,
And to his mod*er* for ovre saluacion.
Of moche myrth now ma we meyne
Thatt we soo well hath done this obblacion.

REX II. Now farewell, S*ir* Jaspar, brothur, to yoeu, [fol. 11v
Kyng of Tawrus, the most worthe;
S*ir* Balthasar, also to you I bow,
And I thanke you bothe of youre good cu*m*pany

Thatt we togeddur haue had.
He thatt made vs to mete on hyll,
I thanke hym now and eyu*er* I wyll,
For now may we goo w*ith*owt yll
And off owre offerynge be full fayne.

REX III. Now syth thatt we mvst nedly goo
For drede of Erode thatt ys soo wrothe,
Now farewell brothur, *and* brothur also;
I take my leve here at you bothe
This dey on fote.
Now he thatt made vs to mete on playne
And offurde to Mare in hir jeseyne,
He geve vs g*r*ace in heyvin agayne
All togeyd*er* to mete.

NUNCIOS. Hayle, kynge, most worthist in wede.
Hayle, manteinar of curt*e*se throgh all þ*is* world wyde.
Hayle, the most myghtyst that eyu*er* bestrod a stede.
Ha<y>ll, most monfullist mon*n* in armor man to abyde.
Hayle, in thyne hoonowre:
Thesse iij kyngis þ*at* forthe were sent
And schuld haue cu*m* ageyne before þe here p*re*sent,
Anothur wey, lorde, whom the went,
Contrare to thyn honowre.

ERODE. Anothur wey—owt! owt! owtt!
Hath those fawls traytvrs done me þ*is* ded?
I stampe! I stare! I loke all abowtt!
Myght I them take, I schuld them bren at a glede!
I rent, I rawe, *and* now run I wode!
A, thatt these velen trayturs hath mard þ*is* my mode!
The schal be hangid yf I ma cu*m* them to! [fol. 12r

Here Erode ragis in þe pagond and *in the strete also.*

E, and thatt kerne of Bedlem he schal be ded,
And thus schall I fordo his p*ro*fece.
How sey you, s*ir* knyghtis, ys not this the best red
Thatt all yong chyldur for this schuld be dede,

Wyth sworde to be slayne?
Then schall I, Erod, lyve in lede,
And all folke me dowt and drede
And offur to me bothe gold, rychesse, *and* mede.
Thereto wyll the be full fayne.

MYLES I. My lorde, Kyng Erode be name,
Thy wordis agenst my wyll schal be.
To see soo ma*n*y yong child*er* dy ys schame;
Therefore consell þ*er*to gettis þ*ou* non of me.

MYLES II. Well seyd, fello, my trawth I plyght.
S*ir* kyng, p*er*seyve right well you may,
Soo grett a mord*er* to see of yong frute
Wyll make a rysyng in þi noone cuntrey.

ERODE. A rysyng! owt! owt! owt!

There Erode ragis ageyne, and then seyth thus:

Owt, velen wrychis, har apon you I cry!
My wyll vtturly loke þ*at* yt be wroght,
Or apon a gallowse bothe you schall dy,
Be Mahownde most myghtyste þ*at* me dere hath boght.

MYLES I. Now, cruell Erode, syth we schall do this dede,
Your wyll nedefully in this realme mvste be wroght:
All the chyld*er* of þ*at* age dy the mvst nede.
Now w*ith* all my myght the schall be vpsoght.

MYLES II. And I woll sweyre here apon your bryght sworde:
All the chyld*er* thatt I fynd sclayne þe schal be,
Thatt make many a mod*er* to wepe
And be full sore aferde
In owre armor bryght when the hus see.

ERODE. Now you have sworne, forth þ*at* ye goo, [fol. 12v
And my wyll thatt ye wyrke bothe be dey *and* nyght.
And then wyll I for fayne trypp lyke a doo,
But whan the be ded I warne you bryng ham before my syght.

ANGELL*US*. Mare and Josoff, to you I sey,
Swete word from the Fathur I bryng you full ryght:
Owt of Bedlem into Eygype forth goo ye þe wey,
And w*ith* you take the Kyng full of myght
For drede of Eroddis red*e*.

JOSOFF. Aryse up, Mare, hastely and sone.
Owre Lordis wyll nedys mvst be done
Lyke ase the angell vs bad.

MARE. Mekely, Josoff, my none spowse,
Towarde that cuntrey let vs reypeyre.
Att Eygyp su*m* tocun off howse;
God grant hus g*r*ace saff to cu*m* there.

*Here the weme*n *cu*m *in wythe there chyldur syngyng them, and Mare* and *Josoff goth awey cleyne.*

WOMON I. I lolle my chylde wondursly swete,
And in my narm*is* I do hyt kepe
Becawse thatt yt schuld not crye.

WOMAN II. Thatt babe thatt ys borne in Bedlem so meke,
He saue my chyld and me from velany.

WOMAN III. Be styll, be styll, my lyttull chylde,
That Lorde of lordis saue bothe the *and* me,
For Erode hath sworne w*ith* wordis wyld
Thatt all yong chyldur sclayne þe schal be.

MYLES I. Sey, ye wyddurde wyvis, whydd*e*r ar ye awey? [fol. 13r
What beyre you in youre arm*is* nedis mvst we se.
Yff the be man*n* chyldur, dy the mvst þ*is* dey,
For at Eroddis wyll all thyng mvst be.

MYLES II. And I in handis wonys them*m* hent
Them for to sley noght woll I spare.
We mvst fullfyll Erodis com*m*andement,
Elis be we asse trayturs *and* cast all in care.

WOMAN I. S*ir* knyghtis of youre curtessee,
Thys dey schame not youre chevaldre,
But on my child haue pytte
For my sake in this styde;
For a sympull sclaghtur yt were to sloo,
Or to wyrke soche a chyld woo
Þ*at* can noder speyke nor goo
Nor neu*er* harme did.

WOMON II. He thatt sleyis my chyld in syght,
Yff thatt my strokis on hym ma lyght,
Be he skwyar or knyght
I hold hym but lost.
Se, thow fawls losyngere,
A stroke schalt thow beyre me her*e*
And spare for no cost.

WOMAN III. Sytt he neyu*er* soo hy in saddull
But I schall make his braynis addull,
And here w*ith* my pott ladull
W*ith* hym woll I fyght.
I schall ley on hym a<s> thog I wode were
W*ith* thys same womanly geyre.
There schall noo man steyre
Wheddur thatt he be kyng or knyght.

MYLES I. Who hard eyu*er* soche a cry [fol. 13v
Of wemen thatt there chyldur haue lost
And grettly reybukyng chewaldry
Throghowt this reme in eyue*r* cost,
Wyche many a mans lyff ys lyke to cost.
For thys grett wreyche þ*at* here ys done,
I feyre moche wengance þ*er*off woll cu*m*.

MYLES II. E, brothur, soche talis may we not tell,
Wherefore to the kyng lett vs goo,
For he ys lyke to beyre the p*er*ell
Wyche wasse the cawser that we did soo.
Yett must the all be broght hym to
W*ith* waynis and waggyns fully fryght.

I tro there wol be a carefull syght.

MYLES I. Loo, Eyrode kyng, here mast thow see
How many M' thatt we haue slayne.

MYLES II. And nedis thy wyll fullfyllid must be,
There ma no mon sey there ageyne.

NUNCIOS. Eyrode kyng, I schall the tell,
All thy dedis ys cu*m* to noght.
This chyld ys gone into Eygipte to dwell.
Loo, S*i*r, in thy none land what wondurs byn wroght.

EROD. Into Eygipte, alas, for woo
Lengur in lande here I canot abyde.
Saddull my palfrey, for in hast wyll I goo;
Aftur yondur trayturs now wyll I ryde
Them for to sloo.
Now all men hy fast
Into Eygipte in hast;
All thatt cuntrey woll I tast
Tyll I ma cu*m* them to.

Fynes lude de taylars and scharmen.

T<h>ys matter
nevly correcte be Robart Croo
the xiiijth dey of Marche
fenysschid in the yere of owre Lorde God
MCCCCC & xxxiiij^{te}
then beyng mayre mastur Palmar
also mastris of the seyd fellyschipp Hev Corbett
Randull Pynkard and
John Baggeley.

Theise Songes
Belonge to
THE TAYLORS *AND* SHEAREMENS PAGANT

THE FIRST AND THE LASTE THE SHEPHEARDS SINGE
AND THE SECOND OR MIDDLEMOST THE WOMEN SINGE

Thomas Mawdycke

die decimo tertio Maij anno do*min*i millessimo quingentesimo nonagesimo primo. Praetor fuit ciuitatis Couentriae D. Mathaens Richardson, tunc Consules Johanes Whitehead *et* Thomas Grauener.

SONG I

As I out rode this enderes night,
Of thre ioli sheppardes I saw a sight,
And all abowte there fold a star shone bright;
They sange "terli terlow";
So mereli the sheppards ther pipes can blow.

SONG II

Lully lulla, þ*o*w littell tine child,
By by, lully lullay, þ*o*w littell tyne child,
By by, lully lullay.

O sisters too, how may we do
For to preserve þis day—
This pore yongling for whom we do singe,
By by, lully lullay?

Herod, the king, in his raging,
Chargid he hath this day
His men of might in his owne sight

All yonge children to slay.

That wo is me, pore child, for thee,
And ever morne and say
For thi parting nether say nor singe
By by, lully lullay.

SONG III

Doune from heave*n*, from heave*n* so hie,
Of angeles þer came a great com*m*panie
W*ith* mirthe and ioy and great solemnitye;
The sange "terly terlow";
So mereli the sheppards þer pipes ca*n* blow.

The Weavers' Pageant

<PRIMUS> P*RO*FETA. E <.>grett astronemars now awake, [fol. 1r
W*ith* youre fam*us* fatheres of folosefy,
And into the oreien<t> reyspecte ye take,
Where nevis *and* strangis be cum of lately,
Affermyng the seyng of old p*ro*fecie
Thatt a star schuld apere
Apon the hyll of Wawse among hus here.

P*RO*FETA II. Ye brethur all, then be of good chere,
For those tythings makyth my hart ful lyght:
We haue desirid many a yere
Of thatt star to haue a syght
And spesschalli of thatt kyng of myght,
Of whose cu*m*yng we haue playne warnyng
Be this same star aftur p*ro*fettis deseri<n>inge.

Yet furthur I p*ra* you for my larnyng
Lett hus hawe su*m* comenecacion
Of this star be oldd p*ro*nostefying,
How hit aperid *and* vndr whatt fassion.

P*RO*FETA I. Sir, aftur a strange deformacion,
As be atorite reyhers I can,
For this same star be int*er*pretacion
Syngnefyid the natevete of a man*n*,
As the p*ro*fett Balam
In his text afarmyth right well,
Seying, "Orietur stella ex Jacobo et exorgit homo de I<sr>aell."

He seyd of Iacobe a star schuld springe,
Wyche syngnefyith only this same kynge
Thatt amongist vs now ys cu*m*,
And as towchyng the letter folloyng:
"Et ipse dominabitur om*ni* gen*era*cioni."

P*RO*FETA II. Sir, here ma be movid a question
Of this nobull prince of soo hi degre,
The wyche of all men*n* schall haue domeneon,
Vndur whatt maner borne he schuld be.

P*RO*FETA I. Ase ye schall here right wondrfull,
Be devine powar of a virgene pure,
Afarmyng the p*ro*feci agenst all nature.

P*RO*FETA II. Where fynde you þ*a*t in wholle scripture
Before p*ro*nostefide this to be done?

P*RO*FETA I. Isaee the p*ro*fett writyth full sure:
"Ecce v*ir*go concipiet apariet filium." [fol. 1v
Balam, seyng of the heyvinly wyssedome
A man*n* schuld spryng here in Isaraell;
The seyd Isayee answeyring to þ*a*t questeon*n*,
"Et vocabit*ur* nomen eius Emanvel."

PROFETA II. Yett haue I grett marvell
How thatt men schuld tell
Off soche strangis before the fell,
And man*n* beyng here but a mortall creature.

PROFETA I. Be devine powar, I make you sure,
The sprete of p*ro*fece to them was sent,
Soo to subscrybe in wholle sc<r>ipture,
And yett them*m*selfe wyst not watt yt ment.

P*RO*FETA II. Now lawde be vnto hym þ*a*t soche knoleyge sent
Vnto hus wreychis of pore symplecete,
Where he ys Lord *and* God om*n*ipotent,
In this hys wyll to make hus preve.

P*RO*FETA I. Did nott þ*a*t profett man Malache
Resite vnto hus on this same wyse
Thatt the sun of lyff schall spring *and* arise?

Wyche cawsid Isaee to cast vp his iees
Toward heyvin, w*ith* all his inward syght,

Seying, "Good Lord, afarmyng thy p*ro*mes,
Send downe to hus thi wonly sun off myght,
Huse to reystore vnto owre right,
Owt of des*er*te from the hard stone,
Reycomfordyng þi doghtur dwyllyng in Sion."

Also Jaramo, thatt wholle mon*n*,
Seyd in heyvin God schuld make seede,
A greyne off Davith thatt now ys c*um*,
Wyche eyu*er* in gracis schall spring *and* spreyde
And kepe Juda owt off drede,
And also Isaraell sett in surenes,
And he schall make Jugementis of rightwesenes.

P*RO*FETA II. I wondr to here you this expres,
Be actoris hi, this worthe mystere,
And spesschalle of this v*er*tu, rightwessenes,
Where hit schal be vsid *and* in whatt p*ar*te.

P*RO*FETA I. Apon the yarthe bothe w*ith* hy *and* loo degre;
And rightwessenes men*n* schall hym call
When he schall cu*m* to sit in the see [fol. 2r
Of Kyng Davit, þ*a*t most riall stall,
And þ*er* schall he before the pristis all
Of Juda *and* Leyve be his powar device,
W*ith* nev insence to do sacrefyce

To God aboue for the grett offence
Of the peple *and* for yngnorance,
W*ith* there offeringe to make reycompence
For the lenage of Adam*is* p*ro*geny.
This schall this childe by the<ym> free
From all the offencis thatt þ*e* haue done
Be cruell deyth and bytt*er* passion.

P*RO*FETA II. Good s*ir*, yett vndr p*ro*dustacion
Owre feyth thereby for to incresse,
Of this star lett hus haue reylacion,
How hit aperid *and* vndur whatt fassion,
Yff hit wold pleyse you for to expresse.

P*RO*FETA I. W*ith* d*iu*er*s* streymis of grett brightnes,
A child þ*er*in of flagrant swetnes,
Wyche apon his bake a crosse did beyre,
And of an eygull hit bare the lykenes,
Beytyng his wyngis into the eyre;
A woise therein off lange fey*re*
Thatt wasse hard throghowt the cuntrey
Seyinge, "Natus est nobis oddie rex Iudeor*um*," *et* sethere.

P*RO*FETA II. Of a farthur declaracion I wold you praye,
Whatt trybus the were *and* in whatt p*ar*te
The were date, *and* whatt maner a wey
They haue made p*ro*bate of this p*ro*fece?

P*RO*FETA I. *And* thatt schall I scho you right eyvedently.
The grett lordis of the land of Caldy
Fowndid twelve masturs of asestronemy
For to se this star apere,
And, when these masturs were eylecte,
On the hill of Wawse þ*er* wache the kepte,
And the all togeddr neu*er* sclepte
Abowe ix C yere.

P*RO*FETA II. And dide the soo longe wache þ*at* hill? [fol. 2v

P*RO*FETA I. Ye, truly, tyll þ*at* hit was this kyngis will
This seyd p*ro*fece for to fullfyll,
Thatt strange star to send them till
Whereof the had intellegence,
Thatt aftur the darkenes of the nyght
In the day hit schone soo bright
Thatt when the sun*n and* the stare
In the yeyre togeythur warre,
Betwyxt them wasse lyttull or non in dyfference.

And soo this stare wasse a s*er*veture,
And vnto iij kyngis a playn cundeture
Vnto the mancion of a v*ir*gin pure.

P*RO*FETA II. But ar you sure for whatt intent?

P*RO*FETA I. For sothe to Bedlem streyght the went,
Whereasse the offurd to thes childe reu*er*ent
W*ith* grett omage a fam*us* present:

The furst wasse gold as most myghte kyng,
The seycond wasse myr asse prist of pristis beyng,
The thryd wasse insence in tokyning of byrring.

P*RO*FETA II. Yet wold I kno the cawse spesschally,
Whatt movid these kyngis to cu*m* so hastely,
And whedur the cam oopun*n* or prevy.

P*RO*FETA I. The star broght them throgh eyu*er*e cuntre,
And eyu*er* as the cam oopunly
The dide inquere of those nevis:
Eyu*er* the axid, "Where ys he
Thatt ys borne for to be the kyng of Juys?"

Therefore lett hus w*ith* all delegence
Vnto þ*a*t chyld geve honowre *and* reyu*er*ence,
And thatt we ma cu*m* vnto his presence
To haue fruyssion of his hi deyit<e>.
And, brothur, I thanke you of youre pacence,
For now att this tyme dep*ar*te wyll wee. *Exceat.*

P*RO*FETA II. Now, brothur, for youre swete sentence,
Att all tym*is* welcu*m* to me —

Loo, fryndis, here may you see
How God in man workith alwey.
Now all we þ*a*t his s*er*vandis be [fol. 3r
Hathe grett cawse in hym to joie,
Wyche sendyth hus knoleyge the truth to sey;
And he soo meraculosly wyrkyng þerw*ith*
Thatt of all seycrettis we wryte þe were pyth:

Wherefore moche cawse haue we to make myrth
When we reyme*m*bur the gloreose birthe
Of this v*ir*gyns sun.
He the seconde p*er*son in Trenete,

Eyquall w*ith* his Fathur in deyite,
And vndr the curteyne of owre vmanete
For hus wold man becu*m*;

Wherefore here I exsorte you all
That in this place here asembulde be,
Vnto this chylde for m*ar*ce cawll,
Wyche schall reydeme vs apon a tre,
And thatt gloreose blys thatt we ma see,
Wyche he hathe ordenide for all men
In his selesteall place to be
In secula seculor*um*, amen*n*.

Here Semeon intrythe and *the last profett gothe owtt.*

SEM*M*EON. The seylesteall soferent, owre hy Gode et*er*nall,
Wyche of this mervelus world ys þe fowndatur,
And create the hy heyvyns his one see em*m*p*er*ell,
W*ith* sun, mone, *and* staris, yorthe, sky, and wattur,
And al for the sustenance of owre vmayne nature,
W*ith* fysche, fowle, best, *and* eyu*er*e othur thyng,
Vndur hus to haue þe naturall cowrs *and* beyng;

Yett owre forme parence at the begynnyng
Throgh dyssobeydence had a grevose fawll
From the hy pales *and* blys eyu*er*lastyng
Downe into þ*is* wale *and* meserabull mvndall,
For the wyche transegression all we ar now mor<t>a<ll>,
Thatt before wasse infynite foreyu*er* to reymayne;
And now schall take yend be deyth *and* cruell payne,

Wyche grevoise s<o>ro ofte dothe me constrayne
Inwardly to syghe *and* byttur teyris to wepe
Tyll thatt I reyme*m*bur the grett comforde ageyne
Of anceant p*ro*fettis w*ith* þ*er* sentens swete, [fol. 3v
Whose fructu*us* syence of p*ro*fownde larnyng depe
In there awturs aperith to hus right manefestly:
Of Isaee, Sebbellam, Balam, *and* Malache.

O Lorde of lordis, in hart beseke I the

Of this infinite worke to send me the tru lyght,
Truly to expownde this seyde whole p*ro*fece,
And also of that Kyng that I ma haue a syght;
The wyche be reydemcion schall hus all reyles,
At whose cu*m*yng the tru ovncion*n* of Juda schall seyse.

Now, Lorde, fullfyll thatt hy tym*me* of pes,
For age draith me fast apon*n*:
Fayne wold I see thatt wholle of whollenes
Or this mortall lyff fro me were gone.
Now, Lorde, ase thow art iij in won,
Grant me grace, yff thatt thy wyl be,
In my nold age that syght for to see.

Then at thy wyll, Lorde, fayne wolde I be,
Yff thow soche grace woldist me sende,
To loove the Lorde w*ith* all vmelyte,
And soo of my lyff then to make an ende.
Yett, Lorde, þi grace to me now extende:
Suffur me rathur yett to lyve in peyne
Then to dy or thatt I thatt solam syght haue seyne.

*Her*e *Ane cu*my*th in to Seme*onn *and seythe:*

ANE. O sufferent Semeon, w*ith* all solemnete,
Thatt of owre gloreose tempull hath þe gou*er*nance,
W*ith* all dev rew*er*ence here beseke I the,
Þ*i* olde frynde in Gode to haue in reyme*m*burance,
The wyche hathe tarrid be a long co*n*tenevance
For the comyng of þe right Messee,
Wycche hathe byn p*ro*mysid vnto hus be p*ro*fece.

O Lorde, thogh þ*a*t I be nothynge worthe,
To see the fassion of þi most p*re*sseose pyctore,
Yett, Lorde, acsepte me of þi grett marce,
Asse thy pore s*er*wand *and* feythfull creature.
To se the, Lorde, yff þ*a*t I myght be sure,
No lenger on grownd wold I reyqu*er*e
In this mortall lyff to contenev here. [fol. 4r

SEMEO*N*. O feythefull frynde and lou*er* dere,
To you this text ofte haue I tolde,
That the lyght of loyve amonge vs here
In Isaraell schuld be boght *and* sold,
Asse avnteant p*ro*fettis hereof hathe told,
That in this lande here he schuld make surenes,
And he to be cawlid the Kyng of Pes,

Asse Isaee hym*m*selfe herein to wyttnes:
"In facie populor*um*," thes did he sey,
"Cu*m* venerit sanctus santor*um* cessabit vnctio vestra."
And soo when owre ryght blod schall seyse,
Moche v*er*tu and g*r*ace then schall incresse,
W*ith* hy jugeme*n*tis of rightwessenes,
Amongest hus evyn here in Isaraell.

ANE. Yff thatt I myght abyde þ*a*t dey
Thatt wholle off wholleis for to see
Wyche thatt I haue desyrid allwey,
In this worlde well were me.
Now, Lord, *and* yff thy wyll hit be,
Grant me my hoope longe lokid fore,
Then joie nor welthe kepe I no more.

SEMEO*N*. Now, Ane, systur and dere frynde,
Lett hus bothe w*ith* a whole intent
In this tru feyth owre lyvis yend,
Lawdyng thatt Lorde wyche ys o*m*nipotent;
Wherefore I thynke hyt full expeydente
In contenuall preyar for to indure,
To kno þerby his graceose plesure.

ANE. O sofferent Semeon, þi fam*us* consell
Inwardely gladyth me in my hart.
Nothyng contentyth my mynd soo well;
Wherefore at þ*is* tyme woll we dep<a>rte.

S<EMEON>. Now, Ane, syth þ*a*t ye wol hence nede,
Vnto the tempull w*ith* all spede [fol. 4v

Owre Lordis wyll for to abyde,
That Lord of lordis be thy gyde,
And sende the þ*a*t wyche thow lovist most,
Bothe heyle *and* bote for the p*ro*vide,
Where eyu*er* thow goo in any cost.

Fryndis, now ys hit tyme to prey
Before that I my rest do take;
My custome hathe yt byn alwey
Asse longe ase eyu*er* I am awake
Intersession vnto that Lorde to make
Of hym to obteyne all my reyquest,
And then full peysable to take my rest.

Now, Lorde, that madist all thyng of noght,
Bothe heyvin *and* hell and eyu*er*e creature,
Asse thow knoist myn inwarde thoght,
Reycomforde when hit ys thy plesure;
For I do covett no more treysure
Then the tyme of thy natevete
W*ith* my mortall yeeis thatt I myght se.

But asse thow wolt, Lorde, all thyng mvst be,
And reysun hit ys thatt hit be soo;
My wyll þ*er*to schall eyu*er* agre:
My wholle desyre now dost þ*o*u kno.
Or thatt I vnto slepe do goo,
I com*m*ytt my warkis w*ith* all the s*ir*cu*m*stanse
Wholly vnto thy lawis *and* ordenance.

*There Semeon settys hym downe to rest, ase hit were, and the Angell seythe to hym*m*:*

I ANGELL. Semeon of thy rest awake!
Owre Lord in heyvyn he sendyght the gretyng
Of my <message>, with the for to make
W*ith* the hys frind a solame metyng. [fol. 5r
Hys blessid bode vnto thi kepyng
W*ith*in schort tyme schal be broght,

And here in thy tempull thow schalte be soght.

SEMEO*N*. Lorde, whence cam this solam noyse
That awoke me here soo suddenly?
I my spretis þ*er*w*ith* did soo reyjoyse
Thatt no leng*er* slepe cowlde I.
Me thoght he seyde right p*er*fettly
Thatt solam sufferent thatt I schulde see,
And haue hym here in my custode.

ANGELL II. Semeon*n*, thatt Lorde in Trenete,
Whom thow hast desirid to see alwey,
At thy tempull offurde schal be
Vnto thy honde this same dey;
Þ*er*fore spede in all thatt thow may
That the tempull in ordur be,
This Prynce to reyseyve w*ith* all vmelete.

SEM*M*EON. Now Lorde of lordis, thankis be to the.
These gloreose tythyngis þ*a*t here be tolde
In my hart soo gladith me
Thatt I am lyghtar a M folde
Then eyu*er* I wasse before.
Therefore wyll I w*ith* al my myght
To se my tempull soo presseoosely pyght
In gorgis araye thatt hyt be dyght
This Prynce for to ownowre.

There Semeon gothe to his clarkis and seyth:

Now, fryndis all, be of good chere,
And to owre tempull draw we nere;
Soche solam nevis now I here
Thatt all my spretis dothe glade.
Thatt babe ys borne of dyngnete
Thatt we soo long hathe desirid to see,
Owre Lord *and* Kyng most myghte
Thatt all this world made.

CLAREC*US*. Now blessid mot that Lorde be,

Thatt dey *and* owre thatt we schall see
His gloreose bodde in Trenete,
Thatt flowre thatt neu*er* schall fade.

SEMEON. No lenger, surs, lett vs abyde,
But to the tempull w*ith* all spede
To reyseyve the Saueower of this world wyde, [fol. 5v
And hym to s*er*ve w*ith* lowe and drede.
Now, sirs, loke thatt ye take good hede
To wayte *and* s*er*ve w*ith* all delegence,
His g*r*ace to ownowre w*ith* humble reu*er*ence.

CLAREC*US*. To s*er*ve a prynce of soche magneffecens,
S*ir*, I wasse neu*er* wont thereto.
Sythe ye þ*er*in hathe more intellegence,
Instructe me, s*ir*, how þat I schuld do
Lest thatt I do offende.
For rathur then I wolde hym grewe
Thatt Lord on whom I do beleve,
Yett had I leyu*er* myself reymeve
Vnto the worldis yende.

SEMEON. Sith thatt ye for knoleyge dothe make sute,
Your wyttis the bettur do I reypute.
W*ith* humble hartis and meke,
Won of hus mvst holde the lyght
Ande the othur the sacrefyce,
And I on kneis asse hit ys right,
The offece to exsersyse
Vnto thatt babe soo swette.

CLAREC*US*. Then hast we this alter to araye,
And clothis off onowre þ*er*on to laye,
<And>e the grownde straw we w*ith* flowris gay
Thatt of oddur swetely smellis.

SEMEON*N*. And when he aprochis nere this place,
Syng then w*ith* me thatt conyng hasse,
And the othur the meyne space,
For joie rynge ye the bellis. *Cantant.*

*There Semeon*n *and his clarkis gothe vp to the tempull, and Gaberell c*um*yth to the tempull dore* and *seyth:*

GABERELL. Hayle, Mare, meke and myld,
The v*er*tu in the schall neyu*er* fade.
Hayle, meydyn, and thy chylde,
Thatt all this world made.

Thy seylesteall Fadur wyche ys om*n*ipotent,
Of his ambassage hethur hathe me sent
Vnto the, lade and v*ir*gyn reyu*er*ent,
W*ith* thy sun, owre heyvin Kynge.
Vnto the tempull thatt thow schuldist goo, [fol. 6r
And to whyt turtuls w*ith* the also,
And present the chyld and them to,
All iij of them in offeryng.
Spede you forth thatt ye were gone,
But leyve nott ye wold Josoff at whome,
For nedely, lade, he mvste be won
In this sacrefyce doyng.

MARE. W*ith* hart and wyll hit schal be done,
In pleysing of that Fathur of myght.
Thyddur wyll I bothe hastely *and* sone,
And take me my child soo bryght.

GABERELL. Then to Josoff goo ye full right,
And make hym preve of this case.
Byd hym hast þ*at* he were dyght
To gyd you theddur into that place.
Now rest well, Mare, w*ith* moche solas,
For I mvst thiddur asse I cam froo.

MARE. He thatt ys ande eyu*er* wasse
Be thy gyde where eu*er* thow goo,
And send hus all of his grace.
I pray here knelynge hit ma be so.

Now cu*m* heddur to me, my darlyng dere,
My myrthe, my joie, and al my chere,

Swetter then eyu*er* wasse blassu*m* on brere.
Thy swete mowthe now wyll I kis.
Now Lorde of lordis be owre gide
Where eyu*er* we walke in cuntreyis wyde,
And these to turtuls for hus p*ro*vide,
Off them thatt we do nott mys.

Here Mare goth to Josoff and *seyis:*

Rest well, Josoff, my spouse soo free.

JOSOFF. Now welcu*m*, Mare, dame, whatt sey yee?

MARE. Swet nevis, husebond, I bryng to thee.
The angell of God w*ith* me hath be
To geve hus bothe warnyng
Thatt you *and* I w*ith* a wholle intent,
Aftur the law thatt here ys ment,
Schuld in the tempull owre chyld present
In Jerusalem, þ*er* to make offeryng.

JOSOFF. Now, Mare, thatt woll I neu*er* deny, [fol. 6v
But aftur my powar for to apply,
And thatt you kno, dame, asse well asse <I>;
You neu*er* cawll but I am reddy.

MARE. Now, husebond, ye speyke full gentylli,
Þ*er*fore loke, Josoff, *and* ye cold spy
To turtyll dowis how thatt we myght cu*m* ny,
For nedely turtullis offur mvst we:
Thatt offeryng fawlyth for owre degre.

JOSOFF. Nay, nay, Mare, thatt wol not be.
Myne age ys soche I ma not well see;
There schall noo duffu*es* be soght for me,
Also God me saue.

MARE. Swette Josoff, fullfyll ye owre Lordis hestes.

JOSOFF. Why, *and* woldist thu haue me to hunt bridis nestis?

I pray the hartely, dame, leve thosse jestis
And talke of thatt wol be.

For, dame, woll I neu*er* vast my wyttis
To wayte or pry whe<re> the wodkoce syttis,
Nor to jubbard among the m*ar*le pyttis,
For thatt wasse neyu*er* my gyse.
Now am I wold *and* ma not well goo;
A small twyge wold me ou*er*throo,
And yche were wons lyggyd aloo,
Full yll then schulde I rys*e*.

MARE. Ye, hardely, Josoff, do nott drede:
Owre Lorde wyll quyte right well youre mede,
And att all tym*is* be youre spede,
And furthur you in youre viage.

JOSOFF. Ey, dame! Ey, God helpe hus all!
Me thynke youre meymorre were small,
On me soo whomly eyu*er* to call.
You mynde nothynge myne age.
But the weykist gothe eyu*er* to the walle.
Therefore go thyself, dame, for me thow schall;
Ye, or ellis get the a nev page.

MARE. Husebande, these be no womens dedis.
Therefore, Jossoff, ye must forthe nedis,
For surely there ys no reymedy.

JOSOFF. Noo remedy, then, but I mvst goo? [fol. 7[r]
Now be my trawthe I ma tell you
Thosse tythingis ar but cold.
Then nedis mvste thatt nedis schall,
And now he thatt ma worst of all
The candyll ys lyke to holde.

MARE. Now, gentyll Josoff, when wyll ye goo
To make an ende of this owre jurney?

JOSOFF. Þ*at* schal be or I haue any lust thereto,

And thatt dare I boldely sey.

How sey ye all this cu*m*pany
Thatt be weddid asse well asse I?
I wene þ*a*t ye suffur moche woo;
For he thatt weddyth a yonge thyng
Mvst fullfyll all hir byddyng,
Or els ma he his handis wryng,
Or watur his jis when he wold syng;
And thatt all you do knoo.

MARE. Why sey ye soo, sir? Ye be to blame.

JOSOFF. Dame, all this cu*m*pany wyll sey the same.
Ys ytt not soo? Speyke, men*n*, for schame!
Tell you the trothe ase you well con.
For the þ*a*t woll nott there wyffis plese,
Ofte tym*is* schall suffur moche dysees;
Therefore I holde hym well att es
Thatt hathe to doo w*ith* non*n*.

MARE. Leyve of these gawdis for my lowe,
And goo for these fowlys, s*ir*, I you pray.
The Fadur of heyvin thatt ys abowe
Wyll spede you well in youre jurney.

JOSOFF. No reymede then, but I mvst forthe nede.
Now owre Lord grant me well for to spede.
Loo, feyre wordis ffull ofte dothe leyde
Men cleyne agen there mynd.
Now, Lorde God, thow sende me feyre weddur,
And thatt I ma fynd those fowlis togeddur,
Whytt or blake, I care nott wheddur,
So thatt I ma them fynde.

MARE. Full well schall you spede hardely,
Yff thatt ye goo abowt hytt wyllyngly.

JOSOFF. Then I woll goo by *and* by, [fol. 7v
Thogh hit be not full hastely,

W*ith* all my hart I wol goo spy
Yff any be in my wey, I wyll them fynd *and* I may,
Or thatt I make an ende.

MARE. Now thatt Lorde thatt best may,
He be your spede in youre jurney,
Ande good tythyngis of you me send.

JOSOFF. Yea, he thatt hatth socheonon hym to crawe,
He schal be sure, asse God me sawe,
Eyu*er* the worse yend of the staff to haue
Att the lattur yend.

Here Josoff gothe from Mare and seyth:

I wandur abowt myself alone;
Turtulis or dowis can I non see.
Now, Kyng of heyvin, thow amend my mone,
For I tro I seke nott where the be.

My myght, my strenth ys worne fro me,
For age I am waxun*n* almost blynd;
Those fowlys the ar full far fro me,
And werie yvill for me to fynde.

I loke fast and neu*er* the nere,
My wynd for feynt ys allmost gone.
Lorde, benedissete, whatt make I here
Among these heggis myself alone?

Forwere I ma no lengur stond,
These buskis the teyre me on eyu*er*e syde;
Here woll I sytt apon this londe,
Owre Lordis wyll for to abyde.

I ANGELL. Aryse vp, Josoff, *and* take no thoght
For these to fowlys thatt thow hast soght:
Evyn to thy hond I haue them broght,
And therefore be off good chere.
Take them here bothe to,

And ageyne to Mare thy wyff thow goo
In all the hast thatt hit be doo;
Thow tarre noo lengur here.

JOSOFF. O lawde be vnto thatt Lorde soo exsellent
For those to fowlis thatt I haue soght.
Fullfyllid now ys myn intent, [fol. 8r
My hart ys evyn*n* asse yt wolde be,
All care fro me ys past.
Now thatt Mare my wyff these briddis had
For to make hir hart asse glad,
To hir wyll I in hast.

Now rest well, Mare, my none darlyng.
Loo, dame, I haue done thy byddyng
And broght these dowis for owre offeryng:
Here be the bothe alyve.
Womon*n*, haue them in thy honde.
I am full glade I haue them fond.
Am nott I a good husbonde?
Ye, dame, soo mot I thryve.

MARE. Now the Fathur of heyvin that ys abowe,
He quyt you, Josoff, for this dede,
And furthur I pray you for my lowe,
Vnto the tempull lett vs make spede.

JOSOFF. Ey, bloo a whyle, dame, I the pray,
For soft *and* essele men goo far.
I haue laburde all this dey,
Yett am I vere lyttull the nar.
I tro thatt I schall neyu*er* bewar.
Soo full of feyre wordis these wemen*n* be
Thatt men thereto must nedis agre,

And therefore, dame, alsoo mote I the,
Aftur my labur fayne wolde I rest.
Therefore goo thyselfe thow schalt for me,
Or tarre att whome wheddur þ*ou* thynkist beste.

MARE. Na, swet husebond, ye do well kno,
To goo alone ys not for me;
Wherefore, good s*ir*, I pray you soo
Thatt I ma haue your*e* cu*m*pany.

JOSOFF. Loo, fryndis, here ma you knoo
The maner of my wyff ys soo
Thatt w*ith* hyr nedis mvst I goo,
Wheddur I wyll or nyll.
Now ys nott this a cu*m*burs lyff?
Loo, sirs, whatt ytt ys to haue a wyff!
Yett had I leyu*er*, nor to lyve in stryff,
Apply evyn to hir wyll

For syth þ*at* here ys no remede.
Take vp youre chylde, I sey, Mare,
And walke we togedur feyre *and* essele,
And soo to stynt all strywe;
And I woll trusse vp thys gere, [fol. 8v
For I se well I mvst hit beyre.
At Jerusalem I wold all ye were,
Also mote I thryve.

MARE. There schall we be when God wyll,
For at his plesure all thyng mvst be.

JOSOFF. Dame, and thatt ys bothe reysun and skill:
Sett forward then and lett me see.

II ANGELL. Awake, Semeon, and drede the noght,
In all the hast thatt eyu*er* ma be,
And reyseyve that Lord thatt all hathe wroght,
W*ith* hym his modur, Mare.
Make spede, Semeon*n*, þ*at* thow were dyght
To reyseyve thatt chyld w*ith* all thy myght.
Now schalt thow see the blessidist syght
Thatt eyu*er* thow didist see. *Cantant.*

SEMEON. O Lord of lordis, this solam noyse
From the Maker of heyvin *and* hell,

My hart therew*ith* soo did reyjoise,
Thatt the myrthe þ*er*off can noo tong tell,
Nor hand w*ith* pen subscrybe.
I thanke þ*at* Lorde *and* Kyng of myght,
Thogh all my lust throgh age be worne,
Thatt I schall see this gloreose syght.
Blessid be the owre thatt thou wast borne
This dey þ*at* eyu*er* I do abide.

Now to reyseve this Kyng of Pes,
Thatt owt of dangyr schall hus reles;
Owre hy merrettis schall he incres
In joiye abundantly;
For here kepe I no more blis,
But thatt he m*ar*ke me for won of his,
And then whan his swete wyll ys
Am I evyn*n* redde to dy.

Now, clarkis, cu*m* forth *and* do your offes,
And this awter hastely þ*at* ye aray;
For here schal be the solamyst sacrefyce
Thatt eyu*er* wasse seyne in Juda.

Make sure, fryndis, *and* all thatt ye may,
Thatt ordur be hade in eyu*er*e place.

CLARECUS. Now þ*at* Lord of lordis thatt best may,
To do owre devteis he grant vs g*r*ace,
And for to plese hym to his paye,
Sey all you, "Deo gracias."

Loo, mastur, bothe man *and* place, [fol. 9r
Be all redde at your byddeng.

SEMEON. Then, surs, cu*m* forthe apase
And myrrele the bellis ryng.

Ane, systur, goo ye w*ith* me
For to reyseyve thatt p*r*ince of onowre
And hym to welcu*m* reu*er*ently,

Ase of this world lorde *and* gou*er*nowre.

ANE. Now, fathur Semeon*n*, I am obeydentt,
Youre g*r*aceose pleysure for to obbey.
To s*er*ve thatt Lorde wyche ys om*n*ipotent,
Lett vs goo mete hym on the wey.

CLAREC*US*. Mastur, now ar the bellis rong,
And redde att hond ys eyu*er*e thyng.

SEMEON*N*. Then lett me see w*ith* hart *and* tonge
How myrrely thatt ye can syng. *Cantant.*

Here the cum *doune* wi*th* *pressession to mete them:*

MARE. Heyle sufferent Semeon so good.
My semely sun here I bryng to the
To offur hym vp in flesche and blode,
Ase be the law he oght to be.

SEMEON*N*. Now, wholle Mare *and* Josoff also,
Ye be ryght welcu*m* vnto this place,
For off God ar ye blessid bothe to
Thatt hath you grondid in soche g*r*ace.
And ye, Josoff, of soo grett age
Thatt soche a babe forth can bryng,
In whom all owre reydemcion doth hyng,
And off this worlde ys Lorde *and* Kyng,
This wase a graceose mareage.

JOSOFF. Now gentill bysschope, I the pray,
Evyn the verre truth thow woldist me sey,
Ys nott this a prete bewey
Asse eyu*er* thow hast knone?
Now, be hym þ*at* made both heyvin *and* hell,
This lyttull myte I lowe as well
Asse thogh he were myn oone.

MARE. Reyseve, Semeon, w*ith* good chere;
The law wyll hit schall so be,

For wyche cawse I bryng hym here.
Here in thi hondis take hym the. [fol. 9v

SEMEON*N*. Now welcu*m*, Lord, vnto <. . .>y <. . .>r <. . .>d.
Now welcu*m*, Prynce, vnto this place.
Welcu*m*, owre sufferent Saweowre.
Welcu*m*, the groundr of owre g*ra*ce.
Welcu*m*, owre joie. Welcu*m*, owre myrthe.
Welcu*m*, owre g*ra*ceose goue*r*nowre.
Welcu*m* to huse, thatt heyvinly flowre.
Now blessid be the dey and owre
Of thy gloreose byrthe.

ANE. Now welcu*m*, Kyng of kyngis all.
Now welcu*m*, Maker of all mankynd.
Welcu*m* to hus, bothe grett and small.
Good Lord, thy sarvandis now haue in mynd,
Thatt longe hath levid here
In clenes pure w*ith*owt offence,
W*ith* grett desyris for to be hence;
But now the syght of thy presence
Hath amendid all owre chere.

CLAREC*US*. Now welcu*m*, Lord, vnto all hus,
Thy none tru s*er*vandis, ase reysun ys.
Welcu*m,* owre God and Kyng of blys,
Owre Lorde longe lokid fore.
All the p*ro*fettis thatt of the spake
Seyd thow schuldist, for owre sake,
Fleysche *and* blod of a meydyn take,
Owre joys to reystore.

SEMEON*N*. Cu*m* on w*ith* me, my fryndis dere,
W*ith* this chylde thatt we haue here,
Of this worlde the lant*er*ne cl*er*e,
Of whom all lyght schall spryng.
W*ith* hoole hartis now lett hus p*ra*ee.
Thatt owre *and* tyme now blesse we may
Þ*a*t eyu*er* we aboode þe dey
Of this chyldis comynge. *Cantant.*

*Here Semeon goth to the awtere wi*th *þe chyld in hys arm*is and *seyth:*

SEMEON. Now art thow cu*m*, Lorde, to my honde,
Thogh thatt I onworthe were;
Yett, Lorde, forgeve þi pore s*er*wande.

. . .

<MARE.> Whyle, whyle the weddur ys soo feyre; [fol. 11r
And I woll cu*m* aftur asse I may.
For now att whome I wolde we weyre.

JOSOFF. To goo before now I woll asaye,
Thogh thatt my fotemanschipe be not full gaye.
I pray God spede vs on owre jurney,
For I schall be were or thatt I cu*m* there.

There Mare and *Josoff depa*rtis *owt of the vpp*er *parte of the pagond.*

SEMEON*N*. Loo, fryndis, how God for vs hathe wroght,
And schode hymself here at this tyde.
Blessid mot he be in word *and* thoght,
Myghtefull Maker of thy world wyde.

I wasse lame of fote *and* hond,
And now am whole ase ye ma see.
I thanke thatt Lorde of his sond,
And eyu*er* his s*er*vande wyll I be,
Thatt Lorde soo moche of myght.
Now Lorde of lordis that hath no pere,
Wyche att this tyme wase offurd here,
Sende you all the fruyssio<n> clere
Of his heyvinly mancion soo bryght.

ANE. And of owre mys he amend vs,
And from owre foys defend vs,
And <to> his hy trone he send vs,
In secula seculor*um*. Amen.

Here gothe Semeon and his clarkis owt of the tempull.

JOSOFF. Now, Mare, my wyff here p*re*sent,
Vnto <God> myche bondon, dame, ar we,
Thatt soo goodly a childe here hath vs sent;
In this world a feyrear þ*er* canott be.

MARE. I thanke þ*a*t Lord om*n*ipotent,
For yt dothe me good hym for to see;
Wherefore, Josoff, I wold he went
Vnto Jerusalem w*ith* you and me.
For now he ys xij yere of age,
Full well reyconid yt ma be,
Of lymys he waxith feyre *and* large,
And moche desyrith cu*m*pane.

JOSOFF. Now, dame, he ys a prette page, fol. 11^{v}
And as ye sey full well cu*m* on;
I kno non soche on of hys age.
I p*ra* God make hym a right good man.

MARE. Now Jh*esus*, my son*n*, w*ith* you whatt chere?
Whatt m<y>rth make <ye,> chyld, this dey?
Thow art he thatt I love most dere,
My joie, my myrthe, and all my pley.

JH*ESUS*. I thanke you, my modur, in all thatt I may,
And at youre hand I am here
To do you s*er*ves bothe nyght and dey,
And redde alwey to make you chere.

JOSOFF. Loo, fryndis, here doth apere,
Yt ys eyrly scharp thatt wol be thorne.
How glad he ys his modr to pleyse,
And eyu*er* hathe byn syth he wasse borne.
Thogh thatt my vthe frome me be vorne,
Yet in his dedis I haue moche joie;
For in feythe he woll p*re*ve evin a prette bwey.
Cu*m*, my sun, well mot thow thee.
Thow schalt to J*er*usalem w*ith* þi modur *and* me,

Su*m* goodly syghtis, sun, for to see
Apon this owre festefawll dey.

MARE. Now truly, Josoff, as ye sey,
And merely for to pase forthe þ*e* wey,
Su*m* v*er*tuos cu*m*pany I wold we had.

JOSOFF. Dame, I kepe noo moo but evyn this lad;
For you nor I canot be sade
Thatt dey þ*at* we hy*m* see.
Mare, you kno thatt I am olde,
And in cu*m*pany canot be soo bolde
Asse I wasse wont to be.
Therefore, Mare, leyde ye the wey,
And essely lett vs togeddr goo;
Thogh yt be far furth on the dey,
Yett all be owre fryndis I dare wel sey,
And neu*er* a won owre foo.

MARE. Now God hold thatt wyche best may,
And, gentyll Josoff, lett vs goo.
Be the hand the chylde wyll I leyde;
I trust the bettur for to spede.
And ye Josoff alsoo.

JOSOFF. Ye hardely, dame, lett hym goo before ye and me,
And be nothyng afrayde.
For the best foteman of hus thre, fol. 12r
In good feyth, dame, thatt ys hee,
Yff he were well asayde.

JH*ESUS*. I am full redde w*ith* you to goo
At your bydding in weyle *and* woo,
And to do you s*er*ves bothe to,
In hart w*ith* all mekenes.
Cu*m* on, my mothur, and dred ye noght,
And on your jurney, ase you oght,
The Fadur of heyvin þ*at* all hat<h> wroght,
He kepe you from dystres.

JOSOFF. Now, Lord, when I to mynde do call
In vthe when I was werre small,
Many wynturs agone,
Lord God, benedicete,
Yong chyldur now more wyser be,
Nor wase then an olde mon*n*.

MARE. Now welcu*m* be owre Lordis sond.
Therefore cu*m* on, gentyll husbond,
The sytte ys evyn*n* at owre honde;
Good cu*m*pany there ma we fynd.

JOSOFF. Ey, ey, dame, in feyth I can noo more.
My leggis byn were, my fete be soore;
That man thatt canot go before
Nedis mvst cu*m* behynd.

There the all goo vp to the awter, and *Jh*es*us* *before.* Þe *syng an antem.*

JOSOFF. Now, Mare my wyff, cu*m* hethur to me.
Al thyng ys done ase yt schulde be,
And s*er*ves song full sollamle
For this owre festefawll dey.

MARE. Now, huseband, then lett vs iij
Make the hast þ*a*t ma be
Whom to goo w*ith* cu*m*pane
To bryng vs on the wey.

*There the goo done into the for-pagond and Jh*es*us* *steylyth awey.*

JOSOFF. Mare, my spretis be rayvisschid cleyne,
And clerely cast owt off all woo,
W*ith* these solam syghtys thatt we haue seyne
In yondur tempull þ*a*t we cam froo.

MARE. Now serten, Josoff, you wolde not wene fol. 12v
Whatt myrthe I make w*ith*owt woo,
Thatt my chylde w*ith* hus hathe bene,

And those solam syghtis seyne alsoo.

JOSOFF. Then whomwarde, Mare, lett vs goo
Whyle thatt we haue the lyght off þ*e* dey;
For you haue eyu*er* lovid cu*m*pany,
For yt dothe schorttun well youre wey.

Yett in good owre we ma bothe sey,
For othur did we neyu*er* fynde.

MARE. Alas, Josoff, and well awey.
Now haue we lafte owre chyld behynd.

JOSOFF. Whatt, Mare, I sey, amend thy chere.
P*ar*dy, dame, he dothe but as othur done.
Chyldur togedur woll draw nere:
He woll, I warrand, ou*er*take vs sone.

MARE. Ou*er*take vs sone, q*uoth*a? Nay, s*er*tes, na!
Whatt nede you me soche talis to tell?
He ys gon su*m* othur wey,
Or s*er*ten, Josoff, he ys not well.

JOSOFF. Dame, he ys nott far awey:
From vs no man wyll hym wyle.

MARE. Hyt helpyth not, Josoff, soche wordis to sey.
My chylde ys gone, alas the whyle.

JOSOFF. We schall haue <hym>, dame, or hit be longe;
Yff we serche well yondur sytte,
Su*m* chyrdur there he ys amonge,
Or elis surely whomwarde ys he.

MARE. Off sorro now schal be my songe,
My chylde ageyne tyll I ma see.

JOSOFF. Dame, of his welfare I wold be glade,
And off the othur I wolde be woo;
Therefore Mare, no more be sade,

But ayene to the sytte lett vs goo.

MARE. Make hast, Josoff, thatt we were there;
For had I neu*er* more lust thereto.
Bake agane lett vs reypeyre,
For thatt ys best for vs to do.

Here Mare and Josoff goth downe in to the tempull warde. fol. 13r

DOCTOR I. Now, lordyngis, lystun to me a whyle,
Wyche hathe the lawis vndur honde,
And thatt no man fawll in soche p*er*ell
Agenst any artyccull for to stand,
For the come*n* statute of this lande
Woll that all soche p*er*sonys schulde be tane,
And in the face of peple ooponn*n*ly slayne.

DOCTOR II. E and the othur wholle decryis ageyne,
Wyche vnto Moyses wonly wasse sent
In tabulis of ston only to reymayne
Vndur an hy and streyte cu*m*mandement,
Wyche at this tyme we thynke convenent
There apon to holde dyssepyssions here,
Be polatike syence of clarge clere.

DOCTOR III. Wherefore, all peple, now draw nere,
And in this place gewe your attendence.
How ye schuld lyve here ma you lere,
Acordyng vnto your aleygence;
For yt ys well knowe vnto this p*re*sence
Thatt doctoris we ar *and* of hy degre,
And haue the lawis in custode.

DOCTOR I. Ley forth youre reysonis, now lett me see
How lawe of leygence oght to be lade,
Wyche of the Eybruys subsc<ri>byd be,
W*ith* othur of Moyses thatt now ys hade.
To contend herein I wold be glade,
Amo<n>ge the peple here manefestly,
And the truthe expowndid to them oopunly.

JH*ES*US. Lordis, moche lowe w*ith* you be lent,
And pes be amonge this cu*m*pany.

DOCTOR III. Su*n*, awe I wold thow went,
For othur hast in hand haue wee.

DOCTOR II. Chylde, whosooeyu*er* the hyddur sent
The were not wyse, thus warne I the,
For we haue othur talis to tent
Then w*ith* chyldur bordyng to bee.

DOCTOR I. Good sun, thow art to yonge to larne
The hy mystere of Mosess law:
Thy reysun canot yt deserne,
For thy wytt ys not worthe a strawe,
And no marvell thogh thow schuldist be rawe
In soche hy pwyntis for to be reysonyng,
For off age art thow a vere yonglyng. fol. 13v

JH*ES*US. E, surs, whattsooeyu*er* to me you sey,
Me nedith not of you to lerne nothyng.

DOCTOR II. This besse bweye of his tong,
All secrettis surely he thynkith he knois.

DOCTOR III. Nay serten, sun, thow art to yonge,
Be clarge clere, to kno owre lawis.

JH*ES*US. Ye doctoris all thatt be present,
Suffyce *and* mvse no more off me;
For off your lawis the wholl intent
Nothyng þ*er*off ys hyde froo me;
For in those placis haue I be
Where all owre lawis furst were wroght.

DOCTOR I. Cu*m* sett the here *and* we schall see
For sarten, sun, soo semys yt noght.

There the doctoris settyth Cryst among them.

Now were yt nott a wondurs thyng
Thys chylde owre reysuns þ*at* he schuld reyche?
And yett he seyth he hath a felyng
Owre lawis truly for to teyche.

JH*ESUS*. Syris, the Whoole Goste in me hath lyght
Thatt my powar ys to preyche,
And of the Godhed most of myght,
Most p*er*fettly here ma I teyche.

DOCTOR III. Whense cam thys chylde, I m*ar*vell soore,
Thatt speykyth to vs this mystecawlly.

JH*ESUS*. Surs, I wasse all you before,
And aftur you agen schal be.

DOCTOR III. Surs, ys nott this a wondurs thyng,
And also a moche more m*ar*vell?
How be yt surely in his workyng
The actis thereof ma follo right well;
For ase Davith in his salme dothe tell
Be chyldur yong, seyng of them,
Ex ore infanciam et lactancium p*er*fesiste laudem.
Of chyldurs mothis ye kno right well
God hathe p*er*formyde loving,
But of sochon hard I neu*er* tell
He beyng but soo yong a thyng. fol. 14r

Yett, sun, su*m*whatt thow schuldest haue let
In this place here to speyke so large:
Where nobull doctors togeddur ar met
There chyldurs wordis ar at no charge.
For sure yff thow woldist neu*er* so fayne
Labur thi wyttis to lerne owre lawe,
Yett art thow nodur of myght nor mayne
To p*er*seyve thatt ase a clarke ma knoo.

JH*ESUS*. My wordis in noo wyse wole I reyfrayne,
The trawthe thereby for to debarre;
I woll them p*ro*ve bothe platt and playne

Be youre one lawis and neu*er* arre.

DOCTOR II. Mastur<s> all, whatt ma this meyne?
I wondur soore how this can be.
Soo yong a chylde haue I nott seyne
W*ith* clarkis to talke so conyngle.

DOCTOR III. Ase wyde in worde asse eyu*er* I went,
Saw I neyu*er* non soche before,
But I troo amonst vs he be sent
To be the salu*er* of owre sore.

JH*ESUS*. Suris, I woll p*ro*ve be actoris evedent
Har mystereis þ*an* eyu*er* you red or saw.

DOCTOR I. Sey, sun, wyche wasse the furst co*m*mandement
Thatt wasse subsc<r>ibyd in Moses lawe?

JH*ESUS*. Sythe all you masturs togethur be sett,
And youre bokys here leyde on breyde,
Ley forthe youre reysuns *and* do nott lett,
How right thatt ye can rede.

DOCTOR II. I rede this in the furst byddyng
Wyche Moses dyd rede vs vntill:
Fyrst honor God aboue all thyng
W*ith* all thy hartt and all thy wyll,
And asse thyself loue thy neybur
And in noo wyse to do hym yll.

JH*ESUS*. Ye nede noo nodur bokis to bryng
But these to pwyntis for to insev,
In whome the whole afecte dothe hynge
Of all owre lawis bothe olde *and* nev.

DOCTOR III. Syth he these to, son, hath the schoide,
Tell me the othur, chylde, I the p*ra*.

JH*ESUS*. The thryd beddyth the in any wey fol. 14v
Thatt of thy labur thou schuldyst reste,

And truly kepe thy Sabett dey,
Thy selfe, þi s*er*wande, *and* thy best.

The forthe bydithe the do thy best
Thy fathur *and* mothur for to honowre,
And when þ*er* goodis ar decrest,
W*ith* all thy myght thou schuldist them succure.

The fyfte cum*m*andythe for any reygur
Man nor woman þ*a*t þ*o*u schuldist kyll.
To fle advltre ys anothure,
And all thatt towchis any yll.

The vijth seyis thow schuldyst nott steyle
Thy neyburis goodis more nor les.
The viijth forbyddyth the to cownsayle
Or to bare any fawls wyttnes.

The ixth forbyddeth othys grett
In any wyse þ*o*u schuldist nott sweyre.
The last wold þ*o*u schuldist no covett
Thy neyburs goodis hym to apere.

And this Mosees amonge vs here
Hathe declarid amonge all men,
Aftur sc<r>ipture þ*a*t we schulde lere
How to kepe these com*m*andementis x.

DOCTOR I. Beholde owre lawis hou he dothe expounde
Thatt neu*er* larny<d> on boke to rede.
Then all we he ys moche more p*ro*founde
In all trawthis yff we take hede.

DOCTOR II. Brether, lett hym goo his weyis;
For yff þ*is* abrode were knone p*er*fettly
The peple wolde geve hym more prese
Then we docturs for all owre clarge.

DOCTOR I. Ye, fryndis bothe, syth yt ys soo,
He knois no farthur of owre lore,

But asse he cu*m* soo let hym goo,
For w*ith* vs he schall medyll no more.

Here cumyth Josoff and *Mare sekyng þis chylde,* and *Mare seyth:*

MARE. A, dere Josoff, what ys youre redde?
Of my grett dolar noo bote ma be.
My hart ys heyve as any leyd
My chylde ageyne tyll I ma see. fol. 15r
We haue hym soght in many a stede,
Vp and downe these deyis iij,
And wheythur that he be quyke or ded
I do not kno, thatt woo ys mee.

JOSOFF. In sorro wasse there neyu*er* man more,
But mornyng ma nott ytt amend.
Mare, wyff, lett vs therefore
Take the g*r*ace thatt God woll send;

Yff chyldurs cu*m*pany he haue coght,
Abowt yondur tempull he ys full ryght.

MARE. A, Josoff, I see thatt I haue soght;
In this worlde wasse neu*er* soche a syght.
See, husebond, where he syttyth aloft
Amonge yondur masturs soo moche off myght.

JOSOFF. Now blessid be hym thatt hethur vs broght,
For now in hart I am full lyght.

MARE. Josoff, ye kno the ordur well:
Goo ye *and* feyche youre chylde *and* myne.
Now I see hym owt of all p*er*yll,
Whom he schall w*ith* vs ageyne.

JOSOFF. Ey, Mare, wyff, ye kno ryght well,
Asse I haue tolde you many a tyme,
W*ith* men of myght durst I neyu*er* mell;
Loo, dame, how the sytt in there furis fyn.

MARE. To them youre arand for to sey,
Therein, Josoff, þ*er* ys no p*er*ell;
The haue reygardid you alwey
Becawse of age, this wott I well.

JOSOFF. To them, wyff, whatt schulde I sey?
In feythe I do nott knoo full wele.
Surely I schall be schamyde todey,
For I cane nothur croke nor knele.

MARE. Then goo we theddur bothe to
To them þ*a*t sytt soo worthe in wede;
Yff ye woll not the arrande doo,
No reymedy but I mvst nede.

JOSOFF. E, dame, goo tell them þi tale furst,
For lyke þ*o*u art to do thatt dede;
I wold tell myne and I durst.
Also God me spede,
My place at this tyme schal be behynd. fol. 15v

MARE. A, Jh*esus*, Jh*esus*, my sun so swete,
Thy gooyng froo me soo sudden*n*ly
Hathe cawsid vs bothe for to wepe
W*ith* byttur teyris abundantly.

Thyn olde fathur here *and* I
For thy sake, sun, hathe lykyd full yll;
Owre yis the were but seldum dry
But now thatt we are cu*m* the tyll.

JH*ESUS*. Modur, why did you seke me soo?
Hyt hathe byn oft seyde vnto you,
My Fathurs wyll I mvst fullfyll
In eyu*er* pwynt for well or woo.

MARE. Sun, these talis thatt you me tell
Ase yet I canot vndurstand,
But my hart, this kno I well,
Yt were glade I haue the fonde.

Doctor I. Now truly, dame, no m*ar*vell ys
Thogh thow in hart were full woo,
To lose soche a chylde asse this.
How long, wyff, hathe he byn the froo?

Mare. Syr, yt ys now these dayis iij
Syth þ*at* he dep*ar*tid furst fro me:
I am full <glade> here hym to see
Alyve w*ith*owt woo.

Jh*esus*. Now farewell masturs of myght *and* mayne,
For w*ith* my modur now mvst I nede,
For to reyco*mm*ford hyr ageyne
Wyche soo longe for me hath levid in drede.

Doctor II. Now thatt Lorde of lordis be thy spede
Where eyu*er* thow goo in any cruoft,
But yff thow wolt tarre thow schalt not nede
Any more to put thy fryndis to cost.

Doctor III. How seyst thow, fathur, for thy goo<d> wyll?
Wolt thow grant þi help thyre tyll fol. 16r
Awey thatt, s*ir*, he do not goo?

Josoff. Noo, s*ir*, in good fayth þ*at* I nyll,
Nor neyu*er* forgoo hym be my wyll,
Nodur for frynde nor foo.
A long whyle we haue hym myst,
And gone he wasse, or thatt I wyst;
But hade I hym wonis be the fyst,
He schall noo more doo soo!

Mare. Now, lordyngis, of your curtesse,
Do ye nott wyll my chylde fro me,
For w*ith* my wyll yt schall nott be
Whyle thatt owre lyvis last.

Doctor I. Then yt ys noo bote for to intreyte,
Thy chylde I see I canot gete;
I tro yt be but wast to speyke,

Thatt tyme I thynke ys past.

JH*ESUS*. Now, lordyngis all, w*ith* youre lysence,
Good tyme yt ys thatt we were hence.
I thanke <you> of youre hy sapence
Thatt I w*ith* you haue hade.

DOCTOR II. Now, sun, wheneyu*er* thow cu*m*yst þ*is* wey,
Be bold of hus, I the p*r*aye.
Yff thow to age lyve may,
Thy fryndis ma be full glade.

MARE. Now farewell, lordis of hy degre;
I take my leyve at you all three.
Thatt Lorde thatt ys in Trenete,
He kepe you all from care.

JOSOFF. And for the fyndyng of this owre sun,
In heyvynis blysse thatt we ma wone,
And geve you well to fare.

Now cu*m* on, Mare, w*ith* myrre chere,
And brynge youre chyld w*ith* you here:
At Naza*re*the now I wolde we weyre.

MARE. S*ir*, in good tyme we schall cu*m* there;
The wey *and* weddur *and* all ys fayre,
Whereoff am I right fayne.

JOSOFFE. In this place whyle we ar here fol. 16v
Loke thatt we haue all owre gere
Thatt we cu*m* nott agayne.

MARE. Josoffe, husebonde, we myse nothyng,
But at youre wyll lett vs be gooyng
Asse faste ase eyu*er* we can.
Ande now att all this cu*m*pany
My leyve I take *and* þ*a*t full humbly,
Vnto thatt Lorde most myghty
Now I betake you eyu*er*e mon*n*.

JOSOFF. Now farewell, my fryndis all,
For I mvst goo whatteyu*er* befall;
Nedis mvst þ*at* nedis schall,
Be me here may you kno.
A*nd* thatt all you ma vse thatt weyis,
At all tym*is* youre wyvis to pleyse,
Then schall you awoide moche dysees:
God grant thatt you ma do soo.

DOCTOR I. Now, ye lordis thatt hathe the lawis to leyde,
Marke well the wordis thatt hathe byn seyde
Be yondur chylde of wysedome grett,
Wyche at this tyme amonge vs here
Declarid owre lawis be clarge clere,
Wyche be his actis dothe apere
Thatt of God he ys eylecte.

DOCTOR II. Now surely yt can no nothur be,
For he ys nott levyng þ*at* eyu*er* see
Soch hy knoleyge of exselence
In soo tendur vthe.
For in owre moste hyist dysspecionis,
To them he gawe tru solyssionys,
And also made exposysionis,
Acordyng to the truthe.

DOCTOR III. Ys not thys a wondurs case,
That þ*is* yonge chylde soche knolege hase?
Now surely he hath asposschall g*r*ace,
Soo hy dowtis des*er*nyng,
Thatt we wyche nobull docturs be,
And gradudis gret of old antequete,
And now on this place w*ith* yonge infance, fol. 17r
Ageyne ar sett to larning.

Doctor I. Now, bredur bothe, be my consell,
These myghtte matters you sett on syde,
And in avoidyng of more p*er*ell
Thatt here apon myght betyde,
Therefore lett vs no lengur abyde

In these cawsis for to contende,
For this dey ys almost at an yende.

DOCTOR II. Now, brethur bothe, syth yt ys soo,
Ase vere nature dothe me compell,
Here my trowthe I plyght you to
In hart foreyu*er* w*ith* you to dwell.

DOCTOR I. Now, masturs all, be won assent,
All owre matters reyjurnyd be,
Tyll thatt a dey of argument
Ma be apwyntyd indyfferentle,
Where all you the come*n*alte,
You ma dep*ar*te on this co*n*dyssion,
Thatt ye atende at the next monyssion.

DOCTOR III. Now, fryndis, tochyng owre festefall dey,
Ys there oght els þ*at* I ma sey?

DOCTOR II. No more now bute evyn awey,
For the nyght drawis fast apon.

DOCTOR. And of youre cu*m*pa<n>y I wolde you p*ar*t,
And hereof take my leve at eyu*er*e mon.

T<h>ys matter nevly translate be Robart Croo,
in the yere of owre Lord God M^{l}v^{c}xxxiiij^{te},
then beyng meyre Mastur Palmar, Beddar,
and Rychard Smythe an<d> < > Pyxley,
masturs of the Weywars. Thys boke yendide
the seycond dey of Ma*r*che in yere above seyde.

The Songs

[fol. 17v

Thomas Mawdycke

[Song I]

Rejoyce, rejoyce, all that here be:
The angell these tythyng<s> hath browght
That Simion, before he dye,
Shalle se the Lorde w*hic*h all hathe wrowght;

Wherefore now let vs all prepare
Owr temple that yn order be,
For he hathe put awey owre care,
The seconde p*er*sone in Trinitye.

Rychard

[Song II]

Beholde, now hit ys come to pase
That manye yeres before was tolde
How þat Christ, owre ryght Messyae,
By Jwdas sholde be bowght and solde.

For owre offence he man became,
His fathers wrathe to pacyfye,
And after mikely as a lamb
—Vpon the crosse then dyd he dye.

O Lorde, as þ*o*u hast bowght vs all,
And suffryd at Mownt Callverye,
Recownfort vs bothe gret *and* small
That yn thy trewth we lyve *and* dye.

James Hewyt

Appendix I
The Weavers' Pageant:
Two Fifteenth-Century Fragments

The two fifteenth-century leaves containing fragments of an earlier text of the Weavers' pageant are contained in Coventry Record Office 11/1. These folios present portions of the Purification section of the play corresponding to lines 1–58 and 181–223 in Croo's text. The text that is presented here is a diplomatic transcription which retains original orthography and punctuation.

FRAGMENT A

I P*RO*FETA ye gret astronemerris now awake [fol. 1r
w*ith* youre fam*us* fadurs of phelossefee
in to the orrent aspecte you take
wherre in nevis & strangis apered latele
ase towching the fraces off the wholle p*ro*fesse
afirmyng þ*at* astar schuld appere
Evin in yseraell amongist vs here

II P*RO*FE*TA* bredur all then be off good chere
those tythingis makis my hart fullight
for we haue desirid many ayere
of þ*at* star to haue a sight
& speschalle off that king off myght
off whose cu*m*yng we haue had warnyng
<be> þe seyd star of p*ro*fettis des*er*nyng
y<e>t furthur more for owre larnyng
<le>t us haue su*m* co*m*mene casion
of this seyd star be old p*ro*nostefying
how hyt apperud & vndur what fassion

I P*RO*FE*TA* aftur awondurfull strange demonstracion
ase be the Exp*er*ence p*ro*ve yt I con*n*
for this star be interp*re*tacion

singnefith the natevete of amon
ase the p*ro*fet <Balam> be the spret off god
~~be the spret off god~~ affirmithe well
orre Etur stella Ex Jacob
et Exvrge homo de yseraell
he seyd of Jacob astar schuld spryng
wyche singnefis only this same thing
wyche amonst vs now ys cu*m*
& ase towching the lettur folloing
et ipse dominabetur omni gen<. . .>

II P*ROFETA* here be youre fau*er* wold I move a questeon [fol. 1v
of this p*r*incis high geneloge
wyche ou*er* the gentilis schuld haue domeneon
where & off what sort born he schuld be

<I> P*RO*FETE ase ye schall here right worthele
be devin powar off a v*er*gin pure
affirmyng the p*ro*fettis agenst all nature

II P*ROFETA* where fynd you þ*a*t in wholle scripture
of any right awter wyche þ*a*t woll mencion

<I> P*ROFETA*. Isae the p*ro*fet wrytith full sure
Ecce v*ir*go consepith aperet fillium*m*
balam seying of þe heyvinle wysedom
amann*n* schuld be reysid here in yseraell
in confirmyng the seyd questeon
et vocatur nomen*n* eiu*us* Emanevell

<II PROFETA> yet to me yt ys moche marvell
vndur whatt sort þ*a*t men schuld tell
soche high mysteres be fore þe fell
he being but a mortall creature

<I> P*ROFETA* be godis p*ro*vedence ye mabe sure
the espret of god to them wassent
& lafft to vs in wholle scripture
& them selvis not knoyng what hit ment

<II PROFETA> presid be to hym wyche þ*a*t espret sent
vnto vs pore wrechis of loo symplessete
he beyng the lord owre god om*n*epotent
in this his workis to make vs preve

<I PROFETA> did not þ*a*t p*ro*fet man callid malache

. . .

FRAGMENT B

<SEMEON> <. . .> [fol. 2r
w*ith* fysche fowle and best <and> Eu*er*e odur thing
vndur man*n* to haue there naturall curse & being
yet owre anceant parence at the beginnyng
throgh þ*i*s dissabeydence had agrevos fall
from the abowndant blis Eu*er* lasting
~~in trihumfe & glore for Eu*er* to reymane~~
~~in to this vale off teyris & meserabull mundall~~
dovn*n* in to the vale off this meserabull mu*n*dall
owre nature creatid be hym to be inmortall
& now throgh syn fallin to in mortallete
and vtturle distroid w*ith*owt the gret marce
this ded most dolorus ofte doth me constreyne
in wardle to sigh & bytturle to weepe
tyll þ*a*t I reme*m*bur the gret c*om*ford agein
off anceant p*ro*fettis w*ith* þe sentencis swete
whose fructuos sencis off p*ro*fonde larnyng depe
wyche apon anceant avters grondid constantle
off Izae the sebbelis balam & maleche
O lord off lordis yff thy swet wylbe
off þ*i*s thi infynit worke send me þe tru light
Iustle to Expond þ*i*s thy whole mystere
& that I wonse ma se that only king of myght
and thatt we ma walke in his weyis vppright
at whose cu*m*yng ase þe p*ro*fettis do Exprese
the right vngcion off Juda schall seyse
Oh lord ffullfyll þ*a*t hy tyme off pes
for my crokid age dravys fast apon
fane wold I see thatt wholle off whollenes
or this mortall lyff fro*m* me were gon

o lord reme*m*bur thy doghtur syon*n*
releve hir lord in þ*is* hir mezere
reyleysche hyr graceose god off hir callamete
Oh lord at þi wyll all thing mvst be
yet lord thy g*ra*ce to vs do Exstend [fol. 2v
the to s*er*ve w*ith* all vmyllete
& w*ith* thy g*r*ace huse rule & defende
owre solis & bodeis to the we co*m*mend
Ernystle loking for thy wholle p*ro*mes
owt off danger yseraell & Juda to reles
Oh lord reyleue owre inbesyllete
& thy only sun*n* off lyff to vs do send
hym to reseyve w*ith* all vmyllete
& off this mortall lyff then to make amend
o lord thy powar no man ma co*m*prehend
yet grant me my peytission to obteyne
not to dy till þ*a*t I thatt solam sight haue seyne

<AN> Oh suffrent semeon*n* w*ith* all vmyllete
wyche art owre gide in gostle gou*er*nance
w*ith* all dev reu*er*e<n>ce be seke I the
thy humble obbeydent off longe contenevance
yet haue me semeon in thy rememburrans
when yt schall plese thatt hy messe
vnto yseraell & Juda reveylid to be
amonst the othur reme<*m*>bur me
wyche this iiij skore yeris & more
in this tempull contenevalle
thatt lord owre god Eu*er* loking fore
wyche yseraell & Juda schall Restore
from dredfull bonde vnto lybarte
ase well apperis be anceant p*ro*fece

<SEMEON> systur an welcu*m* to me
<you>re hoope right hyle I do co*m*mend
wyche wyll appere on dowtedle
when thatt lord the tyme doth send

. . .

Appendix II
Royal Entries

On three occasions in the second half of the fifteenth century when royal visitors came to Coventry the *Leet Book* recorded entertainments prepared for them. The first was the visit in 1456 of Queen Margaret of Anjou, who would again be welcomed by the city in March 1457 and would "pr*eu*ely" return to see the plays at Corpus Christi in June of the same year (*REED: Coventry*, 35–37; *Coventry Leet Book*, 2:285–92).

For her 1456 entry Queen Margaret was accompanied by the child Prince Edward—hence the inclusion of Edward the Confessor among the prophets who greeted her and her son at the first two stations. Edward the Confessor's symbol is a ring, which here was given to the prince. The initial tableau of the Jesse Tree was, as Gordon Kipling notes, "an apt symbol for [the citizens'] complicated allegiances" (*Enter the King*, 68). Subsequent characters which appeared included the Four Cardinal Virtues and Nine Worthies. The Smiths' records transcribed by Sharp indicate that they took out their pageant wagon "at the comyng of the quene, that ys the parell to þe pagent and harneste men and þe harnes to <harnes> hem wyth and a cote armyr for *Arture and* a crest w*ith* iij grevyvyes [leg armor]," for which they spent 17*s* 11½*d* (*Dissertation*, 149n). Ingram deduced that the expenditures indicated that the Smiths presented the King Arthur pageant, which was the sixth among those mounted for Queen Margaret (*REED: Coventry*, 548). The pageants were set up along the route that was taken by the queen through the city. The pageantry culminated in a tableau of St. Margaret, the queen's patron saint. The text is from CRO A3(a), fols. 168^{v}–170^{v}.

1. The Reception of Queen Margaret (14 September 1456)

M*emoran*d*um* that the demene *and* rule that was [fol. 168^{v}
made *and* shewed vnto oure Soue*r*ayn lady the quene at Couentre was thus as it foloweth yn wrytyng, that is for to sey, furst at Bablake there was made a Iesse ou*er* the yate right well, and there were shewed too speches, as foloweth.

YSAY. P*r*inces most excellent, borne of blode riall,
Choson quene of this region, conforte to all hus,
I, Ysay, replete w*ith* þe spirite p*ro*pheticall,
Wordes to yo*ur* magnificens woll I say thus:
Like as mankynde was gladdid by the birght of Ih*es*us,
So shall þis empyre ioy the birthe of yo*ur* bodye;
The knyghtly curage of P*r*ince Edward all men shall ioy to se.

IEREMY. Emp*r*ice, quene, p*r*inces excellent in on p*er*son all iij,
I, Ieromy þe p*ro*phete trew, þies wordes of you wyll say:
This reme shall ioye þe blessyd tyme of yo*ur* natiuyte;
The mellyflue mekenes of yo*ur* p*er*son shall put all wo away.
Vnto the rote of Iesse likkyn you well I may,
The fragrante floure sprongon of you shall so encrece *and* sprede
That alle the world yn ich p*ar*ty shall cherisshe hym, love, *and* drede.

Afturward withinne the yate at the est yende of the chirche was sette a pagent right well arayed, *and* þ*er*in was shewed ij speches, on of Sineynt Edward *and* the other of Seynt Iohn Euang*elist*, as foloweth.

S. EDWARD. Moder of mekenes, dame M*ar*garete, p*r*inces most excellent, [fol. 169r
I, Kyng Edward, welcu*m* you w*ith* affeccion*n* righ<t> cordiall,
Certefying to yo*ur* highnes mekely myn entent.
For the wele of the kyng *and* you hertely p*r*ay I shall,
And for P*r*ince Edwarde, my gostly chylde whom I love p*r*incipall,
P*r*ayng the, Iohn*n* Euangelist, my helpe þ*er*in to be:
On that condicion*n* right humbly I gif þis ryng to the.

IOHN EUANG*ELIST*. Holy Edward, crownyd kyng, brothur in virginyte,
My power playnly I wyll p*re*fer thi wyll to amplifye;
Most excellent p*r*inces, of wymen mortall, yo*ur* bedeman wyll I be.
I knowe yo*ur* lyf so vertuus þat God is plesyd therby;
The birth of you vnto þis reme shall cause grete melody.

The vertu*us* voyce of P*r*ince Edward shall dayly well encrese;
Seynt Edward, his godfader, *and* I shall p*r*ay þ*er*fore dowtelesse.

Afturward <at> the Cundit yn the Smythforde strete was right well arayed, *and* there was shewed iiij speches of iiij Cardynall V*er*tues, as foloweth.

RIGHTWESNES. I, Rightwesnes, that causeth treuth to be had,
Mekely as a maydyn my langage wyll I make
And welcu*m* you, p*r*inces right cherefull *and* glad:
With you wyll I be dwellyng *and* neu*er* you forsake.

TEMP*ER*AUNCE. I, Temp*er*aunce, to plece you warly wyll wake
And welcome you as most worthy to my power,
Besechyng youre highnes þis langage to take:
I wyll feythfully defende you from all man*er* daunger.

STRENGH. I, Strengh, þe iij[e] Vertewe, wyll playnly appere
Clerely to conseyue you yn yo*ur* estate most riall
And welcu*m* yowe, p*r*inces, gladly w*ith* chere,
For to do þ*at* mowe plece you, aray ws we shall.

P*R*UDENCE. I, P*r*udence, of the iiij Verteues highest in degre,
Welcu*m* you, dame M*ar*garete, quene crowned of this lande.
The blessyd babe þ*at* ye haue born, Prynce Edward is he,
Thurrowe whom pece *and* t*r*anquilite shall take þis reme on hand.
We shall endowe both you *and* hym clerely to vnderstonde;
We shall p*rese*rue you p*er*sonally *and* neu*er* fro you disseu*er*.
Doute not, p*r*inces most excellent, we iiij shall do oure deu*er*.

Afturward at the Crosse yn the Croschepyng there [fol. 169[v] were ordeyned diu*er*se angels sensyng a high on the Crosse, *and* there ranne out wyne at mony places a long whyle.

Afturward betwix the seyde Crosse *and* the Cundit beneþe that were sette ix pagentes right well arayed and yn eu*er*y pagent was shewed a speche of the ix Conqueroures; yn the furst was shewed of Hector, as foloweth.

HECTOR. Most plesaunt p*r*inces recordid þ*a*t may be,
I, Hector of Troy, þ*a*t am chefe conqueroure*e*,
Lowly wyll obey yowe *and* knele on my kne
And welcum yowe tendurly to yo*ur* honoure
To this conabull cite, the p*r*inces chaumbur;
Whome ye bar*e* yn youre bosom, joy to þis lande,
Thro whome in p*ro*sperite þis empyre shall stand.

In the secunde pagent was shewed a speche of Alex*ander*, as foloweth.

ALEX*ANDER*. I, Alexander, þ*a*t for chyualry berith þe balle,
Most curi*us* in conquest, thro þe world am ynamed,
Welcu*m* yowe, p*r*inces, as quene p*r*incipall.
But I hayls you ryght hendly, I wer worthy to be blamyd.
The nobilest p*r*ince þ*a*t is born whome Fortune hath famyd
Is yo*ur* souer*a*yn lorde Herry, emp*erour and* kyng,
Vnto whom mekely I wyll be obeying.

In the thridde pagent was shewed of Iosue, as foloweth:

IOSUE. I, Iosue, þ*a*t in Hebrewe reyn p*r*incipall,
To whome þ*a*t all Egipte was fayne to inclyne,
Wyll abey to yo*ur* plesure, p*r*inces most riall,
As to the heghest lady þ*a*t I can ymagyne;
To the plesure of yo*ur* p*er*sone I wyll put me to pyne
As a knyght for his lady boldly to fight
Yf any man of curage wold bid you vnright.

In the fourthe pagent was shewed of Dauid, as foloweth.

DAUID. I, Dauid, þ*a*t in deynteȝ haue led all my dayes,
That slowe þe lyon *and* Goly thorowe Goddys myght,
Will obey to you, lady, youre p*er*sone p*r*ayse
And welcu*m* you curtesly as a kynd knyght
For the loue of yo*ur* lege lorde, Herry that hight,
And yo*ur* laudabull lyfe that vertuus eu*er* hath be;
Lady, most lufly, ye be welcu*m* to þis cite.

In the fyth pagent was shewed a speche of Iudas, as foloweth. [fol. 170r

IUDAS. I, Iudas, þ*a*t yn Iure am called the belle,

In knyghthode *and* conquest haue I no pere,
Wyll obey to you, p*r*inces, ell*es* did not I well,
And tendurly welcu*m* you yn my manere;
Y*our* own souu*er*ayn*n* lorde *and* kynge is p*re*sent here
Whome God for his godenes p*reser*ue yn good helthe,
And ende you w*ith* worship to this landys welthe.

In the sixt pagent was shewed a speche of Arthur, as foloweth.

ARTHUR. I, Arthur, kynge crownyd *and* conqueroure
That yn this lande reyned right rially;
With dedes of armes I slowe the Emp*erour*;
The tribute of this ryche reme I made downe to ly;
Ihit vnto <you>, lady, obey I mekely
As your*e* sure s*er*uande; plesure to yo*ur* highnesse
For the most plesaunt p*r*inces mortall þ*at* es.

In the vij pagent was shewed a speche of Charles, as foloweth.

CHARLES. I, Charles, chefe cheftan of þe reme of F*ra*unce
And emp*erour* of grete Rome made by elleccion,
Which put mony paynym to pyne *and* penaunce:
The holy relik*es* of Criste I had in possession—
Ihit, lady, to yo*ur* highnes to cause dieu refeccion,
Worshipfully I welcu*m* you aft*ur* yo*ur* magnificens;
Yf my s*er*uice mowe plece you, I wyll put to my diligence.

In the viij pagent was shewed a speche of Iulius, as foloweth:

IULIUS. I, Iulius Cesare, souu*er*ayne of knyghthode
And emp*erour* of mortall men, most hegh *and* myghty,
Welcu*m* you, p*r*inces, most benynge *and* gode.
Of quenes þ*at* byn crowned so high non knowe I;
The same blessyd blossom þ*at* spronge of yo*ur* body
Shall succede me yn worship—I wyll it be so;
All the landis olyue shall obey hym vnto.

In the ix pagent was shewed a speche of Godfride, as foloweth.

GODFRIDE. I, Godfride of Bollayn, kynge of Ierusalem,

Weryng þe thorny crowne yn worship of Ih*es*u,
Which yn batayle haue no pere vnder the sone beme,
Yhit, lady, right lowlely I loute vnto yowe.
So excellent a p*r*inces, stedefast *and* trewe,
Knowe I none c*r*istened as you yn yo*ur* estate:
Ih*es*u for his m*er*ci incresse *and* not abate.

Afturward *and* last the Cundit yn the Crossechepyng [fol. 170v was arayed right well with as mony virgyns as myght be þ*er*vppon, and there was made a grete dragon, *and* Seynt Marg<ar>et sleyng hym be myracull, *and* there was shewed full well this speche that foloweth.

S. MARGARET. Most notabull p*r*inces, of wymen erthle,
Dame M*ar*garete, þe chefe myrth of þis empyre,
Ye be hertely welcu*m* to þis cyte;
To the plesur*e* of yo*ur* highnes I wyll sette my desyre.
Bothe nature *and* gentilnes doth me require,
Seth we be both of one name, to shewe you kyndnes;
Wherfore by my power ye shall haue no distresse,
I shall p*r*ay to the p*r*ince þ*a*t is endeles
To socour you w*ith* solas of his high g*r*ace;
He wyll here my peticion, this is doutles,
For I wrought all my lyf þ*a*t his wyll wace.
Therfore, lady, when ye be yn any dredefull cace,
Calle on me boldly, þ*er*of I p*r*ay you,
And trist to me feythfully, I woll do þ*a*t may pay you.

M*emorandum* that the seyd Richard Braytoft, meyre, resseyued of Thomas Bradmedowe *and* Iohn Straunge, late wardens of the fote, of her acounte xxi li. xiij s ij d, of the which the seyde meyre payde to Iohn Wedurby of Leycet*ur* for þe p*ro*vicion *and* makyng of these p*re*misses of the welcomyng of oure Soue*r*ayn lady the quene, *and* for his labour inne *and* out xxv s.

In 1474 Prince Edward, who was three years old at this time, came to Coventry accompanied by his mother and was entertained with pageants around the city. He was given a substantial gift (the city annals reported £100 "*and* a Cup" [*REED: Coventry*, 55], while the *Leet Book* specifies a third less than that amount), and the pageantry was undoubtedly lavish as well. The records of this visit in the *Leet Book* (CRO A 3(a), fol. 221^{r}–221^{v}) are less complete than the account of the reception of Queen Margaret, but nevertheless are of considerable interest. Mary Dormer Harris, in her edition of the *Leet Book* (4:855), believed that the *Childer of Issarell* pageant was the Holy Innocents section of the Shearmen and Taylors' pageant. Ingram notes that "[t]his accords with the following pageant which calls for the 'iij kynges of Colen'" (*REED: Coventry*, 553). No conjecture is required with regard to the Smiths, however, since their accounts list expenditure of 7 *d* "for bryngyng furth the pagent aȝenst the comyng of the Quene *and* the prince" (ibid., 56); as Ingram remarks, this is a remarkably small amount compared with their expenses for the visit of the queen in 1456. The entry concluded with St. George's defeat of the dragon. This scene perhaps used the same dragon that had appeared with St. Margaret before the queen in 1456.

2. Receiving Prince Edward (28 April 1474)

Memorand*um* that the xxviiith day of the moneth of [fol. 221^{r} Aprill cam*m* oure lorde Prince Edward out of Walys so by Warrewik to Couentre, and the meire *and* his brethern*n* w*ith* the diuers of the cominalte of the seide citie, clothed in grene and blewe, metyng oure seid lorde prince vpon horsbake by yonde the Newe Crosse, in a chare, beyng of age of iij yere, there welcomyng hym to his chaumbr and yevyng hym there a C mark in a gilt coppe of xv ounceȝ w*ith* a kerchyff of plesaunce vpon*n* the seid coppe. And then*n* comyng into <the> citie, and at Babulake yate ther*e* ordeyned a stacion*n*, therin beyng Kyng Richard w*ith* xiij other arrayed lyke as dukes, mark*is*es, erles, vicouns, and barons *and* lordis w*ith* my*n*strallcy of the wayt*es* of the cite, and Kyng Richard there havyng this speche her*e* ffolowyng.

Rex Ric*ard*us. Welcom, full high and nobull prince, to vs right speciall,
To this yo*ur* chaumbr*e*, so called of antiquite. 14
The p*re*sens of yo*ur* noble p*er*son*n* reioyseth yo*ur* hart*es* all.
We all mowe blesse the tyme of yo*ur* natiuite:

The right lyne of the royall blode ys now as itt schulde be,
Wherfore God of his goodnes p*rese*rue you in bodily helth,
To vs and yo*ur* tenaunt*es* here p*er*petuall ioy, and to all the londis welth.

Also at the Condite afore Richard Braytoft the Elder another stacion w*ith* iij P*at*riarkes there stondyng vpon*n* the seid Condite w*ith* Iacobus xij sonnes w*ith* mynstralcy of harpe and dowsemeris, *and* there rennyng wyne in on*n* place; and there on*n* of the seid pat*r*i-arkes havyng this speche vnder writtyn*n*:

O God most glorious, grounder and gyder of all g*r*ace,
To vs iij P*at*riarkes thou p*ro*mysed (as scriptur*e* maketh rehersall)
That of oure stok lynially schuld p*ro*cede and passe
A prynce of most nobull blode and kyng*es* sonne imp*er*iall;
The wich was fullfylled in God, and nowe referre itt we schall
Vnto this nobull prynce that is here p*re*sent,
Wich entreth to this his chaumbr as prynce full reu*er*ent.

Also at the Brodeyate a pagiont, and Seint Edward beyng therin w*ith* x astates with hym*m*, w*ith* mynstralcy of harpe *and* lute, and Kyng Edward havyng this speche next foloyng:

Nobull Prynce Edward, my cossyn *and* my knyght
And v*er*y prynce of our*e* lyne com yn dissent.

I, Seint Edward, haue pursued for yo*ur* faders imp*er*iall right, [fol. 221v
Wherof he was excluded by full furi*us* intent.
Vnto this yo*ur* chaumbr as prynce full excellent
ȝe be right welcom, thanked be Crist of his sonde,
For þ*at* that was oures is nowe in yo*ur* faders hande.

Also at the Crosse in the Croschepyng were iij p*ro*phett*es* standyng at the Crosse seynsyng, and vpon the Crosse aboven were Childer of Issarell syngyng and castyng out whete obles *and* ffloures, and iiij pypis rennyng wyne.

Also in the Croschepyng afore the Panyer, a pagent and iij Kyng*es* of Colen therin w*ith* other diu*er*s arraied and ij knyght*es* armed w*ith* mynstralsy of small pypis and on*e* of the kyng*es* havyng this speche vnder writtyn:

O splendent Creator, in all our*e* speculacion*n*,
More bryghter then Phebus, excedent all lyȝt,
We thre kyng*es* beseche the w*ith* meke mediacion*e*
Specially to p*re*s*er*ue this nobull prynce þi knyght,
Wich by influens of thy grace p*ro*cedeth aright
Of on of vs thre lynnyally we fynde
His nobull moder Quene Elizabeth ys comyn*e* of þ*a*t kynde.

Also vpon the Condite in the Croschepyng was Seint George armed and a kyng*es* dought*er* knelyng afore hym*m* w*ith* a lambe, and the fader *and* the moder beyng in a toure aboven*n* beholdyng Seint George savyng their*e* dought*er* from*m* the dragon*e*; and the Condite rennyng wyne in iiij placeȝ, and mynstralcy of orgon pleyinge, and Seint George havyng this speche vnder writtyn:

O myghty God, our*e* all socour*e* celestiall,
Wich þis royme hast geven*e* to dower*e*
To thi moder and to me, George, p*ro*teccion p*er*petuall,
Hit to defende from enimies ffere *and* nere.
And as this mayden defended was here
Bi thy g*r*ace from this dragon devour*e*,
So, Lorde, p*re*s*er*ue this noble prynce and eu*er* be his socour*e*.

On 17 October 1498 Prince Arthur was welcomed to Coventry by the Nine Worthies, but unlike their appearance to Queen Margaret in 1456, the only character among them to have a speech was King Arthur. The role of Arthur is discussed by Sydney Anglo, who notes that the tableau did not make any extravagant claim for the descent of the Tudors from the ancient British king (*Spectacle, Pageantry, and Early Tudor Policy*, 55–56). The similarities with earlier entries did not end with Arthur and the other Worthies, however, since St. George, who had also appeared to Prince Edward in

1474, was again the concluding figure in the pageantry. Again the city annals report that the gifts to the prince were £100 "*and* a cup" (*REED: Coventry*, 91). The text is from CRO A3(a), fol. 281^{v}.

3. The Reception of Prince Arthur (17 October 1498)

M*emoran*d*um* that this ȝer*e* the Wensday the xvij day of Octobr*e* a*nno* xiiij° R*egis* H*enre* vij, Pr*ince* Arthur, the ffirst begoton son of Kyng Henr*e* the vijth, then beyng of þe age of xij ȝer*es and* mor*e*, cam first to Couentr*e and* there lay in þe p*r*iory fro Wensday vnto þe Munday next suyng, at which tyme he removed toward*es* London. Ayenst whos co*m*myng was þe Sponstrete ȝate garnysshed with the ix worthy, and Kyng Arthur then hauyng thus spech as foloweth:

Hayle prynce roiall, most amyable in sight,
Whom the court ete*r*nall thurgh p*r*udent goue*r*na<u>nce
Hath chosen*n* to be egall ons to me in myght
To sprede our*e* name Arthur *and* act*es* to aua*u*nce,
And of meanys victorious to haue such habundaunce
That no fals treito*u*r ne cruell tirrant
Shall in eny wyse make profer to your lande,
And rebelles all falce quarels shall eschewe
Thurgh þe fere of Pallas that fauoreth yo*ur* lynage
And all outward enmyes laboreth to subdue
To make the*m* to do to yewe as to me dyd homage.
Welcome therfor*e* the solace *and* comfort of my olde age,
Prince pereles, Arthur, icome of noble p*ro*geny,
To me *and* to your*e* chambr*e* with all þis hole companye.

And at the turnyng into þe Croschepyng before Mr Thru*m*ptons durr*e* stode þe Barkers paiant well appareld in which was the Quene of Fortune with dyu*er*s other virgyns, whech quene has þis spech folowyng:

I am Dame Fortune, quene called, full expedient
To emprours *and* p*r*inc*es*, prelat*es*, with other moo
As Cesar, Hecto*u*r, and Sabius most excellent,
Scipio, exalted Nausica, *and* Emilianus also;
Valerius, also Marchus, with sapient Cicero.
E and noble men*n*, breuely the truth to conclude all,
My fauo*u*r verily had, as storys maketh rehersall,

Withoute whom*m* sithen*n* non*n* playnly can*n* prosp*er*e
That in þis muitable lyfe as nowe p*ro*cedyng
I am come thurgh love; truste me intiere
To be with yewe *and* yours evirmor*e* enduryng,
Prynce most vnto my pleasur*e* of all þ*a*t ar nowe reynyng;
Wherfor*e*, my nowne hert *and* best beloued treasur*e*,
Welcome to þis, your*e* chambr*e* of whom ye be inh*er*itur*e*.

And the Crosse in the Croschepyng was garnysshed *and* wyne ther*e* rennyng, and angels sensyng *and* syngyng with orgayns and other*e* melody *etc*.

And at þe Cundyt there was Seynt George kyllyng the dragon*n*, and Seynt George had this speche folowyng:

O most sou*er*aign lorde, be dy<vy>ne p*ro*vision to be
The ruler of cruell Mars *and* kyng insup*er*able,
Ye reioyce my corage, trustyng hit to se,
That named am George, yo*ur* patron*n* fauorable,
To whom ye ar *and* eu*er* shal be so acceptable
That in felde or cite, wher*e*soever ye rayne,
Shall I neu*er* fayle yewe, thus is my purpose playn*e*:
To protect yo*ur* magnyficence myself I shall endev*ou*r,
In all thyng*es* that yo*ur* highnes shalt concerne,
Mor*e* tenderly then I ȝit did ever;
Kyng, duke, yerle, lorde, or also berne,
As ye be myn*e* assistence in p*ro*cesse shall lerne,
Which thurgh yo*ur* vertue, most amorous knygh<t>,
I owe to yo*ur* p*re*sence be due *and* very right.
Likewyse as þis lady be grace I defended,
That thurgh myschaunce chosen was to dye
Fro this foule s*er*pent whom I sor*e* wonded,
So ye in distresse p*re*serve ever woll I
Fro all parell and wyked veleny,
That shuld yo*ur* noble p*er*sone in eny wyse distrayn*e*
Which welcome is to þis yo*ur* chambr*e* *and* to me right fa<ayn>.

And this balet was song at þe Crosse:

Viuat le Prynce Arthur

Ryall P*r*ince Arthur,
Welco*m*me nowe, tresur*e*,
W*ith* all our*e* hole cur
    to þis yo*ur* cite.

Sithen in vertue der*e*,
Lorde, ye haue no per*e*
Of yo*ur* age tendr*e*,
    as all we may see.

Cunyng requyred,
All hath cont*r*ived,
And so receyued
    yo*ur* intelligence.

That Yngland all playn
May nowe be right fayn
Yewe long to remayn*e*
    to their*e* extollence.

Syng we þ*er* foll all;
Also let vs call
To God immortall
    that he yewe defend.

In this breue beyng
Youre astate supporting,
And vertue ay spredyng
    to yo*ur* lyfes yend.

Appendix III
The Songs
for the Shearmen and Taylors' Pageant

The music of the songs as presented here is reprinted from JoAnna Dutka, *Music in the English Mystery Plays*. Dutka's transcriptions rationalize the notation as it appears in Thomas Sharp's *Dissertation on the Pageants or Dramatic Mysteries Anciently Performed at Coventry* (1825), the only source of the songs since the original manuscript was destroyed in a fire that devastated the Birmingham Free Library. The texts are transcribed here, however, as they appear in the individual parts in the music so far as possible. Song I combines Songs I and III in Sharp's *Dissertation* since they represent two stanzas of the same item. Textual variants are listed by Dutka.

Song I

5
lit - tell tyne childe, by by lul - ly, lul -
lit - tell ty - ne childe, by by lul - ly, lul -
lit - tell tyne childe, by by lul - ly, lul -
10
lay, thow lit - tel tyne child, by by lul -
lay, thow lit - tel tyne childe, by by lul -
lay, thow lit - tel tyne childe, by by lul -
15
ly, lul - lay.
O sis - ters
He - rod the
That wo is
ly, lul - lay.
O sis - ters
He - rode the
That wo is
ly, lul - lay.
O sis - ters
He - rode the
That wo is

too, how may we do for to pre -
King, in his ra - ging char - ged he
me, pore child, for thee and e - ver
two, how may we do for to pre -
King, in his ra - ginge char - ged he
me, pore child, for thee and e - ver
two, howe maie we do for to pre -
Kinge, in his ra - ginge char - ged he
mee, pore child, for thee and e - ver

20
serve this day this pore yong - ling, for
hath this day his men of might, in
morne and say for thi par - ting nether
serve this day this pore yong - linge, for
hath this day his men of might, in
morne and saye for thi par - tinge nether
serve this daye oure pore yonge - linge, for
hathe this daie his men of mighte, in
morne and say for thi par - tinge nether

SONG II

* Should be ◇. in the original

5
– this ende - res night,
– from hea - ven so hie,
– this ende - res night, of thre io - li
– from hea - ven so hie, of an - geles ther
– this end - ers night, of
– from he - ven so hie, of
10
of thre io - li shep - pards I saw a
of an - geles ther came a great com - pai -
shep - pards I saw a sight, I sawe a sighte,
came a great com - pa ni, a great com - pa -
thre io - li shep - pardes I saw a
an - geles ther came a gret com - pa -
15
sight, and all a
nie, with mirthe and
– and all a - boute there fold a
ni, with mirthe and ioy and gret so -
sighte, and all a - bout there
ni, with mirthe and ioy and

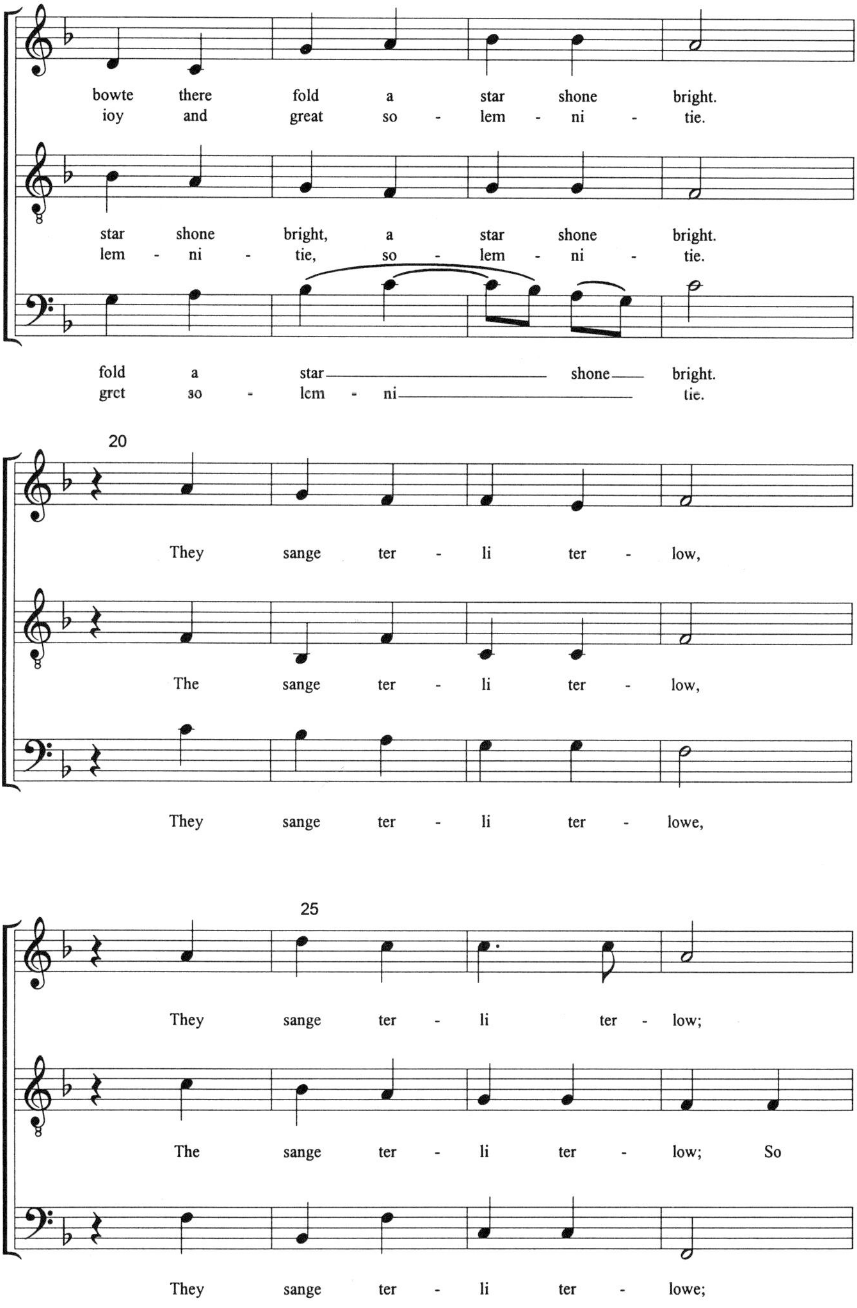

bowte there fold a star shone bright.
ioy and great so - lem - ni - tie.

star shone bright, a star shone bright.
lem - ni - tie, so - lem - ni - tie.

fold a star shone bright.
gret so - lem - ni tie.

20

They sange ter - li ter - low,

The sange ter - li ter - low,

They sange ter - li ter - lowe,

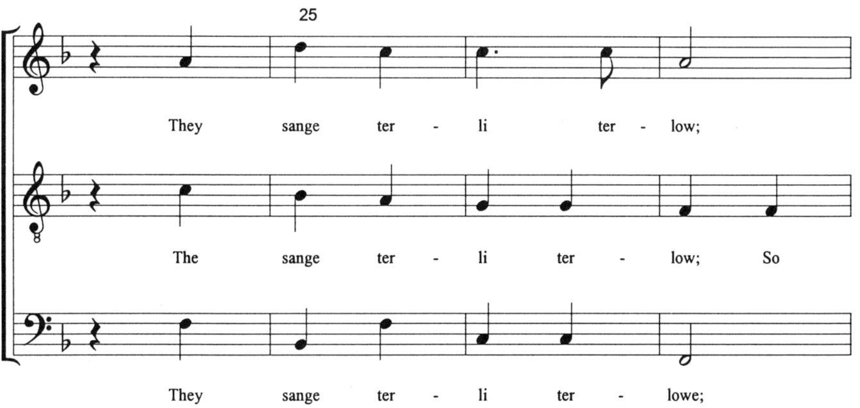
25
They sange ter - li ter - low;
The sange ter - li ter - low; So
They sange ter - li ter - lowe;

30
So me - re - li the shep - pards there
me - re - li the shep - pards ther pipes can—— blow, so
So me - re - li the shep - pardes there pipes can
35
pipes can blowe, ther pipes can blowe, so
me - re - li the shep - pards ther pipes can blow,
blow, ther pipes can blowe,——
me - re - li the shep - pards, so me - re - li the
so me - re - li the shep - pards ther pipes can
so me - re - li the shep - pards ther

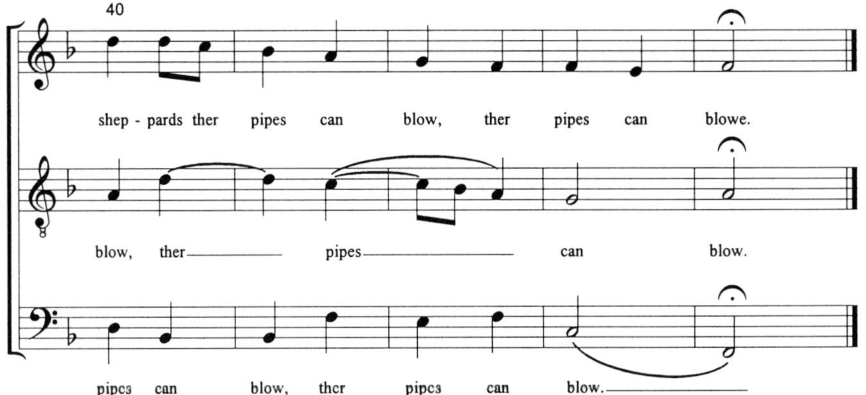
40
shep - pards ther pipes can blow, ther pipes can blowe.
blow, ther pipes can blow.
pipes can blow, ther pipes can blow.

Appendix IV
Versions of the Doctors Pageants

As W. W. Greg asserted in an article in the Malone Society volume devoted to the Chester plays in 1935, "One of the most intriguing problems in the whole of the English religious drama concerns the play of Christ's Disputation with the Doctors in the Temple . . ." (101). The degree of overlap between the Coventry Weavers' play and the other Doctors plays in the English cycles (excluding N-Town) will be demonstrated by presenting for comparison the text of the York Spurriers and Lorimers' play, collated with the Doctors play in the Towneley manuscript and the Doctors segment of the Chester Blacksmiths' play. York, copied into the Register in the 1460s, apparently represents the earliest version among these. Both the Towneley play and the Coventry Weavers' play, although they follow York's order, expand on it in different ways. Coventry's is the most elaborated version and also contains the most changes in versification, for Croo's rewriting resulted in a highly irregular metrical structure. This version especially may be seen to alter vocabulary from York's which is distinctively Northern—a vocabulary which also was possibly perceived as archaic by all the dedactors. Greg developed at some length the argument that all versions (except, of course, N-Town) derived from a now missing (and earlier) original that lay immediately behind the text preserved in the York Register ("Bibliographical and Textual Problems of the English Miracle Cycles, III—Christ and the Doctors," 298–99). Clearly this is the case. The Chester episode can be observed to be drawing on a related original, but is much shorter and includes some radical reordering of the lines which renders it more overtly didactic and expository than the other versions.

The selection from the York Doctors play which follows is presented in abbreviated form (omitting passages which have no parallel in the Coventry pageant) up to line 73, and thereafter the unabbreviated text is included since the correspondences between the two plays become more pronounced. Quotations from the Towneley and Chester plays are by permission from the Leeds Texts and Monographs: Medieval Drama Facsimiles editions.

Line number references to the Coventry Weavers' pageant (W) are listed in the left-hand column, then will appear the corresponding lines from the text of the York Doctors play (Y); in the right-hand column are variants in the Towneley (T) and Chester (Ch) plays. The Chester play readings are from the Huntington manuscript.

W		Y	T / Ch
811	*Joseph*	Marie, of mirthis we may vs mene,	[*The beginning of the Towneley play is lost;*
812		And trewly telle betwixte vs twoo	*for the beginning of the Chester play, see below.*]
813		Of solempne sightis þat we haue sene	
814		In þat cité where we come froo.	
		. . .	
816		Hamward I rede we hye	
		In all þe myght we maye,	
818		Because of company	
819		Þat will wende in oure waye	
		. . .	
	Maria	To go ouer-fast we haue begonne	
823		And late þat louely leue behynde.	
824	*Joseph*	Marie, mende thy chere,	
		For certis whan all is done	
		He comes with folke in feere,	
827		And will oueretake vs sone.	
828	*Maria*	Oueretake vs sone sir? Certis nay,	
		. . .	
	Joseph	I wende he hadde bene with vs aye,	
833		Awaye fro vs how schulde he wyle?	
834	*Maria*	Hit helpis nought such sawes to saie,	

835 My barne is lost, allas þe whille,

. . .

Joseph Agaynewarde rede I þat we gang
The right way to þat same citee,
To spire and spie all men emang,
839 For hardely homward gone is he.
840 *Maria* Of sorowes sere schall be my sang,
841 My semely sone tille I hym see,
He is but xij ȝere alde.

. . .

II Magister For maistirs in þis lande ar we,
And has þe lawes lelly to lede,
869 And doctoures also in oure degree
Þat demyng has of ilka dede.
871 Laye fourthe oure bokes belyue, late see,
What mater moste were for oure mede.

[*The text of T begins with II Magister, but this speech and those immediately following differ from York.*]

. . .

[*T interpolates:* Tu*n*c venit Iesus.]

878 *Jesus* Lordingis, loue be with ȝou lentte
879 And mirthis be vnto þis mené.
880 *I Magister* Sone, hense away I wolde þou wente,
881 For othir haftis in hande haue we.
882 *II Magister* Sone, whoso þe hedir sente,
883 They were nouȝt wise, þat warne I þe,
884 For we haue othir tales to tente
885 Þan nowe with barnes bordand to be.

Lordingis] Masters *T*
mirthis] mensk T
whoso] whosoeuer *T*
þat warne] thus tell *T*

886 *III Magister* Sone, yf þe list ought to lere
887 To lyve by Moyses laye,
Come hedir and þou shalle here
þe sawes þat we shall saye,

For in som mynde itt may þe brynge,
To here oure reasouns redde by rawes.
894 *Jesus* To lerne of you nedis me nothing,
896 For I knawe both youre dedys and sawes.

I Magister Nowe herken ȝone barne with his bowrdyng,

He wenes he kens more þan we knawes.
897 We, nay, certis sone, þou arte ouere-ȝonge
898 By clergy ȝitt to knowe oure lawes.

yf] *omit;* to] *omit T*

shall] wyll *T*

reasouns] sawes *T*

[*Ch opens with the following stanza prior to taking up the text from Y:*
Deus: You clearkes that be of great degree,
Vnto my talkinge you take good heede:
My Father that sitteth in maiestie,
Hee knowes your workes in thought and deede.
My Father and I together bee
In on godhead withouten dread;
We be both on in certayntie,
All these workes to rule and reade.]

Nowe herken ȝone barne with] Hark yonder barn w*ith T;* Hearkes this child in *Ch*

we] he *T;* hee *Ch*

We, nay, certis] Nay, certis *T;* Certes *Ch*

ȝitt] cleane *Ch*

[*Ch interpolates:*
Therefore, if thou wouldest never so fayne,

			Further in age tyll thou have drawe: Yett art thou neither of might nor mayne To knowe yt as a clarke might knowe. *Secundus Doctor:* And thou wilt speake of Moyses lawe, Take good heede and thou may see, In case be that thou can knowe, Here in this booke that written bee.]
	Jesus	I wote als wele as yhe	*omit line Ch*
904		Howe þat youre lawes wer wrought.	wer] was *T; omit line Ch*
905	*II Magister*	Cum sitte, sone schall we see,	*omit line Ch*
906		For certis so semys it noght.	*omit line Ch*
907		Itt wer wondir þat any wight	þat] if *T; omit line Ch*
908		Vntill oure reasouns right schulde reche.	*omit line Ch*
909		And þou sais þou hast insight	*omit line Ch*
910		Oure lawes truly to telle and teche?	*omit line Ch*
911	*Jesus*	The holy gost has on me light	The holy gost on] The kingdome of heaven is in *Ch*
		And has anoynted me as a leche,	has anoynted me as] has anoynt me lyke *T;* hath me annoynted as *Ch*
912		And geven me pleyne poure and myght	me pleyne] to me *T*
913		The kyngdom of heuene for to preche.	for] *omit T;* for to preche] to tell and teach *Ch*
			[*Ch reorders from this point to* § *preceding the exposition of the ten commandments.*]
915	*I Magister*	Whens-euere this barne may be	
916		That shewes þer novellis nowe?	þer] thise *T*

917	*Jesus*	Certis, I was or ȝe,	Certis] Certan, syrs, *T*
918		And schall be aftir ȝou.	
	I Magister	Sone, of thy sawes, als haue I cele,	haue I] we haue *T*
920		And of thy witte is wondir thyng,	
		But neuere the lesse fully I feele	
921		Itt may falle wele in wirkyng.	Itt] That it; wele] *omit T*
923		For Dauid demys of ilka dele,	of ilka] euerilk *T*
924		And sais þus of childir ȝing:	sais þus] thus he says *T*
			[*T interpolates:*
925			Ex ore infanciu*m* et lactenciu*m* p*er*fecisti laude*m*]
926		Of ther mouthes, he wate full wele,	he wate full] sayth Dauid *T*
927		Oure lord has parformed loving.	has] he has *T*
930		But ȝitt sone, schulde þou lette	But ȝitt] Neu*er*theles, son, yit *T*
931		Here for to speke ouere-large,	ouere-large] in large *T*
932		For where maistirs are mette	
933		Childre wordis are noȝt to charge,	
934		And if þou wolde neuere so fayne,	And if] For certys if *T*
935		Yf all þe liste to lere þe lawe,	
936		Þou arte nowthir of myght ne mayne	
937		To kenne it as a clerke may knawe.	kenne] know *T*
938	*Jesus*	Sirs, I saie ȝou for sartayne	for] in *T*
939		That suthfast schal be all my sawe,	
940		And poure haue playnere and playne	haue] haue I *T*
		To say and aunswer as me awe.	

942	*I Doctor*	Maistirs, what may þis mene?	
943		Meruayle methynke haue I,	
944		Whens-euere þis barne haue bene	Whens-] Where; haue] has *T*
		That carpis þus connandly?	
			[§*Here Ch again corresponds briefly to the text of Y.*]
946	*II Doctor*	Als wyde in worlde als we haue wente	Als wyde in worlde] In warld as wyde *T;* als we] as I have *Ch*
947		ȝitt fande we neuere swilke ferly fare,	ȝitt fand] Fand *T;* found *Ch;* swilke] sich *T;* we] I; swilke] so *Ch*
948		For certis I trowe þis barne be sente	For certis] Certys; þis] the *T; omit line Ch*
949		Full souerandly to salue oure sare.	Full souerandly] Sufferanly *T; omit line Ch*
950	*Jesus*	Sirs, I schall proue in youre present	*omit line Ch*
951		Alle þe sawes þat I saide are.	*omit line Ch*
952	*III Doctor*	Why, whilke callest þou þe firste comaundement	Why, whilke] Which *T; omit line Ch*
953		And þe moste in Moyses lare?	*omit line Ch*
954	*Jesus*	Sirs, sen ȝe are sette on rowes	sen ȝe are sette] synthen ye syt *T; omit line Ch*
955		And has youre bokes on brede,	has] hafe *T; omit line Ch*
956		Late se sirs, in youre sawes,	*omit line Ch*
957		Howe right þat ȝe can rede.	*omit line Ch*
958	*I Doctor*	I rede þis is þe firste bidding	þis] that this *T*
959		Þat Moyses taught vs here vntill:	taught] told *T;* and is the most in Moyses lawe *Ch*
960		To honnoure God ouere all thing	To] *omitted T;* all] ilka *T;* To honnoure God ouere] to love oure God aboue *Ch*
961		With all thy witte and all þi will,	thy witte] our might; þi will] our lawe *Ch*

And all thyn harte in hym schall hyng,
Erlye and late, both lowde and still.

thyn] thi *T; omit line Ch*
omit line Ch

[*Ch departs from the other two texts here as Jesus expounds the commandments:*
That for to do, looke yee be bayne
W*it*h all your harte w*it*h good intent:
Take you not his name in vayne;
This is my Fathers commandment.

Alsoe you honour your holye daye;
No workes save almes deedes you doe.
These three, the certayne for to saye,
The first table belongen to.
Alsoe father and mother worshippe aye.
Take no mans goodes w*it*hout the right.
All false witnesse you put awaye,
and slea no man by day nor night.

Envy do by no woman
To do her shame by night or daye.
Other mens wives desyre you not:
All such desyres you put awaye.
Looke ye ne steale by night nor daye,
Whatsoever that you be lent.
These wordes vnderstand you maye:
They are my Fathers commandment.]

964	*Jesus*	Ʒe nedis non othir bokes to bring,	[*From this point omit Ch, which takes up again at* **§§**.]
		But fandis þis for to fulfill.	fandis] fownd; for] *omit T*
		The secounde may men preve	
		And clerly knawe, wherby	wherby] therby *T*
963		Ʒoure neghbours shall ȝe loue	
		Als youreselffe, sekirly.	Als] Right as; sekirly] truly *T*
		This comaunded Moyses to all men	This] Thus; to] tyll *T*
		In his x comaundementis clere,	x comaundementis] co*m*maundes *T*
965		In þer ij biddingis, schall we kene,	þer] thise; we] ye *T*
966		Hyngis all þe lawe þat we shall lere.	þat we shall] we aght to *T*
		Whoso ther two fulfilles then	ther two fulfilles] fulfylles thise two *T*
		With mayne and myght in goode manere,	myght in] mode and *T*
		He trulye fulfillis all þe ten	trulye fulfilles] fulfyllys truly *T*
		Þat aftir folowes in feere.	aftir] after thaym *T*
		Þan schulde we God honnoure	
		With all oure myght and mayne,	
		And loue wele ilke a neghboure	a] *omit T*
		Right as oureselfe, certayne.	
968	*I Doctor*	Nowe sone, sen þou haste tolde vs two,	sen] synthen *T*
969		Whilke ar þe viij, can þou ought saye?	Whilke] Which *T*
970	*Jesus*	The iij biddis whareso ȝe goo	
971		Þat ȝe schall halowe þe halyday;	
			[*T interpolates:*
			From bodely wark ye take youre rest;

Than is þe fourthe for frende or foo
975 That fadir and modir honnoure ay.

978 The v^te you biddis noght for to sloo
979 No man nor woman by any way.

The vj^te, suthly to see,
Comaundis both more and myne
980 That thei schalle fande to flee
981 All filthes of flesshely synne.

982 The vij^te forbedis you to stele
983 Ȝoure neghboures goodes, more or lesse,
Whilke fautez nowe are founden fele
Emang þer folke, þat ferly is.

984 The viij^te lernes ȝou for to be lele,
985 Here for to here no false witnesse.

Youre household looke the same thay do,
Both wyfe, chyld, seruande, and beest.]

The fourt is then: In weyll and wo *T*
Thi fader, thi moder thou shall honowre *T*
[*T interpolates:*
Not only w*ith* thi reuerence
Bot in thare nede thou thaym socoure,
And kepe ay good obedyence.]
biddis noght for to sloo] bydys the: No man slo, *T*
Ne harme hym neuer in word ne dede *T*
[*T interpolates:*
Ne suffre hym not to be in wo
If thou may help hym in his nede.]
[*T continues:*
The sext bydys the thy wyfe to take,
Bot none othere lawfully;
Lust of lechery thou fle and fast forsake,
And drede ay God whereso thou be.

The vii bydys the be no thefe feyr,
Ne nothyng wyn w*ith* trechory;
Oker ne symony thou com not nere,
Bot conscyence clere ay kepe truly.

The viii bydd*es* the: Be true in dede,
And fals wytnes looke thou none bere;

		Ȝoure neghbours house, whillis ȝe haue hele,	Looke thou not ly for freynd ne syb, Lest to thi saull that it do dere.']
		The ix[te] biddis take noȝt be stresse.	The ix byddes the not desyre
		His wiffe nor his women	Thi neghburs wyfe ne his women, [*T interpolates:* Bot as holy kyrk wold it were, Right so thi purpose sett it in.]
988		The x[te] biddis noȝt coveyte.	The x byddes the for nothyng [*T continues:* Thi neghburs goodys yerne wrongwysly, His house, his rent, ne his hafyng, And Crysten fayth trow stedfastly.' Thus in tabyls, shall ye ken, Oure Lord to Moyses wrate;]
		Thez are þe biddingis x, Whoso will lelly layte.	biddingis] commaundementes *T*
994	*II Doctor*	Behalde howe he alleggis oure layse,	[§§ *Ch inserts earlier*] allegis] lege *T;* hase learned *Ch*
995		And lered neuere on boke to rede;	And lered] and he learned *Ch*
996		Full subtill sawes methinkeþ he saies,	methinkeþ] methynk *T;* Methinkes hee sayes suttle suwes [*other MSS.:* sawes] *Ch*
997		And also trewe, yf we take hede.	also trewe] very trueth; we] you *Ch*
998	*III Doctor*	Ȝa, late hym wende fourth on his wayes,	wende] *omit T;* Ȝa] *omit Ch*
999		For and he dwelle, withouten drede,	and] if *T*
1000		The pepull schall full sone hym prayse	schall] will *T;* schall full sone] full sonne will *Ch*
1001		Wele more þan vs for all oure dede.	vs] wee *Ch*
	I Doctor	Nay, nay, þan wer we wrang,	wer] wyrk *T;* This is nothinge to my entent *Ch*

		Such speking wille we spare.	speking wille we spare] speach to spende I read *Ch*
			[§ *End of section inserted before commandments in Ch; Ch then inserts:* *Tertius Doctor:* Syr, this child of mycle pryce W*hi*ch is yonge and tender of age, I hould him sent from the high iustice To wynne agayne our heritage.]
1004		Als he come late hym gang,	*omit line Ch*
1005		And move vs nowe no more.	nowe] not *T; omit line Ch*
1006 *s.d.*			[*T inserts:* Tunc venient Ioseph et Maria, *et* dicet Maria]
1006	*Maria*	A, dere Joseph, what is youre rede?	*omit line Ch*
1007		Of oure grete bale no bote may be,	*omit line Ch*
1008		Myne harte is heuy as any lede	Myne] My *T; omit line Ch*
1009		My semely sone tille hym I see.	tille] to *T; omit line Ch*
1010		Nowe haue we sought in ilke a stede	ilke a] euery *T; omit line Ch*
1011		Boþe vppe and doune ther dayes thre,	ther] thise *T; omit line Ch*
1012		And whedir þat he be quyk or dede	þat] *omit T; omit line Ch*
1013		Ʒitt wote we noght, so wo is me.	*omit line Ch*
1014	*Joseph*	Mysese had neuere man more,	Mysese] Sorow *T; omit line Ch*
1015		But mournyng may not mende;	mournyng] mowr[n]yng, Mary; mende] amende *T; omit Ch*
1016		I rede forther we fare	I rede forther] Farther do I red *T; omit line Ch*
1017		Till God som socoure sende.	Till] To *T; omit line Ch*
		Aboute ȝone tempill if he be ought	ȝone] the *T; omit line Ch*
		I wolde we wiste þis ilke nyght.	That wold I that we wyst this nyght *T; omit Ch*

1020	*Maria*	A, sir, I see þat we haue sought,	sir] certys *T; omit line Ch*
1021		In worlde was neuere so semely a sight.	*omit line Ch*
1022		Lo where he sittis, se ȝe hym noght	See where hee sittes thatt wee haue sought *Ch*
1023		Emong ȝone maistiris mekill of myght?	ȝone] yond *T;* yonder *Ch* [*Ch transposes this couplet with the following one*]
1024	*Joseph*	Now blist be he vs hedir brought,	Now blist] Blyssyd *T; this line and next attributed to Mary in Ch*
1025		For in lande was neuere non so light.	In land now lyf*es* there non so light *T;* In land lyves non so bright *Ch*
1026	*Maria*	A, dere Joseph, als we haue cele,	A] Now; we haue] haue ye *T;* Wend forth, Josephe, vpon your waye *Ch*
1027		Go furthe and fette youre sone and myne.	fette] fetche *T;* And fetch our sonne, and lett us fare *Ch* [*Ch interpolates:* That sytteth w*it*h yonder doctours gaye; For we have had of him great care]
		This daye is done nere ilke a dele	done] goyn *T; omit line Ch*
1029		And we haue nede for to gang hyne.	gang] go *T; omit line Ch*
1032	*Joseph*	With men of myght can I not mell,	can I] I cannot *Ch*
		Than all my trauayle mon I tyne;	That I must all my traveyle teene *Ch*
		I can noȝt with þem, þis wate þou wele,	þis] that; þou] ye *T;* Marye, wife, thou wottes right well *Ch* [*this line and the preceding two are taken in reverse order in Ch*]
1033		They are so gay in furres fyne.	They are] That syttes *Ch*
1034	*Maria*	To þam youre herand for to say	*omit Ch*
1035		Suthly ȝe thar noȝt drede no dele,	Suthly ȝe] Surely that; noȝt] ye *T; omit line Ch*

1036		They will take rewarde to you allway	rewarde] hede *T; omit line Ch*
1037		Because of elde, þis wate ȝe wele.	ȝe] I *T; omit line Ch*
1038	*Joseph*	When I come there what schall I saye?	*omit line Ch*
1039		I wate neuere, als haue I cele.	I wate neuere] For I wote not *T; omit line Ch*
1040		Sertis Marie, þou will haue me schamed for ay,	Sertis Marie] Bot *T; omit line Ch*
1041		For I can nowthir croke nor knele.	nor] ne *T; omit line Ch*
1042	*Maria*	Go we togedir, I halde it beste,	*omit line Ch*
1043		Vnto ȝone worthy wysse in wede;	wysse] wyghtes *T; omit line Ch*
1044		And yf I see — als haue I reste	*omit line Ch*
1045		Þat ȝe will noȝt, þan bus me nede.	bus me] must I *T; omit line Ch*
1046	*Joseph*	Gange on Marie, and telle thy tale firste,	Gang on Marie] Go thou *T; omit line Ch*
		Thy sone to þe will take goode heede.	*omit line Ch*
		Wende fourth Marie, and do thy beste,	*omit line Ch*
1049–50		I come behynde, als God me spede.	*omit line Ch*
1051	*Maria*	A, dere sone Jesus,	*omit line Ch*
		Sen we loue þe allone,	Sen] Sythen *T; omit line Ch*
1052		Why dosse þou þus till vs	till vs] tyll vs thus *T; omit line Ch*
1054		And gares vs make swilke mone?	swilke] this *T; omit line Ch*
1055		Thy fadir and I betwyxte vs twa,	*omit line Ch*
1056		Son, for thy loue has likid ill.	*omit line Ch*
1058		We haue þe sought both to and froo,	*omit line Ch*
1057		Wepand full sore as wightis will.	Wepand full sore] Wepeand sore *T* [*Ch interpolates:* *Maria:* My deareworthy sonne, to mee so deare,

			Wee have you sought full wonder wyde; I am right glad that you be here, That we found you in this tyde.]
1059	*Jesus*	Wherto shulde ȝe seke me soo?	ȝe seke] ye, moder, seke *T; omit line in Ch*
1060		Ofte tymes it hase ben tolde you till,	Mother, full ofte I tould you tyll *Ch*
1061		My fadir werkis, for wele or woo,	
1062		Thus am I sente for to fulfyll.	Thus am] Hither was *Ch* [*Ch interpolates:* That must I needes doe or I goe.] [*The following four lines following are attributed to Joseph in the Towneley MS.*]
1063	*Maria*	There sawes, als haue I cele,	There] Thise *T;* They *Ch;* als] sonne, as *Ch;* cele] heale *Ch*
1064		Can I noȝt vndirstande.	Can I] I can *T;* Can nothinge *Ch*
1065		I schall thynke on þam wele	wele] full well *Ch*
1066		To fonde what is folowand.	fonde] fownd *T;* And fownd to doe that the command *Ch* [*Ch here ends the episode with an expository stanza from an angel.*]
	Joseph	Now sothely sone, þe sight of þe	
		Hath salued vs of all oure sore.	salued] comforthed; sore] care *T*
1116		Come furth sone, with þi modir and me,	sone] now *T*
1118		Att Nazareth I wolde we wore.	
1101	*Jesus*	Beleves wele, lordis free,	wele, lordis] then, ye lordyng*es T*
1102		For with my frendis nowe will I fare.	
	I Doctor	Nowe sone, wher þou schall bide or be,	Now sone wher] Son, whereso; bide] abyde *T*
		Gode make þe gode man euermore.	

		No wondir if ȝone wiffe	ȝone] thou *T*
		Of his fynding be full fayne,	full] *omit T*
1107		He schall, and he haue liff,	and] if *T*
1108		Proue till a praty swayne.	till] to; praty] full good *T*
		But, sone, loke þat þou layne for gud or ill	But, sone, loke þat þou] Son, looke thou *T*
		Þe note þat we haue nemed her nowe,	note] noytt*es*; nemed her] nevened *T*
1081		And if it like þe to lende her stille	if it like þe to lende] if thou lyke to abyde *T*
		And wonne with vs, welcome art þowe.	wonne with vs] with vs won *T*
	Jesus	Graunte mercy sirs, of youre gode will,	Graunte mercy] Gramercy *T*
		No lenger liste me lende with ȝou,	me lende] I byde *T*
		My frendis thoughtis I wol fulfille	wol] shall *T*
		And to þer bidding baynely bowe.	
	Maria	Full wele is vs þis tyde,	vs] me *T*
		Nowe maye we make goode chere.	
	Joseph	No lenger will we bide,	
		Fares wele all folke in feere.	

Textual Notes

ABBREVIATIONS:

Craig : Hardin Craig, ed. *Two Coventry Corpus Christi Plays*, 2nd ed., EETS, e.s. 87. London: Oxford University Press, 1957.

Harris : Mary Dormer Harris, ed. *The Coventry Leet Book*. EETS, o.s. 134–35, 138, 146. London: Kegan Paul, Trench, Trübner, 1907–13.

Holthausen : F. Holthausen, ed. "Das Spiel der Weber von Coventry," *Anglia* 25 (1902): 209–50.

LB : *Leet Book*, CRO A 3(a)

Manly : John M. Manly, ed. *Specimens of the Pre-Shaksperean Drama*. 2 vols. Boston: Athenaeum Press, 1897.

MS. : Coventry Record Office 11/2

MS. Frag. : Coventry Record Office 11/1

REED: Coventry : R. W. Ingram, *Records of Early English Drama: Coventry*. Toronto: University of Toronto Press, 1981.

Sharp 1817 : Thomas Sharp, ed. *The Pageant of the Sheremen and Taylors*. Coventry: William Reader, 1817.

Sharp 1825 : Thomas Sharp. *A Dissertation on the Pageants or Dramatic Mysteries Anciently Performed at Coventry*. Coventry, 1825; facs. reprint, with foreword by A. C. Cawley, Wakefield: EP, 1973.

Sharp 1836 : Thomas Sharp, ed. *The Presentation in the Temple: A Pageant, as Originally Represented by the Corporation of Weavers in Coventry*. Edinburgh: Abbotsford Club, 1836.

THE PAGEANT OF THE SHEARMEN AND TAYLORS:

Sharp's text in his *Dissertation* is intended as a diplomatic transcription with typographic equivalents for abbreviations in the manuscript and omitting punctuation. Lacking an extant manuscript of the pageant, this must be the copy text and its readings preferred over Sharp's earlier transcription of 1817. In collating the copytext with both the earlier and subsequent editions, minor orthographic differences (e.g., fayne/feyne) and differences in word divisions have not been noted for this pageant. Punctuation and capitalization follow modern practice.

1. *Craig inserts stage direction: <Enter Isaiah as prologue.>* evere] *Sharp 1825; probably Sharp's misreading of Croo's* eyuere, *his normal spelling of this word*

3. geven*us*] *Sharp 1825;* geue us *Sharp 1817;* geve us *Manly*

6. for to] forto *MS.*

8. incresse] in cresse *Sharp 1825*

12. Into] In to *Sharp 1825*

13. abownde] a bownde *Sharpe 1825*

15. Wherefore] Where fore *Sharp 1825*

16. eyu*ere*] *Manly;* eyer*ue* *Sharp 1825*

24. Beholde] Be holde *Sharp 1825*

26. meydin<h>od] meydin od *Sharp 1825;* meydin-<h>od *Manly*

34. schal be] schalbe *Sharp 1825*

42. schal be] schalbe *Sharp 1825*

43. *Manly and Craig insert stage direction: <Exit Isaiah; enter Gabriel to Mary.>*

46. Allmyght] All myght *Sharp 1825*

51. abowe] a bowe *Sharp 1825*

56. schal be] schalbe *Sharp 1825*

59. wyl be] wylbe *Sharp 1825;* wit*h*owt] wi*th* owt *Sharp 1825*

62. ma be] mabe *Sharp 1825*

70. schal be] schalbe *Sharp 1825*

76. Beholde] Be holde *Sharp 1825*

79. schal be] schalbe *Sharp 1825*

80. Wherefor] Where for *Sharp 1825*

81. ma be] mabe *Sharp 1825*

83. for to] forto *Sharp 1825*

84. for to] forto *Sharp 1825;* fullfyll] full fyll *Sharp 1825*

85. handemayde] hande mayde *Sharp 1825*

90. farewell] fare well *Sharp 1825*

91. Godhed] god hed *Sharp 1825;* beteyche] be teyche *Sharp 1825*

98. for to] forto *Sharp 1825*

109. my nynee] *Sharp 1825;* myn ynee *Sharp 1817*

113. schal be] schalbe *Sharp 1825;* seyne] *Sharp 1825;* seyne, <ywis> *Manly, Craig*

116. Begyld] Be gyld *Sharp 1825;* anothur] a nothur *Sharp 1825*

117. begylde] be gylde *Sharp 1825*

119. husebonde] huse bonde *Sharpe 1825*

120. Husebond] Huse bond *Sharp 1825*

125. Behynd] Be hynd *Sharp 1825*

127. begylid] be gylid *Sharp 1825*

129. farewell] fare well *Sharp 1825*

130. Worthe] *Sharpe 1825;* <Wo> worthe *Manly, Craig;* yche one] ycheone *Sharp 1825*

131. begylid be] be gyldid be *Sharp 1825;* be be-gylid *Manly*

134. *Manly and Craig insert stage direction: <Lies down to sleep; to him enters an angel.>*

138. w*it*h*o*wt] w*ith* owt *Sharp 1825*

140. schal be] schalbe *Sharp 1825*

141. be not agast] *printed on a separate line by Manly, followed by Craig.*

146. *Manly and Craig insert stage direction: <Returns to Mary.>*

150. Thogh] *Manly, Craig;* Thoght *Sharp 1817, 1825;* mysname] mys name *Sharp 1825*

154. forgeve] for geve] *Sharp 1825;* foreu*er*more] for eu*er*more *Sharp 1825*

157. myself] my self *Sharp 1825*

162. allmyghte] all myghte *Sharp 1825*

167. togedur] to gedur *Sharp 1825*

168. *Manly and Craig insert stage direction: <They set out, and travel a while.>*

171. groue] *Sharp 1825, Craig;* grone *Manly, who, however, suggests* growe *as the meaning*

175. wol be] wolbe *Sharp 1825*

179. abyde] a byde *Sharp 1825*

184. husebond] huse bond *Sharp 1825*

186. schal be] schalbe *Sharp 1825*

190. wemen*n*] wem*m*en *Sharp 1825*

192. *Manly and Craig insert stage direction: <In another part of the place a shepherd begins to speak.>*

204. Wit*h*] *Sharp 1825;* W*ha*t *Manly, Craig*

205. *Manly and Craig insert stage direction: <Two other shepherds appear (in the street).>*

207. Therefore] There fore *Sharp 1825*

208. aright] a right *Sharp 1825*

212. this nyght hit ys soo cold] *Sharp 1825;* hit ys soo cold this nyght *Manly, Craig*

215. in made I] *Sharp 1825;* in made/ I *Sharp 1817;* then made I *Manly, Craig*

216. afrayde] *Sharp 1825;* afryght *Manly, Craig*

217. for to] forto *Sharp 1825*

222. wit*h*in] wit*h* in *Sharp 1825*

236. schal be] schalbe *Sharp 1825*

237. wit*h*owt] wit*h* owt *Sharp 1825*

239. a chylde] *Manly, Craig;* I chylde *Sharp 1825*

258. wase þer] *Sharp 1825;* wast þey *Sharp 1817*

260. wel seyd] welseyd *Sharp 1825*

267. wol be] wolbe *Sharp 1825*

277. hymselfe] hym selfe *Sharp 1825*

281. schal be] schalbe *Sharp 1825;* anon] *Sharp 1825; omit Sharp 1817*

282. warmyd well] warmyd <hym> well *Manly, Craig*

283. *Manly and Craig insert stage direction: <Angels appear to the shepherds.>*

291. *Manly and Craig insert stage direction: <The shepherds approach and worship the Babe.>*

295. Wherein] Where in *Sharp 1825*

299. a pore] *Sharp 1817, Manly, Craig;* apore *Sharp 1825*

317. for to] forto *Sharp 1825*

325. becum*m*] be cum*m* *Sharp 1825*

327. Into] In to *Sharp 1825;* ondefyld] on defyld *Sharp 1825*

327. *Manly suggests a line missing after l. 327.*

334. wondurfull] wondur full *Sharp 1825*

337. be jonyd] *Sharp 1825;* jonyd be *Manly, Craig*

340. schal be] schalbe *Sharp 1825*

348. opp*er*acion] opp*ro*acion *Sharp 1825;* ap'pacion *Sharp 1817*

360. subscryve] *Sharp 1825;* subscrybe Manly, Craig; chy<l>dis] chy<*l*>dis *Sharp 1825*

364. feymyne] *Sharp 1825, Craig;* feymy<ny>ne *Manly*

367. schuld be] schuldbe *Sharp 1825;* wit*h*ow<t>] w^{t} ow<*t*> *Sharp 1825*

371. inded] in ded *Sharp 1825*

373. stede] sede *Sharp 1817, 1825*

375. for to] forto *Sharp 1825*

379. schall] *Manly, Craig;* schalld *Sharp 1817, 1825*

381. thereof] there of *Sharp 1825*

397. Na, na] *Sharp 1825;* Nay, nay *Sharp 1817*

398. thereof] there of *Sharp 1825*

403. pyle] *Sharp 1825;* pallays *Sharp 1817. Sharp explains* (Dissertation, *120) that "Over the word Pyle, some later hand has written Pallays" in the manuscript.*

410. fullfyll] full fyll *Sharp 1825*

411. Betwyxt] Be twyxt *Sharp 1825*

415. Into] In to *Sharp 1825*

420. the<m>] *Manly, Craig;* the *Sharp 1825*

422. þerin] þer in *Sharp 1825*

425 *s.d. gothe*] *Sharp 1825;* dep*ar*the *Sharp 1817*

436. *Qui statis*] *written in red ink in manuscript*

440. the] *Sharp 1825;* the<m> *Manly, Craig*

441. onsundr] on sund'r *Sharp 1825*

442. wondr] wond'r *Sharp 1825*

443. thundr] thund'r *Sharp 1825*

446. þerof] þer of *Sharp 1825*

452. vndr] vnd'r *Sharp 1825*

456. a twynke] *Sharp 1825;* at wynke *Sharp 1817*

462. allwey þeron] all wey þer on *Sharp 1825*

463. the] Sharp *1817, 1825, Craig;* he *Manly*; allwey wit*h*owt] all wey wit*h* owt *Sharp 1825*

464. abownde] a bownde *Sharpe 1825*

465. Throghowt] Throgh owt *Sharp 1825*

472. eyue*r*] *Sharp 1825;* eyue*r*<e> *Manly;* eyue*re Craig;* aryve] a ryve *Sharp 1825*

473. aleond] *Sharp 1825;* aleoud *Sharp 1817*

477. schal be] schalbe *Sharp 1825*

481. schal be] schalbe *Sharp 1825*

483. throghowt] throgh owt *Sharp 1825*

484. eyue*r*] *Sharp 1825;* eyue*r*<e> *manly;* eyue*re* Craig

486. schal be] schalbe *Sharp 1825*

492. amonge] a monge *Sharp 1825*

493. p*ro*fettis] *Sharp 1825;* profet *Manly, Craig*

494. Aseyd] *Sharp 1825;* A seyd *Manly, Craig*
496. forlorne] for lorne *Sharp 1825*
503. into] in to *Sharp 1825*
510. methynke] me thynke *Sharp 1825*
511. betocunyth] be tocunyth *Sharp 1825*
513. a mayde] *Sharp 1817, Manly, Craig;* amayde *Sharp 1825*
514. intent] in tent *Sharp 1825*
518. Towarde] To warde *Sharp 1825*
520. Into] In to *Sharpe 1825*
522. intent] in tent *Sharp 1825*
525. <you>] <you> *Sharp 1825*
528. frankinsence] frank in sence *Sharp 1825*
534. A, yondur] *Sharp 1825;* Yondur *Sharp 1817;* besemyng] be semyng *Sharp 1825*
535. betocuns] be tocuns *Sharp 1825*
536. methynke] me thynke *Sharp 1825*
539. For to] Forto *Sharp 1825*
542. intent] in tent *Sharp 1825*
543. betocuns] be tocuns *Sharp 1825*
547. Allmyghte] all myghte *Sharp 1825*
551. Into] In to *Sharp 1825*
560. therefore] there fore *Sharp 1825*
564. Jerusalen] *Sharp 1817, 1825;* Jerusalem *Manly, Craig*
566. mast] *Sharp 1825;* must *Manly, Craig;* wey<lde>] *Manly, Craig;* wey *Sharp 1817, 1825*
567. fordo] for do *Sharp 1825;* shal be] shalbe *Sharp 1825*
570. thereof] there of *Sharp 1825*
577. *Manly and Craig insert stage direction: <The messenger goes to the kings.>*
585. *Manly and Craig insert stage direction: <They go to Herod>*; withowt] w*ith* owt
591. Wherein] Where in *Sharp 1825;* harie] *Sharp 1825, Craig;* harting *Manly*
598. for to] forto *Sharp 1825*
600. be west] *Sharp 1817;* to be west *Sharp 1825, Manly, Craig*
615. paseporte] pase port *Sharp 1825*
619. farewell] fare well *Sharp 1825*
625. *Manly and Craig insert stage direction: <Exeunt the three kings.>*
626. Onwysely *and* onwyttely] On wysely & on wyttely *Sharp 1825*

628. schal be] schalbe *Sharp 1825*
632. into] in to *Sharp 1825*
635. where] *Sharp 1825;* were *Sharp 1817*
637. Besekyng] Be sekyng *Sharp 1825*
639. wyl be] wylbe *Sharp 1825*
641. whereby] where by *Sharp 1825*
644 *s.d. into*] *in to Sharp 1825*
645. togedur] to gedur *Sharp 1825*
647. Albeyt] Albe yt *Sharp 1825*
648. <of>] *<of> Sharp 1825, Craig*
649. w*ith*owt] w*ith* owt *MS.*
651. p*re*ste<h>od] p*re*ste<h>od *Manly, Craig;* p*re*steod *Sharp 1825*
652. insence] in sence *Sharp 1825*
653. behovith] be hovith *Sharp 1825*
656. tocunyng] to cunyng *Sharp 1825*
660. p*ro*vyssion] *Sharp 1825;* puyssim *Sharp 1817*
662. *Manly and Craig insert stage direction: <As the kings go away, they say:>*
664. berthur] *Sharp 1817, 1825; brethur Manly, Craig*
665. far wachid] *Sharp 1825;* for-wachid *Manly, Craig*
667. wherefore] where fore *Sharp 1825*
670. *Manly inserts stage direction: <While they sleep, the angel appears.> Craig inserts a variant of Manly's stage direction: <They lie down, and while they sleep, an angel appears.>*
675. Into] In to *Sharp 1825*
676. schal be] schalbe *Sharp 1825*
677. thus] *Sharp 1825;* thys *Craig*
683. betraye] be traye *Sharpe 1825*
684. for to] forto *Sharp 1825*
686. farewell] fare well *Sharp 1825*
688. togeder] to geder *Sharp 1825*
702. w*ith*owt] w*ith* owt *Sharp 1825*
703. fayne] *Sharp 1825;* glad *Manly, Craig*
706. farewell] fare well *Sharp 1825*
708. fote] *Sharp 1825;* fete *Manly, Craig*
710. offurde] *Sharp 1825;* offur *Manly, Craig*
711. agayne] a gayne *Sharp 1825*
712. togeyder] to geyder *Sharp 1825*
713. *Manly and Craig insert stage direction: <They go out, and Herod and his train occupy the pageant.>*

714. curtese] *Manly;* curterse *Sharp 1825*
716. Ha<y>ll] Ha<y>ll *Sharp 1825, Manly, Craig*
722. Anothur] A nothur *Sharp 1825*
728. schal be] schalbe *Sharp 1825*
729: schal be] schalbe *Sharp 1825*
730. thus] *Sharp 1825;* this *Sharp 1817;* fordo] for do *Sharp 1825*
739. schal be] schalbe *Sharp 1825*
741. þerto] þer to *Sharp 1825*
755. sworde] *Sharp 1825, Craig;* swerde *Manly*
756. schal be] schalbe *Sharp 1825*
763. ham] *Sharp 1825; <t>ham Manly;* before] be fore *Sharp 1825*
764. *Manly and Craig insert stage direction: <Herod and his train go away, and Joseph and Mary are, while asleep, addressed by an angel.>*
766. into] in to *Sharp 1825*
769. Aryse] A ryse *Sharp 1825*
774. su*m* tocun off] *Sharp 1825;* to su*m* cun off *Manly, Craig* (*Kittredge's emendation*)
778. Becawse] Be cawse *Sharp 1825*
784. schal be] schalbe *Sharp 1825*
785. awey] a wey *Sharp 1825*
790. for to] forto *Sharp 1825*
791. fullfyll] full fyll *Sharp 1825*
805. Se . . . fawls losyngere] *Sharp 1825;* So . . . fowls losyn gere *Sharp 1817*
806. here] *Manly, Craig;* herer *Sharp 1825*
812. a<s> thog] athog *Sharp 1825;* <as> thogh *Manly*
816. *Craig inserts stage direction: <Here they kill the children.>*
819. Throghowt] Throgh owt *Sharp 1825;* eyuer] *Manly;* eyueer *Sharp 1825*
822. þeroff] þer off *Sharp 1825;* woll] *Sharp 1825;* wull *Sharp 1817*
824. Wherefore] Where fore *Sharp 1825*
829. wol be] wolbe *Sharp 1825; Manly inserts stage direction:* <They go to Herod.>
832. fullfyllid] full fyllid *Sharp 1825*
834. *Manly inserts stage direction: <Enter Nuncius.>*
836. into] in to *Sharp 1825*

844. Into] In to *Sharp 1825*
Colophon. Th<y>s] *Sharp 1825*

SONGS:

I.3. abowte] a bowte *Sharp 1825*
II.13. may] *Manly (Kittredge's emendation), Craig;* say *Sharp 1825*

It has not been practical to collate the text underlay in the songs as these appeared in score in Sharp 1825*; see Appendix IV.*

THE PAGEANT OF THE WEAVERS:

Sharp's text in his Abbotsford Club edition of 1836 is close to a diplomatic transcription of the manuscript (CRO 11/2) but has some misreadings. Typographic equivalents were supplied by him for abbreviation marks in the manuscript, but punctuation was omitted. Holthausen's text is problematic as it includes a number of attempts to correct and improve on Sharp's text without the assistance of the manuscript which had still to be rediscovered. For instance, Holthausen normalizes *u* and *v* throughout, emends *wyche* to *w<h>yche*, *watt* to *w<h>att*, *pra* to *pra<y>*, *ma* to *ma<y>*, and *the* to *the<y>*. It has not been considered necessary to note his habitual orthographic emendations, silent and acknowledged; only his genuinely variant readings which attempt to clarify or alter the meter or sense of a line have been included. Craig's text is primarily a reprint of Sharp's, but in his case collated with the manuscript: it thus corrects some misreadings but perpetuates others and introduces some new ones. Craig adopts some of Holthausen's emendations, particularly words added to achieve metrical regularity. Minor differences in spelling (e.g., most/moste, oure/owre, hym/hym*m*) have not been noted unless significant. As for the Shearmen and Taylors' pageant, modern conventions of punctuation and capitalization have been adopted.

The manuscript lacks an identifying title at the head of the text.

1. E < . > grett] *MS. damaged;* Grett *Sharp 1836, Holthausen;* Ye grett *Craig*

2. W*ith* youre] *MS.;* Youre *Sharp 1836;* Ye *Holthausen*

3. into] in to *MS.;* oreien<t>] oreien *MS. (damaged);* oreient *Sharp 1836*

6. a star] *MS.;* a star <of Jacob> *Holthausen*

9. makyth] *MS.;* in wyth *Sharp 1836;* ful lyght] fullyght *MS.*

10. a yere] ayere *MS.*

14. deserni<n>ge] desernige *MS.;* desernynge *Sharp 1836;* desernyng *Craig;* desarnyng *Holthausen*

17. oldd p*ro*nostefying] olddp*ro*noste fying MS.; p*ro*<g>noste-fying *Holthausen;* prognostefying *Craig*

18. aperid] *MS.;* aperie *Sharp 1836*

22. Syngnefyid] *MS.;* Syngnefyn *Sharp 1836;* Syngnefyth *Holthausen, Craig*

25. Jacobo] *MS.;* Jacob *Sharp 1836, Holthausen;* exorgit] ex orgit *MS.;* exsurget *Sharp 1836, Holthausen, Craig;* I<sr>aell] *MS. (damaged);* Israel *Sharp, Holthausen, Craig*

26. a star] astar *MS.*

30. gen*era*cioni] *MS.;* gen*era*cione *Sharp 1836, Holthausen, Craig*

31. here] here here *MS.;* ma be] mabe *MS.*

35. wondrfull] *MS.;* wonderfull *Sharp 1836;* wonderfull<é> *Holthausen;* wonderfulle *Craig*

39. Before] be fore *MS.;* p*ro*nostefide] *MS.;* p*ro*<g>nostedfide *Holthausen;* prognostefide *Craig*

41. apariet] aparet, *MS. emended to* apariet; pariet *Sharp 1836, Craig; <et> pariet Holthausen*

42. *Holthausen places this line in a footnote.*

43. A man*n*] Aman*n* *MS.*

44. The] *MS.;* The<n> *Holthausen*

46–47. *Holthausen prints as one line.*

48. before] be fore *MS.*

51. was sent] wassent *MS.*

51–52. *Holthausen transposes these two lines.*

52. sc<r>ipture] scipture *MS.*

53. them*m*selfe] them*m* selfe *MS.;* watt] *MS.;* whatt *Sharp 1836, Holthausen*

56. Where] *MS.;* Where<as> *Holthausen*

62. Toward] to ward *MS.*

64. thi] *MS.;* this *Sharp 1836, Holthausen, Craig*

67. Reycomfordyng] rey comfordyng *MS.*

68. Jaramo] *MS.;* Jaremé *Holthausen*

73. surenes] sure nes *MS.*

78. schal be] schalbe *MS.*

82. stall] *MS.;* of all *Sharp 1836; omit Holthausen*

83. before] be fore *MS.*

85. insence] in sence *MS.*

87. for yngnorance] *MS.;* for <their> yngnorance <hi> *Holthausen*

93. Good] *MS.;* God *Holthausen;* p*ro*dustacion] *MS.;* p*ro*testacion *Holthausen*

94. for to incresse] forto in cresse *MS.*

96–97. *Holthausen transposes these lines.*

97. for to] forto *MS.*

99. A child] achild *MS.;* þerin] þer in *MS.;* swetnes] swet nes *MS.*

100. a crosse] acrosse *MS.*

102. into] in to *MS.*

103. lange] lang<ag>e *Holthausen*

104. throghowt] throgh owt *MS.*

105. oddie] *MS.; <h>odie Holthausen*

113. For to] forto *MS.*

116. togeddr] to geddr *MS.*

118. wache þ*at*] *MS.;* wache <on> þ*at* *Holthausen*

119. tyll þ*at* hit] *MS.;* tyll hit *Sharp 1836, Holthausen*

120. for to fullfyll] forto full fyll *MS.*

121. them till] *MS.;* them there *Holthausen*

122. Whereof] where of *MS.;* intellegence] in tellegence *MS.*

126. togeythur] to geythur *MS.*

127. Betwyxt] be twyxt *MS.;* in dyfference] *MS.;* dyfference *Sharp 1836, Holthausen;* indyfference *Craig*

129. a playn] aplayn *MS.*

131. intent] in tent *MS.*

133. thes] *MS.;* this *Sharp 1836, Holthausen, Craig*

137. insence] in sence *MS.*

143. inquere] in quere *MS.*

144. the] *MS.;* the<y> *Holthausen*

144–45. *Single line in MS.; Craig follows Holhausen in splitting line into two after* he

145. for to] forto *MS.*

149. deyit<e>] deyit *MS.;* deyite *Sharp 1836;* deyit<é> *Holthausen*

150. pacence] *MS.;* pacyence *Holthausen, Craig*

154. here] *MS.;* there *Sharp 1836, Craig;* <dere>, there *Holthausen*

159. þerw*ith*] þer w*ith MS.*

160. wryte] *MS.;* wyte *Holthausen*

161. Wherefore] where fore *MS.*

164. in Trenete] in trenete *MS.;* in the trenete *Sharp 1836, Craig;* in the trenetè *Holthausen*

166. And vndr] *MS.;* Und<e>r *Holthausen;* And under *Craig*

167. becu*m*] be cu*m MS.*

171. apon] a pon *MS.*

172. ma see] masee *MS.*

176 *s.d. Semeon intrythe*] Seme on in trythe *MS.*

176. seylesteall soferent] sey lesteall so ferent *MS.*

178. And create] *MS;* Create<d> *Holthausen;* em*m*perell] *MS.;* emp*er*ell Sharp 1836, Craig; emp*ere*<a>ll *Holthausen*

179. yorthe] *MS.;* þorthe *Sharp 1836;* for the *Holthausen;* wattur] mattur *Sharp 1836, Holthausen*

180. al for] alfor *MS.*

183. forme] *MS. (extra minim);* formee*r Sharp 1836;* form*ere Holthausen, Craig;* begynnyng] be gynnyng *MS.*

185. eyu*er*lastyng] eyu*er* lastyng *MS.*

186. Downe into þ*is* wale] Downe in to þ*is* wale *MS.;* Doune into vile *Holthausen; and*] & *MS.;* off *Craig*

187. transegression] *MS.;* transgression *Sharp 1836, Holthausen, Craig;* mor<t>a<ll>] mor<.>a<..> *MS. (obscured by repaired cut in manuscript);* mortall *Sharp 1836, Holthausen, Craig*

188. before] be fore *MS.;* infynite foreyu*er*] in fynite for eyu*er MS.*

189. yend] *MS.;* þend *Sharp 1836;* þ'end *Holthausen*

190. grevoise] *MS.;* grevuse *Holthausen;* s<o>ro] s<.>ro *MS. (obscured by repaired cut in manuscript);* sorro *Sharp 1836, Holthausen, Craig;* constrayne] con strayne *MS.*

191. Inwardly] in wardly *MS.*

197. beseke] be seke *MS.*

199. whole] *MS.;* wholle *Sharp 1836, Holthausen, Craig*

200. *Craig adds a line following l. 200 from earlier version in MS. Frag.:* And that we ma walke in his weyis upright; *Holthausen inserts a row of dots to suggest a lacuna.*

203. fullfyll] full fyll *MS.*

204. apon*n*] a pon*n MS.*

208. wyl be] wylbe *MS.;* wyl <hit> be *Holthausen*

209. for to] forto *MS.*

213. an ende] anende *MS.*

219. rew*e*rence] *MS.;* reu*e*rance *Sharp 1836, Holthausen, Craig*

220. þ*i*] MS.; þi<n> *Holthausen*

221. a long] along *MS.;* co*n*tenevance] *MS.;* co*n*tenvance *Sharp 1836, Craig;* co*n*tenuance *Holthausen*

227. se*r*wand] *MS.;* se*r*vand *Sharp 1836, Holthausen*

233. loyve] *MS.;* Leyve *Sharp 1836, Craig;* Leyvé *Holthausen*

235. avnteant] *MS.;* avnceant *Sharp 1836, Holthausen, Craig;* hereof] here of *MS.*

238. hym*m*selfe herein] hym*m* selfe here in *MS.*

239. thes] *MS.;* this *Sharp 1836, Holthausen, Craig*

242. incresse] in cresse *MS.*

245. abyde] a byde *MS.*

246. for to] forto *MS.*

248. worlde well] *MS.;* worlde <so> well *Holthausen*

254. tru feyth] trufeyth *MS.*

256. expeydente] *MS.;* expeydent *Sharp 1836;* expedyent *Holthausen*

257. contenuall] *MS.;* conteniall *Sharp 1836, Holthausen, Craig;* preyar for to] preyarforto *MS.*

258. þerby] þer by *MS.*

260. Inwardely] in wardely *MS.*

261. contentyth] con tentyth *MS.*

262. dep<a>rte] depte *MS., Sharp 1836*; dep*a*rte *Holthausen, Craig; Holthausen inserts a row of dots after this line to suggest a lacuna.*

263. nede] *MS.;* ȝede *Sharp 1836;* <I> rede *Holthausen*

264. Vnto the tempull w*ith* all spede] *first line on fol. 4^{v}; canceled at base of previous page;* Unto the tempull <to go> w*ith* all spede *Holthausen*

265. for to abyde] forto a byde *MS.*

268. heyle *and* bote] *MS. corrected in later hand to* heylth *and* lyfe

269. *Craig silently inserts a stage direction here: "Ane goes out." A horizontal line has been drawn under l. 265, and a speaker's name in the left hand margin has been written, then erased.* "Annis" *is then written in brown opposite l. 268 in the left margin, then there is another horizontal line under l. 269. Craig may have been right in his assumption that Anna was meant to exit*

at this point, but there is no explicit stage direction in the usual form in the text.

271. Before] be fore *MS.*

273. awake] a wake *MS.*

274. Intersession] in tersession *MS.*

275. obteyne] ob teyne *MS.*

276. *Omitted Sharp 1836 and Holthausen, who nonetheless detects a lacuna and adds a row of dots;* my rest] myrest *MS.*

280. Reycomforde] rey comforde *MS.;* Reycomforde <me> *Holthausen, Craig*

281. no more] nomore *MS.*

286. þerto] þ*er* to *MS.*

290. ordenance] *MS.;* ordonance *Sharp 1836, Holthausen, Craig*

291. *s.d. hit were*] hitwere *MS.*

291. awake] a wake *MS.*

292. sendyght] *MS., Sharp 1836;* sendyth *Holthausen, Craig*

293. <message>] s<...>er *MS. (word scored out, with* message *written in above in later hand);* message *Sharp 1836, Holthausen, Craig;* for to] forto *MS.*

296. Wi*th*in schort tyme schal be] Wi*th* in schorttyme schalbe *MS.*

299. awoke] a woke *MS.*

300. I my] *MS.;* My *Sharp 1836, Holthausen, Craig;* þerwi*th*] þer wi*th MS.;* reyjoyse] rey joyse *MS.*

301. slepe] *Sharp 1836, Holthausen, Craig;* shepe *MS.*

307. schal be] schalbe *MS.*

311. *Craig inserts stage direction: <Exeunt the two angels.>*

316. before] be fore *MS.*

317. Therefore] there fore *MS.;* I wi*th* al my] I wi*th* almy *MS.*; I <spede> wi*th* al my *Holthausen*

320. for to] forto *MS.*

321 *s.d. clarkis*] *MS.;* Clarks *Sharp 1836, Holthausen, Craig*

327. Kyng most] *MS.;* kyng, <þat> most *Holthausen*

328. made] *MS.;* <hath> made *Holthausen*

329. Lorde] *MS.;* lord<ing>e *Holthausen*

336. lowe] *MS.;* loue *Sharp 1836, Holthausen*

340. a prynce] aprynce *MS.*

341. thereto] there to *MS.*

342. þerin] þ*er* in *MS.*

345. grewe] *MS.;* greive *Sharp 1836, Holthausen, Craig*

347. myself] my self *MS.*

351. and meke] *MS.;* and <full> meke *Holthausen*

359. <And>e] and *scored out in MS.;* straw] *MS.;* strew *Holthausen*

365 *s.d. clarkis*] *MS.;* Clarks *Sharp 1836, Holthausen,Craig. Craig adds an additional stage direction here: <Mary and Joseph with the child have occupied the front part of the pageant.>*

368. world made] *MS.;* world <hath> made *Holthausen*

370. ambassage] *MS.;* ambassaye *Sharp 1836, Holthausen, Craig;* me sent] mesent *MS.*

373. Vnto . . . goo] *The line appears (partly obliterated) at the bottom of fol.* 5^{v} *in MS. and is repeated at the top of the next page (fol.* 6^{r}*);* schuldist] schalist *Sharp 1836, Holthausen*

381. schal be] schalbe *MS.*

384. take] *MS.;* take <with> *Holthausen, Craig*

388. into] in to *MS.*

390. *Craig inserts stage direction: <Gabriel goes out.>*

393. all of] all <the gift> of *Holthausen*

395. *Craig inserts stage direction: <Addresses Jesus.>*

397. blassu*m*] *MS.;* blossu*m* *Sharp 1836, Holthausen, Craig*

408. intent] in tent *MS.*

413. for to] forto *MS.*

414. <I>] *Sharp 1836, Holthausen, Craig; omit MS.*

416. husebond] huse bond *MS.;* gentylli] *MS;* gentylle *Sharp 1836, Craig;* gentyllé *Holthausen*

417. þerfore] þ*er* fore *MS.*

421. wol not] wolnot *MS.*

424. Also] *MS.;* Alse *Sharp 1836, Holthausen;* saue] *MS.;* saue <so fre> *Holthausen*

428. wol be] wolbe *MS.*

430. whe<re>] whe *MS.;* wh*ere* *Sharp 1836, Holthausen, Craig*

431. m*ar*le] *MS.;* merle *Craig*

433. ma not] manot *MS.*

434. oue*r*throo] oue*r* throo *MS.*

437. do nott] donott *MS.*

442. were] *MS.;* veré *Holthausen*

444. nothynge] no thynge *MS.*

446. Therefore] there fore *MS.;* thyself] thy self *MS. Holthausen inserts a row of dots following l. 446 to suggest a lacuna.*

449. Therefore] there fore *MS.*

452. trawthe] *MS.;* trowthe *Sharp 1836, Holthausen, Craig*

458. an ende] anende *MS.*

459. schal be] schalbe *MS.;* thereto] there to *MS.;* thereta *Sharp 1836*

467. jis] *MS.;* iis *Sharp 1836, Holthausen, Craig*

471. men*n*, for] men*n*for *MS.*

475. Therefore] there fore *MS.*

477. lowe] *MS.;* love *Sharp 1836, Holthausen*

479. abowe] *MS.;* above *Sharp 1836, Holthausen*

481. then] *MS.; omit Holthausen, Craig*

482. for to] forto *MS.*

486. togeddur] to geddur *MS.*

488. them] them *Holthausen, Craig;* then *MS. (missing minim)*

492. Thogh] *Holthausen, Craig;* thoght *MS.*

493. wol goo] wolgoo *MS.*

494. *Holthausen and Craig print as two separate lines, dividing at* wey*;* them] *Sharp 1836, Holthausen, Craig;* then *MS. (missing minim)*

495. an ende] anende *MS.*

496. best may] *MS.;* best <so> may *Holthausen*

498. me sende] mesende *MS.*

499. socheonon] soche on on *MS.;* crawe] *MS.;* crave *Sharp 1836, Holthausen*

500. schal be] schalbe *MS.;* me sawe] mesawe *MS.;* me save *Sharp 1836, Holthausen*

501–02. *Holthausen divides after* staff

505. amend] a mend *MS.*

506. the be] thebe *MS.*

507. fro me] frome *MS.*

508. age] *MS.;* adge *Sharp 1836, Holthausen*

509. fro me] frome *MS.*

512. allmost gone] all mostgone *MS.*

518. for to] forto *MS.*

529. Fullfyllid] full fyllid *MS.;* intent] in tent *MS.*

530. yt wolde be] *MS.;* yt oght *Craig, following suggestion by Manly;* hyt wold be <thoght> *Holthausen*

532–33. *Holthausen divides after* wyff*, then adds* <as fast> *to complete the second line.*

532. briddis] *MS.;* birddis *Sharp 1836, Holthausen, Craig*

533. glad] *MS.;* blith *Holthausen*

534. *Craig adds stage direction: <Returns to Mary.>*

537. dowis] *MS.;* dovis *Sharp 1836, Holthausen*

538. alyve] a lyve *MS.*
541. husbonde] hus bonde *MS.*
542. *Written on same line as l. 541 in MS.*
543. abowe] *MS.;* above *Sharp 1836, Holthausen*
545. lowe] *MS.;* love *Sharp 1836, Holthausen*
551. bewar] be war *MS.*
554. therefore] there fore *MS.;* alsoo] *MS.;* alse *Sharpe 1836, Holthausen*
556. Therefore] there fore *MS.;* thyselfe] thy selfe *MS.*
558. husebond] huse bond *MS.*
560. Wherefore] where fore *MS.*
562. fryndis] *MS.;* fryndis <dere> *Holthausen*
566. a cu*m*burs] acu*m*burs *MS.*
568. I leyu*er*] *MS.;* leu*er Sharp 1836;* <I> leu*er Holthausen*
572. togedur] to gedur *MS.*
576. ye] *MS.;* we *Holthausen*
577. Also mote I thryve] *Canceled in a later hand, and correction added:* also well that ye might thryve; Also mote I thryve *Holthausen, Craig*
578. wyll] *MS.;* <it> wyll *Holthausen*
581. forward] for ward *MS. Following this line Craig adds stage direction: <They continue in the front part of the pageant as if making a journey. An angel appears in the temple.>*
589. *Cantant*] *omit Sharp 1836, Holthausen, Craig; instructions to sing are added in a different hand in margin but are integral to the meaning of the original text.*
592. therew*ith*] there w*ith MS.*
593. þ*er*off] þ*er* off *MS.*
602. incres] in cres *MS.*
603. abundantly] a bundantly *MS.*
605. he m*ar*ke me] *MS.;* he <me> m*er*ke *Holthausen*
606. wyll ys] *MS.;* wyll <hit> ys *Holthausen*
609. aray] a ray *MS.*
610. schal be] schalbe *MS.*
616. for to] forto *MS.*
618. bothe] *MS.;* <now> bothe *Holthausen*
619. byddeng] *MS.;* byddyng *Sharp 1836, Holthausen, Craig*
620. apase] *MS.;* <with me> apase *Holthausen*
622. w*ith* me] *MS.;* <alse> w*ith* me *Holthausen*
623. For to] forto *MS.*
627. for to] forto *MS.*

634 *s.d.* pressession] *MS.*; prossession *Holthausen*

649. a prete] aprete *MS.; a* prette *Sharp 1836, Craig;* a pretté *Holthausen*

654. Reyseve] *MS.;* Reyseve <him> *Holthausen, Craig*

655. wyll hit] *MS.;* <hit> wyll *Holthausen*

658. vnto <. . .>y <. . .> <. . .>d] *MS. (half-line canceled);* vnto my hand *Sharp 1836;* unto my hand *Holthausen;* of honowr *added to the end of the next line by later hand and imported into l. 658 by Craig.*

660. sufferent Saweowre] *MS.;* saveowre sufferant *Holthausen*

662. *Holthausen omits second* Welc*um in this line.*

666. Of] *MS.;* Child, of *Holthausen*

672. wit*h*owt] wit*h* owt *MS.*

673. for to] forto *MS.*

677. *Holthausen inserts a row of dots after l. 677 to indicate a lacuna.*

682. a meydyn] ameydyn *MS.*

684. Cu*m* on] *MS.;* On, on *Sharp 1836, Holthausen, Craig*

692. honde] *MS.;* hande *Holthausen*

693. onworthe] on worthe *MS.*

694. *A leaf (fol. 10) is missing in the manuscript following this line.*

695. Whyle, whyle] *MS.;* Whyle *Sharp 1836, Holthausen, Craig. Across the top of fol. 11ʳ a later hand has written:* Jhesus in geare of scarlete ys put in

698. To goo] *Holthausen, Craig;* to to goo *MS.;* before] be fore *MS.*

699. fotemanschipe] *MS.;* fetmanschipe *Sharp 1836*

705. Mightefull] mighte full *MS.;* <The> mightefull *Holthausen, Craig;* thy] *MS.;* thy<s> *Sharp 1836, Holthausen, Craig*

708. Lorde] *MS.;* <hi> lorde *Holthausen;* Lord *Craig*

713. fruyssio<n>] fruyssio *MS.;* fruysso*n Sharp 1836, Craig;* fruyss<i>o*n Holthausen*

715. ANE.] *Holthausen and Craig, following a marginal notation in a later hand in the MS., attribute this speech to* Clarec*us.*

716. foys defend] foys de fend *MS.;* foys <he> defend *Holthausen*

717. And <to> his] *Holthausen;* and his *MS.*

719. *Holthausen inserts the heading* <Jesus bei den Schriftgelehrten.> *Craig adds a row of asterisks suggesting a break here, but none is indicated in the MS. Following the asterisks he adds a*

stage direction: <Mary and Joseph enter the lower front-part of the pageant.>

720. Vnto <God>] *Craig; MS., Sharp 1836 omit* God*;* Unto <God> *Holthausen*

724. for to] forto *MS.*

725. Wherefore] where fore *MS.*

730. moche desyrith] *MS.;* moche he desyrith *Sharp 1836, Holthausen, Craig*

734. man] *MS.;* mon *Sharp 1836, Holthausen, Craig*

736. m*y*<r>th make <ye>] mrth make *MS.;* <ye> *inserted below line in MS.*

738. pley] *scored out in later hand;* glee *substituted*

740. I am] *MS.;* <lo,> I am *Holthausen*

742. redde] *MS.;* reddy *Sharp 1836, Holthausen. An added line, written in different hand, appears in the margin:* Now Gods blyssyng haue *and* myne*; retained in parentheses in Sharp 1836; omit Holthausen; Craig imports and emends:* haue you *and* myne

743. fryndis, here] fryndis here *MS.;* fryndis <dere>, here *Holthausen*

744. wol be] wolbe *MS.*

747. vorne] *MS.;* worne *Sharp 1836, Holthausen, Craig*

749. evin] *omit Holthausen*

750. thow thee] *MS.;* thriv thee *Sharp 1836;* thriv<e> yee *Holthausen;* thou thee *Craig*

752. for to] forto *MS.*

755. for to] forto *MS.*

757. *In the right margin of MS. is a line written by a later hand* Ye dame he schalbe orre gyde, *integrated by Craig into text prior to l. 757; retained and placed in parentheses in Sharp 1836; omit Holthausen*

763. Therefore] there fore *MS.*

764. togeddr] to geddr *MS.*

766. dare wel sey] darewelsey *MS.*

768. hold] *MS.;* wold *Holthausen;* may] *MS.;* may <rede> *Holthausen*

771. for to] forto *MS.*

772. ye] *MS.;* yo *Sharp 1836*

773. *Incomplete line in MS.;* before [*MS.* be fore] ye and me *added to complete line taken from variant line written in a later hand in margin* Ye dame lytt hym goo be fore ye and me. *Holthausen reads:* Ye hardély, dame, lett hym goo <fre>. *Craig imports*

the entire marginal line, omitting hardely

774. And be] *MS.;* And, <Mare>, be *Holthausen*

784. hat<h>] *Sharp 1836;* hat *MS.*

786. *Line in different hand in right margin of MS.:* Now thys ys wyttele sayd *and* wyll; *imported into text by Holthausen (who changes* wyll *to* wall*) and Craig.*

791. Craig adds stage direction: <*They set out and travel a while.*>

793. Therefore] there fore *MS.*

798. before] be fore *MS.*

799. behynd] be hynd *MS. Line in right margin of MS. in different hand:* Now Mare harke what I schall saye*; retained by Craig in parentheses following l. 800.*

804. huseband] huse band *MS.*

805. ma be] *MS.;* <made> ma<y> be *Holthausen*

808 *s.d. into*] in to *MS.*; *for-pagond*] for pagond *MS.*

813. w*ith*owt] w*ith* owt *MS.;* w*ith*owt<en> *Holthausen*

816. whomwarde] whom warde *MS.;* homwarde *Sharp 1836, Holthausen;* goo] *MS.* (*canceled*)*;* hye *Holthausen*

823. behynd] be hynd *MS.*

826. togedur] to gedur *MS.*

827. ou*er*take] ou*er* take *MS.*

828. Ou*er*take] ou*er* take *MS.*

836. <hym>] *Sharp 1836, Holthausen, Craig; omit MS.*

838. chyrdur] *MS.;* chyldur *Sharp 1836, Holthausen, Craig*

839. whomwarde] whom warde *MS.*

840. schal be] schalbe *MS.*

844. Therefore] there fore *MS.*

846. MARE.] *MS. ascribes speech to Joseph.*

847. thereto] there to *MS.*

848. reypeyre] rey peyre *MS.*

853. for to] forto *MS.*

856. of peple] *MS.;* of <þe> peple *Holthausen*

862. dyssepyssions] *MS.;* dyssepu<ta>ssions *Holthausen*

864. Wherefore] where fore *MS.;* draw nere] drawnere *MS.*

865. gewe] *MS.;* geve *Sharp 1836, Holthausen*

867. aleygence] aley gence *MS.*

868. knowe] *MS.;* knone *Sharp 1836, Holthausen, Craig*

869. degre] de gre *MS.*

872. be lade] belade *MS.*

873. subsc<ri>byd] subscbyd *MS.*

875. herein] here in *MS.*

876. Amo<n>ge] Amoge *MS.;* Amo*n*ge *Holthausen, Craig;* manefestly] mane festly *MS.*

877. truthe expoundid] *MS.;* truthe <were> expoundid *Holthausen;* truthe expownd *Craig*

878. *Craig adds stage direction: <Jesus comes in.>*

881. hast] *MS.;* haft *Holthausen, Craig*

882. whosooeyu*er*] who soo eyu*er* *MS.*

886. thow art] thowart *MS.*

887. Mosess] *MS.;* Mosees *Sharp 1836, Holthausen, Craig*

889. wytt ys] *MS.;* wyttys <ar> *Holthausen;* a strawe] astrawe *MS.*

891. pwyntis] *MS.;* poyntis *Sharp 1836, Holthausen, Craig;* be reysonyng] bereysonyng *MS.*

893. whatsooeyu*er*] what soo eyu*er* *MS.*

895. bweye of] *MS.;* bweye, <proud> of *Holthausen*

896. knois] *MS.;* kna<w>is *Holthausen*

901. intent] in tent *MS.*

902. Nothyng þeroff] no thyng þer off *MS.*

904. owre] *MS.;* <y>owre *Holthausen*

906. sun] *MS.;* sur *Sharp 1836, Holthausen*

907. wondurs] *MS.;* wondrus *Holthausen*

910. for to] forto *MS.*

911. Syris] *MS.;* Suris *Craig*

913. Godhed] god hed *MS.*

918. schal be] schalbe *MS.*

919. DOCTOR III] *emendation in margin of MS.; Sharp 1836, Holthausen, and Craig retain* I DOCTOR*;* wondurs] *MS.;* wundrus *Holthausen*

920. a moche] amoche *MS.*

922. actis thereof] actisthere of *MS.*

925. infanciam] in fanciam *MS.;* infancium *Sharp 1836, Holthausen, Craig;* p*er*fesiste] p*er* fesiste *MS.;* p*er*fecisti *Sharp 1836, Holthausen, Craig*

927. p*er*formyde] *MS.;* p*er*formyde <him> *Holthausen*

931. here to] hereto *MS.*

932. togeddur] to geddur *MS.*

937. ma knoo] *MS.;* ma knoe *Sharp 1836, Craig;* ma<y> kna<w>e *Holthausen*

939. for to] forto *MS.*

940. p*r*ove] *MS.;* p*r*eve *Sharp 1836*

942. Mastur<s>] mastur *MS.;* Mastur<s> *Holthausen, Craig*
946. worde] *MS.;* wor<l>de *Holthausen, Craig*
947. before] be fore *MS.*
951. Har] *MS.;* H<i>ar *Holthausen*
953. subc<r>ibyd] subscibyd *MS.;* subscribyd *Holthausen, Craig*
954. togethur] to gethur *MS.*
956. reysuns] *MS.;* reysunis *Sharp 1836, Holthausen, Craig*
958. this in] *MS.;* this is *Holthausen*
959. rede] *MS.;* teche *Holthausen*
960. Fyrst] fyrst *MS.;* Furst *Sharp, Holthausen, Craig*
962. thyself] thy self *MS.*
963. noo wyse] noowyse *MS.*
965. for to insev] forto in sev *MS.*
966. afecte] *MS.;* ef<f>ecte *Holthausen*
967. owre] *MS.;* <y>owre *Holthausen*
974. *Holthausen replaces the entire line with* <The fourthe beddith þe, alderbest>
980. anothure] a nothure *MS.*
984. forbyddyth] for byddyth *MS.*
985. Or to] orto *MS.;* bare] *MS.;* bere *Holthausen;* wyttnes] *MS.;* wyttines *Sharp 1836, Craig*
988. no] *MS.;* no<t> *Holthausen, Craig*
989. apere] *MS.;* impere *Holthausen*
991. declarid] de clarid *MS.; Sharp 1836 gives the first half of l. 991 followed by the second half of l. 992:* amonge all men] þ*a*t we schulde lere, *then omits l. 992 altogether; Holthausen conflates both lines:* Hathe declarid, þat we schulde ken
992. sc<r>ipture] scipture *MS.;* scripture *Craig*
994. expounde] ex pounde *MS.;* expownde *Sharp 1836, Holthausen, Craig*
995. larny<d>] *Holthausen, Craig;* larny *MS.*
996. all we] allwe *MS.*
997. trawthis] *MS.;* trowthis *Holthausen*
998. Brether] *MS.;* Brother *Sharp 1836, Holthausen, Craig*
1001. we] *MS.;* us *Holthausen*
1002. DOCTOR I.] *originally unnumbered in MS., but* I *added in later hand; Sharp 1836, Holthausen, and Craig attribute to* DOCTOR III.
1003. no] *MS.;* mo *Holthausen*
1004. cu*m*] *MS.;* ca*m* *Holthausen*

1005. no more] nomore *MS.*

1006 *s.d. Here*] Here *MS;* There *Sharp 1836, Holthausen, Craig; þ*is] þis *MS.; þ*e *Sharp 1836, Holthausen, Craig*

1007. dolar] *MS.;* dolor *Sharp 1836, Holthausen, Craig*

1009. ma see] masee *MS.*

1016. therefore] there fore *MS.*

1019. *Craig adds stage direction: <They turn toward the temple.>*

1024. hym] *MS.;* he *Holthausen*

1029. ageyne] *MS.;* go hyne *Holthausen*

1035. Therein] there in *MS.*

1040. todey] to dey *MS.*

1041. croke] *MS., Holthausen, Craig;* troke *Sharp 1836*

1049. Also God me spede] *Emended by Craig on basis of York:* <I come be-hynde> also God me spede.

1050. schal be] schalbe *MS. The line is legible in the MS. although an attempt has been made to erase it. Sharp 1836 and Holthausen omit; for Craig's solution, see textual note to l. 1049, above. Craig adds stage direction: <They go up toward the altar.>*

1053. for to] forto *MS.*

1057. seldum] seldun *MS. (missing minim);* seldum *Holthausen, Craig*

1060. vnto you] *MS.;* you untill *Holthausen*

1061. fullfyll] full fyll *MS.*

1061–62. *Holthausen emends to read:* My fathurs wyll for well or woo/ In eyu*er*<y> pwynt I must fullfyll.

1066. Yt were] *MS.;* Ys veré *Holthausen;* Ys were *Craig*

1070. the froo] thefroo *MS.*

1073. <glade>] *Sharp 1836, Holthausen, Craig; omit MS.*

1074. Alyve w*ith*owt] A lyve w*ith* owt *MS.;* Alyve w*ith*-owt<en> *Holthausen*

1075. farewell] fare well *MS.*

1077. For to] forto *MS.*

1079. Doctor II] Doctor I *Holthausen, Craig*

1080. cruoft] *MS.;* quost *Sharp 1836, Craig;* chest *Holthausen*

1082. cost] *MS.;* quest *Holthausen*

1083. seyst] *MS.;* seyhst *Sharp 1836, Craig;* goo<d>] goo *MS.;* goo<d> *Sharp 1836, Holthausen*

1085. s*ir*] *MS.; omit Holthausen, Craig*

1089. A long] along *MS.*

1094. Do] *MS.;* De *Sharp 1836*

1097. for to intreyte] forto in treyte *MS.*

1102. tyme] tyme yet ys were *MS. (words* yet ys were *scored out)*

1103. <you>] *Sharp 1836, Holthausen, Craig; omit MS.*

1105. wheneyu*er*] when eyu*er MS.*

1109. farewell] fare well *MS.*

1114. we] *MS.;* ye *Holthausen. Holthausen indicates by a row of dots that a line is missing between ll. 1114 and 1115; Craig finds that a line seems to be missing between 1113 and 1114.*

1117. chyld] *Holthausen, Craig;* chydl *MS.*

1121. Whereoff] where off *MS.*

1125. husebonde] huse bonde *MS.;* nothyng] no thyng *MS. Holthausen indicates by row of dots that he believes a line is missing after l. 1125.*

1131. betake] be take *MS.*

1132. farewell] fare well *MS.*

1133. whatteyu*er* befall] whatt eyu*er* be fall *MS.*

1136. A*nd*] *MS.;* A! *Holthausen, Craig*

1139. *Craig adds stage direction: <They go out.>*

1142. wysedome] wyse dome *MS.*

1144. Declarid] de clarid *MS.*

1151. dysspecionis] *MS.;* dysspu<ta>cionis *Holthausen*

1155. a wondurs] awondurs *MS.;* a wondrus *Holthausen*

1157. asposschall] *MS.;* a spesschall *Holthausen*

1160. gradudis] *MS.;* graduatis *Holthausen;* old] *MS.; omit Holthausen*

1161. And now] *MS.;* Now *Holthausen;* yonge] *MS.; omit Holthausen*

1163. bredur] *MS.;* brodur *Sharp 1836*

1165. avoidyng] a voidyng *MS.*

1168. for to] forto *MS.*

1169. an yende] and yende *MS.*

1173. foreyu*er*] for eyu*er MS.*

1174. now brethur bothe the same I sey *crossed out line in MS. in Croo's hand;* III *canceled and* I *added in the speech attribution.*

1175. reyjurnyd] rey jurnyd *MS.*

1178. all you] *MS.;* you <teche> all *Holthausen*

1181. I *canceled and* III *added in speech attribution.*

1186. cu*m*pa<n>y] cu*m*pay *MS.;* cu*m*pany *Sharp 1836, Holthausen, Craig;* par*t*] *MS.;* pra<y> *Holthausen;* p*ra Craig*

1187. hereof] here of *MS.;* here I *Sharp 1836, Holthausen, Craig;* eyuere mon] eyueremon *MS.*

Colophon. T<h>ys] Tys, *MS., Craig;* Robart] *MS.;* Robert *Sharp 1836, Holthausen, Craig;* < > Pyxley] *MS. (blank for missing name),* Sharp 1836; <Herre> Pyxley *Holthausen, Craig*

SONGS:

I.2. tythyng<s>] tythyng *MS., Sharp 1836*

II.1 now] *MS.;* how *Sharp 1836, Holthausen*

II.3. Messyae] *MS.;* Messyas *Sharp 1836, Holthausen, Craig*

II.7. mikely] *MS.;* mekely *Sharp 1836, Holthausen*

II.8 crosse] *MS.;* crose *Sharp 1836, Craig;* cros<s>e *Holthausen*

II.9. þou] *MS.;* þu *Sharp 1836, Holthausen*

APPENDIX I

FRAGMENT A

14. <be>] *MS. Frag. text obscured by ink smudge*

15. y<et>] *MS. Frag. text obscured by ink smudge*

16. <le>t] *MS. Frag. text obscured by ink smudge*

23. <Balaam>] *canceled in MS. Frag.*

24. be the spret of God] *repeated from previous line in MS. Frag. and canceled here*

25–26. *Craig prints as one line*

31. gen< . . . >] *MS. frag. reading unclear;* generacione *Craig*

FRAGMENT B

1. best] *written above the line as an insertion in MS. Frag.*

3. beginnyng] *MS. Frag. missing minim in* nn

5a–5b. *Lines canceled in MS. Frag.*

8. to in] into *Craig*

47. reuere<n>ce] reuerece *MS. Frag.*

60. <you>re] *text obscured by a smudge in MS. Frag.*

APPENDIX II
1. THE RECEPTION OF QUEEN MARGARET

4. well] *LB;* well<arayed>] *Sharp 1825*
7. choson] *LB;* chosen *REED: Coventry*
8–9. *Lines transposed in LB*
17. rote of Iesse likkyn] *Craig;* rote of Iesse rote likkyn *LB, Sharp 1825, Harris*
20–23. *These lines are also entered, incorrectly, prior to Jeremiah's speech, as follows:* Afturward withinne the yate at the est yende of the chirche was a pagent right well arayed *and* þ*er*in was shewed a speche of Seynt Edward *and* an oþ*er* of Seynt Iohn the Euang*elist*, as foloweth
24. righ<t>] righ *LB, Sharp 1925;* right *Craig;* righ*t REED: Coventry*
34. vnto] vn to *LB*
37. <at>] *scored out in LB*
62. beneþe] be neþe *LB*
76. curi*us*] *LB, REED: Coventry;* cur*agious Harris*
88. a knight] aknight *LB*
111. vnto <you>, lady] *Sharp 1825; LB omits* <you>
130. shall] *LB; omit REED: Coventry;* vnto] vn to *LB*
140. Marg<ar>et] Marget *LB;* Marg*a*ret *Craig*
151. is doutles] is ~~endle~~ doutles *LB*

2. RECEIVING PRINCE EDWARD

8. into] in to *LB;* <the> citie] *Sharp 1825; LB omits* the
15. o*u*r] *Harris;* our *Craig;* you*r LB*
20. another] a nother *LB*
24. *Two lines which follow are canceled:* Nobull P*r*ince Edward, my cossyn and my knyght / And v*er*y prynce of oure lyne / comen by dissent
25. glorious, grounder] glorious ~~and~~ grounder *LB;* glorious! Grounder *Craig*
29. fullfylled] full fylled *LB*
43. aboven] a boven *LB*
46. afore] a fore *LB*
58. afore] a fore *LB*
59. aboven*n*] a boven*n LB*

61. orgon pleyinge] orgonpleyinge *LB*

64. royme hast] *words separated by canceled* d *LB;* Reyme hast *Sharp 1825*

3. THE RECEPTION OF PRINCE ARTHUR

6. ȝate] ȝarte *LB;* ȝayte *Sharp 1825*

9. gou*er*na<u>nce] gou*er*na*u*nce *Harris, Craig;* gou*er*naince *REED: Coventry*

27. Fabius] *Craig, Harris;* Sabius *MS, REED: Coventry;* Sabins *Sharp 1825*

32. Withoute] With oute *LB*

44. dy<vy>ne] *Harris;* divyne *Craig;* dyne *LB*

48. shal be] shalbe *LB*

49. whe*re*soever] whe*re* so ever *LB*

51. 51. myself] my self *LB*

56. knygh<t>] knigh *LB*

58. Likewyse] like wyse *LB*

64. fa<ayn>] *Harris;* fayn *Craig;* fa<...> *LB*

83. þ*er* foll] *LB, REED:Coventry;* the*r*for *Craig*

Commentary

Full bibliographic references for works cited are given in the Select Bibliography when not included below.

The Pageant of the Shearmen and Taylors

Dramatis Personae: Isaiah, Gabriel, Mary, Joseph, Angel, Pastor I, Pastor II, Pastor III (Sym), Profeta I, Profeta II, Nuncius (Calcas), Herod, Rex I (Jaspar), Rex II (Balthasar), Rex III (Melchior), Miles I, Miles II, Woman I, Woman II, Woman III. Also required (dolls or puppets): the Innocents. The Infant Christ may also have been a doll or puppet, but we should not rule out the possibility that a real baby was used.

1–42. A prologue by the prophet Isaiah opens the Shearmen and Taylors' pageant with a speech invoking God, who knows all the secret thoughts of humans. Isaiah's prophecy of the coming of Christ here stresses the function of the Savior in history and in the redemption of the individual. Cf. *York Plays* XII.1–144 in which the Doctour quotes the prophecies of the Incarnation from the Vulgate text of the Old Testament and comments upon them. A second prophet scene in the Coventry Shearmen and Taylors' pageant will be introduced at ll. 313–424, following the adoration of the Christ Child by the shepherds; in both instances in this play the prophet or prophets most likely addressed the audience from the *platea* rather than from a pageant wagon or scaffold.

4. in grett mesere mankynd ys bownd. A commonplace. The classic statement is Pope Innocent III's *De Miseria Humanae Conditionis*.

5. The sarpent . . . soo mortall a wonde. In Genesis 3:1–6 the temptation by the devil, disguised as a serpent, resulted in the Fall, which was frequently described as a lesion or wound that required medication in the form of Christ, here referred to in l. 7 as God's "right vncion of Jvda." Theologians taught that God's grace and mercy in the Christian era were the only source of freedom from the spiritual sickness and bondage which had afflicted the human race on account of the Fall.

9. the right rote in Isaraell sprynge. The image derives from Isaiah 11:1: "there shall come forth a rod [virga] out of the root of Jesse, and a flower shall rise up out of his root." This prophecy was developed visually in depictions of the Tree of Jesse, originating at its root in the reclining figure of the patriarch Jesse and rising up through his descendants to the fruit (here, in l. 10, "the greyne off whollenes," probably derived from Numbers 17:8) of Mary's womb. The iconography was common; an example in the Coventry church of St. Michael appeared on a misericord (destroyed in bombing in World War II), and there are examples in Warwickshire painted glass at Merevale and Mancetter; see Davidson and Alexander, *The Early Art*, 18–19, 106–10, figs. 3, 37–38. The first king calls attention to the prophecy that a child should "be borne,/ Comyng of the rote of Jesse" when he enters at ll. 494–95, below.

11. owt of danger. Salvation from the danger of life confined in hell throughout eternity.

12. thatt reygeon. Heaven, bliss, which exists above and transcends time.

20–21. thogh that Adam . . . Abell *and* Seythe. In Genesis, Adam and his descendants are judged and condemned to die for his disobedience. Those who, like Abel and Seth, are worthy of redemption will be consigned to Limbo until after the death of Christ on the cross has taken place. No mention is made here of Cain, the first permanent resident of hell. Isaiah was traditionally one of those released from Limbo at the Harrowing; see, for example, *York Plays* 37.49–60.

22. Ecce v*irg*o consepeet. Isaiah 7:14: "Behold, a virgin shall conceive [concipiet]." Rogerson observes ("The Coventry Corpus Christi Play," 156) that Isaiah "is traditionally associated with Article 3 of the Apostles' Creed ('that he was conceyuyd of the holy goost Borne of the vyrgyn Mary')." See also the Weavers' Play, l. 41.

26. hir meydin<h>od nothing defylid. A reference to the perpetual virginity of Mary. See, for example, the *Golden Legend*, 1:38, which proclaims that Mary was a virgin both before and after the birth of Christ. This doctrine, affirmed by the *Protevangelium* and the Church Fathers (the proof text was Ezekiel 44:2), was an important element in the popular cult of the Virgin which in Coventry included the veneration of her image at the Whitefriars (W. G. Fretton, "Memorial of the Whitefriars, Coventry," *Transactions of the Birmingham Archaeological Society* 3 [1872]: 72). She was one of the patrons of the important Coventry guild of the Holy Trinity, Mary, St. John the Baptist, and St. Catherine. The cult of Mary was, of course, a point of conflict in the increasing Protestantization of cities such as Coventry in the 1530s and subsequently.

27. Sche ys deputyd to beare the sun, almyghte God. That Mary was the mother of God (*Theotokos*, or *Mater Dei*) had been affirmed in the fifth century by the Council of Ephesus. See also ll. 57–58, 70–71, below.

30–32. For Adam . . . From bondage and thrall. Isaiah prophesies the Harrowing of Hell and the release of Adam from limbo; this in turn will have been made possible by the birth of Jesus, Mary's Son, who will rescue the first human being from bondage. Cf. "Adam lay I-bowndyn," which places the Harrowing within the framework of the "happy Fall"; if Adam had not fallen, "ne hadde neuer our lady a ben heuene qwen" (*Religious Lyrics of the XVth Century*, no. 83). The popular iconography of the Harrowing may be illustrated by a fifteenth-century alabaster in the Victoria and Albert Museum (Cheetham, *English Medieval Alabasters*, no. 198); cf. the untypical illumination in *The Holkham Bible Picture Book*, fol. 34^{r}. A fragmentary Harrowing appears in glass now in the Bishop Haigh Chapel in the ruins of St. Michael's, Coventry; see Rackham, "The Glass Paintings of Coventry," pl. XVI, and Davidson and Alexander, *The Early Art*, 32. The Harrowing was included in the Coventry Cappers' pageant; see Introduction, above.

42. in secula seculor*um*. I.e., "world without end." In the liturgy the concluding words of the *Gloria Patri*.

43–45. Hayle, Mare, full of grace . . . blesside mote thow be. See

Luke 1:28: "And the angel being come in, said unto her: Hail, full of grace, the Lord is with thee: blessed art thou among women." The salutation of the angel Gabriel begins the Annunciation, which continues to l. 93. The account follows the narrative in Luke with variations and additions. Examples in the visual arts were ubiquitous before the Reformation, and many survived the Protestant iconoclasm of the sixteenth and seventeenth centuries. A sculpture of the Annunciation appears on a corbel at the entrance to St. Mary's Hall; though very worn, the figure of Mary, wearing a waisted gown, holds her hands together over her lap; see Davidson and Alexander, *The Early Art*, 21–22, fig. 5. The usual lily pot appears between Mary and the angel in this representation of the Annunciation, and it may be fairly confidently asserted that it also was part of the setting for the Annunciation in the Shearmen and Taylors' play. An account book of the Coventry Corpus Christi Guild records payment of 4*d* to "gabryell for berying the lilly" in the Corpus Christi procession (*Records of Early English Drama: Coventry*, 155). For other representations of the Annunciation in the county of Warwickshire surrounding Coventry, see Davidson and Alexander, *The Early Art*, 88, 112–13. As Gail McMurray Gibson notes, the feast of the Annunciation on 25 March appears to have been "in many ways . . . the single most important liturgical event in late medieval Christian piety" (*The Theater of Devotion*, 166–67).

51–59. Gabriel comes down from heaven as an ambassador to the Virgin Mary, whose virtue is exemplary among humans; grace inherent in her has prepared her for being the Mother of the God who will be born without sin on her part. See also commentary on l. 27, above.

61. But eyu*er* to lyve in v*ir*genete. An addition to the biblical account. See commentary on l. 26, above.

66. The Wholle Gost in the schall lyght. A promise of the descent of the Holy Spirit to Mary, which will happen shortly; see ll. 86–89, below.

67. And schado thy soll. See Luke 1:35: "and the power of the most High shall overshadow [obumbrabit] thee." Concerning this passage, the *Golden Legend* (1:199) quotes the *Glossa Ordinaria*: "A shadow ordinarily is formed by light falling on a solid body, and neither the Virgin nor any pure human being could contain the fullness of the deity: but '*the power of the Most High will overshadow thee*,' and in her the incorporeal light of the godhead took on the body of mankind, in order that she might bear God."

72–73. He schall saue . . . the fyndis powar dystroie schall he. The reference to Christ's role in the salvation in the course of the Annunciation event is consistent with the popular understanding of the Incarnation; Nicholas Love speaks of the Annunciation as "þe gronde of sauacion of mankynd" (*Mirror of the Blessed Life of Jesus Christ*, 30). The Annunciation implies in itself the later event of the Crucifixion—a connection that is demonstrated visually in the iconography of the lily with the crucifix that sometimes occurred in the scene with Gabriel and Mary. See W. L. Hildburgh, "An Alabaster Table of the Annunciation with the Crucifix," *Archaeologia* 74 (1923–24): 203–34, and "Some Further Notes on the Crucifix on the Lily," *Antiquaries Journal* 12 (1932): 24–26; Davidson and O'Connor, *York Art*, 39–40; Anderson, *The Imagery of British Churches*, 103, pl. 13. The reference to the "fyndis powar" alludes to the Harrowing of Hell; see the note on ll. 20–21, above. Rogerson suggests an allusion to Article 5 of the Creed ("The Coventry Corpus Christi Play," 163).

75–79. *And* furthur, lade, here in thy noone lenage/ Beholde Eylesabeth . . . schal be sene. Reference to the Visitation, when Mary visited her cousin Elizabeth, who is "of [Mary's] own lineage" and, in spite of being past child-bearing age, is pregnant with John the Baptist. The Visitation scene, which is included in fuller dramatized Nativity sequences, as in the N-Town plays, was not performed in Coventry's single long Nativity play.

86–89. Now blessid . . . in Trenete. An addition to Luke. Following Mary's submission to her role (l. 85), she receives the Holy Spirit. Traditionally this action was visualized by a dove, representing the Holy Spirit, descending on beams of light. In the N-Town Salutation and Conception, "þe Holy Gost discendit with iij bemys to oure Lady, the Sone of þe Godhed nest with iij bemys to þe Holy Gost, the Fadyr godly with iij bemys to þe Sone. And so entre all thre to here bosom" (11.293 *s.d.*). At Barcelona in 1453 a mechanical dove issued from the mouth of the Father and descended "with its wings extended" to the Virgin; "it is to emit certain rays of light or fire which are to do no damage when it is before Mary," and thereafter it flapped its wings and returned to God (Meredith and Tailby, *The Staging of Religious Drama*, 119). Somewhat less common (no examples are extant from Coventry or the surrounding region) was the descent also of a small figure of the soul of the Second Person of the Trinity, as in an illumination in York Minster Library MS. Add. 2, fol. 35v (Davidson and O'Connor, *York Art*, 43, fig. 9), and in painted glass at St. Peter Mancroft in Norwich (Gibson, *The Theater of Devotion*, fig. 6.5). At this point, Gabriel says, the Savior is conceived "in Trenete." In sculpture noted by Gibson (ibid., 144, fig. 6.2) Mary is shown in her pregnancy in such a manner that, when the hinged statue depicting her is opened, within her the Trinity may be seen.

93. be my leyche. God is regarded as healer, the bringer of health and wellbeing.

94. Mare, my wyff. In Luke 2:5 Mary is described as Joseph's "espoused wife" (cf. Matthew 1:18). The legend of Joseph's troubles about Mary was suggested by Matthew 1:19–24, but the fleshing out of the episode and the introduction of dialogue may be traced to the apocryphal *Protevangelium* 13.1–14.2 (*Apocryphal New Testament*, 94). The Shearmen and Taylors' pageant picks up in the middle of the story of Mary and Joseph, but it omits the portions of the apocryphal account that treat prior events; for this material as it appears in other English plays, see Woolf, *The English Mystery Plays*, 160–64. The audience could have been expected to know in general terms the circumstances immediately surrounding the scene of Joseph's troubles as it was presented. Accounts in the other English play cycles vary considerably. In the Shearmen and Taylors' pageant, Joseph must not at first see that Mary is pregnant and only recognize the change in her condition as she speaks (ll. 97–98). The explanation for his lack of knowledge is provided in l. 100: "who hath byn here sith I went"—implying an absence on his part of some duration (the *Protevangelium* specifies that he returns when she is in the sixth month of her pregnancy). In the play there is an immediate problem in production, since upon Gabriel's departure the youth playing the role must suddenly appear to be pregnant. At Mons, a stage direction indicated that Mary is to be reminded "to raise her belly to show that she is pregnant" (Meredith and Tailby, *The Staging of Religious Drama*, 171). The depiction of Joseph's doubts is rare in the visual arts; see Schiller, *Iconography of Christian Art*, 1:56–57, figs. 67, 141, and Gibson, *The Theater of Devotion*, fig. 6.13.

109. w*ith* my nynee. I.e., "with my eye(s)."

116–28. Begyld as many anothur ys . . . wed soo yong a chyld. Joseph fears that, as an old man married to a young woman, he is a typical cuckold; hence old men ought to take him as an example and be properly warned. Like other English plays which treat this episode, the scene is handled as essentially comic and is reminiscent of the fabliau. It was accepted that Mary was not more than fifteen years of age.

120. þ*at* acold. "Called that" (Sharp, *Dissertation*, 119); cf. *MED*, *s.v.* 'i-called' (verb); but another possibility is that the word signifies 'numbed' (adj.), as if with cold and referring to "Husebonde."

122. stand *and* truse. Sharp may be correct in suggesting that "this appears to have been a colloquial phrase," meaning "truss, tie up my points" (*Dissertation*, 119).

134–41. Aryse up . . . be not agast. The angel has appeared to Joseph in a vision after he has retired from Mary's presence and appeared to seek to go to sleep. The appearance of the angel, who tells Joseph that Mary is not only innocent but also that she is to be the Mother of God, elaborates on Matthew's account, which specifies the name to be given to Jesus and indicates that he will "save his people from their sins" (Matt. 1:21). The words "be not agast" are an addition (by Robert Croo?) to the stanza; Craig, following Manly, prints them on a separate line.

145–46. to Mare I woll in hast. . . . I knele full loo. Embedded stage directions.

156. to Bedlem must I wynde. Joseph must go to Bethlehem and, he believes, leave Mary behind; the reason for his journey is not specified here.

167–69. Goo we togedur . . . yt drawyth toward nyght. The staging here is unclear. Mary and Joseph have left their home and have traveled toward Bethlehem, which in l. 168 is three leagues away. Night is approaching, and by l. 180 he will have led Mary to the stable where Jesus will be born.

178. The lyght of the Fathur ou*er* hus both spreyde. Mary's prayer, apparently not foreshadowing the star of Bethlehem but referring to the light which appeared in the cave (later, stable) when Mary entered according to the account in Pseudo-Matthew (*Apocryphal New Testament*, 74).

182, 185. I for help to towne. . . . goo now fro me. Embedded stage directions. Joseph will go, as he indicates, to town for assistance. In the extant text of the York Nativity (Play XIV), Joseph similarly goes away, but he does so for a different reason; when he returns the Child has already been born in the manner described in St. Birgitta's *Revelations* (see Cornell, *Iconography of the Nativity*, 12–13). In the Shearmen and Taylors' pageant, Joseph's absence is for the purpose of obtaining the assistance of women, midwives for Mary in her hour of need (ll. 190–91). Here Joseph's leaving the stage serves to clear the way for the next scene (ll. 192–312), which initially focuses on the shepherds and the heavenly song that they hear. Because no midwives are present, the presentation of the birth seems to imply dependence on St. Birgitta's account, in which the mandorla-encircled Child appears miraculously and painlessly before her; this iconography, influenced by the *Meditations on the Life of Christ*, was popular in England after c.1420 and occurs, for example, in an alabaster at Coughton Court, Warwickshire (Davidson and Alexander, *The Early Art*, 115–16, fig 39; Philip B. Chatwin, "Three Alabaster Tables," *Transactions of the Birmingham Archaeological Society* 48 [1925]: 178, pl. XXXIV), and in painted glass at Great Malvern (Rushforth, *Medieval Christian Imagery*, 278–80, fig. 136). See also Love, *Mirror of the Blessed Life of Jesus Christ*, 37. In the Shearmen and Taylors' play, the birth of the Child most likely took place as the audience's attention was directed elsewhere. The Child is already born by the time that the angels sing the *Gloria* at l. 250. In fact, the moment of birth probably coincided with the appearance of the star to the shepherds at l. 229 *s.d.*—a cunning device to distract the audience from the event in the stable.

194–99. For I kno nott wheyre my scheepe nor the be . . . on this wold. The first shepherd illustrates the disorientation of the world before the birth of Christ. He is lost, depressed, and afraid, and the night is bitter cold. It is wintertime. His sheep are not in his sight, and his fellow shepherds are out of sight. He hopes to cheer the others up, however, and shouts to them from "this wold" or, as he indicates in l. 201, "this looe," implying a raised spot in the *platea* or on a scaffold. The two other shepherds must be some distance away when they hear Pastor I shouting (l. 205), but they are able to come quickly. For comment on their costumes, see the Introduction, above. They may also have been distinguished by shepherds' crooks, as in a misericord at Gloucester Cathedral (Remnant, *Catalogue of Misericords*, 50). In the Shearmen and Taylors' pageant the first shepherd has a musical instrument, the pipe that he will give to the Christ Child at ll. 294–95.

213. a pyrie of wynd w*yth* a myst. A blast of wind with rain, a sudden storm. The first shepherd has been given a fright by his fellows; see l. 216: "*And* wase full sore afrayde." Cf. the *Pepysian Gospel Harmony*, 5: "hij weren so sore adradde. . . ." But this passage, like the biblical text in Luke 2:9, describes their reaction to the appearance of the angel and the "brightness of God [which] shone round about them."

222–23. hit ys far . . . day lyght. See Luke 2:8. An indication that the birth of Christ took place in the depths of the night (Mirk, *Festial*, 21, like Love, *Mirror of the Blessed Life of Jesus Christ*, 36, places the time at midnight), and that as morning approached the star would appear to the shepherds in the sky.

229 s.d. *There the scheppardis drawys furth there meyte . . . the fynd the star.* The source of the shepherds' feast is Joseph's vision in the *Protevangelium* 18:2. Also suggested here is breaking of the pre-Christmas fast, which was obligatory in England from the first Sunday in Advent until midnight on Christmas eve; see James Ryman, "Farewele, Aduent," in Green, *The Early English Carols*,

1–2. As they are feasting, the shepherds discover the star over Bethlehem. The following dialogue indicates that Pastor III, whose name has been given as Sym, sees the star first and calls the others' attention to it. The biblical account requires a star in the story of the three Magi, not the narrative of the shepherds watching their flocks, who are, however, said at Luke 2:9 to have been enwrapped in light: "the brightness of God [claritas Dei] shone round about them." Love's *Mirror of the Blessed Life of Jesus Christ* only specifies the appearance of an angel "wiþ gret liȝt" (39). However, the star is presumably meant by the shepherd in the Shrewsbury Fragments who says, "Ȝone brightnes wil vs bring/ Vnto þat blisful boure" (*Non-Cycle Plays and Fragments*, 2), and it appears similarly to the shepherds in the York and Chester cycles and in the Towneley collection. It also occurs in the Annunciation to the Shepherds in painted glass at Norwich and East Harling (Woodforde, *The Norwich School*, frontispiece and pl. XI). In the Shearmen and Taylors' pageant the star presumably required for a bright light was a device that would be visible in daylight performances. One way to produce such a bright light would involve the use of glasses filled with liquid as condensers to intensify light from candles or torches; such a way of representing stars was apparently used by the Lincoln cordwainers for their pageant of Bethlehem; see *Records of Plays and Players in Lincolnshire, 1300–1585*, ed. Stanley Kahrl, Malone Society Collections 8 (Oxford, 1974), 96, and for discussion Butterworth, *Theatre of Fire*, 68–76. The *Golden Legend* described the star as "suspended at a level of the air close to earth" and "so bright indeed that sunlight could not dim it and even at midday it appeared brightest of all" (1:81). In the Shearmen and Taylors' pageant, Profeta I will report that, as the shepherds have announced, the star is a thousand times brighter than the sun at midday (ll. 392–94).

233–36. now ys cu*m* the tyme þ*a*t old fathurs hath told . . . In whom all p*ro*feciys schal be fullfyld. See, for example, Isaiah 7:14, 9:2; Hosea 14:6; etc. Micah 5:2 was regarded as specifying the place of birth in Bethlehem.

238–41. Soo seyd the p*ro*fett Isaye . . . myddis of the nyght. Invoking Isaiah's prophecy, Pastor I claims that the birth should be on the "schortist dey" of the year or in the middle of the night. In the early sixteenth century, however, the shortest day under the

Julian calendar was closer to the feast of St. Lucy (13 December) than to Christmas. St. Lucy's day is still elaborately celebrated as a festival of lights in Sweden.

250 *s.d. the angelis syng "Glorea in exselsis Deo."* In answer to the prayer of Pastor II, the angels appear above in the clouds and sing "Glory to God in the highest . . . " (Luke 2:14). The word "altissimis" of the Vulgate is replaced by "excelsis," as in liturgical usage and Luke 19:38. Music for this item was presumably not preserved in the manuscript transcribed by Sharp, but may have been, as at Chester, not the *Gloria* of the Mass Ordinary but the first responsory of Christmas Matins. The music for the beginning portion of this item in the Chester play is provided in British Library MS. Harley 2124, fol. 42[r]; see Dutka, *The Music of the English Mystery Plays*, 28–29. For discussion of the Chester *Gloria* and dating of its music in Queen Mary's reign, see Rastall, *Heaven Singing*, 1:152–59. In the Shearmen and Taylors' pageant, the *Gloria* will be repeated as the scene shifts briefly to Joseph's return to Mary at l. 268. The angels must appear on a higher staging level representing heaven; while, as indicated above, clouds can be confidently assumed, the nature of the heaven scaffold or pageant cannot be determined.

252–53. draw we nere/ To here there armony. The shepherds, who have been sharing a meal, are apparently to move close together in a group. The term 'armony' does not imply harmony in the modern sense but simply "the act of singing or making music; music or song" (Dutka, *Music in the English Mystery Plays*, 95).

258. "Glore glorea in exselsis." The second shepherd attempts to remember the angels' song, and is closer in his imitation than the shepherds in the *Holkham Bible Picture Book*, fol. 13[r], who begin "Glum glo ceo ne est rien," or in the N-town pageant whose attempts are "Gle, glo, glory" and "Gle, glo, glas, glum" (16.65, 69). See also York (XV.60–64 and the following *s.d.*) and the Towneley *Secunda Pastorum* (13.952–54).

263. "Et in tarra pax omynibus." "And on earth peace to all people." The words follow "Gloria in exselsis Deo"; presumably the shepherd attempts to mimic the angels' song. The song that the shepherds sing thereafter, however, is not the *Gloria* responsory but *Ase I Owt Rodde*. The text of this song appears at the end of the play; for the music see Appendix III.

264. this noise þ*at* I do here. Music, not undifferentiated noise in the modern sense. Joseph hears the singing of the shepherds as they approach. For shepherds singing on their way to worship the Christ Child, see also, for example, the York Nativity, which has them attempting to imitate the angelic song and also singing as they approach with "myrthe and melody," and "[w]ith sange . . . seke oure savyour" (XV.84–85), and Chester VII.472–79. M. D. Anderson observes that shepherds were traditionally regarded as musical (*Imagery of British Churches*, 107). Though Joseph had left Mary to seek assistance, as in the *Protevangelium* and Pseudo-Matthew, he returns here without midwives. It might be speculated that his return instead is meant to allow for Brigittine iconography, which would have him bringing back a lighted candle; in this iconography the space occupied by the Child and his Mother, however, is illuminated by divine light that is more bright than candlelight (see Twycross, "As the sun with his beams when he is most bright," 44–47). But the play text is insufficiently explicit for us to know the specifics of the visual display here.

270–72. Now welcu*m* to me, the Makar of mon . . . here woll I kys. Joseph picks up and kisses the Child, but otherwise again the text, lacking stage directions, is unclear about how the episode is to be staged. Does he take the infant up from the ground into his own arms in front of Mary, or from her lap, or from the manger? The Child is "the Makar of mon" since the Second Person was regarded as the member of the Trinity who created the universe, including humankind.

276. be fyld *and* fryth. Sharp glosses: "by land and sea" (*Dissertation*, 120).

278. the breythyng of these bestis to warme hy*m* wi*th*. As Mary has explained, there is no fire in the stable. The Child is warmed by the ox and the ass. In Love's *Mirror of the Blessed Life of Jesus Christ*, these animals knelt down and "leiden hir mouþes on þe craches [manger], breþing at hir neses vpon þe child" in order to provide warmth for him (37). This detail is derived from Pseudo-Matthew (*Apocryphal New Testament*, 74); the ox and the ass involve a misunderstanding of Habakkuk's prophecy (3:2) that Christ would be born "in the midst of the years," reading "beasts" for "years." At l. 279 Mary asks Joseph to bring her the Child, but at l. 289 the second angel promises the shepherds that he is "Lyinge in a crybbe." It is, however, more likely that she held her son during the scene of the adoration of the shepherds that follows.

290. of Davithis lyne cu*mon*n ys hee. See Matthew 1:6 and Luke 3:31, but in the biblical text David figures as the ancestor of Joseph, not Mary. David, playing a harp, appears in the genealogical Jesse trees at Merevale and Mancetter in Warwickshire (Davidson and Alexander, *The Early Art*, 106–10).

291–308. Hayle, mayde, modur . . . Othur treysure haue I non to present the wi*th*. Conventional *Hail* lyrics (cf. *Religious Lyrics of the XVth Century*, nos. 19, 23, 25, 30, 33) are commonly directed to Mary but here spoken not only to the Virgin (mother) but also to the (human) Child and (divine) Lord. A para-liturgical connection should be noted in that Hail lyrics additionally were directed to the Host at the elevation at Mass; see Rossell Hope Robbins, "Levation Prayers in Middle English," *Modern Philology* 40 (1942–43): 131–46. There is some precedent in liturgical drama. In a fourteenth-century *Officium Pastorum* from Rouen, the shepherds adored the Child and then sang *Salve, virgo singularis* (Young, *The Drama of the Medieval Church*, 2:17). As in the Towneley *Prima Pastorum* and *Secunda Pastorum* and in the Chester play, Hail lyrics accompany the giving of gifts. The shepherds' gifts make no appearance in the biblical text but, except for N-Town, occur in the other English plays on the subject. The gifts are clearly intended to be a parallel to the gifts of the Magi. The first shepherd gives a pipe, which he may have played in the procession of the shepherds to the Child as in a roof boss noted by Anderson at Norwich Cathedral (*Drama and Imagery in British Churches*, 95). The pipe is placed in the baby's hand, while amusingly the second shepherd puts his gift, a hat, on Jesus' head as a protection against the cold. Finally, the third shepherd gives him mittens "to pytt on þi hondis." The hat and mittens do not seem to have symbolic signification except insofar as they stress the cold of the winter season. However, the first gift, the pipe, is particularly appropriate since the Savior was widely associated with harmony, which was often seen in musical terms; for the fifteenth-century Flemish music theorist Joannes Tinctoris, for example, Jesus Christ was the greatest musician because "in duple proportion" he united "two natures," the human and the divine (*Proportionale musices*, in *Scriptorum ecclesiastici de musica*, ed. C. E. H. Coussemaker, 4 vols. [Paris, 1864–76], 4:154, as quoted in translation by Strunk, *Source Readings*, 194). The devil, on the other hand, was frequently seen as an incompetent musician; see Reinhold Hammerstein, *Diabolus in musica* (Bern: Francke Verlag, 1974). On a roof boss at Salle, Norfolk, and in painted glass at Great Malvern, St. Peter Mancroft in Norwich, and East Harling shepherds are playing pipes of various types for the Child; see Cave, *Roof Bosses in Medieval Churches*, 190; Rushforth, *Medieval Christian Imagery*, 380; Woodforde, *The Norwich School of Glass-Painting*, frontispiece and pl. XI.

311. Asse he ys heyvin Kyng, to grant you his blessyng. Mary asserts the Child's kingship and urges him to bless the shepherds who have come to see him. A doll could have been manipulated to simulate blessing, but in any case a real baby may have been used.

313 *s.d. the scheppardis syngith ageyne and goth forth of þe place.* The shepherds apparently are intended to sing a stanza, designated in Sharp's edition as Song III (actually a continuation of Song I); the text is printed at the end of the play, and, for music see Appendix III. The text of the continuation is not, however, as appropriate for the shepherds after their visit to the Child as before. See also Profeta I's description (at ll. 416–24) of their singing, which matches this stanza only in part.

313–424. Nothing is said in the stage directions about the members of the Holy Family, who seem to have remained visible to the audience, but the exit of the shepherds and the entrance of the prophets nevertheless signal a break in the action that may be interpreted as a point where two pre-existing plays were joined together, either by Robert Croo or by an earlier writer. From a practical standpoint the break would seem to have provided opportunity for the setting up of Herod's court since the prophets appear to have been positioned in the *platea* rather than on a pageant wagon or scaffold. The dialogue of the prophets returns to prophecies of the Nativity of Christ at a time when he has already been born (see ll. 380ff). They therefore fit the definition of 'prophet' in the *OED* as a "person who speaks for God or for any deity, as the inspired revealer or interpreter of his will. . . ." Prophet II acts as a foil to the first prophet. Both probably hold books of scripture. For further discussion, see King, "Faith, Reason and the Prophets' Dialogue," 37–46.

329. Owre frayle nature ys now begilde. The Virgin Mary's participation in the Incarnation is an act which beguiles frail human nature; her Son will be the beguiler of Satan, the original beguiler, and will thus reverse the primordial Fall. Cf. the Towneley *Secunda Pastorum*, ll. 1030–31: "The fals gyler of teyn,/ Now goys he begylde."

332. a mayde evin asse sche wasse. In birth the Child had passed forth from her womb even like light through glass (a common explanation) and had left her virginity intact. See also the note to l. 26, above.

334–37. A wondurfull marvell . . . thatt the Trenete . . . Schuld be jonyd vnto owre mortallete. The Christological doctrine that Jesus was both God ("of one substance with the Father") and man simultaneously, thus joining two natures, had been affirmed by the Council of Nicaea in 325 A.D.

339–40. Throgh whose vmanyte all Adam*is* p*ro*gene . . . owt of p*er*dyssion. As Anselm had stressed in his *Cur Deus Homo*, Christ had carried out the work of salvation by becoming our brother. All of Adam's children, however, were not redeemed from Limbo at the Harrowing, but only those who were worthy (see notes to ll. 20–21, 30–32, above). Nor, of course, will salvation be given to all at the Last Day of history.

341–42. who schuld amend/ But the seyd mon*n*. As one man through his disobedience offended, so only another by his perfect obedience might adequately atone for Adam's crime. As certain of the Church Fathers had taught, the devil had been afforded rights over humankind on account of the Fall; these rights could then only be abrogated by one who had not inherited the lapsarian condition.

344. asse man*is* one brother. See note to ll. 339–40, above.

345–48. vnto the deyite, I beleve p*er*fettle . . . or wyrkyng. Profeta II is a fideist who places faith before reason.

350. Yet dowtis oftym*is* hathe derevacion. "Yet doubts often are productive."

351–53. Thatt ys be þe meynes of comenacacion*n* . . . Be þe same dowts reysoning. "That occurs when the truth is communicated, being given appropriate examination by means of applying reason to the same doubts" (King, "Faith, Reason and the Prophets' Dialogue," 41).

359. the same lyne joynid to hir be mareage. In answer to Profeta II's doubts and questions, Profeta I explains Mary's noble heredity, which she has through her marriage to Joseph. Below, at ll. 362–65, Profeta I explains that the practice in ancient Israel was to trace one's family through the male line, as in the case of Jesus in Matthew 1:1–16 and Luke 3:23–38.

367. naturis p*re*judyse. Referring to conception outside of wedlock, which was regarded as against nature. Profeta I will explain (l. 369) that it is a logical impossibility for an act of the King of Nature to be against nature.

370. Dyd not þe powar of God make Aronis rod beyre frute in on day? See Numbers 17:8: "on the following day . . . the rod of Aaron . . . was budded: and . . . the buds swelling it had bloomed blossoms, which spreading the leaves, were formed into almonds." Regarded as prophetic; see *Biblia Pauperum*, 51.

373. sede. Sharp's reading. Craig glossed "sede" as ?seed (meaning "germ"). Profeta I has referred to a specific *place* in Scripture, and Profeta II then would presumably have opened his book to a specific *place* as if to find the biblical text to which reference has been made. This raises the possibility that Croo may have erroneously written "sede" instead of "stede" (i.e., place).

375–76. his blod he schuld schede amens . . . For owre transegression. The Atonement requires the death of the one without sin (Christ) just as the sin of Adam brought death into the world. The English *Speculum humanae salvationis* affirmed that humankind was not "delivred onene *þat* Crist was borne,/ Bot wyne of Cristis blode p*re*ssed in the Crosses horne" (*Mirour of Mans Saluacioune*, ll. 1049–50). Much was made in late medieval popular religion of Christ's blood, relics of which were allegedly present in England at Westminster and Hayles Abbey. The shedding of his blood was an important part of the Passion sequences staged in medieval England, and it was prominently displayed in the visual arts. In a wall painting at Coventry now in fragmentary condition, angels capture the precious blood at the Crucifixion in chalices (see Pierre Turpin, "Ancient Wall Paintings in the Charterhouse, *Burlington Magazine* 35 [1919]: 246–50, pl. facing 252); thus the blood shed at the Crucifixion is identified with the wine of the Eucharist. The doctrine of transubstantiation, of course, insisted that the wine indeed was transformed into the substance of Christ's blood (though not the appearance, or accidents). For a general discussion, see Davidson, "Sacred Blood and the English Medieval Stage." Early Protestantism affirmed the importance of the sacrifice of Christ's blood for salvation, but denied transubstantiation (though not the real presence) and condemned the element of sacrifice in the Mass. The passage here may be seen as consistent with both Catholic and Protestant theology.

377–79. Ase yt ys seyd in p*ro*fece . . . wee schall haue reydemcion. As if referring to a specific Old Testament text (not identified).

385–95. This othur nyght . . . these tythyngis tolde. An amplification of Luke 2:20; the singing and rejoicing of the shepherds has been overheard both describing the star and giving praise to the King of Israel (see l. 401).

403. In what pyle or castell. As a king, he should have been found in a great house or castle. Much is made in the various accounts of the poverty of the surroundings of Christ's birth. See, for example, the illustrations in the *Speculum humanae salvationis* (Wilson and Wilson, 156, 158) which show the stable as the barest of shelters, and the passage quoted by Owst, *Literature and Pulpit*, 501–02, from the sermon in British Library Add. MS. 41,321. This sermon remarks: "Wher weren the grete castellis and hye toures, with large halles and longe chaumbres" that would be appropriate for "the birth of so hiʒ an emperoure? . . . In stude of the real castel arayed with riche clothes, thei hạdden a stinkynge stable in the hyʒe wey."

410–13. The p*ro*feci to fullfyll/ Betwyxt an ox and an as . . . borne he was. The prophecy to which reference is made here occurs in Isaiah 1:3: "The ox knoweth his owner, and the ass his master's crib: but Israel hath not known me, and my people hath not understood." See also the note on l. 278, above.

424. there song hit ys neowell. I.e., "their song is 'noël'," as in Christmas carols; see, for example, Green, *The Early English Carols*, no. 29: "Nowel syng we both al *and* som. . . ."

425 *s.d.* Stage directions indicate that the prophets leave the playing area and Herod enters with his messenger. The relationship between his stage and the Nativity scene is unclear, but possibly he and his court occupied the wagon recently vacated by Mary and Joseph when they set out for Bethlehem. When he exits at l. 490 *s.d.*, the three Magi will enter in the street, not on the stage where he has presumably displayed himself.

425–35. The messenger, named Calcas (see l. 471, below), speaks in Anglo-Norman French, which appears written out in Croo's erratic spelling. The penultimate line is not entirely decipherable. The following translation is by Deborah McGrady:

> Be quiet, worthy barons of great renown,
> Compatriots, lords, and knights of noble worth.
> Quiet, gentlemen, countrymen both great and small.
> I ask that you remain silent,
> Compatriots, while your king and sire is present.
> That all show deference,
> That no one start a fight, but remain patient:
> And revere in your heart your lord,
> For all strength goes to your king.
> In the name of <. . .>, I request this of you;
> And King Herod, the great abolisher, commands you.

436. *Qui statis.* As a sign of his own exaggerated self-importance, Herod here misquotes the offertory verse *Qui statis in domo domini*. See Rastall, *Heaven Singing*, 1:202.

436–70. Herod is presented here as clearly demonic, and as such his movements on stage would have been quick and jerky rather than dignified. He brags about being the greatest conqueror in history and about being the creator of heaven and hell. This is the kind of speech that we might expect from Lucifer. It is absurd but also blasphemous to insist that his rule sustains the world; in this he claims for himself power that is only God's. He brandishes a sword or scimitar, as he often does in the visual arts (in painted glass at Fairford he impales an infant on the point of his weapon; see Wayment, *The Stained Glass of the Church of St. Mary, Fairford*, 80, pl. XXXIX), and in this speech claims to have used it to defeat Magog and "Madroke" (derived from the biblical Gog and Magog), whose bones he has broken in his cruelty. Herod is a braggart whose claims are comically exaggerated, yet with his sword in his hand he also must seem to be formidable. Even if he cannot literally make the earth shake for dread, the actor playing this role can give the impression of a fearful king to those standing by in the audience. He calls attention to his complexion and "colur" (l. 457), but there is reason to believe that he may have appeared with a painted face, in dark colors, to emphasize his anger as well as the absurdity of his claims. In painted glass of c.1285 showing him with the Magi in the Chapter House at York Minster, Herod has a dark face, and A. F. Leach has published a reference to "black Herod" in dramatic records from Beverley ("Some English Plays and Players," 213). Face painting is recorded in 1477 and 1508 in the Coventry Smiths' pageant accounts for Herod Antipas, whose identity was frequently confused with his father Herod the Great (*REED: Coventry*, 59, 104). Herod's bragging about his accouterments—his fashionable clothes and sword—also may be ironic, as one iconographic tradition illustrates: in painted glass in the church of St. Michael Spurriergate, York, Herod has been given a devil crown (see Miriam Skey, "Herod's Demon-Crown," *Journal of the Warburg and Courtauld Institutes* 40 [1977]:274–76). His god in any case is Mahownd, who anachronistically not only is the deity favored by Herod elsewhere (most loyally in the York and Towneley plays), but also appears invoked frequently by other unregenerate characters in the English plays. Mahownd here is a blasphemous replacement for Christ. Herod, who for Shakespeare was the archetypal raging tyrant, had almost certainly been seen by him at Coventry when he was a boy living in nearby Stratford-upon-Avon (see *Hamlet* 3.2.13–14). Shakespeare was fifteen years old when the Coventry Corpus Christi plays were played for the last time in 1579.

472–74. Warne thow eyu*er* porte . . . do pay markis fyve. Herod demonstrates his xenophobic fear of aliens by setting a high fee for permission to enter the country. A mark was equivalent to two-thirds of a pound sterling. Failure to pay the required fee would be a capital offense (l. 477).

483–86. Now schall owre regeons throghowt be soght . . . for there best. Not only are ports to be guarded, but also are aliens within the realm to be arrested and brought before the king. The word 'katyffis' (l. 485) here signifies both "prisoners" and "miserable persons"; see *OED*, *s.v.* caitiff.

488. Trompettis, viallis, and othur armone. As Herod goes off to rest, he specifies an assortment of instruments to play when he awakens. Trumpets, which were considered to be particularly appropriate for royalty, and viols would not be likely to have been played together. The mention of such instruments may, however, indicate that the intent was to use them in the course of the play, though no records are extant that might verify or contradict this. Possibly a trumpet sounded at Herod's entries, for example, just as this instrument would have been used to announce the entry of a real king.

490 s.d. *the iij kyngis speykyth in þe strete.* The Magi are typically called kings, as in the *Pepysian Gospel Harmony*, 4. In Matthew 2:1, however, they are referred to as "magi" ("wise men") only. They are identified as kings in the *Glossa Ordinaria* (*PL*, 114:73), which is quite unusually questioned in a sermon in British Library MS. Royal 18.B.xxiii; the sermon concludes that the Magi were "men of gret co*n*nynge, and not kyng*us*, all-be-it þat þei wer*e* myghty p*r*inces in arm*us* and men also of right gret lettur*e*" (*Middle English Sermons*, ed. Ross, 226). Schiller notes (*Iconography of Christian Art*, 1:105) that after the tenth century they are normally depicted as kings in the visual arts; most but not all wear crowns. This came about through their identification with the kings mentioned in Psalm 71:10–11 (*AV*: 72:10–11): "The kings of Tharsis and the islands shall offer presents: the kings of the Arabians and Saba shall bring gifts: And all kings of the earth shall adore him. . . ." In the pageant they enter and speak separately before they meet. Horses are not specified here but apparently were used for their entry since subsequently there are references in the text to riding. The kings also ride horses elsewhere, as in the Chester Magi play where one stage direction specifies that they "goe downe to the beastes and ryde abowt" (VIII.113 *s.d.*), and, to cite a Continental example, at Lucerne the horses seem to have been disguised as a camel, an elephant, and a dromedary (Meredith and Tailby, *The Staging of Religious Drama*, 120). Nevertheless, in the visual arts, as in the *Speculum humanae salvationis* (Wilson and Wilson, 158), the kings are typically on horseback as they follow the star. The Shearmen and Taylors' kings are not given names until ll. 670–72, when the angel calls their names: Jaspar of Tarsus, Balthasar of Arabia, and Melchior of "Aginare." They will not identify themselves by name until they depart from each other for home (ll. 695–97). Sometimes in the visual arts the third and youngest (unbearded) king is depicted as an African; see, for example, Cheetham, *English Medieval Alabasters*, no. 114, and also, for an example in Continental drama, Evans, *The Passion Play of Lucerne*, 201.

491. yondur a feyre bryght star I do see. The star has reappeared, probably on cue as Herod left his stage and the Magi appeared in the street. At Lucerne the "operator of the Star" lowered it when the kings rode into the square, but drew it up again when they were at Herod's court in Jerusalem; thereafter, "when they have been with Herod and remount, he lowers the star again . . . over the Hut of the Nativity" (Meredith and Tailby, *The Staging of Religious Drama*, 148). Though the king has come from a pagan land, he has heard the prophecies concerning the baby that would be born for the salvation of humankind.

494–95. a babe be borne,/ Comyng of the rote of Jesse. See note to l. 9, above.

499. God and man thatt all made of noght. The Second Person of the Trinity, here said from before the Incarnation to have combined the two natures of the divine and the human, is also the Creator who has created all things out of nothing (*ex nihilo*).

504. Thatt I ma hym worschipe w*ith* umellete. A contrast is immediately established between the three kings, who come in humility to see the Child, and Herod, whose pride is central to his character. The third king, Melchior, also stresses his humility (l. 545) as he asks to ride with the others to seek the precious Child.

510. a feyre bryght star . . . The wyche betocunyth the byrth of a chyld. In answer to the king's prayer for "su*m* knoleyge," he sees the star, which, as verified in l. 536, has the image of the Child in it. Mirk repeats the legend that there was "yn þe sterre a fayre chyld, and vndyr hys hed a bryght crosse of gold . . ." (*Festial*, 48). Cf. *The Three Kings of Cologne*, 34; the *Golden Legend*, 1:82; and, for the early development of this image, Trexler, *The Journey of the Magi*, 27.

528. To hym wyll I offur frankinsence. The first mention of the kings' gifts. Frankincense is offered here for the Child's future role as head of the Church. The incense might have been carried in an incense boat, as in the painted glass at Great Malvern (*Medieval Christian Imagery*, 285, fig. 137), in the wall painting formerly in St. Stephen's Chapel, Westminster (Tristram, *English Wall Painting of the Fourteenth Century*, fig. 2), and in three alabasters in the Victoria and Albert Museum (Cheetham, *English Medieval Alabasters*, nos. 109, 112–13) and another in the Burrell Collection in Glasgow (Robinson, *Studies in Fifteenth-Century Stagecraft*, fig. 11). When the second king presents the gift (ll. 650–53, below), the incense signifies Christ's priestly role and has associations with sacrifice. According to Mirk, *Festial*, 49, incense represented his deity; other explanations are provided by the *Golden Legend*, 1:83, and, most curiously, by the *Stanzaic Life*, which explains that the "Encense" was given to alleviate the "stenche of stabul" (ll. 2053–54).

536. a chyld peryng in a stare. The Child appears in the star; see note on l. 510, above.

544. thys present. Frankincense, as noted above, l. 528.

549 s.d. *Here Erode cumyth in ageyne.* The kings have already been met by Herod's messenger, who will ask permission to bring them into his presence.

552. a grett cumpany. Love reports that the kings were accompanied by a "gret multitude *and* a wirchipful company of lordes *and* oþer seruantes" (*Mirror of the Blessed Life of Jesus Christ*, 43). In the Shearmen and Taylors' pageant the three kings would have needed attendants for their horses, which were probably led away as they arrived at Herod's court, and in a wall painting at Croughton, Northamptonshire, an attendant is leading two horses away while the kings adore the Child (Tristram, *English Wall Painting of the Fourteenth Century*, 163; Borenius and Tristram, *English Medieval Painting*, fig. 50). No evidence of the presence of horses appears in the pageant after the meeting with Herod. The kings will leave Herod's court, then reappear, and kneel in prayer; also, when the time comes for the kings to leave for their home countries, they are on foot (see l. 708, spoken by the third king). On the other hand, in the Towneley play the kings retain their horses until they arrive before the Christ Child (14.505 *s.d.*). At Coventry a large number of extras would have been extremely unlikely for the simple reason that costumes would have been required. Was the reference to a great throng of people a nod to the members of the audience who were crowded around?

553. Whatt make those kyngis in this cuntry? What are those kings doing in this land?

555–56. Of whatt age . . . twellve deyis old. The twelfth day of Christmas, the feast of Epiphany, was traditionally regarded as the date of the visit of the Magi to the holy family in the stable.

558. the schode me. "They showed me. . . ." I.e., they either pointed to the star before it disappeared over Herod's court, or they opened a book to point out the prophecy. The action may have been staged, but there is also the possibility that it was merely reported.

560. hy the in hast. "Go, hurry." A sign of Herod's impatience and anxiety. He is anxious both to hear what the kings have to say and to trick them.

577. Hayle, syr kyngis. The kings must be nearby. There is no stage direction between Herod's order sending the messenger forth and his arrival before the kings. The messenger must descend from the pageant into the street and quickly walk to the kings, who would probably have dismounted. After a brief speech by the first king who ironically hopes for Herod's help in their search for the Child (ll. 581–84), the messenger then must lead the three kings back to the tyrant, who will welcome them with oily hypocrisy.

588. of my bryght ble . . . bassche ye noght. Don't be abashed by my bright appearance. Such self-praise by Herod also appears in other English plays, as, for example, N-Town 18.9: "I am þe comelyeste kynge clad in gleterynge golde."

599. This same ys evin the xijth dey. Epiphany, the twelfth day of Christmas when the kings traditionally arrived out of the East to worship Christ.

600. be west. I.e., out of the west.

603–06. cu*m* whom by me this same wey . . . bankett w*ith* me. Herod insists that after they have found the Child, they should return home by way of his court so that he might hear the news and share a banquet with them. See Matthew 2:8. The pageant omits Herod's consultation with the wise men of his realm who tell him that the Child is to have been born in Bethlehem. Cf. Towneley 14.405–68 for Herod's use of consultants and his cursing of them for providing information that is hardly to his liking concerning the fulfillment of the prophecy. When the Doctors in Chester VIII rehearse the prophecies for the birth of Christ, Herod becomes so angry that he breaks his sword.

611–13. He thatt weldith all thyng . . . in pes. God, as the wielder or controller of all things, will teach the kings the way to pass through Israel in peace. There is an element of irony here, since the angelic warning will assist them to avoid returning to the fate that the demonic Herod has planned for them.

615. Youre paseporte for a C deyis. Herod grants them a visa for safe passage for a hundred days in order to encourage their (false) feeling of security. In ll. 621–24 Herod continues his hypocritical hospitality, which is calculated only to trick them. After they have left, he at once announces his plan to execute them summarily upon their return to his court (l. 627). His view of law is entirely arbitrary, as demonstrated in ll. 629–33.

636. Now knele we downe. The Magi kneel in prayer (embedded stage direction).

640. Yondur . . . I see the star. The star has now reappeared to lead the kings to the Nativity scene, which is pronounced to be not far away (l. 641).

644 s.d. *There the iij kyngis gois into the jesen.* The kings enter the stable, identified as "þ*is* pore place" (l. 643), then approach the gesine or childbed. The scene in the pageant is one that replicates the design of the seal of the guild of Shearmen and Taylors which shows the first king, uncrowned, before the Child, whom his mother holds as she sits on a throne.

Text encirling seal omitted

In the seal, the Child is reaching out to receive the gift that is being offered to him (see also Davidson and Alexander, *The Early Art*, 23–24, fig. 6). Evidence from the visual arts contemporary with the play would indicate that the kings kneel before the Child in succession, beginning with the oldest and concluding with the youngest, as also in painted glass at Great Malvern (*Medieval Christian Imagery*, 284–85), the *Speculum humanae salvationis* (Wilson and Wilson, 158), and alabasters in the Victoria and Albert Museum (Cheetham, *Medieval English Alabasters*, nos. 107, 109–10, 112–

15); when each kneels, he removes his crown or hat and presents his gift. These examples bear comparison with painted glass by John Thornton of Coventry in York Minster in which the second king is removing his crown as the first kneels, bare headed, before a nude figure of the Child, who is blessing as he is being held on his mother's lap; a third king still has his crown on his head (Davidson and O'Connor, *York Art*, 54, fig. 13). The gifts given by the kings are specified in Matthew 2:11.

644. Hayle, Lorde. Hail lyrics are spoken by each of the kings just as was the case with the three shepherds, above. The first (ll. 644–49) addresses Christ as God and Creator.

648. A cupe full <of> golde. The first king's gift is indicative of the Child's lordly preeminence in spite of his humble lodging; hence he has given a cup of gold as a sign of his preeminence in the cosmic order. The gold is usually in the form of coins, which themselves became the focus of legend (Melchior's thirty gold pennies have been made from Alexander's golden apple in *The Three Kings of Cologne*, 74). Mirk explains that this gold acknowledged that the Child was in fact "kyng of all kynges" (49)

652. a cupe full off insence. On the gift of frankincense, see note to l. 528, above.

655. myre. Myrrh was used for embalming, and hence Mirk says that it was given to the Child because he "was veray man, þ*a*t schuld be ded, and layde in graue wythout rotyng" (*Festial*, 49). In the third king's speech here (ll. 654–57), myrrh is specifically given to the child "for mortalete." The Crucifixion is thus foreshadowed.

667. Lett all vs rest. The three kings have left the stable and plan to return to Herod, but at this point decide they need rest. Prior to the twelfth century the convention had already been established that the three kings lay on the ground side by side with their crowns in place on their heads (see Mâle, *Religious Art in France*, 1:72, figs. 60–62); for an English example from the fourteenth century, see George Warner, *Queen Mary's Psalter* (London: British Museum, 1912), pl. 174.

670–72. Identification of the three kings by name and country of origin; see note to l. 490 *s.d.*, above. The angel appears to the kings in a dream vision while they are sleeping.

674. goo you west whom. The kings of the East are to go home by way of a western route.

676. Ye schal be byrrid *with* gret reynowne. Relics believed to be the bodies of the Magi were transferred to Cologne in 1164, and their shrine would become a major pilgrimage site; see Trexler, *The Journey of the Magi*, 44.

685–712. The kings take leave of each other and depart separately. For their identification by name in ll. 695–97, see the note to l. 490 *s.d.*, above.

686. the feyrist of schapp soo swete. It was generally assumed that Jesus was the most perfect of body among men. The application of the word *sweet* to Jesus was commonplace in the century prior to the Reformation.

691–92. Vnto this kyngis son . . . for ovre saluacion. The Christ Child is described as "clensid so cleyne," for he is utterly pure. The gifts, presented to by the kings to both the Son and the Virgin Mother for their "saluacion," are called "this obblacion" (l. 694), terminology which is suggestive of the offertory in the Mass though it also has a wider application.

697. S*ir* Balthasar. A mistake for Melchior, since Rex II is himself Balthasar.

700. on hyll. Cf. the third king's identification of the space where they originally met as "on playne" (l. 709).

705. drede of Erode thatt ys soo wrothe. They rightly dread Herod because of the angel's warning (ll. 670–77), but they have not been told about his explosive anger. The statement, however, anticipates Herod's choleric mood when he is seen a few lines later in the pageant.

713. There is no stage direction to indicate that the three kings have left and that Herod has positioned himself on his pageant, presumably on a throne. The messenger's recital of Hail lyrics as he approaches his sovereign seems ironic not only because Herod is neither a model of courtesy nor the mightiest man alive, but also because they represent an ironic reversal of the Hail lyrics spoken by the shepherds and those recently recited by the three kings before the Child. Two soldiers have also positioned themselves near Herod, for they must be present to speak at ll. 738ff.

716. mon*n* in armor. Herod may have worn armor, but surely not a full suit. It is quite possible that this reference is only rhetorical, like the envisioning of him on "a stede" in l. 715—a line which echoes N-Town 18.10: "þe semelyeste syre þat may bestryde a stede."

722–30. The three kings indeed have marred Herod's mood by not returning to his court. The speech contains embedded stage directions which call for Herod to "stampe," "stare," "loke all abowtt," tear at his clothes, rave, and run mad. The famous stage direction following l. 728 calls for him to rage both on his pageant and in the street. Anderson calls attention to the series of bosses in the transept of Norwich Cathedral which show scenes from the narrative of the Magi and Herod, including a boss that shows him in rage (*Drama and Imagery*, 95–97, fig. 11b).

729–33. thatt kerne of Bedlem he schal be ded . . . slayne? Herod devises a plan for murdering all the children of Bethlehem in order to be sure that the Christ Child is slain. According to Matthew's account as it was paraphrased in the *Pepysian Gospel Harmony*, when Herod saw that the three kings had "so bigiled hym, þan wex he wel wroþ, and sent ou*er*al his men *and* dude sle all þe children in Bedleem and of al þe cuntre aboute þat were of lesse age þan of two yere . . ." (7). In contrast to the York play, for example, Herod bears full responsibility for the plan.

744–45. Soo grett a mord*er* . . . a rysyng in þi noone cuntrey. Herod's tenuous claim to authority was asserted by early writers. While the first soldier has objected to the slaughter as a "schame" (l. 740) and wishes to avoid involvement, the second soldier only sees unpleasant political consequences in such an act. The suggestion that there may be a rebellion in the Bethlehem area, however, only causes Herod to lose his temper again; see l. 747 *s.d.* for the continuation of his raging. His threat of capital punishment for not doing his bidding (ll. 748–50) will convince them to proceed with the slaughter.

755. your bryght sworde. Herod still has a sword, as at l. 441; the soldiers swear on it to do their sovereign's will.

759. owre armor bryght. The soldiers are wearing plate armor. See the depiction of the Massacre of the Innocents in a panel of painted glass in the East Window of St. Peter Mancroft, Norwich (Woodforde, *The Norwich School*, 27, pl. III). The plate armor in this glass is datable prior to the middle of the fifteenth century. In the earlier wall painting of the Massacre of Innocents at Croughton, the soldiers wear surcoats; one has a helmet, and the other is wearing chain mail, which would have been out of fashion long before the Shearmen and Taylors' pageant (see Tristram, *English Wall Painting of the Fourteenth Century*, 163; Borenius and Tristram, *English Medieval Painting*, pl. 51).

760–63. Now you have sworne . . . before my syght. Herod reminds the soldiers of their oath, and expects their full allegiance in order that he might be released from his fear of the King born at Bethlehem. When the children have been killed, their bodies are to be brought to him. At ll. 827–28, the second soldier says that the bodies are to be loaded into "waynis and waggyns." In the visual arts, Herod sometimes oversees the carnage and even participates in it, as in painted glass at York Minster (Davidson and O'Connor, *York Art*, 59–60, fig. 16) and at St. Peter Mancroft in Norwich (Woodforde, *The Norwich School of Glass-Painting*, 27, pl. III), and as in a wall painting at Chalgrove (Tristram, *English Wall Painting of the Fourteenth Century*, 153). In the Shearmen and Taylors' pageant, however, Herod would apparently need to watch the killing field from afar. The soldiers must now take their leave of Herod, and their journey to the Bethlehem pageant stage must require sufficient time for Joseph, Mary, and the Child to escape.

764–75. The Flight to Egypt is handled very briefly, with the action merely switching (without a stage direction in the text) to the Bethlehem pageant and Joseph's vision of the angel who orders the holy family to go away; then Joseph awakens Mary with news of the angel's message, and they set forth. While an ass was part of the stage setting for the stable where Jesus was born, there is no indication here that it would become the beast of burden to carry the Mother and Child off to Egypt or that it was even a live animal. Perhaps Joseph and Mary merely descended from the pageant wagon and walked away together. It is unclear whether the angel simply withdrew or followed them to provide protection along the way.

774. su*m* tocun of howse. Meaning unclear. Kittredge's emendation, adopted by Manly ("su*m* cun off" = *some kind of*), is not very helpful.

776 *s.d. Here the wemen* cum *in wythe there chyldur syngyng them.* At this point Song II, *Lully lulla, þow littell tine child*, was to be sung as the soldiers approached. It is a lullaby with a recurring refrain. The text of the song was printed at the end of the play by Sharp; for the music, see Appendix III.

777. in my narm*is*. The woman is holding her child in her arms. The soldiers will be required to tear the children away from their mothers' arms.

791. We mvst fullfyll Erodis com*m*andement. A sign that the soldiers are reluctant to do what they feel must be done; if they fail to carry out Herod's orders, they will be treated as traitors to the realm (l. 792). This is in contrast to the rough brutality of N-Town's Primus Miles who moves in and impales a child on his spear with a taunt to the mothers: "Lett moderys howte!" (20.105–12).

794. schame not youre chevaldre. An appeal to the ideals of chivalry, which ought to include protecting women and children. The soldiers here differ significantly from the character of Watkin in the Digby *Killing of the Innocents* who believes that he merits a knighthood for his exploits in infanticide. Though there is no stage direction to signify the killing of the first woman's child, we cannot doubt but that this in fact is what takes place. The cries "reybukyng chewaldry" of this woman and the others are remarked on in the first soldier's speech at ll. 816–18.

801–02. He thatt sleyis . . . my strokis on hym ma lyght. The second woman threatens the soldier, "Be he skwyar or knyght" (l. 803), who is about to kill her child. She delivers a blow at the soldier. In the Towneley and Chester plays and in illustrations of the Slaughter of the Innocents such as the painted glass in St. Peter Mancroft, Norwich, the mothers fight back. In the Norwich glass, a mother has one of the soldiers in a choke hold as he holds up his sword with her nude infant spitted upon it. An alternative possibility for portraying the women was taken up at York, which was to make the women passive and grieving rather that violent as a way of anticipating in their laments the Virgin Mary's *planctus*. In either case, rag dolls seem to have been used for this scene; see Anderson, *Drama and Imagery*, 136–37, and cf. Oosterwijk, "Of Mops and Puppets," 169–71; as Woolf notes (*The English Mystery Plays*, 392), Hildburgh's suggestion ("English Alabaster Carvings," 61) of wooden dolls "would obviously not serve in this scene."

808. Sytt he neyu*er* soo hy in saddull. Rhetorical; there is no evidence that the soldiers were on horseback, but rather this is a reference to high social class.

810. w*ith* my pott ladull. She threatens the soldier with a typical woman's weapon, a cooking ladle. Normally incidents in which feisty women beat their husbands with such "womanly geyre" were regarded as comic and not unusually appeared on misericords; for a woman striking her husband with a ladle at Nantwich, Cheshire, see Remnant, *Catalogue of Misericords*, 27. An example which shows a woman beating a man with a cooking pan appears on a misericord at Holy Trinity Church in nearby Stratford-upon-Avon (Davidson and Alexander, *The Early Art*, 80). The woman in the Shearmen and Taylors' pageant who is attempting to protect her child is, however, highly sympathetic. The cruelty of the entire scene seems to have been retained in the memory of one youthful spectator of the Coventry plays who years later depicted a historical king of England describing what would happen to the citizens of a French city unless they surrender:

> Your naked infants spitted upon pikes,
> Whiles the mad mothers with their howls confus'd
> Do break the clouds, as did the wives of Jewry
> At Herod's bloody-hunting slaughter-men.
> (Shakespeare, *Henry V* 3.3.38–41)

821–22. For thys grett wreyche . . . moche wengance þ*e*roff woll cu*m*. The *Golden Legend*, 1:58, cited the *Historia Scholastica* in reporting that "God, the most just Judge, did not allow Herod's great wickedness to go without further punishment" through being deprived of his own son along with the other children. In other accounts, especially those that follow Peter Comestor, the terrible death that ultimately overcame him is instead immediately inflicted upon him (see *PL*, 198:1546, as quoted by Woolf, *The English Mystery Plays*, 393). The Chester, Digby, and N-Town plays dramatize Herod's end, but it is not included in the conclusion to the Shearmen and Taylors' pageant. Nevertheless, the second soldier's claim in l. 825 that Herod "ys lyke to beyre the p*er*ell" seems to point toward such a catastrophe for him. Instead, at the end of the play Herod announces that he will dash off on his horse to Egypt in pursuit of "yondur trayturs" (l. 841)—that is, the holy family.

827–28. Yett must the all . . . fully fryght. A wagon was to be loaded with the bodies of the children and taken to Herod; see note on ll. 760–63, above. Some kind of contrivance must have been used to convey the slain children to the presence of Herod, since the first soldier announces that the tyrant may see the thousands that they have killed (ll. 830–31).

833. There ma no mon sey there ageyne. The sight is so terrible that no one will ever see such a sight again.

845–46. All thatt cuntrey woll I tast . . . them to. He will search out all parts of Egypt until he finds the Child and his parents.

Colophon. For Robert Croo and his role in "correcting" the playbook, see the Introduction, above. 14 March 1534 is an old style date (= new style 1535). The year is also identified by citing the mayor, in this case Roger Palmer, a mercer whose name appears frequently in the *Coventry Leet Book* between 1521 and 1544; see also the annals printed by Bliss Burbidge, *Old Coventry*, 227, which list him as a bedder. The names of the masters of the Shearmen and Taylors Guild do not appear in the *Leet Book*. John Baggeley was probably related to Richard Baguley, a tailor residing in Jordan Well ward in 1538.

The Songs. The songs were copied by Thomas Mawdyke in 1591, well after the final performance of the plays in 1579, but reflect usage during the years when the Shearmen and Taylors' pageant was still being produced. See the commentary on the songs in the Introduction, above, and, for the music and musical transcriptions, see Appendix III, below.

Song I. Dutka, no. 1 (English Songs).

Song I.3. there fold. This does not seem right, since the shepherds should be imagined to be out on the countryside, not in their sheepfold. The song, however, may not have been composed specifically for the pageant but rather may have been adapted from a preexisting text and melody.

5. mereli the sheppards ther pipes can blow. While here only one shepherd seems to have a pipe, the song may refer to shepherds generically, as it was their traditional role to be musicians at, for example, country weddings.

Song II. Dutka, no. 4 (English Songs).

Song II.6. This pore yongling. Apparently a reference to Jesus, but ambiguously also to the women's own children, who are doomed to Herod's "raging."

Song III. Continuation of Song I, sung by the shepherds. See note to l. 313 *s.d.*, above. The final line with its reference to the shepherds' pipes seems even more out of place here, since the first shepherd has given away his pipe as a gift to the Christ Child.

The Weavers' Pageant

Dramatis Personae: Profeta I, Profeta II, Simeon, Anna, Angel I, Angel II, Clerk, Gabriel, Mary, Jesus (at age twelve), Joseph, Doctor I, Doctor II, Doctor III. Non-speaking roles: Infant Jesus, two clerks (singers?).

1–175. The pageant opens with a long dialogue between two "prophets," who comment on the action that has been presented in the Shearmen and Taylors' play. They begin with attention to the star of Bethlehem which appeared to the Magi in the East as the fulfillment of prophecy. Thereafter they rehearse the Old Testament prophecies that predicted the Incarnation. The first fifty-eight lines also appear in an earlier version in CRO MS. 11/1; see Appendix I.

1. grett astronemars. The twelve astronomers; see below, ll. 112–17.

2. fatheres of folosefy. In *The Golden Legend*, the Magi are identified with the Latin term "*sapiens*, wise man" (1:79), but the reference to early philosophers here is ambiguous.

6–7. star . . . Apon the hyll of Wawse. The star will appear over the hill of Vaus. Also known as the hill of Victory, it is the highest hill in the East. See *The Three Kings of Cologne*, 6, 18, and also l. 115, below.

20. be atorite. According to (the) authority (of Scripture). Cf. CRO MS. 11/1: "be the Exp*e*rence" (Fragment A, l. 20).

23. the p*ro*fett Balaam. Balaam, who prophesied the appearance of a star which should signify a king of Israel in Numbers 24:15–19.

25. "Orietur stella . . . I<sr>aell." The form of Balaam's prophecy that also appears in *The Chester Mystery Cycle* 5.320 *s.d.*; the source is liturgical (a responsory for Advent 3, feria 4, in *Antiphonale Sarisburiense*, 6: pl. j), as Rastall has pointed out (*Heaven Singing*, 1:295); see also *Stanzaic Life*, ll. 1721: "*Orie*tur *stella ex Iacob, exurget homo de Israel.*" This form differs from the Vulgate in Numbers 24:17: "orietur stella ex Iacob et consurget virga de

Israhel." The quotation in the play is glossed in ll. 26–27 ("He seyd of Iacobe a star schuld springe" that signifies "this same kynge") and l. 43 ("A man*n* schuld spryng here in Isaraell").

30. "Et ipse dominabitur om*n*i gen*era*cioni." "And he will rule all generations." Cf. *The Three Kings of Cologne*, 4. The *Stanzaic Life* has "*erit omnis terra possessio ei*us" (l. 1721), which is also the liturgical form; see *Antiphonale Sarisburiense*, 6: pl. j.

41. "Ecce v*ir*go concipiet apariet filium." Isaiah 7:14 ("Behold, a virgin shall conceive, and bear a son"), slightly misquoted ("apariet" for "et pariet").

45. "Et vocabit*ur* nomen eius Emanvel." Isaiah 7:14 ("and his name shall be called Emmanuel").

53. yett them*m*selfe wyste not watt yt ment. Prior to the coming of Christ, even the prophets did not have a full understanding of what they themselves predicted; full knowledge and illumination would come only with the Incarnation.

58–60. þ*a*t profett . . . schall spring *and* arise. See Malachi 4:2: "the Sun of justice shall arise, and health in his wings."

63–67. "Good Lord . . . Sion." The prophecy is attributed to Isaiah but has not been identified.

68. Jaramo. Jeremiah. For the citation in the following lines, see Jeremiah 22:30; Jesus will be the king descending from the seed ("greyne") of David.

85. sacrefyce. The sacrifice on the cross, which will atone for the sins of all humankind since Adam's fall; see ll. 86–92.

98. streymis of grett brightnes. According to Jacobus de Voragine, following Fulgentius, the star was "so bright indeed that sunlight could not dim it" (*The Golden Legend*, 1:81). See also *A Stanzaic Life*, ll. 2004–20.

99–100. A child . . . apon his bake a crosse. . . . See note to the

Shearmen and Taylors' pageant, l. 510.

101. an eygull. Elsewhere, as in the *Stanzaic Life*, ll. 1873–76, writers are said to have believed the Holy Spirit (in the sign of a dove?) to have been present in the star. The eagle, however, was the symbol of St. John the Evangelist.

103–05. A woise therein . . . Seyinge. In *The Golden Legend*, the star addresses the Magi.

105. "Natus est nobis oddie rex Iudeor*um*." "Born to us today is the King of the Jews." Cf. Luke 2:11.

111. the land of Caldy. Chaldea.

112–17. twelve masters . . . yere. For the legendary twelve "masturs of asestronemy," see *The Three Kings of Cologne*, 37, 39.

124–27. See commentary on l. 98, above.

130. mancion of a v*ir*gin pure. The three kings or Magi do not, of course, find the Child in a mansion but in a stable, but the Virgin Mary's body has served as a mansion to house the Son of God.

135–37. The second and third gifts are given different symbolic significance than in the Shearmen and Taylors' pageant; here incense is identified with burial and myrrh with priestly functions.

144–45. Eyu*er* the axid, "Where ys he . . . the kyng of Juys?" Matthew 2:2.

166. vndr the curteyne of owre vmanete. Christ took on the form of a human but retained his divine nature; he was at once God and humankind but in appearance was fully human. St. Augustine explained: "God himself remains God; man is added to God, and there is made one person, so that there is not a semi-God, as it were in one part God and in one part man, but wholly God and wholly man" (Sermon 293, as quoted in translation in *An Augustine Synthesis*, ed. Erich Przywara [New York: Harper, 1958], 184).

171. schall reydeme vs apon a tre. Christ will redeem humankind upon the cross.

175. In secula seculor*um*. "World without end."

176–718. Purification episode, based on Luke 2:22–39. The stage direction preceding l. 176 specifies that Profeta II, who has been speaking directly to the audience, should leave and that Simeon should enter. Simeon will begin by rehearsing the creation story and the Fall, which brought mortality into the world. As in various other accounts, Simeon, who is awaiting the coming of Christ which has been prophesied by the "anceant p*ro*fettis," is identified as a priest associated with the temple (in contrast to Luke 2:25, where he is merely a devout man); indeed, Anna refers to him as the one who "of owre gloreose tempull hath þe goue*r*nance" (l. 218). Because of his great age, he fears that he may not live long enough to see the Messiah. At l. 647 he is called "bysschope." The Weavers' Account Book reports payment of 8*d* in 1542 for "makyng of Symyons mytor" and 2*d* in the year before for an amice (*REED: Coventry*, 156, 161). In the visual arts, his vestments are often vaguely adapted from contemporary styles. In the *Speculum humanae salvationis* he appears in a mitre (cf. Leviticus 8:13 for the use of the term *mitras* for the headgear of Jewish priests) and cope (Wilson and Wilson, 160), but in the *Biblia Pauperum*, 53, he wears a fanciful hat similar to that which is worn by a Jewish priest in the adjoining illustration. In a mid-fifteenth-century book of hours (British Library, Harley MS. 2887, fol. 58), he wears a particularly fanciful mitre and a cope (Scott, *Later Gothic Manuscripts*, fig. 478). The figure of Simeon in painted glass at Wroxall—the only example of the Purification in the county of Warwickshire—appears in a portion of this panel that is restored and unreliable (Davidson and Alexander, *The Early Art*, 118, fig. 40). See Appendix I for the fragment of text (parallel to ll. 181ff) preserved in CRO MS. 11/1.

184–85. a grevose fawll/ From the hy pales *and* blys eyue*r*-lastyng. The Fall of Adam and Eve from Paradise. It will, however, be a "happy Fall" since at the Harrowing of Hell they are released from Limbo and taken to everlasting bliss. The Fall was the cause of humankind's subjection to pain, misery, and mortality.

196. Isee, Sebbellam, Balam, *and* Malache. Isaiah, the pagan Sybil ("Sabbellam"; see *Mirour of Mans Saluacioune*, 73), Balaam, and Malachi, who prophesied the coming of Christ. Their prophecies are comforting to those who hear them.

198. tru lyght. Christ is the light of the world. The theme is particularly appropriate for the feast of Candlemas when the Purification in the temple is called to mind in the liturgy. Lighted candles are carried in procession on this day. See also Jacobus de Voragine, *The Golden Legend*, 1:149. The dramatic records for the Weavers' pageant record on occasion the supplying of candles and incense (see *REED: Coventry*, 208, 210).

202. At whose cu*m*yng the tru ovncion*n* of Juda schall seyse. With the coming of Christ the foreshadowing of events by the Jewish religion will have been complete and the role of the Jews as the chosen people will have ceased.

203. hy tym*me* of pes. The coming of Christ will be during a time of universal peace, and one of his titles will be "Prince of Peace."

209. my nold age. Mirk conventionally describes Simeon as "a passyng old man" (*Festial* 58), but according to the *Cursor Mundi* he is of "sex scor yeire" (l. 11,315). See also Shorr, "The Iconographic Development," 20.

217–30. The widow and prophetess Anna is Simeon's "dere frynde" of long standing who, according to the biblical account, at eighty-four years of age "departed not from the temple, by fastings and prayers serving night and day" (Luke 2:37). In CRO MS. 11/1 she does not greet Simeon as the governor of the temple but as one who "art owre gide in gostle goue*r*nance" (Fragment B, l. 46)

233–34. the lyght of loyve . . . schuld be boght *and* sold. The rite that is dramatized in the pageant involves the Purification in which Mary comes to the temple for ritual purification after childbirth, though in her case, as *The Golden Legend* [1:144] and other sources indicate, it is not really necessary, since she has not been polluted in the process of bringing a child into the world. But the play also is simultaneously a dramatization of the Presentation, in which according to the Jewish law the firstborn son is offered up in the temple and then redeemed again by his parents.

239–40. "In facie populor*um* . . . cessabit vnctio vestra." Attributed to Isaiah.

264. Vnto the tempull w*ith* all spede. Simeon and Anna are not in the Temple as yet. Anna will depart for this location at l. 270 *s.d.*

270–71. to prey/ Before that I my rest do take. He will pray the following prayer before sleeping. In this prayer he will express his humility before God and his laws.

277. Lorde, that madist all thyng of noght. The world was created out of nothingness, not out of pre-existent atoms.

291 *s.d. the Angell.* One angel appears to Simeon, but the speech tag at l. 305 identifies the presence of a second angel. Croo's text may not have been followed in early performances since the sixteenth-century Weavers' Account Book consistently lists payment of 8*d* to only two angels, and one of these would need to be Gabriel. To be sure, since some players were paid, others were not, while yet others paid to be allowed to play (see Rogerson, "Casting the Weavers' Pageant," 138–47), we can never be absolutely certain that the absence of a character from the accounts means that he had been dropped from the cast. But further corroboration for only two actors playing the angels' roles is the citation in the Weavers' accounts of the repair of only two angels' crowns at the cost of 2*d* (*REED: Coventry*, 285). It seems here that Croo's intention was that the speech of the first angel would awaken Simeon, and the second would announce what will transpire at the temple.

307–08. offurde schal be/ Vnto thy honde. The Christ Child will be offered into Simeon's hands.

315. I am lyghtar a M folde. "I am a thousand times lighter. . . ."

319. In gorgis araye. Simeon promises that the temple will be made gloriously ready for the Prince of Peace.

322. to owre tempull draw we nere. Simeon, who is speaking to his clerks (see 321 *s.d.*), indicates that they now are setting out to go to the temple; they arrive at the temple after bells are rung, and they sing at l. 364. More than one clerk is also specified at l. 608, when Simeon asks them to perform their roles in the rite which is to be done. Only one clerk speaks, and according to the sixteenth-century Weavers' Account Book the payment of between 1*s* 8*d* and 2*s* seems large for this role unless this clerk was the leader of the singers. Singers are regularly noted in the sixteenth-century Weavers Account Book, where payments of 16*d* were normally paid to them; they are also identified as "clarkes" (*REED: Coventry*, 183).

352–53. Won of hus mvst holde the lyght/ Ande the othur the sacrefyce. The candle and the sacrificial animals that Joseph and Mary will bring. Concerning candles, see Shorr, "The Iconographic Development," 27.

354. I on kneis. Simeon indicates that he will kneel as he performs the rite or "offece" involving the Child Jesus.

357–60. hast we this alter to araye . . . smellis. They will place altarcloths on the altar (see also l. 609, below), and strew flowers on the "grownde." With regard to the latter detail, see Shorr, "The Iconographic Development," 30.

364. *Cantant.* The music to be sung during the ringing of the bells is not specified. Payments that were entered in the sixteenth-century Weavers' Account Book to singers indicates the availability of singers, and from 1554 to 1573 the wait James Hewet was also on hand to play the regals. The text of Song I at the end of the Weavers' manuscript may have been intended to be sung here.

365 *s.d.* *Semeon*n *and his clarkis gothe vp to the tempull, and Gaberell cumyth to the tempull dore.* The temple is apparently on a wagon stage, and the previous action has most likely been played on the platea. The temple has an entry door and presents an interior to the audience. According to Ludolphus of Saxony, whose *Vita Jesu Christi* was well known in England, the temple was a round structure with eight sides and marble columns (1.12, as cited by

Shorr, "The Iconographic Development," 30n). The architectural design of the Weavers' pageant wagon is not recorded. The stage direction that has Gabriel coming to the door of the temple to greet Mary seems entirely wrong unless it is from this position that he addresses her as she remains in a nearby location such as a supplementary stage. Still, this placement would be extremely odd, since at l. 373 he orders her to go to the temple. Whatever the staging, the appearance of Gabriel would have been reminiscent of the Annunciation—an appearance also stressed by the text "Hayle, Mare," which echoes the words of the angel to her on the earlier occasion.

374. to whyt turtuls. See Luke 2:24. Turtledoves, required in the Purification rite, as specified by Leviticus 12:8 if "she is not able to offer a lamb." Young pigeons were also allowed as an alternative to turtledoves, but *The Golden Legend* explains that this bird would have been unsatisfactory in this circumstance since it is "lascivious" in contrast to the dove which is a "virtuous bird" (1:146). The choice of turtledoves instead of a lamb verifies the poverty of Joseph and Mary (see Jacobus de Voragine, *The Golden Legend*, 1:146, and Love, *Mirror of the Blessed Life of Jesus Christ*, 47).

378–80. Josoff . . . mvste be won/ In this sacrefyce doyng. Joseph as the (presumed) father is required to take part in the ritual.

394. I pray here knelynge. Mary kneels during her prayer (ll. 391–94). Was she in a posture of kneeling before Gabriel during his speech to her?

395–402. cu*m* heddur to me . . . we do nott mys. Mary takes up the Child Jesus, and at l. 398 kisses him. When she "*goth to Josoff*" (l. 403 *s.d.*) the text following indicates that he has been sleeping. The role of the Christ Child was taken by a "lettell chyld" in 1549, and in the 1550s the Weavers' Account Book indicates that payments, usually of 4*d*, actually were paid to the child's mother (*REED: Coventry*, 183, 189, 196, 199). Payments to the "chylde," who is distinguished in the records from "Ihesu" in the Doctors segment, continue until the suppression of the Coventry cycle in 1579.

412–15. Now, Mare . . . You neu*er* cawll but I am reddy. Joseph responds testily to Mary. This response introduces the fabliau-like scene that is to follow in which Joseph resumes the aged- and aggrieved-husband role. His speech is characterized by frequent use of proverbs (see Whiting, *Proverbs in the Earlier English Drama*, 30–31, and, more comprehensively, Ishii, "Joseph's Proverbs").

420. Thatt offeryng fawlyth for owre degre. They must provide two turtledoves but are not responsible for a lamb on account of their low "degre" or socio-economic level. Joseph will object his eyesight is so poor (l. 422) that he will not be able to obtain the birds. He is also so weak that he may fall over a twig and would have trouble getting up if he should fall (ll. 434–36).

429–30. woll I neu*er* vast my wyttis/ To wayte or pry whe<re> the wodkoce syttis. The allusion is to a proverbial saying mentioning the woodcock: "As wise as a Woodcock" (see Tilley, W746). Ishii provides a gloss: "Joseph says that he will never be so witless as to seek a woodcock's hiding place; he is a fool who goes looking for a woodcock nest, since they are so hard to find" (51).

445. the weykist gothe eyu*er* to the walle. Proverbial. Tilley, W185. Ishii ("Joseph's Proverbs," 50) cites John Heywood, *A Dialogue of Proverbs*, ed. Rudolph E. Habenicht (Berkeley and Los Angeles: University of California Press, 1963), ll. 1864–65: "That dede without words shal dryue him to the wal,/ And further than the wall, he can not go."

453. Thosse tythingis ar but cold. Incomplete proverb (Ishii, "Joseph's Proverbs," 50).

455–56. he thatt ma worst of all/ The candyll ys lyke to holde. Proverb. Whiting, *Proverbs, Sentences, and Proverbial Phrases*, C23.

464–65. he thatt weddyth a yonge thyng/ Mvst fullfyll all hir byddyng. Proverb. Cf. Whiting, *Proverbs, Sentences, and Proverbial Phrases*, M254.

466. handis wryng. A symbol of despair, sometimes, as in the Wenhaston Doom painting, represented by clasped hands; see Charles E. Keyser, "On a Panel Painting of the Doom Discovered in 1892, in Wenhaston Church, Suffolk," *Archaeologia* 54 (1894): 124.

467. watur his jis. Weep.

470. all this cu*m*pany. The audience, toward which Joseph presumably gestures.

473–74. For the þ*a*t woll nott there wyffis plese,/ . . . dysees. Proverbial.

483–84. feyre wordis ffull ofte . . . mynd. Proverbial.

489–90. Full well schall you spede . . . wyllyngly. Proverbial.

501. Eyu*er* the worse yend of the staff to haue. Proverbial. Whiting, *Proverbs, Sentences, and Proverbial Phrases*, E89; Tilley, E132.

514. Among these heggis. Most likely Joseph is asking the members of the audience to engage their imaginations in visualizing hedges. But the text does indicate that Joseph has moved away from Mary and the Child, and at l. 517 he sits, whereupon the angel demands that he should arise to receive the birds.

539. haue them in thy honde. Embedded stage direction. Joseph, who has received the doves from the angel at l. 523, now will hand them over to Mary.

552–53. Soo full of feyre wordis . . . must nedis agre. Proverbial.

571–72. Take vp youre chylde . . ./ And walke we . . . essele. Embedded stage directions. At l. 574 Mary will also take up "thys gere"—i.e., the doves—herself since Joseph is too feeble to carry it as they set out for the temple in "Jerusalem." Presumably she also carries the Child.

582. Awake. The angel awakens Simeon, who seems to have been sleeping at the temple, where he has been waiting.

593–94. can noo tong tell,/ Nor hand *with* pen subscrybe. Cf. I Corinthians 2:9: "That eye hath not seen, nor ear heard, neither hath it entered into the heart of man, what things God hath prepared for them that love him."

605. thatt he m*ar*ke me for won of his. Cf. Ephesians 4:30: "whereby you are sealed unto the day of redemption."

609. this awter . . . aray. Usually the altar is freestanding and covered by an altarcloth, as in the *Biblia Pauperum*, 53, and the *Speculum humanae salvationis* (Wilson and Wilson, 160). In these examples Simeon appears as the high priest at the right, while Mary at the left places her child upon the altar. The Smiths' records from Chester for 1571–72 list payment of 10*d* "for lone of a Cope an Altercloth *and* tunecle" for their Purification play (*REED: Chester*, 91). In the illumination in British Library MS. Harley 2887, fol. 58, the altar has a frontal and white altarcloth. The initial in the Carmelite Missal (British Library, MS. Add. 29704–5, fol. 93) has a small square altar of the Greek type (Rickert, *The Reconstructed Carmelite Missal*, 103, pl. IX).

621. myrrele the bellis ryng. Embedded stage direction. The bell ringing concludes at l. 630. Bells also ring in the Towneley Purification pageant (see *Towneley Plays* 17.102–14), and in that play their ringing is spontaneous.

633. How myrrely thatt ye can syng. *Cantant.* They sing. The music is not specified, but it appears that processional music is used as Simeon, his clerks, and Anna go forth to meet Mary, Joseph, and the Child, probably at the door of the temple (placed, according to l. 702 *s.d.*, on the "*vpp*er *parte*" of the pageant wagon), as the holy family approaches in procession, presumably across the platea. The second of the songs at the end of the manuscript seems not exactly appropriate in this case (see Rastall, *Heaven Singing*, 1:264), and in earlier years Latin liturgical music would most likely have been used. The procession here and to the altar is an important one, since it was regarded as the model for Candlemas processions; see the *Stanzaic Life*, ll. 2941–72. Mirk notes the practice of bearing "a candyll yn processyon, as þagh þay ȝedyn bodyly w*yth* oure lady to chyrch, and aftyr offyr wyth hyr yn worschip and high reuerens of hur" (*Festial* 59). Candlemas was a red letter day in the calendar and remained so after the Reformation.

636. in flesch and blode. A reminder of the connection between the incarnate Christ, his Passion, and the Eucharist. The presentation of the Child in this play represents a type of the Mass.

654–57. Reyseve . . . Here in thi hondis take hym the. Mary hands the Child to Simeon, who will hold him in his arms as he speaks (see l. 692 *s.d.*), and as he holds him Anna likewise welcomes the "Kyng of kyngis" (ll. 667–75). This moment, as the Child is received into the temple by Simeon, involves the fulfillment of prophecy. The *Biblia Pauperum* displays the figure of the prophet Malachi above with a scroll containing Malachi 3:1: "veniet ad templum suum dominator quem vos quaeritis" ("the Lord, whom you seek, shall come to his temple"). For the iconography of this scene, see Shorr, "Iconographic Development," 24, 26. Simeon may have had his hands ceremonially covered as in Byzantine depictions of the scene and in the Carmelite Missal, fol. 93 (Rickert, *The Reconstructed Carmelite Missal*, 103, pl. IX).

668. Mak*er* of all mankynd. Jesus, though now a child, nevertheless as the second person of the Trinity is identified as the Creator.

686–87. Of this worlde the lant*er*ne cl*er*e,/ Of whom all lyght schall spryng. The mention of light echoes the *Nunc dimittis*: "Now thou dost dismiss thy servant, O Lord, according to thy word in peace; Because my eyes have seen thy salvation, Which thou hast prepared before the face of all people: A light to the revelation of the gentiles, and the glory of thy people Israel." Attention also was thus directed to the candle carried in the procession (see l. 352). In the *Biblia Pauperum* the candle is held at the altar by the prophetess Anna.

692 *s.d. Semeon goth to the awtere.* Simeon takes the Child to the altar, upon which the Child will be placed. Unfortunately the text is missing at this point in the play since fol. 10 was lost in the manuscript before it was transcribed by Thomas Sharp. Rastall believes that this lacuna appears when Simeon "may be about to sing *Nunc dimittis*" (*Heaven Singing*, 1:263), which appeared in English service books as a canticle, a tract, and an antiphon (Dutka, *Music in the English Mystery Plays*, 35). For the visual effect in this scene, compare the examples in the visual arts in which the Child is frequently naked, as may have been the case in the example in painted glass at Wroxall (see Davidson and Alexander, *The Early Art*, fig. 40); however, the *Biblia Pauperum* has the Child clothed in a simple robe, and this is the most likely manner in which Jesus would have been displayed on the altar in the Coventry pageant. At Wroxall, a figure, probably Joseph (whose body appears above in the restored glass), holds the basket with the two turtledoves. In painted glass in the north clerestory at Great Malvern, the child Jesus, who has been placed on a square altar, is clad in a red garment (Rushforth, *Medieval Christian Imagery*, 106, fig. 39).

695. For the interpolated stage direction designating the introduction of Jesus in a scarlet gown at the top of fol. 11^r, see Textual Notes.

698. To goo before now I woll asaye. Joseph will go ahead, leaving Mary and the Child to follow. In processions the rule was that "the last shall be first"; see Matthew 19:30.

719–1187. The episode of Jesus before the Doctors in the Temple follows on directly from the Presentation in mid-folio with no indication of a pause in the action. This part of the play, drawing on the account in Luke 2:40–52, falls into three distinct actions: the Holy Family's journey to Jerusalem and Jesus' separation from Mary and Joseph; Jesus' disputation with the Doctors; and then Jesus' reunion with Mary and Joseph and their departure for Nazareth. In the gospel account, Mary and Joseph are not given distinct actions and reactions to the loss of their son, but the Coventry playwright, by maintaining the characterization he has established already in the play, constructs a more vivid and accessible account of the parents' anguish at losing their child and the joy at his rediscovery than is the case in any of the other versions of the episode in the cycles with which this episode is closely related. See Kline, "Structure, Characterization, and the New Community in Four Plays of the Doctors," 344–57.

In the first action (ll. 719–807) Jesus, now a child of twelve, will accompany his parents to Jerusalem, which according to the biblical account they visit every year faithfully "at the solemn day of the pasch." The dramatization of this part of this biblical story is unique, and appears in no other English play. In the sixteenth century the Weavers' Account Book records consistent payments of 1*s* 8*d* to the actor who played Jesus, who is differentiated from the child who played the infant in the Purification. That these payments begin in the extant accounts before Croo's revisions to the Weavers' pageant proves that the two segments of the Purification and the Doctors in the Temple were joined prior to 1535. The earliest Weavers' accounts to record payments to Jesus, however, are from 1525 (*REED: Coventry*, 124), a date later than the revisions that were made to the plays when they were described as new in 1519 (ibid., 114). The payments for "solyng of Iesus hose," "for settyng one of Ihesus sleues," and "for payntyng of Iesus heade" noted in the Weavers' Rentgatherers' Book in 1564 refer to the twelve-year-old boy (ibid., 226). At Chester payments were frequently made "for gelldinge of Gods fase" (*REED: Chester*, 53 and passim), so it is possible that the twelve-year-old Jesus at Coventry also wore a mask or had his face gilded directly; for the connection between the Chester and Coventry plays, see the note on l. 808, below.

721. soo goodly a childe. See Luke 2:40, where Jesus is described as "strong, full of wisdom; and the grace of God was in him." In contrast, the speaker, Joseph, should rightly have been presented as even older than in the previous Purification scenes, and on their journey to Jerusalem would have been walking with the help of a walking staff.

727. he ys xij yere of age. This is the only indication of the lapse of time between this section of the play and the preceding Purification.

735. Now Jh*esus* . . . whatt chere? It seems likely that the boy-actor playing Jesus enters on this line of greeting from Mary.

742. An emendation in a later hand gives the words "Now Gods blyssyng haue *and* myne" in the margin; if these words were used in later productions of the play, Jesus would have been seen dispensing his blessing, undoubtedly with the appropriate gesture, in the name of the Father and the Son.

744. Yt ys eyrly scharp thatt wol be thorne. Proverbial.

745. How glad he ys his modr to pleyse. An important conception in late medieval popular theology. Jesus will not deny anything to his mother, and even in depictions of the Last Day of history she is present as intercessor on the behalf of sinners.

747. my vthe frome me be vorne. Joseph is again harping on his extreme old age.

753. this owre festefawll dey. Mary and Joseph will take Jesus with them to Jerusalem for the celebration of the Passover: "in die sollemni pasche" (Luke 2:41).

754–799. The structure of the Doctors' play is here given a more elaborate framework than in the other versions. Jesus is created as the plausibly childlike son of the elderly Joseph, who finds domestic duties burdensome, and Mary, his gentle but firmly persuasive wife.

763. Mare, leyde ye the wey. Imbedded stage direction. Mary goes ahead, with Jesus whom she holds by the hand (see l. 770, but cf. l. 773 as emended by a later hand), and the aged Joseph follows.

765. far furth on the dey. The time is late in the day.

766. owre fryndis. A reference to others who are also going to Jerusalem; these do not appear as characters in the play.

773. lett hym goo before ye and me. The words "before ye and me," added in by a later hand in the margin in the manuscript, suggest that the child shall go ahead.

778–79. I am full redde . . . bydding in weyle *and* woo. Jesus demonstrates his proper obedience to his parents.

789. benedicete. Here meaning "praise God."

790–91. Yong chyldur . . ./ Nor wase then an olde mon*n*. "If young children are not wiser nowadays, I am not an old man."

792. Now welcu*m* be owre Lordis sond. Mary's words remind the audience that her obedient child is also the Second Person of the Trinity, as she acknowledges the efficacy of her son's blessing.

797. My leggis byn were . . . soore. These words serve as an imbedded stage direction to indicate that Joseph should be even more uncertain on his legs than at the beginning of the journey to Jerusalem—a journey which in fact has been only a short distance for the actors to walk.

798–99. That man thatt canot go before/ . . . behynd. Proverbial.

800 s.d. ***all goo vp to the awter . . . syng an antem.*** The altar, located in the "temple," would presumably utilize the same stage setting on the pageant wagon as for the scene of the Purification. In this scene Jesus goes up first. There is no indication of the nature of the anthem that was sung, but prior to the Reformation it was conventional that an item appropriate to the occasion might be chosen from liturgical usage. The question has been raised whether the anthem was a processional item, but Rastall observes that the movement of the actors to the altar and the singing need not have been simultaneous (*Heaven Singing* 1:224). The lines which follow do not suggest any further ritual, and hence a sung procession to the altar without anything further done at that location would appear anti-climactic. Rastall is therefore likely to be correct about envisioning a silent procession prior to the singing at the altar. The procession and singing at the altar must be seen as symbolic of the "pompe *and* solempnite" of the eight-day festival to which Love makes reference in *The Mirror of the Blessed Life of Jesus Christ*, 57. The singers and instrumentalists to whom payments by the Weavers were recorded must have been involved again in the music here.

808 s.d. ***the goo done into the for-pagond and Jhes*****us** ***steylyth awey.*** The "for-pagond" would seem to have been the same as the "forp*ar*te" mentioned in the Coventry Cappers' records. If so, the Weavers' pageant would have utilized a more complex wagon stage than offered by a single wagon. As for Jesus' disappearance, however, no complicated effect is necessary; he seems merely to slip away when Mary and Joseph go down from the altar.

808. Beginning with this line, the play follows the Spurriers and Lorimers' play in the York Register, which Greg claimed contains the "most original form" of the pageant ("Bibliographical and Textual Problems," 298), though this text seems not to have been the direct source of the Coventry pageant. The actual source of the Coventry play may have been a lost York guild copy which existed independently from the compilation in the possession of the Corporation. The same guild copy may then also have been the source of the Doctors play in the Towneley collection. Greg notes, however, that the Coventry version of the play has been "practically rewritten in a different and very irregular metre. Comparatively few lines have escaped more or less profound alteration, but there remain yet considerable sections in which the text is in a general way parallel" (ibid., 300). In turn, Coventry and Chester are said by Greg to appear to have been the derived from a common source (ibid., 313). For further discussion, see Kline, "Structure, Characterization, and New Community," 344–57. Joseph's opening lines in the York play are given here for comparison:

> Marie, of mirthis we may vs mene,
> And trewly telle betwixte vs twoo
> Of solempne sightis þat we haue sene
> In þat cite where we come froo. (*York Plays* 20.1–4)

For further comparison of the Coventry Doctors' episode with the York, Towneley, and Chester texts, see Appendix IV.

The imbedded stage direction in the Coventry version implies merely that the holy family have left the temple, not that they have already gone out of the city. Their ecstasy provides sufficient motivation to make credible their subsequent failure to notice that Jesus is missing. In contrast, Love's narrative (*Mirror of the Blessed Life*, 58) has Joseph and Mary taking different routes on the first day of their return journey as the reason for not noticing that Jesus was missing.

812–15. Now serten . . . alsoo. Mary's lines here indicate that a period of time has elapsed during which the Holy Family has participated in the Passover celebrations and Jesus has become separated from his parents, something enacted in dumb-show as indicated by the stage direction at l. 808.

816–49. Mary and Joseph speak while traveling, possibly through the audience between two playing locations.

820–21. Yett in good owre . . . fynde. Cf *York Plays*, 20.13–14: "For gode felawshippe haue we fone/ And ay so forward schall we fynde." Joseph assumes that the child is with others in the group that is returning home from Jerusalem and that he will "ou*er*take" them shortly (see ll. 824–27). There is again no reason to assume that the actors are here accompanied by others to make up such a "cu*m*pany"; instead, the actor probably gestures to the audience standing around.

840. Off sorro now schal be my songe/ . . . I ma see. Love stresses Mary's tender love for her child and her intense anxiety at their loss of him (*Mirror of the Blessed Life*, 58), but also mentions Joseph's weeping as, going about the city, they look for him.

845. ayene to the sytte lett vs goo. Imbedded stage direction. Joseph has suggested the possibility that Jesus has remained in the "sytte" to play with other children (or else he has gone on ahead toward home) at ll. 837–39. Now the actors return to the Jerusalem set. The stage direction following l. 849 has them walking toward the temple precincts, while the focus of attention has turned to the young Jesus and the Doctors. Joseph and Mary will, however, not yet enter the "*tempull*" but rather will go about searching until l. 1020.

850–77. The Doctors are given four stanzas in which to introduce themselves as upholders of the Old Law of Moses. Like others who assert earthly power in the cycles (e.g., Herod, Pilate), Doctor I opens by threatening the audience. Then Doctor II establishes their line of authority back to Moses, and Doctor III enjoins the audience to gather round and listen. Doctor I challenges all comers to enter the debate, which provides Jesus with his cue to intervene. These stanzas thus serve as a springboard for the central scene of the Doctors pageant which follows.

851. Wyche hathe the lawis vndur honde. Who has mastered Jewish law.

852–56. thatt no man fawll . . . ooponnly slayne. Even denial of a single article of Jewish law, according to the legal code, demands capital punishment.

857–59. othur wholle decryis . . . to reymayne. The holy decrees are the Ten Commandments given to Moses; upon them the Doctors will hold a disputation (see ll. 862–63). The choice of the Ten Commandments has been seen to be influenced by the Gospel of Thomas, which reported that Jesus "put to silence the elders and teachers of the people, expounding the heads of the law and parables of the prophets" (*The Apocryphal New Testament*, 54). See Cawley, "Middle English Metrical Versions of the Decalogue," 133–34.

863. Be polatike syence of clarge clere. Cf. *York Plays* 20.54: "Be clargy clere if we couthe knawe. . . ."

864–67. all peple . . . aleygence. The audience is asked to pay attention to the didactic matter which is to be expounded. Ironically, it will not be the Doctors but Jesus who will do the teaching.

878ff. Unlike Mary and Joseph's search for Jesus which is not represented in iconography, the scene with the Doctors, selecting the moment when his parents arrive, is fairly common, though there are no extant examples from Coventry or indeed from anywhere in Warwickshire. However, the scene appears in painted glass at Great Malvern, York, and East Harling, and there are manuscript illuminations as well as roof bosses at Norwich Cathedral. The Great Malvern glass, dated c.1501, depicts Jesus with a white-and-gold cross nimbus and in a gold-bordered blue tunic, while the Doctors appear in fur-lined hoods and academic caps and gowns. One doctor holds a book, another a parchment roll. Jesus is placed on a high seat, which is also designated in the Coventry play at l. 1022: "he syttyth aloft" (cf. *The N-Town Play* 21.145 *s.d.*). In this glass the gestures indicate that an argument is taking place just as Mary and Joseph appear at the left rear (Rushforth, *Medieval Christian Imagery*, 382, fig. 174). In glass of c.1375 in the choir of York Minster the elders in the temple are reading from books on lecterns (Davidson and O'Connor, *York Art*, 60). At Fairford Jesus is raised very high above the Doctors (Wayment, *The Stained Glass*, pl. VI), while at East

Harling a purple-robed Christ sits in a seat, also raised up very high, which is in fact a throne (Woodforde, *The Norwich School*, 47, pl. XIII). In British Library MS. 2887 an enthroned Christ holds an open book, while the Doctors, in their distinctive academic caps, also hold open books (Scott, *Later Gothic Manuscripts*, fig. 478); in another mid-fifteenth-century book of hours in the British Library, MS. Add. 62,523, fol. 26^{v}, Jesus has his index finger of his right hand raised to make a point, while the other hand also is raised in a conventional rhetorical gesture as he speaks in response to his parents' arrival. In the latter miniature one of the Doctors studies a parchment roll, while others are gesturing in surprise (ibid., fig. 378). A. C. Cawley calls attention to a roof boss at Norwich Cathedral that shows the boy Jesus seated on a throne, with an open book on his lap, and with his right hand raised before four Doctors who also hold books and who wear ermine tippets (*The Revels History of Drama*, 1: fig. 2). The boy Jesus conventionally has bare feet. For a general discussion of the iconography of this scene, see Schiller, *Iconography of Christian Art* 1:124–25.

The text of the Weavers' play reveals only that the Doctors' costumes include fine furs (l. 1033), that they have books (l. 955), and that they are seated during the session with the boy Jesus (ll. 1033, 1043). Interestingly, there are no payments noted in the Weavers' accounts to the Doctors, who must have played without fee. In contrast, Chester's Doctors were paid regularly for playing in the Smiths' pageant in the sixteenth century.

878–79. Lordis . . . pes be amonge this cu*m*pany. Jesus' entry, presumably making the sign of blessing, perhaps to the audience as well as the Doctors (the Coventry play substitutes "pes" for York's "mirthis" [20.74]). In contrast, the Chester play extends the substance of these two lines into an explicit statement of his divinity which alters the balance and emphasis of the ensuing disputation in the play. For further comparison of the section of the play which follows with close parallels in the York, Towneley, and Chester versions, see Appendix IV.

880–906. In the Coventry play as in York, Chester, and Towneley, the Doctors respond in the same way to Jesus' intervention. He is precocious, sent to them by foolish adults who do not realize that he is too young, but nonetheless he is invited to stay to learn about

Moses' law. Jesus' response that he need learn nothing from them is dismissed, and he is invited to join them.

903–04. in those placis haue I be/ Where all owre lawis furst were wrought. He has participated in the divine Being, the origin of all law. Cf. *The Chester Mystery Cycle* 11.233–38 for an explicit statement concerning his relation to the Godhead. Below, at ll. 911–14, Jesus claims the inspiration of the Holy Ghost, and at ll. 917–18 he affirms his eternity, answering Doctor III's question "Whense cam thys chylde[?]"

907 *s.d. the doctoris settyth Cryst among them.* See commentary on ll. 878ff, above, and the note on l. 1020, below. Jesus is placed on a raised seat or throne.

911. the Whoole Gost in me hath lyght. Jesus affirms his divine parentage. Mary conceived by the power of the Holy Ghost. The Holy Ghost is also associated with the gift of preaching, particularly in connection with the gift of tongues conferred upon the apostles at Pentecost.

923–27. For ase Davith in his salme . . . lovyng. Citation of Psalm 8:3: "Out of the mouths of infants and sucklings thou hast perfected praise." The Latin text is not quoted in the York Spurriers and Lorimers' play but appears in the Towneley pageant (*Towneley Plays* 18.90a), which is closely based on York; however, the translation of the text in the Weavers' play, ll. 926–27, follows *York Plays* 20.115–16 closely. See Appendix IV. In the Coventry play, as in the other versions, one of the doctors is prepared to accept that Jesus may have something to teach them in fulfillment of this verse from the Psalms (see ll. 928–29). The same verse is later to be quoted by Jesus, according to Matthew 21:16, in his attack on the temple in Jerusalem.

933. ar at no charge. Cf. *York Plays* 20.120: "are noȝt to charge."

941. neu*er* arre. Jesus astoundingly promises that his interpretation of the law will be infallible.

946. Ase wyde in worde asse eyu*er* I went. "As widely as I have traveled in the world." Cf.*York Plays* 20.133: "Als wyde in worlde als we haue wente."

948–49. But I troo amonst vs he be sent . . . saluer of owre sore. Doctor III, who was prepared to accept Jesus as teacher above, seems willing here to consider that he may be the Messiah, the "healer of the wound" of the Fall. The attribution of these two speeches to Doctor III by the dramatist creates for him a distinct character as the least dismissive of the three.

952–1005. There is no direct source in the Gospels for the central section of the disputation, common to Coventry, York, Towneley, and Chester; see note to ll. 857–59, above, and especially Cawley, "Middle English Versions of the Decalogue with Reference to the English Corpus Christi Cycles," 129–45. The Ten Commandments formed part of staple material with which every lay Christian in the period of the pageants was supposed to be familiar and on which every priest was expected to offer instruction.

955. youre bokys here leyde on breyde. Imbedded stage direction; cf. *York Plays* 20.142: "And has youre bokes on brede." See commentary on ll. 878ff, above, for examples in the visual arts in which the Doctors hold books.

958–63. I rede . . . yll. Doctor II recites the summary of the law from Matthew 22:37–40 (derived from Deuteronomy 6:5 and Leviticus 19:18) rather than the first two of the Ten Commandments. Jesus will explain in the lines following (ll. 966–67) that these two great commandments are the foundation not only of the Old Law of Moses but also of the New Law of Christ.

970–89. Jesus recites the third through the tenth Commandments.

980–81. To fle advltre . . . yll. Cf. *York Plays* 178–80, where the command is "to flee/ All filthes of flesshely synne."

986. forbyddeth othys grett. Swearing of oaths is forbidden.

988–89. þou schuldist no covett/ Thy neyburs goodis. *York Plays* 20.188–89 forbids instead the taking "be stresse" thy neighbor's "wiffe nor his women"—i.e., a prohibition against rape.

994–95. Beholde owre lawis . . . to rede. The remarkable thing is that he is able to "expounde" the Ten Commandments even though he has not been taught to read. For this assertion concerning Jesus' literacy at age twelve, see *York Plays* 20.194; it is suppressed in the Chester play. Woolf, however, comments that "in the Middle Ages it cannot have been a feat for a twelve-year-old boy to be able to rehearse such a standard piece of Christian teaching" (*The English Mystery Plays*, 213). The Coventry Doctors, as in the biblical text, are "astonished at his wisdom and his answers" (Luke 2:47), but they also are envious of the boy's learning. They are now ready to send Jesus on his way, but this does not agree with the biblical text which has Mary and Joseph discover him in the midst of discussion with the Doctors in the temple (Luke 2:46). Love too explains that they "fonden him sittyng among þe doctours of lawe heryng hem ententlv, *and* askyng hem questiones wisyly" (*Mirror of the Blessed Life*, 59). In the Coventry play as the Doctors discuss letting Jesus go, his mother and Joseph have appeared "*sekyng þis chylde*" (l. 1006 *s.d.*). Later, at ll. 1081–82, Doctor II seems comfortable with inviting Jesus to stay with them in the temple.

1006ff. The third and final action of the Doctors play is greatly expanded in the Coventry version. In it Mary and Joseph arrive at the temple to rediscover Jesus, and after their reunion set off with him for Nazareth again, while the Doctors discuss the encounter.

1014–15. In sorro wasse there neyu*er* man more . . . amend. Proverbial. See Whiting, *Proverbs in the Earlier English Drama*, 32.

1018–19. Yff chyldurs cu*m*pany . . . full ryght. Dramatic irony. The reason that Jesus is "[a]bowt yondur tempull" is very different from his having found children with whom to play. At l. 1071 it is revealed that Mary and Joseph's search has taken three days.

1020. I see thatt I haue soght. Embedded stage direction. Mary and Joseph have now arrived back at the temple, where they see the Child with the Doctors. At l. 1022 Mary comments that he is sitting "aloft"; see commentary on ll. 878ff, above.

1027. Goo ye *and* feyche youre chylde *and* myne. Mary commands Joseph to fetch Jesus out of the temple, but to little effect.

1031–32. Asse I haue tolde you . . . mell. Joseph, a simple and aged carpenter, is intimidated by the Doctors, who are of higher social class, and he wishes quite simply to avoid meeting them. His inability, because of his physical condition, to kneel before his social superiors is also a factor; in ll. 1040–41 he states that he is likely to be shamed because he cannot any longer bow or kneel.

1033. furis fyn. The Doctors' academic garments include fur, presumably fur tippets.

1042. Then goo we theddur bothe to. Embedded stage direction. As Mary indicates in ll. 1044–45, however, if Joseph refuses she must go into the temple alone.

1050. My place . . . schal be behynd. Joseph reiterates that his status is inferior to Mary's. Embedded stage direction.

1051–58. Based on Luke 2:48: "And his mother said to him: Son, why hast thou done so to us? behold thy father and I have sought thee sorrowing."

1059–62. Modur, why did you seke me soo?/ . . . for well or woo. For Jesus' words to his mother, see Luke 2:49. The York version differs slightly: "My fadir werkis, for wele or woo,/ Thus am I sente for to fulfyll" (*York Plays* 20.259–60).

1067–74. Added by the Coventry dramatist, these lines have two adults discussing Jesus over his head, as it were, and thus adding to the play's characterization of him as plausibly childlike.

1081–82. yff thow wolt tarre . . . cost. Doctor II invites Jesus to stay in the temple; see comment on ll. 994–95, above. In the following speech, Doctor III turns to Joseph to see if he will allow Jesus to stay. Both Joseph and Mary refuse permission.

1086–92. Noo, *sir*, . . . But hade I hym wonis be the fyst . . . doo

soo. Another extrapolation by the Coventry dramatist adding substance to relationships within the Holy Family, particularly Joseph's threat to keep hold of Jesus "be the fyst" to prevent him from wandering off again.

1107–08. Yff thow to age lyve may,/ . . . glade. Cf. *York Plays* 20.275–76: "He schall, and he haue liff,/ Proue till a praty swayne." The Coventry play retreats from the symbolism implied by the York text and merely is suggestive of high childhood mortality.

1115–18. And geve you well to fare. . . . Joseph's farewell to the Doctors; this is parallel to Joseph's final line in the York play: "Fares wele all folke in feere" (*York Plays* 20.288). In the Coventry play, Joseph and Mary with Jesus now prepare to depart from the temple pageant and set out for Nazareth after a more extended leave-taking.

1132–39. Now farewell, my fryndis all . . . do soo. Joseph's farewell to the members of the audience, who are enjoined to please their wives, maintains the fabliau characterization of him as an elderly hen-pecked husband, established in the beginning of the play, right up to the end.

1140–85. The Coventry playwright adds the concluding dialogue in which the Doctors discuss their encounter with Jesus. Kline notes that, rather than having the Doctors relate different views of Jesus as at York, this dialogue "homogenizes their characterization" as the play closes ("Structure, Characterization, and the New Community," 352).

1173. In hart foreyu*er* w*ith* you to dwell. I.e., in eternity.

Colophon. See commentary on the Colophon to the Shearmen and Taylors' pageant, above. The date of completion of this manuscript by Robert Croo is 2 March 1535 (1534 old style). The masters of the Weavers' guild in this year were Richard Smith and a Mr. Pyxley (possibly Harry Pixley; see Introduction, above).

The Songs. The name Thomas Mawdycke appears at the top of the page, presumably here, as for the songs accompanying the Shearmen and Taylors' pageant, the copyist. The songs are, however, written in different hands. See the commentary on the songs in the Introduction, above.

Song I. Dutka, no. 2 (English Songs).

Song II. Dutka, no. 5 (English Songs). Where this song would have been intended for use in the Weavers' play is a very good question. It is a Passion lyric consistent with the Protestant theology of the atonement, and could have been written during either Catholic or Protestant times. For Christ's dying on the cross like a meek lamb, see James Marrow, *Passion Iconography* (Kortrijk: Van Ghemmert, 1979), 96–99.

APPENDIX II

1. THE RECEPTION OF QUEEN MARGARET

Queen Margaret's entry into Coventry on 14 September 1456 came during the period of dynastic struggle between the houses of Lancaster and York. In the previous year the mayor and council had responded to a request by the Crown for troops before the battle of St. Albans by sending one hundred men along with equipment for them (*Leet Book*, ed. Harris, 2:282–83). Margaret's husband, King Henry VI, was effectively unable to rule in 1456 on account of a bout of madness, and Margaret was attempting to assert her power in the realm. The author of the speeches presented in this pageantry may have been John Wedurby of Leicester, who was paid (see ll. 160–61) for his work in "makyng" and staging them. The sum of £21 13*s* 2*d* suggests that he was a pageant master responsible for the expenses of the pageantry, and that he was paid on a contract basis to handle all the finances. Nothing further is known of Wedurby.

4. a Iesse ou*er* the yate. Jesse tree; genealogical tree growing up from Jesse to the Virgin Mary and Christ, positioned over Bablake Gate (Spon Gate on Map). Jeremiah refers to "the rote of Iesse" in l. 17, below, where the queen and her son Prince Edward are "likkyn[ed]" to the Virgin Mary and her Son. The comparison has already been made in Isaiah's speech which at ll. 10–11 compares the birth of Edward in 1453 to the Nativity. See also comment on the Shearmen and Taylor's pageant, l. 9, above, and also similar use of the Jesse tree iconography in the Entry of the Duke of Burgundy into Bruges in 1440 (Kipling, *Enter the King*, 54–56).

21. a pagent right well arayed. Here designating a pageant wagon, which was positioned at the east end of Bablake Church. This location seems to have been a favored one, and as late as 1566 the Tanners' pageant wagon stood "Att Saint John's Church" for the entry of Queen Elizabeth I (*REED: Coventry*, 234).

40–58. Speeches of the Four Cardinal Virtues. Rightwesnes is Justice, normally depicted from Carolingian times holding a set of scales or balances but later given a related instrument such as a carpenter's square; Temperaunce's usual iconography included a torch and a container of water, as at Canterbury Cathedral; Strengh[th] is Fortitude, who is usually armed with sword and shield; Prudence often holds a snake and a dove. See Katzenellenbogen, *Allegories of the Virtues and Vices*, 55–56; Madeline Harrison Caviness, *The Early Stained Glass of Canterbury Cathedral* (Princeton: Princeton University Press, 1977), figs. 106–07; and also Mâle, *Religious Art in France*, 2:112.

23–29. The speaker represented St. Edward, i.e., Edward the Confessor, whose shrine stands in Westminster Abbey which was completed during his lifetime. The ring which he gives to the prince replicates his identifying symbol. Edward is said to have given a ring to a beggar, and later pilgrims from the Holy Land returned it to him with the explanation that it had been given to them by an old man claiming to be St. John the Evangelist. St. John will deliver the next speech, again addressing the prince (ll. 30–36).

37–38. the Cundit yn the Smythforde strete was right well arayed. London had very likely provided the model for the conversion of water conduits into stages; see Wickham, *Early English Stages,* 1:58, and Withington, *English Pageantry*, passim. For the location of Smithford Street, see Map.

57. We shall p*reser*ue you . . . disseu*er*. A pledge of loyalty, normally expected of a city when receiving a king or prince.

59–61. at the Crosse yn the Croschepyng . . . diu*er*se angels sensyng a high on the Crosse . . . there ranne out wyne. Nothing is said of a speech or singing at this station, but it is hard to believe that the spectacle did not include sounds as well as sights. For angels in the visual arts from Coventry which have survived, see Davidson and Alexander, *The Early Art*, 15–17. Fountains running wine were intended to show the largess of the city but also had a symbolic significance in that they were to be regarded as reflecting Isaiah 12:3: "You shall draw waters with joy out of the saviour's fountains"; see the discussion in Kipling, *Enter the King*, 165–66.

62–63. betwix the seyde Crosse *and* the Cundit . . . were sette ix pagents . . . ix Conqueroures. Nine pageant wagons were lined up; from them were spoken the speeches of the Nine Worthies, figures frequently represented as accompanying Dame Fortune, with whom they are shown in a woodcut in Stephen Hawes, *The Example of Vertu* (London, 1530), sig. A2[r] (reproduced in Chew, *The Pilgrimage of Life*, fig. 62). See the mention of Fortune in the speech of Alexander (l. 79). Withington notes that the Worthies were first presented in civic pageantry in Paris in 1431 (*English Pageantry*, 1: 80).

70. this conabull cite, the p*r*inces chambur. Thomas Sharp explains the reference: "As London was called the *Kings Chamber*, and Bristol the *Queens Chamber*, so in numerous instances Coventry is termed the *Princes Chamber*. Sir John Throgmorton, the Recorder of Coventry, in his oration to Queen Elizabeth, in 1565 [sic], says that 'this auncient Citie hath bine of longe tyme called the princes Chamber the iij[de] Citie of youre Realme'" (*Dissertation*, 148n). For the London context and the political use of the imagery of the Song of Songs, see Kipling, *Enter the King*, 16–17. In Coventry, the prince is the Bridegroom and the city is *sponsa*, the mystical body (cf. ibid., 46).

79–81. nobilest p*r*ince . . . Herry . . . I wyll be obeying. Alexander expresses his loyalty to King Henry VI, Queen Margaret's "sou*er*ayn."

83–84. Iosue . . . þ*at* all Egipte was fayne to inclyne. Conqueror of the land of Israel; the text here seems to confuse him with Joseph (see Gen. 41:41).

100. Iudas, þ*a*t in Iure am called the belle. Judas Maccabaeus.

108–10. Arthur, kynge . . . I slowe the Emp*erour*. King Arthur of Britain. The pageant wagon used for Arthur belonged to the Smiths (*REED: Coventry*, 35).

116–18. Charles, chefe cheftan . . . penaunce. Charlemagne, elected as Holy Roman Emperor, was according to legend a hero of battles against pagans and the rescuer of the Holy Land.

119. holy relik*es* of Criste I had in possession. The crown of thorns, wood of the cross, and a nail of the Passion; see Mâle, *Religious Art in France*, 1:306–07.

128. blessyd blossom þ*a*t spronge of yo*ur* body. Prince Edward, again referred to in the context of Jesse Tree symbolism.

132–34. Godfride of Bollayn . . . sone beme. Godfrey of Bouillon, who distinguished himself in the battle for Jerusalem and was appointed its first Latin ruler after its fall in 1099.

139–42. last the Cundit yn the Crossechepyng . . . myracull. The conduit in Cross Cheaping was turned into a stage on which many "virgyns" were positioned. Apparently St. Margaret of Antioch appeared on this set with the dragon, which she killed miraculously, perhaps as in the Coventry Tapestry in St. Mary's Hall merely by stepping on it (Davidson and Alexander, *The Early Art*, 50) though in other cases she thrusts a spear through the creature. This act seems to have been done as mime, followed by her speech, in which she stresses her "power" to relieve "distresse" (l. 150). While in the pageantry for Queen Margaret this saint would have been felt to be most appropriate, she also seems to have been popular in Coventry since she appeared along with St. Catherine and several virgins (usually six or eight) in Corpus Christi processions in 1539–42 and 1544–46 (*REED: Coventry* 152, 155, 157, 162, 170, 173, 174). The queen is encouraged to call upon the saint if she should in future "be yn any dredefull cace" (l. 155).

158. Richard Braytoft. Elected mayor on 25 January 1456. Braytoft personally paid for a ton of wine for the king at the time of the queen's visit; other gifts are listed in the *Leet Book* (ed. Harris, 292).

159. Thomas Bradmedowe *and* John Straunge, late wardens of the fote. Local officials; listed among the ninety-one councillors who met with the mayor in St. Mary's Hall on 28 August 1456 in preparation for the queen's visit. A gift of 100 marks was agreed upon, to be divided between the queen and the prince (*Leet Book*, ed. Harris, 2:285–86).

161. Iohn Wedurby. See headnote to the Reception of Queen Margaret, above.

2. Receiving Prince Edward

Coventry had supported Edward IV in 1460 and had agreed to send troops for his army against the Lancastrians, though there are signs that the city was not entirely united (see *Leet Book*, ed. Harris, 2:308–16). When the king came to Coventry later that year the Leet voted to give him £100 and the customary cup "to his welcome . . . from the felde yn the North" (*Leet Book*, 2:316). No pageantry is recorded for Edward's entry in the *Leet Book*, but the Smiths' accounts include payment of 3*s* 6*d* "for the havyng owght of the pagent when the pryns came yn brede and ale and to Samson wythe hys iij knyghtys and to an harper" as well as 3*d* for "golde for Samsons garments and poyntys" (*Dissertation*, 152; cf. *REED: Coventry*, 40). The city subsequently defected to the cause of the Earl of Warwick, who would be defeated at Barnet in 1471, but the king, following his own victory at Tewkesbury and his reinstatement to the throne, issued a pardon to the mayor, citizens, and other inhabitants of Coventry on 20 June 1472 upon the payment of a heavy fine (*Leet Book*, ed. Harris, 2:367–71, 381). Loyalty of the city to the crown is one of the motifs that appears in the account, which includes texts of speeches, for the entry of Prince Edward and Queen Elizabeth (Woodville) in 1474. The *Leet Book* (ed. Harris, 2:393–94) reports the loyalty oath sworn on 3 May 1474 to Prince Edward that declared him to be the "verray and vndoubted heire" to the throne (*Leet Book*, ed. Harris, 2:394). However, the exact date of the prince's entry is ambiguous, and the day specified in the *Leet Book* may not be correct; see *REED: Coventry*, 554.

2–8. It was customary that upon the arrival of a king or prince that the mayor (in this case Richard Braytoft, Jr.) and other members of the corporation, all of them dressed in livery, should meet him outside the city gates, in this case beyond the New Cross at Stivichall. See also for comparison the entry of Queen Elizabeth I in 1566 (*REED: Coventry*, 232–33).

6. his chaumbr*e*. See note on the Reception of Queen Margaret, l. 70. The terminology appears frequently in the lines which follow.

9. at Babulake yate . . . a stacion*n*. Presumably the prince and his party had entered through Greyfriars gate, had gone up to Smithford Street, and had crossed over to Spon Gate near Bablake Church. The spectacle here probably made use of the architecture of the city gate, where an actor represented King Richard while thirteen others costumed like members of the aristocracy served as supporters of a brief scene in which this king was to speak. The city waits, however, played and undoubtedly provided the trumpet fanfares expected upon the arrival of royalty. The primacy of the trumpet among the waits' instruments was legislated by the Leet; see *REED: Coventry*, 12.

16. We all mowe blesse . . . natiuite. As in the case of Prince Edward, the infant prince here is being told that his birth is, like the Nativity of Jesus, a cause for rejoicing. The speaker is Richard II, the last of the Plantagenet line, who blesses the Yorkist succession.

17. The right lyne of the royall blode. An affirmation of the Yorkist claim to the throne as opposed to the Lancastrian.

20. at the Condite afore Richard Braytoft the Elder another stacion. The station was before the house of the mayor's father, which must have been located in Smithford Street—i.e., the location of the conduit in the Reception of Queen Margaret eighteen years before.

21–22. iij P*at*riarkes . . . w*ith* Iacobus xij sonnes. These figures were standing on the conduit. Also present on the conduit were musicians who were playing harp and dulcimers.

26. as scriptur*e* maketh rehersall. An appeal to biblical authority. The "Patriarkes" are probably the prophets Isaiah, Balaam, and Malachi.

29–31. and now referre itt . . . full reu*er*ent. A parallel between the prince and Christ is given explicit statement here; the entry of a prince into a city was frequently designed to contain echoes of the Palm Sunday liturgy in which the Church calls to mind the entry of Jesus as King into the gates of Jerusalem. The prince is presented *in imitatio Christi*, an important factor for understanding the history of the idolatry directed toward the monarch that continued its existence beyond the Reformation.

32. at the Brodeyate a pagiont. Passing to the end of Smithford Street, the procession with the prince stopped at Broad Gate, where a pageant wagon was waiting with the scene of St. Edward and ten estates. Minstrels, presumably two of the city waits, played harp and lute in this tableau.

37–38. I, Seint Edward, haue pursued for yo*ur* faders imp*er*iall right . . . intent. Edward the Confessor, the prince's and his father's patron saint, refers to the exclusion of King Edward IV from the throne in favor of Henry VI (1461–71).

41. þ*at* that was oures is nowe in yo*ur* faders hande. England, once Edward the Confessor's kingdom, is now in possession of Edward IV.

42–45. at the Crosse in the Croschepyng were iij p*ro*phett*es* . . . seynsyng, and . . . aboven were Childer of Issarell . . . wyne. No speech is recorded for this station, but the "Childer" sing and throw out unconsecrated hosts as well as flowers before the prince. If, as conjectured in our introduction to the text of this royal entry, the scene is related to the entry into Jerusalem, the singing may well have been the chants sung by children in the widespread quasi-dramatic Palm Sunday liturgy in the Sarum rite. In London boy choristers were commonly employed. The boys would sing *Gloria laus et honor* from above, sometimes from specially erected stages, which might also be used to elevate prophets (Davidson, *Illustrations of the Stage and Acting*, 15–17). The use of incense for an anointed one, or in the case of the prince one who is to be anointed as king, would have been thought appropriate. The running of wine from pipes at the Cross would likewise have been an expression of joy over the coming of the prince into the city.

46–48. afore the Panyer, a pageant and iij King*es* of Colen . . . ij knyght*es* armed . . . small pypis. According to Sharp, the Panyer was an "Inn very near to the Cross" (*Dissertation*, 153). It was here that the pageant wagon was set up. The Three Kings of Cologne are, of course, the three Magi who arrive to find the Christ Child at Epiphany. As Craig observes (115), the Shearmen and Taylors would have had costumes in hand for the Magi and hence may have been the sponsors of this pageant. Kipling plausibly believes that each of the Magi presented the prince "with his traditional gift" (*Enter the King*, 32). Such gifts would have affirmed the epiphanal nature of the scene. Music in this instance is of "small pypis."

55–56. Of on of vs thre . . . His nobull moder Quene Elizabeth . . . kynde. The queen is said to be lineally descended from one of the Magi; that is, she is an instrument of epiphany with regard to the prince whom she has brought into being in her womb.

57–60. vpon the Condite in the Croschepyng was Seint George . . . dragon*e*. Finally the conduit in Cross Cheaping was used as a stage to show St. George, who had displaced Edward the Confessor as patron saint of England. The scene that is described is the conventional one in which he is shown in armor killing the dragon and saving the princess while her parents look on from a tower. St. George was particularly popular in Coventry. A woodcarving roughly contemporary with the entry of Prince Edward stood in the Chapel of St. George, Gosford Gate (Davidson and Alexander, *The Early Art*, 47–48, fig. 17), but this only shows the saint, in plate armor, with his sword raised while his horse tramples the dragon, who is clasping a spear in his claws. However, an early sixteenth-century wall painting, now severely faded, at nearby Stratford-upon-Avon does show the entire scene; see Davidson, *The Guild Chapel Wall Paintings at Stratford-upon-Avon*, fig. 15. Music for the St. George pageantry was provided by an organ. This musical instrument was probably not a portative but a small positif played by one of the waits; see Remnant, "Musical Instruments in Early English Drama," 154–56.

3. THE RECEPTION OF PRINCE ARTHUR

4. þe p*r*iory. Priory Church of St. Mary (Cathedral), destroyed at the Reformation.

6–7. Sponstrete ȝate garnysshed with the ix worthy. For Prince Arthur's entry into Coventry, the Nine Worthies were shown on Spon Gate, but, unlike in the entry of Queen Margaret in 1456, only King Arthur among them has a speech. The choice of Arthur is of course logical because he is the one for whom the prince has been named.

16. Pallas. Probably Pallas Athena, representing wisdom.

21. your*e* chambr*e*. See commentary on the Reception of Queen Margaret, l. 70. The welcome to Coventry as the "prince's chamber" will be repeated at ll. 38 and 64 by Fortune and St. George.

22. Croschepyng before Mr Thru*m*ptons durr*e*. Mr. Thrumpton may be John Thrumpton, a mercer, who had been mayor in 1472 (see Sharp, *Dissertation*, 77, citing accounts of the Trinity Guild that are now lost; *REED: Coventry*, 582).

23–24. þe Barkers paiant well appareld . . . virgyns. The Barkers' pageant wagon, but set out for the display of Fortune and other "virgyns" without specifying musicians. The word 'paiant' here does not necessarily signify the subject matter of the Barkers' play. On the other hand, the Mercers' pageant wagon which "Gallantly trimed stood in the Cross Cheaping" at Princess Mary's entry in 1526 (*REED: Coventry*, 125) may have had a connection with the subject matter of their play.

25. Dame Fortune, quene. Fortuna, Lady Luck who has two faces, commonly depicted turning the wheel of fortune. She is normally invoked in connection with people in high places, or aspiring to high places. High place on Fortune's wheel is, of course, impermanent, for in the iconography the aspirant, even the one who is successful, is doomed in the end to fall.

27. Cesar, Hecto*ur*, and Fabius. Julius Caesar, Hector, and possibly Fabius Maximus (fl. 121 B.C.), famous for a Roman victory in Gaul. These and the others listed in the next two lines are Nine Worthies, but the list differs from those in the entry for Queen Margaret. The names in fact may be arbitrary and designed merely to give the impression of famous figures from classical antiquity. For the association of the Worthies with Fortune, see the commentary above on the Reception of Queen Margaret, ll. 62–63.

28. Scipio, exalted Nausica, *and* Emilianus. Scipio Africanus Major, conqueror of Hannibal; Publius Cornelius Scipio Nasica Serapio, consul and leader of a rebellion by the mob in Rome; Publius Cornelius Scipio Aemilianus Africanus Numantinus, grandson of Scipio Africanus Major.

29. Valerius, also Marchus, with sapient Cicero. The first two in this list are possibly Varius Maximus and Marcus Aurelius; Marcus Tullius Cicero is the famous orator.

34–35. trust me intiere . . . enduryng The promise is out of keeping with Fortune's character.

36. nowe reynyng. Those who reign are positioned at the top of Fortune's wheel, which is inherently unstable. But Fortune here promises stability. See the woodcut in Hawes's *The Example of Vertu* (Chew, *Pilgrimage of Life*, fig. 62) which shows blindfolded Fortune poised on her wheel and holding a sail that represents the conquering of the winds of chance for the Nine Worthies who stand by on each side.

39–41. And the Crosse . . . other*e* melody. Again there is wine running from pipes at the Cross in Cross Cheaping, and as in the entry for Queen Margaret a generation before angels are swinging thuribles with incense. On this occasion specific mention is made of singing and organ playing as well as "other*e* melody." The "9 orders of Angells" at Jordan Well for the entry of Henry VIII and

Catherine of Aragon in 1511 (*REED: Coventry*, 107) may have been a refashioning of this scene at a different location.

42. at þe Cundyt. The conduit in Cross Cheaping. For the battle of St. George with the dragon—a scene repeated from the Receiving of Prince Edward in 1474—a platform seems to have been erected, if Sharp's citation (*Dissertation*, 156) of Chamberlains' accounts drafted in 1499 are an indication:

> It*em* pa*i*d for settyng of the posts in þe Croschepyng when þe kyng [i.e., prince] was here, in gret ij[s]
> It*em* for takyng down of þe same posts ageyn x[d]
> It*em* for pavyng in þe Cros Chepyng ther as þe posts stode, of viij yards viij[d]

45. ruler of cruell Mars. Apparently a reference to the peace which has been brought to England by the house of Tudor.

47. George, yo*ur* patron*n*. St. George as the patron saint of England.

51. magnyficence. Kingly virtue, which here seems to be understood as a joining together in perfection of all other virtues and the expression of generosity. Its result is honor, as for Aristotle (*Nicomachian Ethics* 4.3). Chaucer in his Parson's Tale (735) defines magnificence as "whan a man dooth and parfourmeth grete werkes of goodnesse" (*The Riverside Chaucer*, gen. ed. Larry Benson [Boston: Houghton Mifflin, 1987], 313).

58. þis lady be grace I defended. The Princess Cleodolinda's presence in the scene, which had been specified in the earlier Receiving of Prince Edward, is verified here as well.

65. balet. In this case, a lyric poem set to music with a refrain that differs for each stanza. It was sung at the Cross where previously the angel choir had been singing, so the same singers probably sang this ballet.

Select Bibliography

Manuscripts:

British Library, MS. Add. 43645. Annotated copy of Sharp's *Dissertation*.
Coventry Records Office, Acc. BA/e/f/37/1. Leet Book.
Coventry Records Office, Acc. 99/6/1. Drapers' Ordinance.
Coventry Records Office, Acc. 154 Drapers 12, 1c 1950/33.
Coventry Records Office, Acc. 15. Mercers' Account Book.
Coventry Records Office, Acc. 11/1. Weavers' Play (fifteenth-century fragments).
Coventry Records Office, Acc. 11/2. Weavers' Play.
Coventry Records Office, Acc. 34/1. Weavers' Record Book.
Coventry Records Office, Acc. 17/1. Weavers' Account Book.
Records of Early English Drama, University of Toronto. Ingram Papers.
Leuven, Stedelyk Museum, MS. Boonen.
Public Record Office, Prob. 11/19. Will of William Pysford.

Printed Works:

Anderson, M. D. *Drama and Imagery in English Medieval Churches*. Cambridge: Cambridge University Press, 1963.
__________. *The Imagery of British Churches*. London: John Murray, 1955.
Anglo, Sydney. *Spectacle, Pageantry, and Early Tudor Policy*, 2nd ed. Oxford: Clarendon Press, 1997.
Antiphonale Sarisburinese, ed. Walter Howard Frere. 6 vols. London: Plainsong and Mediaeval Music Society, 1901–24.
Apocryphal New Testament, The, ed. Montague Rhodes James. 1924; reprint Oxford: Clarendon Press, 1980.
Aston, Margaret. *England's Iconoclasts*, vol. 1. Oxford: Clarendon Press, 1988.
Baldwin, Elizabeth. "Some Suggested Emendations to *REED: Coventry*," *REED Newsletter* 16, no. 2 (1991): 8.
__________. "Who was the Mother of Death?" *Notes and Queries* 237 (1992): 157–58.

__________. "'The Worship of the Cyte and the Welthe of the Craft': The Cappers of Coventry and Their Involvement in Civic Drama 1494–1591." Ph.D. diss., University of Leeds, 1991.

Beadle, Richard, ed. *The Cambridge Companion to Medieval English Theatre*. Cambridge: Cambridge University Press, 1994.

Berger, Ronald M. *The Most Necessary Luxuries: The Mercers' Company of Coventry, 1550–1680.* University Park: Pennsylvania State University, 1993.

Biblia Pauperum, ed. Avril Henry. Ithaca: Cornell University Press, 1987.

Biblia Sacra iuxta Vulgatam Versionem, ed. Robert Weber, 3rd ed. Stuttgart: Deutsche Biblelgesellscaft, 1983.

Bolton, J. L. *The Medieval English Economy, 1150–1500*, 2nd ed. London: Dent, 1985.

Borenius, Tancred, and E. W. Tristram. *English Medieval Painting*. Florence: Pantheon-Casa Editrice, n.d.

Bridbury, A. R. "English Provincial Towns in the Later Middle Ages," *English Historial Review* 34, no. 1 (1981): 1–24.

Burbidge, F. Bliss. *Old Coventry and Lady Godiva*. Birmingham: Cornish, 1952.

Butterworth, Philip. *Theatre of Fire*. London: Society for Theatre Research, 1998.

Calendar of Close Rolls: Henry V. 5 vols. 1927–38.

Calendar of Papal Registers Relating to Great Britain and Ireland: Papal Letters, XII: *1458–1471*, ed. J. A. Tremlow. London: HMSO, 1933.

Carter, John. *Specimens of the Ancient Sculpture and Painting Now Remaining in the Kingdom*. 2 vols. London, 1780.

Cave, C. J. P. *Roof Bosses in Medieval Churches*. Cambridge: Cambridge University Press, 1948.

Cawley, A. C. "Middle English Metrical Versions of the Decalogue with Reference to the English Corpus Christi Cycles," *Leeds Studies in English* n.s. 8 (1975): 129–45.

__________, *et al. The Revels History of Drama in English: Medieval Drama*. London: Methuen, 1983.

Chambers, E. K. *The Mediaeval Stage*. 2 vols. London: Oxford University Press, 1903.

Chatwin, Philip B. "Medieval Stained Glass from the Cathedral, Coventry," *Transactions of the Birmingham Archaeological*

Association 66 (1950): 1–5.
Cheetham, Francis. *English Medieval Alabasters, with a Catalogue of the Collection in the Victoria and Albert Museum*. Oxford: Phaidon, Christie's, 1984.
Chester Mystery Cycle: A Reduced Facsimile of Huntington MS 2. Leeds Texts and Monographs, Medieval Drama Facsimiles. Leeds: University of Leeds, School of English, 1980.
Chester Mystery Cycle, The, ed. R. M. Lumiansky and David Mills. EETS, s.s. 3, 9. London: Oxford University Press, 1974–86.
Colthorpe, Marion. "Pageants before Queen Elizabeth I at Coventry in 1566," *Notes and Queries* 230 (1985), 458–60.
Cornell, Henrik. *The Iconography of the Nativity of Christ*. Uppsala Universitets Årsskrift. Uppsala, 1924.
Coventry Leet Book, The, ed. Mary Dormer Harris. EETS, o.s. 134–35, 138, 146. London: Kegan Paul, Trench, Trübner, 1907–13.
Craig, Hardin. *English Religious Drama*. Oxford: Clarendon Press, 1955.
__________, ed. *Two Coventry Corpus Christi Plays*, 2nd ed.. EETS, e.s. 87. London: Oxford University Press, 1957.
Cursor Mundi, ed. Richard Morris. EETS, o.s. 57, 59, 62, 68, 99, 101. London: Oxford University Press, 1874–93.
Davidson, Clifford. "Civic Drama for Corpus Christi at Coventry: Some Lost Plays." In *The Stage as Mirror*, ed. Alan E. Knight, pp. 145–64. Woodbridge: Boydell and Brewer, 1997.
__________. *From Creation to Doom: The York Cycle of Mystery Plays*. New York: AMS Press, 1984.
__________. *The Guild Chapel Wall Paintings at Stratford-upon-Avon*. New York: AMS Press, 1988.
__________. *Illustrations of the Stage and Acting in England to 1580*. Early Drama, Art, and Music, Monograph Series 16. Kalamazoo: Medieval Institute Publications, 1982.
__________. *On Tradition: Essays on the Use and Valuation of the Past*. New York: AMS Press, 1992.
__________. "Sacred Blood and the Medieval Stage," *Comparative Drama* 31 (1997): 436–58.
__________. *Technology, Guilds, and Early English Drama*. Early Drama, Art, and Music, Monograph Series 23. Kalamazoo: Medieval Institute Publications, 1996.
__________, ed. *The Iconography of Heaven*. Early Drama, Art, and Music, Monograph Series 21. Kalamazoo: Medieval In-

stitute Publications, 1994.

———— and Jennifer Alexander. *The Early Art of Coventry, Stratford-upon-Avon, Warwick and Lesser Sites in Warwickshire*. Early Drama, Art, and Music, Reference Series 4. Kalamazoo: Medieval Institute Publications, 1985.

———— and David E. O'Connor. *York Art: A Subject List of Extant and Lost Art*. Early Drama, Art, and Music, Reference Series 1. Kalamazoo: Medieval Institute Publications, 1978.

———— and Ann Eljenholm Nichols, eds. *The Iconography of Heaven*. Early Drama, Art, and Music, Monograph Series 11. Kalamazoo: Medieval Institute Publications, 1988.

———— and Thomas Seiler, eds. *The Iconography of Hell*. Early Drama, Art, and Music, Monograph Series 17. Kalamazoo: Medieval Institute Publications, 1992.

Deasy, C. Philip. *St. Joseph in the English Mystery Plays*. Washington, D.C.: Catholic University of America, 1937.

Duffy, Eamon. *The Stripping of the Altars: Traditional Religion in England, 1400–1580*. New Haven: Yale University Press, 1992.

Dugdale, William. *The Antiquities of Warwickshire*. London, 1656.

Dutka, JoAnna. *Music in the English Mystery Plays*. Early Drama, Art, and Music, Reference Series 2. Kalamazoo: Medieval Institute Publications, 1980.

Edwards, A. S. G. "Middle English *Pageant* 'Picture'," *Notes and Queries* 237 (1992): 25–26.

Evans, M. Blakemore. *The Passion Play of Lucerne*. New York: Modern Language Association, 1943.

Farmer, David Hugh. *The Oxford Dictionary of Saints*. Oxford: Clarendon Press, 1978.

Gibson, Gail McMurray. *The Theater of Devotion: East Anglian Drama and Society in the Late Middle Ages*. Chicago: University of Chicago Press, 1989.

Green, R. L. *The Early Christmas Carols*, 2nd ed. Oxford: Clarendon Press, 1977.

Greg, W. W. "Bibliographical and Textual Problems of the English Miracle Cycles: III.—Christ and the Doctors: Interrelations of the Cycles," *The Library*, 3rd ser. 5 (1914): 280–319.

————. *The Trial and Flagellation with Other Studies in the Chester Cycle*. Malone Society Studies. Oxford: Oxford University Press, 1935.

Halliwell-Phillips, J. O. *Illustrations of the Life of Shakespeare*, 9th ed. London: Longmans, Green, 1890.

Harris, Mary Dormer. "The Misericords of Coventry," *Transactions of the Birmingham Archaeological Society* 52 (1927): 246–66.

__________. *A Selection from the Pencil Drawings of Dr. Nathaniel Troughton*. London: Batsford, n.d.

__________. *The Story of Coventry*. London: Dent, 1911.

__________, ed. *The Register of the Guild of the Holy Trinity, St. Mary, St. John the Baptist, and St. Katherine of Coventry*. Dugdale Society, 13. London, 1935.

Hart, Charles J. "Old Chests," *Transactions of the Birmingham Archaeological Association* 20 (1895): 80.

Hildburgh, W. L. "English Alabaster Carvings as Records of the Medieval Religious Drama," *Archaeologia* 93 (1949): 51–102.

__________. "Iconographic Peculiarities in English Medieval Alabaster Carvings," *Folk-Lore* 44 (1933): 32–56, 123–50.

__________. "Note on Medieval English Representations of 'The Resurrection of Our Lord'," *Folk-Lore* 48 (1937): 95–98.

Holkham Bible Picture Book, The, ed. W. O. Hassall. London: Dropmore Press, 1954.

Holthausen, F. "Das Spiel der Weber von Coventry," *Anglia* 25 (1902): 209–50.

Holy Bible Translated from the Latin Vulgate, The (Douay-Rheims). Baltimore: John Murphy, 1914.

Hone, William. *Ancient Mysteries Described, Especially the English Miracle Plays*. London: William Hone, 1823.

Hoskins, W. G. "English Provincial Towns in the Early Sixteenth Century," *Transactions of the Royal Historical Society*, 5th ser. 6 (1956): 1–21.

Hulton, Mary H. M. *"Company and Fellowship": The Medieval Weavers of Coventry*. Dugdale Society, 31. Oxford, 1987.

C Mery Tales, A. London, 1526.

Hussey, S. S. "How Many Herods in the Middle English Drama?" *Neophilologus* 48 (1964): 252–59.

Ingram, R. W. "The Coventry Pageant Waggon," *Medieval English Theatre*, 2 (1980): 3–14.

__________. "Fifteen Seventy-Nine and the Decline of Civic Religious Drama in Coventry." In *The Elizabethan Theatre VIII*, ed. G. R. Hibbard, pp. 114–28. Port Credit, Ontario: P. D. Meany, 1982.

__________. "'Pleyng geire accustomed belongyng & necessarie':

Guild Records and Pageant Production at Coventry." In *Records of Early English Drama: Proceedings of the First Colloquium*, ed. JoAnna Dutka, pp. 60–100. Toronto: Records of Early English Drama, 1979.

__________. "'To find the players and all that longeth therto': Notes on the Production of Medieval Drama in Coventry." In *The Elizabethan Theatre V*, ed. G. R. Hibbard, pp. 17–44. Hamden, Conn.: Archon Books, 1975.

Ishii, Mikiko. "Joseph's Proverbs in the Coventry Plays," *Folk-Lore* 93 (1982): 47–60.

Jacobus de Voragine. *The Golden Legend*, trans. William Granger Ryan. 2 vols. Princeton: Princeton University Press, 1993.

James, Mervyn. "Ritual, Drama and Social Body in the Late Medieval English Town," *Past and Present* 98 (1983): 3–29.

Katzenellenbogen, Adolf. *Allegories of the Virtues and Vices in Mediaeval Art*, trans. Alan J. P. Crick. London: Warburg Institute, 1939.

Kendrick, A. F. "The Coventry Tapestry," *Burlington Magazine* 44 (1924): 83–89.

King, Pamela M. "Calendar and Text: Christ's Ministry in the York Plays and the Liturgy," *Medium Ævum* 67 (1998): 30–59.

__________. *Coventry Mystery Plays.* Coventry and County Heritage Series 22. Coventry: Coventry Branch Historical Society, 1997.

__________. "Faith, Reason and the Prophets' Dialogue in the Coventry Pageant of the Shearmen and Taylors." In *Drama and Philosophy*, ed. James Redmond, pp. 37–46. Themes in Drama 12. Cambridge: Cambridge University Press, 1990.

__________. "Corpus Christi, Valencia," *Medieval English Theatre* 15 (1993): 103–10.

__________. "The York and Coventry Mystery Cycles: A Comparative Model of Civic Response to Growth and Recession," *REED Newsletter* 22 (1997): 20–26.

Kipling, Gordon. *Enter the King: Theatre, Liturgy, and Ritual in the Medieval Civic Triumph.* Oxford: Oxford University Press, 1997.

Kline, Daniel T. "Structure, Characterization, and the New Community in Four Plays of Jesus and the Doctors," *Comparative Drama* 26 (1992–93): 344–57.

Kolve, V. A. *The Play Called Corpus Christi.* Stanford: Stanford

University Press, 1966.

Lancashire, Ian. *Dramatic Texts and Records of Britain: A Chronological Topography*. Toronto: University of Toronto Press, 1984.

Late Medieval Religious Plays of Bodleian MSS Digby 133 and E Museo 160, ed. Donald Baker, John L. Murphy, and Louis B. Hall, Jr. EETS, 283. Oxford: Oxford University Press, 1982.

Leach, A. F. "Some English Plays and Players." In *An English Miscellany Presented to Dr. Furnivall on the Occasion of His Seventy-Fifth Birthday*, pp. 205–34. Oxford: Clarendon Press, 1901.

Leland, John. *The Itinerary*, ed. Lucy Toulmin Smith. 5 vols. 1907; reprint Carbondale: Southern Illinois University Press, 1964.

Love, Nicholas. *Mirror of the Blessed Life of Jesus Christ*, ed. Michael G. Sargent. New York: Garland, 1992.

Luxton, Imogen. "The Lichfield Court Book: A Postscript," *Bulletin of the Institute of Historical Research* 44 (1971):

Mâle, Émile. *Religious Art in France*, trans. Marthiel Mathews. 3 vols. Bollingen Series, 90. Princeton: Princeton University Press, 1978–86.

Manly, John M., ed. *Specimens of the Pre-Shaksperean Drama*, 2 vols. Boston: Ginn, 1897.

May, Steven. "A Medieval Stage Property: The Spade," *Medieval English Theatre* 4 (1982): 77–92.

Meditations on the Life of Christ, trans. and ed. Isa Ragusa and Rosalie B. Green. Princeton: Princeton University Press, 1961.

Meredith, Peter, and John E. Tailby, eds. *The Staging of Religious Drama in Europe in the Later Middle Ages*. Early Drama, Art, and Music, Monograph Series 4. Kalamazoo: Medieval Institute Publications, 1983.

Middle English Sermons, ed. Woodburn O. Ross. EETS, o.s. 209. London: Oxford University Press, 1960.

Mills, David. *Recycling the Cycle: The City of Chester and Its Whitsun Plays*. Toronto: University of Toronto Press, 1998.

Mirk, John. *Festial*, ed. Theodor Erbe. EETS, e.s. 96. 1905; reprint Millwood, N.Y.: Kraus, 1987.

Mirour of Mans Saluacioune, The, ed. Avril Henry. Philadelphia: University of Pennsylvania Press, 1987.

Nelson, Alan H. *The Medieval English Stage*. Chicago: University of Chicago Press, 1974.

Non-Cycle Plays and Fragments, ed. Norman Davis. EETS, s.s. 1. London: Oxford University Press, 1970.

N-Town Play, The, ed. Stephen Spector. EETS, s.s. 11–12. Oxford: Oxford University Press, 1991.

Oosterwijk, Sophie. "Of Mops and Puppets: the Ambiguous Use of the Word 'Mop' in the Towneley Plays," *Notes and Queries*, 242 (1997): 169–71.

Owst, G. R. *Literature and Pulpit in Medieval England*, 2nd ed. Oxford: Basil Blackwell, 1966.

Oxford Dictionary of the Christian Church, The, ed. F. L. Cross; 2nd ed., ed. F. L. Cross and E. A. Livingstone. 1974; reprint Oxford: Oxford University Press, 1978.

Palliser, D. M. *Tudor York*. Oxford: Oxford University Press, 1979.

Pepysian Gospel Harmony, The, ed. Margery Goates. EETS, o.s. 157. London: Oxford University Press, 1922.

Pevsner, Nikolaus, and Alexandra Wedgwood. *Warwickshire*. 1966; reprint Harmondsworth: Penguin, 1974.

Phythian-Adams, Charles. "Ceremony and the Citizen: The Communal Year at Coventry 1450–1550." In *Crisis and Order in English Towns, 1500–1700*, ed. Peter Clark and Paul Slack, pp. 57–85. Toronto: University of Toronto Press, 1972.

———. *Desolation of a City: Coventry and the Urban Crisis of the Late Middle Ages*. Cambridge: Cambridge University Press, 1979.

Rastall, Richard. *The Heaven Singing: Music in Early English Religious Drama*. 2 vols. Cambridge: D. S. Brewer, 1996– .

Rastell, John. *Three Rastell Plays*, ed. Richard Axton. Cambridge: D. S. Brewer, 1979.

Rackham, Bernard. "The Glass Paintings of Coventry and Its Neighbourhood," *Walpole Society* 19 (1931): 89–110.

Records of Early English Drama: Chester, ed. Lawrence M. Clopper. Toronto: University of Toronto Press, 1979.

Records of Early English Drama: Coventry, ed. R. W. Ingram. Toronto: University of Toronto Press, 1981.

Records of Early English Drama: Norwich 1540–1642, ed. David Galloway. Toronto: University of Toronto Press, 1984.

Records of Early English Drama: York, ed. Alexandra F. Johnston and Margaret Rogerson. 2 vols. Toronto: University of Toronto Press, 1979.

Religious Lyrics of the XVth Century, ed. Carleton Brown. 1939; reprint Oxford: Clarendon Press, 1967.

Remnant, G. L. *A Catalogue of Misericords in Great Britain*. Oxford: Clarendon Press, 1969.

Remnant, Mary. "Musical Instruments in Early English Drama." In *Material Culture and Medieval Drama,* ed. Clifford Davidson, pp. 141–94. Kalamazoo: Medieval Institute Publications, 1999.

Rickert, Margaret. *The Reconstructed Carmelite Missal*. Chicago: University of Chicago Press, 1952.

Robinson, J. W. "The Late Medieval Cult of Jesus and the Mystery Plays," *PMLA* 80 (1965): 508–14?

__________. *Studies in Fifteenth-Century Stagecraft*. Early Drama, Art, and Music, Monograph Series 14. Kalamazoo: Medieval Institute Publications, 1991.

Rogerson, Margaret. "Casting the Coventry Weavers' Pageant," *Theatre Notebook* 48 (1994): 138–47.

__________. "The Coventry Corpus Christi Play: A 'Lost' Middle English Creed Play?" *Research Opportunities in Renaissance Drama* 36 (1977): 143–77.

Rushforth, Gordon McN. *Medieval Christian Imagery*. Oxford: Clarendon Press, 1936.

Schiller, Gertrud. *Iconography of Christian Art*, trans. Janet Seligman. 2 vols. Greenwich, Conn.: New York Graphic Society, 1971.

Scott, Kathleen. *Later Gothic Manuscripts, 1390–1490*, 2 vols., Survey of Manuscripts Illuminated in the British Isle. London: Harvey Miller, 1996.

Shakespeare, William. *The Riverside Shakespeare*, ed. G. Blakemore Evans. Boston: Houghton Mifflin, 1974.

Sharp, Thomas. *A Dissertation on the Pageants or Dramatic Mysteries Anciently Performed at Coventry*. 1825; facs. reprint, with foreword by A. C. Cawley, Wakefield: EP, 1973.

__________. *Illustrative Papers on the History and Antiquities of the City of Coventry*, ed. W. G. Fretton. Coventry, 1871.

__________, ed. *The Pageant of the Sheremen and Taylors*. Coventry: William Reader, 1817.

__________, ed. *The Presentation in the Temple: A Pageant, as Originally Represented by the Corporation of Weavers in Coventry*. Edinburgh: Abbotsford Club, 1836.

Sheingorn, Pamela. *The Easter Sepulchre in England*. Early Drama, Art, and Music, Reference Series 5. Kalamazoo: Medieval Institute Publications, 1987.

__________. "The Moment of the Resurrection in the Corpus Christi Plays," *Mediaevalia et Humanistica* n.s. 11 (1982): 111–29.

Shorr, Dorothy C. "The Iconographic Development of the Presentation in the Temple," *Art Bulletin* 28 (1946): 17–32.

Smith, Toulmin, ed. *English Gilds*, EETS, o.s. 40. London: N. Trübner, 1870.

Staines, David. "To Out-Herod Herod: The Development of a Dramatic Character," *Comparative Drama* 10 (1976): 29–53.

Stanzaic Life of Christ, A., ed. Frances A. Foster. EETS, o.s. 166. Oxford: Oxford University Press, 1926.

Strunk, Oliver, ed. *Source Readings in Music History*. New York: W. W. Norton, 1950.

Three Kings of Cologne, The, ed. C. Horstmann. EETS, o.s. 85. London: Trübner, 1886.

Thrupp, Sylvia. "The Gilds." In *Cambridge Economic History of Europe*, ed. W. M. Postan and H. J. Habakkuk, 3:230–80. Cambridge: Cambridge University Press, 1979.

Tilley, Morris Palmer. *A Dictionary of the Proverbs in England in the Sixteenth and Seventeenth Centuries*. Ann Arbor: University of Michigan Press, 1950.

Towneley Cycle: A Facsimile of Huntington MS 1. Leeds Texts and Monographs, Medieval Drama Facsimiles. Leeds: University of Leeds, School of English, 1976.

Towneley Plays, The, ed. Martin Stevens and A. C. Cawley. EETS, s.s. 13–14. Oxford: Oxford University Press, 1994.

Travis, Peter. *Dramatic Design in the Chester Cycle*. Chicago: University of Chicago Press, 1982.

Tretise of Miraclis Pleyinge, A, ed. Clifford Davidson. Early Drama, Art, and Music, Monograph Series, 19. Kalamazoo: Medieval Institute Publications, 1993.

Trexler, Richard C. *The Journey of the Magi: Meanings in History of a Christian Story*. Princeton: Princeton University Press, 1997.

Tristram, E. W. *English Wall Painting of the Fourteenth Century*, ed. Eileen Tristram. London: Routledge and Kegan Paul, 1955.

Twycross, Meg. "As the sun with his beams when he is most bright," *Medieval English Theatre* 12 (1990): 34–79.

__________. "The Flemish *Ommegang* and Its Pageant Cars," *Early*

English Theatre 2 (1980): 15–41.

__________ and Sarah Carpenter. "Masks in Medieval Mystery Plays," *Medieval English Theatre* 3 (1981): 7–44.

Underhill, Jacqueline Joan. "The Staging of Biblical Drama in Coventry 1390–1579." Unpublished Ph.D. diss. University of Toronto, 1995.

Victoria History of the County of Warwick, ed. W. B. Stephens. 8 vols. London: Oxford University Press, 1909–69.

Wayment, Hilary. *The Stained Glass of the Church of St. Mary, Fairford, Gloucestershire*. London: Society of Antiquaries, 1984.

Whiting, Bartlett Jere. *Proverbs in the Earlier English Drama*. 1938; reprint New York: Octagon Books, 1969.

__________. *Proverbs, Sentences, and Proverbial Phrases*. Cambridge: Harvard University Press, 1968.

Wickham, Glynne. *Early English Stages, 1300 to 1660*. 3 vols. London: 1959–81.

Wilson, Adrian, and Joyce Lancaster Wilson. *A Medieval Mirror: Speculum humanae salvationis, 1324–1500*. Berkeley and Los Angeles: University of California Press, 1984.

Withington, Robert. *English Pageantry*. 2 vols. Cambridge: Harvard University Press, 1918–20.

Woodforde, Christopher. *The Norwich School of Glass-Painting in the Fifteenth Century*. London: Oxford University Press, 1950.

Woolf, Rosemary. *The English Mystery Plays*. Berkeley and Los Angeles: University of California Press, 1972.

Wright, Stephen K. "'The Historie of King Edward the Fourth': A Chronicle Play on the Coventry Pageant Wagons," *Medieval and Renaissance Drama in England* 3 (1986): 69–81.

York Plays, The, ed. Richard Beadle. London: Edward Arnold, 1982.

Young, Karl. *The Drama of the Medieval Church*. 2 vols. Oxford: Clarendon Press, 1933.

Glossary

References to line numbers in the Shearmen and Taylors' pageant (*ST*), the Weavers' play (*W*), the Weavers' play fragments in Appendix I (*Wa* and *Wb*), and the documents in Appendix II (*1-Mar, 2-Ed, 3-Ar*) are provided except for common words that appear frequently and unambiguously. A great many of the words appear unfamiliar only because of the orthography of the texts. In alphabetizing the words in this glossary, the letter *y* is treated as *i* when it would so appear in the modern spelling of a word.

abaye, *ST* 610: *v.,* obey
Abell: Abel, son of Adam, killed by Cain
abey, *1-Mar* 85: *v.,* put in abeyance
aboode *W* 690: *v.,* awaited
abowe, *ST* 13, 51, 250, *W* 117, 479, 543: *prep.,* above
abull, *ST* 6: *adj.,* able
acold, *ST* 120: *see Commentary*
actis, *W* 1145: *n., pl.,* deeds
actoris, *W* 76, 950: *n., pl.,* authors
addull, *ST* 809: *adj.,* confused
adev, *ST* 621: adieu
afarmyth, *W* 24: affirms; afarmyng, *W* 37, 63: *pr.p.,* affirming
afecte, *W* 966: *n.,* effect
aferde, *ST* 758: *adj.,* afraid
agast, *ST* 141: *adj.,* surprised, frightened
age, *W* 892: *n.,* age; *W* 204, 422, 508, 596, 642, 1037: (old) age; *W* 1107: maturity
agen: *adv.,* again
agen *W* 484: *prep.,* against, contrary to
agrevos: *see* grevoise
ayen, *W* 845: *adv.,* again
albeyt: *conj.,* albeit
aleygence, leygence, *W* 867, 872: *n.,* allegiance
aleond, *ST* 473: *adj.,* alien, foreign
Allmyght, allmyghte, *ST* 46, 162, 547: *adj.,* almighty
allwey, allwe, *ST* 462, 463, *W* 247: *adv.,* always
alter, *W* 357: *n.,* altar

amacid, *ST* 49: *adj.*, bewildered
ambassage, *ST* 52, *W* 370: *n.,*mission, embassy, message bearing
amend, *ST* 341, *W* 715, 824, 1015; *v.*, rectify, make satisfaction; amendid, *ST* 266, *W* 675: *p.p.*, amended, restored
amens, *ST* 375: *n.*, satisfaction, amends
and, *ST* 277, *W* 1048: *conj.*, if
antem, *W* 800 *s.d.*: *n.,*anthem
antequete, *W* 1160: *n.*, antiquity
apere, appere, *W* 6, 113, 743, *Wb* 51: *v.*, appear; apperis, *Wb* 58: appears; apereth, *ST* 247, *W* 195, 1145: appears; aperid, *ST* 389, 600, *W* 18, 96: appeared
apere, *W* 989: *v.*, damage, impair
apon, apon*n*: *prep.*, upon
apply, *W* 569: *v.*, submit
apwyntyd, *W* 1177: *v.*, designated
arand, arrande, *W* 1034, 1044: *n.*, errand
araye, aray, *ST* 461, *W* 319, 357, 609: *n.*, attire
aryve, *ST* 472: *v.*, arrive
armony, *ST* 253, 488: *n.*, melodious music; *see Commentary note on* ST *253*
Aronis, *ST* 370: *gen.*, Aaron's
arre, *W* 941: *v.*, err
artyccull, *W* 853: *n.*, article, section of legal document
as, *ST* 411: *n.*, ass
asaye, *W* 698: *v.*, attempt
ase, asse: *adv.*, as
asayde, *W* 777: *v.*, tested
a seyde, *ST* 494: *v.*, ?they said
asposschall, *W* 1157: *adj.* especial
aspy, *ST* 366: *v.*, see (*i.e.*, understand)
astates, *2-Ed* 33: *n.*, *pl.,*estates
atorite, *W* 20: *n.*, authority
attendence, *W* 865: *n.*, attention
auaunce, *3-Ar* 11: *v.*, advance
augent, *ST* 540: *adj.*, high in status, noble
autors, *Wb* 15: *n.*, *pl.*, authors
avnteant, *W* 235: *adj.*, old
awe, *W* 880: *adv.*, away
awter, awtere, *W* 609, 692 *s.d.*, 800 *s.d.*: *n.*, altar
awter, *Wa* 40: *n.*, author; awturs, *W* 195: *pl.*, authors

axid, *W* 144: *v.*, asked

bad, *ST* 682, 771: *v.*, ordered
bayne, *ST* 581: *adj.*, willing, ready
bake, *ST* 125, *W* 100, 848: *n.*, back
bankett, *ST* 606: *v.*,feast; have a sumptuous banquet, implying entertainment
bare; *see* beyre
bassche, *ST* 588: *v.*, be abashed, disconcerted
be: *prep.*, by
beddyth; *see* bydithe
bedeman, *1-Mar* 32: *n.*, a person who prays
Bedlem, *ST* 156, 729, 766, 799, *W* 132: Bethlehem
beforne, *ST* 559: *prep.*, before
begyld, begylide, begild, begilde, begylid, *ST* 116–17, 127, 131, 329, 567: *v.*, beguiled, cheated
behovith, *ST* 653: *v.*, is needful for
beym*is*, *ST* 592: *n.*, *pl.*, beams
beyre, bare, *ST* 173, 370, 574, 786, 806, 825, *W* 100, 575, 985: *v.*, bear, carry; *W* 101: bore
beytyng, *W* 102: *pr.p.*, beating
belyff, *ST* 349: *n.*, belief, faith
be noo wysse, *ST* 366: in no manner
benynge, *1-Mar* 126: *adj.*, benign, without evil
berthur; *see* brethur
beseke, *ST* 383, *W* 197, 219, *Wb* 47: *v.*, pray, beseech; besekyng, *ST* 637: *pr.p.*, entreating
besemyng, *ST* 534: *pr.p.*, appearing
besse, *W* 895: *adj.*, busy
best, *W* 181, 973: *n.*, animal; bestis, *ST* 278: *pl.*, animals (the ox and the ass)
betake, *W* 1131: *v.*, entrust
beteyche, *ST* 91: *v.*, entrust, hand over
betocuns, betocunyth, *ST* 511, 535, 543: *v.*, signifies
betraye, *ST* 683: *n.*, betrayal
bewey, bwey, bweye, *W* 223, 649, 749, 895: *n.*, boy
byddyng, byddeng, *W* 465, 536, 619, 779, 958: *n.*, commandment
bydithe, beddyth, *W* 970, 974: *v.*, commands
byn, *ST* 100, 211, 837, *W* 223, 272, 746, 797, 1060, 1070, 1141: *p.p.*, been

byrrid, *ST* 676: *v.*, buried
byrryng, *W* 137: *pr.p.*, burying, burial
bysschope, *W* 647: *n.*, bishop, high priest
betyde, *W* 1166: *v.*, happen
birght, *1-Mar* 10: *n.*, birth
byttur, *W* 191, 1054: *adj.*, bitter
blake, *W* 487: *adj.*, black
blassum, *W* 397: *n.*, blossom
ble, *ST* 588: *n.*, complexion, color
blod, blode, *W* 241, 636, 682: *n.*, blood
bloo, *W* 547: *v.*, breathe, provide time to catch (one's) breath
bodde, bode, *ST* 83, *W* 295, 331: *n.* body
boke, *W* 995, 1191: *n.*, book; bokis, bokys, *W* 955, 964: *pl.*, books
bold, *W* 1106: *adj.*, forthright
bondon, *W* 720: *v.*, bound
bordyng, *W* 885: *pr.p.*, talking idly, jesting
bote, *W* 268, 1007, 1097: *n.*, compensation, reward
breyde; breyde on, *W* 955: spread out
bren, *ST* 725: *v.*, burn
brere, *W* 397: *n.*, briar
brethur, brether, bredur, berthur, *ST* 221, 229, 601, 663, 668, *W* 8, 998, 1163, 1170, *Wa* 8: *n.*, *pl.*, brothers
breuely, *3-Ar* 30: *adv.*, ?briefly
briddis, *W* 532: *n.*, *pl.*, birds; bridis, *W* 426: *gen.*, bird's
bryffly, *ST* 34: *adv.*, in a short time, very soon
brond, bronde, *ST* 441, 447: *n.*, blade, sword
buskis, *W* 576: *n.*, *pl.*, bushes
bwey, bweye; *see* beweye

Caldy, *W* 111: Chaldea
can, *ST* 664, *W* 796: *v.*, can do
cane, *W* 1041: *v.*, can, am able
care, *W* 1112: *n.*, care, despondency; caris, *ST* 632: *pl.*, cares, sorrows
carefull, *ST* 829: *adj.*, full of care, mournful
cawl, *W* 170, 415: *v.*, call, cry; cawlid, *W* 237: called
cawse, *W* 157, 161: *n.*, reason; cawsis, *W* 1168: *n.*, *pl.*, causes, in philosophical disputation
cawser, *ST* 826: *n.*, instigator
cawsid, *W* 61, 1053: *v.*, caused

charge, *W* 933: *n.,* account, value
cheff, *ST* 181, 453: *adj.,* principal
chere, *W* 8, 1116: *n.,* demeanor, mood
chevaldre, chewaldry, *ST* 794, 818: *n.,* chivalry
childur, chyldur, childr, chyldr, chyrdur: *n., pl.,* children; chyldurs, *W* 926, 933, 1018: *gen.*, children's
clarge, *W* 863, 898, 1001, 1144: *n.,* scholarship, wisdom in religious matters
cleyne, *ST* 137, 691: *adj.,* pure, innocent, undefiled
cleyne, *ST* 776 s.d., *W* 484, 808: *adv.* entirely
cleynist, *ST* 181: *adj.,* most innocent
clenes, *W* 672: *n.,* cleanness, innocence, purity
clensid, *ST* 691: *v.,* cleansed, purified
clere, *ST* 250: *adv.,* clear (musical term), in tune without vibrato
clere, *W* 863, 898, 1144: *adj.,* with certainty, definitely
clere, *ST* 327: *adj.,* innocent, not defiled
clere, *ST* 393: *adj.,* clear, not cloudy
coght, *W* 1018: *p.p.,* found, encountered
cold, *W* 417: *v.,* could
Colen, *2-Ed* 47: Cologne
comand, *ST* 576: *v.,* commend
comen, *W* 854: *adj.,* common, as in *common law*
comen, com*m*on, cu*m*on*n*, *ST* 290, 492, 497: *v.,* come (among us); comyn, *ST* 551: *p.p.* (has) come; cumyng, *ST* 306, 309: *pr.p.,* coming, arrival
comenalte, *W* 1178, *2-Ed* 3: *n.,* the common people
comenecacion, comenecacion*n*, *ST* 351, *W* 16, *Wa* 16: *n.,* communication, conveying
comford, *ST* 16, 136, *Wb* 12: *v.,* comfort
comford, *ST* 187, *W* 192: *n.,* comfort
con, *ST* 271, *W* 472: *v.,* can, know how to
conabull, *1-Mar* 70: *adj.,* suitable
condite, cundit, *1-Mar* 37, 63, 139, *2-Ed* 20, 21, 57, 60: *n.,* water conduit
conyng, *W* 362: *n.,* knowledge, ability, understanding
conyngle, *W* 945: *adv.,* shrewdly
conquorde, *ST* 606: *n.,* concord, harmony
conseyue, *1-Mar* 49: *v.,* perceive
consell, *W* 259, 1163: *n.,* counsel, advice
conte, *ST* 363: *v.,* count, reckon

contenev, *W* 230: *v.*, continue
contenvalle, *Wb* 54: *adv.*, continually
co*n*tenevance, *W* 221, *Wb* 48: *v.*, continuance, continuing for a long time
convenent, *W* 861: *adj.*, convenient
cost, *ST* 92, 520, 819, *W* 269: *n.*, coast, esp. border area; region
cost, *ST* 820: *v.*, cost
cost, *ST* 807, 820, *W* 1082: *n.*, expense
cownsayle, *W* 984: *v.*, give counsel (as in court)
cowrs, *W* 182: *n.*, custom, direction
crafte, *ST* 566: *n.*, skill, *here* implying deception
crawe, *W* 499: *v.*, demand
croke, *W* 1041: *v.*, bow
cruoft, *W* 1080: place
cum, cumyst: *v.*, come
cumyng; *see* comen
cumon*n*; *see* comen
cundeture, *W* 129: *n.*, conductor, guide
cundit; *see* condite
cuntre, cuntrey, *W* 104, 141: *n.*, country; cuntreyis, *W* 400: *pl.*, countries
cur, *Ar-3* 69: *n.*, heart, from coër
curse, *Wb* 2: *n.*, course
curtesse, *W* 1093: *n.*, politeness
custode, *W* 304, 870: *n.*, custody, guardianship

dalis, *ST* 531: *n.*, *pl.*, valleys, dales
dam, *ST* 130: *n.*, mother
darke, *ST* 347: *adj.*, obscure, ambiguous
date, *W* 108: *n.*, day
Davith, Davit, *ST* 258, *W* 70, 82, 923: David; Davithis, *ST* 290: *gen.*, David's
debarre, *W* 939: *v.*, deny, exclude
decryis, *W* 858: *n.*, *pl.*, decrees
decrest, *W* 976: *p.p.*, decreased
ded, *ST* 34, 132, 723, 751, *Wb* 10: *n.*, action, circumstance, thing performed; dedis, *ST* 835, *W* 448, 748: *pl.*, doings
ded, dede, *ST* 729, 732, 763: *adj.*, dead
deformacion, *W* 19: *n.*, formation
defuce, *ST* 314: *adj.*, confusing, obscure

degre, *W* 32, 79, 420, 869, 1109: *n.,* status
dey: *n.,* day; deyis: *pl.,* days
deyite, *ST* 345, *W* 149, 165: *n.,* deity
deynteȝ, *1-Mar* 91: *n.,* honor
deyth, deythe, *ST* 20, 559, 628, 633, 657, *W* 92, 189: *n.,* death
deme, *ST* 506: *v.,* deem, judge; demid, *ST* 20: judged
depe, *W* 194: *adj.,* profound
deputyd, *ST* 27: *adj.,* chosen, ordained
derevacion, *ST* 350: *n.,* source
desent, *ST* 467: *n.,* descent, heredity
deserne, *W* 888: *v.,* detect; desernyng, *W* 1158: *pr.p.*, perceiving
desyrith, *W* 730: *v.,* wishes; desyrid, *W* 247: *p.p.,* desired, wished for
desyre, *W* 287: *n.,* hope; desyris, *W* 673: *pl.,* desires, urgent hopes
deuer, *1-Mar* 58: *n.,* duty
dev, *ST* 352, *W* 219, *Wb* 47: *adj.,* due
device, *W* 84: *v.,* devise
devin, *Wa* 37: *adj.,* divine
devteis, *W* 615: *n., pl.,* duties
dy, *ST* 627, 740, 749, 753, 787: *v.,* die
dyght, *ST* 561, *W* 319, 387, 586: *adj.,* ready, prepared
dyngnete, *ST* 651, *W* 325: *n.,* dignity
discomforde, *ST* 80: *v.*, be distressed, upset
dissent, *2-Ed* 36: *n.,* descent
dyssepyssions, dysspecionis, *W* 862, 1151: *n., pl.* disputations
dysses, dysees, *ST* 47, *W* 474, 1138: *n.,* disease (of spirit), uneasiness
disseuer, *1-Mar* 57: *v.,* separate
distroid, *Wb* 9: *v.,* destroyed
dolar, *W* 1007: *n.,* sorrow
domeneon, *W* 33: *n.,* dominion, mastery
done, *W* 808 *s.d.*: *adv.,* down
doo, *ST* 762: *n.,* doe
doo: *v.,* do; doo, *W* 525: done
doghtur, *W* 67: *n.,* daughter
dowis, *W* 418, 504, 537: *n.., pl.,* doves
dowsemeris, *2-Ed* 22: *n.,* dulcimers
dowt, *ST* 735: *n.,* fear, anxiety; dowtis, dowts, *ST* 350, 353, *W* 1158: *pl.,* doubts
dowtelesse, *1-Mar* 36: *adv.,* without doubt

draith, *ST* 174, *W* 204: *v.*, draws; dravys, *Wb* 25: draws
drede, *W* 72, 331, 437, 582, 1078: *n.*, fear
dreyme, *ST* 679: *n.*, dream, vision
dresse, *ST* 167: *v.*, address, set off
drev, *ST* 390: *v.*, drew, beckoned
duffues, *W* 423: *n.*, *pl.*, doves
dull, *ST* 132: *adj.*, depressed, miserable
durre, *3-Ar* 22: *n.*, door
durst, *W* 1032: *v.*, dared
dwyllyng, *W* 67: *n.*, dwelling

E, *W* 857, 893: *exclamation*
egall, *3-Ar* 10: *adj.*, equal
Eybruys, *W* 873: Hebrews
eygull, *W* 101: *n.*, eagle
eylecte, *W* 114, 1146: *adj.*, chosen
eyquall, *W* 165: *adj.*, equal
eyre, yeyre, *W* 102, 126: *n.*, air
eyrly, *W* 744: *adv.*, soon
eyuer, eyuere: every
eyvedently, *W* 110: *adv.*, according to the evidence, demonstrably
eyvin, *ST* 102: *n.*, likeness, equal, peer
eyvin, evin, *ST* 332, 600, 615: *adv.*, even
eyvinly, *ST* 574: *adv.*, evenly, temperately (in appearance)
elis: *adj.*, else
em*m*per*e*all, *W* 178: *adj.*, imperial
endleles, *1-Mar* 151: *adj.*, eternal
enderes, *ST* Song I, 1: *adj.*, recently finished, last
en*n*myis, *ST* 455: *n.*, enemies
ernyst, *ST* 152: *n.*, seriousness
Erod, Erode, Eyrodde, Eroddis, Erood: Herod
es, *ST* 170, 614, *W* 475: *n.*, ease, leisure
espret, *Wa* 52, 55: *n.*, spirit
essele, *W* 548, 572, 764: *adv.*, easily
est, *ST* 227, 484: *n.*, east
expeydente, *W* 256: *adj.*, expedient
exposysionis, *W* 1153: *n.*, *pl.*, detailed explanations
exsort, *W* 168: *v.*, exhort
extollence, *3-Ar* 82: *n.*, lifting up of spirits

fadur, *W* 369, 479, 784: *n.,* father
fayne: *adj.,* glad
fayne, *ST* 762: *n.,* gladness
fayre, feyre: *adj.,* fair, attractive in appearance
farwachid, *ST* 665: *v.,* tired, weary (with lack of sleep, watching)
fassion, *ST* 461, *W* 18, 96, 225: *n.,* appearance, fashion
fathurs, *ST* 233: *n., pl.,* patriarchs
fawcun, *ST* 461: *n.,* falchion, curved single-edged sword
fawl, *W* 184: *n.,* fall (of Adam and Eve)
fawl, *W* 852: *v.,* fall; fawlyth, *W* 420: *v.,* falls, is ordained
fawls, *ST* 683, 723, 985: *adj.,* false
feyche, *W* 1027: *v.,* fetch
feymyne, *ST* 364: *n.,* female side
feynt, *W* 512: *n.,* faintness
feyre; *see* fayre
feyre, *ST* 822: *v.,* fear, anticipate
feyrear, *W* 722: *adj.,* fairer, more attractive
feyrefull, *ST* 445: *adj.,* frightening, inspiring terror, awesome
feyrist, *ST* 686: *adj.,* fairest, most attractive
feyth, *W* 94, 254: *n.,* faith, belief; *W* 749, 1039: truth
felyng, *W* 909: *n.,* perception, knowledge of something
fellois, *ST* 193, 204, 259: *n., pl.,* fellows, co-workers
fere, *ST* 587, 645: *n.,* company
festefawll, festefall, *W* 753, 803, 1181: *adj.,* festival, feast (day)
fet, *ST* 279: *v.,* bring, fetch
fyld, *ST* 232, 276: *n.,* field, open land
fyn, *W* 1033: *adj.,* fine, fittingly
fynd, *ST* 229 *s.d.,* 756: *v.,* discover
fyndis, *ST* 73: *n., gen.,* fiend's
fyst, *W* 1091: *n.,* fist
flagrant, *W* 99: *adj.,* radiant, burning
foys, *W* 716: *n., pl.,* foes
fold, *ST* 231, 387, Song I, 3: *n.,* a pen for animals, *here a* sheepfold
fold, *ST* 275: *v.,* clasp, hold (in arms)
folde, *ST* 392, *W* 315: times; M folde: a thousand times
fole, *ST* 122: *n.,* fool
foll all, *3-Ar* 83: fa la
fond, fonde, *ST* 210, 292, 295, 591, *W* 540, 1066: *v.,* found
foo, *W* 767, 1088: *n.,* enemy
fordo, *ST* 567, 730: *v.,* prevent, abort, destroy

forgeve, *ST* 154: *v.,* forgive
forme, *W* 183: *adj.,* former, first
forwere, *W* 515: *adj.,* very weary
fote, *W* 706: *n.,* foot
foteman, *W* 777: *n.,* one who walks
fotemanschipe, *W* 699: *n.,* ability to walk
fowle, *W* 181: *n.,* bird; fowlis, fowlys, *W* 478, 486, 509, 520, 528: *pl.,* birds
fowndatur, *W* 177: *n.,* creator, founder
fowndid, *W* 112: *v.,* established
fracis, *Wa* 5: *n., pl.,* phrases, details
fryght, *ST* 828: *adj.,* freighted, loaded
frynd, frind: friend; fryndis: *n., pl.,* friends
fryth, *ST* 276: *n.,* wooded area
froo: *prep.,* from
fructu*us*, fructuos, *W* 194, *Wb* 14: *adj.,* delightful
fruyssion, *W* 149, 713: *n.,* enjoyment
frute, *ST* 370, 744: *n.,* fruit
fure, *ST* 444: *n.,* fury, uncontrolled anger
furis, *W* 1033: *n., pl.,* furs
furth, *W* 765: *adv.,* forth, forward in time
furst, *W* 135: *n.,* first; *ST* 596, *W* 952, 958: *adj.,* first; *W* 904, 1046, 1072: *adv.,* first

gamboldyng, *ST* 571: *pr.p.,* gamboling, leaping, as in dancing
game, *ST* 152: *n.,* recreation, fun
gawdis, *W* 477: *n., pl.,* jests
gawe, *ST* 635, *W* 1152: *v.,* gave
geyre, *ST* 813: *n.,* equipment, *here* fighting gear
gentilis, *Wa* 34: *n., pl.,* gentiles
gere, *W* 574, 1123: *n.,* personal effects
geve, gewe, *ST* 248, *W* 147, 407, 865, 1115: *v.,* give; *ST* 711: may (he) give; geven*us*, gevin, *ST* 3, 5: gave
gyde, gyd, gide, *ST* 92, 685, *W* 388, *Wb* 46: *v.,* lead, guide; gydid, *ST* 590: guided, led; gydyng, *ST* 659: *pr.p.,* guiding
gyde, gyd, *ST* 532, *W* 266, 392, 399: *n.,* guide
gysse, gyse, *ST* 362, *W* 432: *n.,* guise, manner
glade, *W* 540, 842, 875, 1066, 1073, 1108: *adj.,* happy
glade, *ST* 36, *W* 324: *v.,* make glad; gladyth, gladith, *W* 260, 314: makes glad

glede, *ST* 725: *n.,* (hot) fire, ember
gloreose, *ST* 31, 296, 505: *adj.,* glorious
goo: *v.,* go, walk
gorgis, *ST* 461, *W* 319: *adj.,* splendid, showy, magnificent
Gost, *see* Wholle Gost
gostely, gostle, *ST* 661, *Wb* 46: *adv.,* spiritually
gostly, *1-Mar* 27: *adj.,* spiritual
grace: *n.,* spiritual favor (from God)
gracis, *W* 71: *n., pl.,* graces, virtues
gradudis, *W* 1160: *n.,* graduates, persons possessing advanced degrees
grant: *v.,* grant, give
grante, *ST* 618: *n.,* grant, decree, conferring something by a formal act
greyne, *ST* 10, *W* 70: *n.,* grain
grett: *adj.,* great
greve, grewe, *ST* 152, *W* 345: *v.,* grieve
grevoise, *W* 190: *adj.,* oppressive; agrevos, *Wb* 4: a grievous, debilitating
grondid, *W* 641: *v.,* grounded
groue, *ST* 171: *v.,* grow

ham, *ST* 763: *pron.,* them
handemayde, *ST* 85: *n.,* attendant
har, *W* 951: *adj.,* higher
har apon you, *ST* 747: ?out upon you
hard, *ST* 251, 420, 679, 816, *W* 104, 928: *v.,* heard
hardely, *ST* 397, *W* 437, 489, 773: *adv.,* with difficulty
hareode, harrode, *ST* 471, 554: *n.,* messenger, herald
harie, *ST* 591: *n.,* distress
hartele, *ST*: *adv.,* heartily
hasse, *W* 362: *v.,* has
hast, *W* 357, 387: *v.,* hasten
hawe, *ST* 369: *v.,* have
heddur, hether, hidder, hiddur, hydder: *ST* 51, 218, 268, 659, *W* 370, 395, 800, 1024: *adv.,* hither
hede, *ST* 566: *v.,* act carefully; take hede, *W* 996: take heed
heggis, *W* 514: *n., pl.,* hedges

heyve, *W* 1008: *adj.,* heavy
heyvin, heyvin*n*, hevin, hevyn, hyvyn: *n.,* heaven; heyvin, *ST* 311: *gen.,* heaven's; heyvynis, *W* 1114, *gen.*, heaven's
heyvinly, *ST* 323, *W* 42, 664, 714: *adj.,* heavenly
hendly, *1-Mar* 78: *adv.*, courteously
hent, *ST* 789: *v.,* seize
here, *ST* 205, 253, 264, *W* 75, 323, *Wa* 36, *1-Mar* 153: *v.,* hear; heryng, *ST* 314, 319: *pr.p.,* hearing
hestes, *W* 425: *n.,* commands
hy, *ST* 198: *pron.,* I
hi, hy: *adj.,* high
hy, *ST* 287, 560, 843: *v.*, hie, go quickly; *ST* 582: let us hurry
hyde, *W* 902: *p.p.,* hidden
hidder, *see* heddur
hyght, *ST* 68: *n.,* high place
hyist, *W* 1151: *adj.,* highest
hyl, *Wb* 60: *adj.,* high
hylist, *ST* 464: *adj.,* highest, most mighty
hynd, *ST* 283, 309: *adj.,* courteous, gracious, humble
hyndly, *ST* 176: *adv.,* graciously, kindly
hyng, hynge, *W* 644, 966: *v.*, depend
hir, hyr, *ST* 592, *Wb* 30: *pron.,* her
hit, hyt, hytt: *pron.,* it
hole, *3-Ar* 21, 69: *adj.,* whole
hond, honde, *W* 308, 521, 539, 631, 694, 706, 851: *n.,* hand; hondis, *W* 657: *pl.,* hands
honowre, hoonowre, oonowre, *ST* 717, 721, *W* 147, 358, 623: *n.,* honor
honowre, onowre, oonowre, *ST* 296, *W* 320, 339, 975: *v.,* honor
hoole, *W* 688: *adj.,* whole
hoope, *W* 250, *Wb* 60: *n.,* hope, expectation
howse, *ST* 358: *n.,* dynasty
hus, huse: *pron.,* us
husebond: *n.,* husband

yche, *W* 435: I
yche one, *ST* 130: each one
iee, nynee, *ST* 109, 456: *n.,* eye; *n., pl.,* jis, yis, *W* 467, 1057: eyes
ihit, yhit, *1-Mar* 112, 120, 135: *conj.,* yet
inbesyllete, *Wb* 38: *n.,* imbecility, stupidity

incresse, incres, *ST* 8, *W* 94, 602: *v.*, increase
inded, *ST* 371: *adv.*, indeed
indyfferentle, *W* 1177: *adv.*, arbitrarily
yngorance, *W* 87: *n.*, ignorance
innevmerabull, *ST* 450: *adj.*, unnumbered, infinite, innumerable
insampull, *ST* 126: *n.*, sign, example
insev, *W* 965: *v.*, follow
intiere, *3-Ar* 34: *adv.*, entirely
intreyte, *W* 1097: *v.*, entreat, beg
intrythe, *W* 176 *s.d.*: *v.*, enters
Isaee, Isae, Izae, *W* 40, *Wa* 41, *Wb* 16: Isaiah
yvill, *W* 510: *n.*, evil

Jaramo, *W* 68: Jeremiah
jesen, jeseyne, *ST* 644 *s.d.*: *n.*, childbed
jonyd, *ST* 337: *v.*, joined
jubbard, *W* 431: *v.*, jeopard, to court danger
Jubytor: Jupitor
Juda: Judea, land of
Jugementes, jugementis, *W* 74, 243: *n.*, *pl.*, judgments

katyffis, *ST* 485: *n.*, *pl.*, caitiffs, prisoners, miserable persons
kneis, *W* 354: *n.*, *pl.*, knees
keysar, *ST* 631: *n.*, caesar
kerne, *ST* 729: *n.*, rascal
kynde, *2-Ed* 56: *n.*, kin
knev, *ST* 63: *v.*, knew (in sexual sense)
knytt, *ST* 88: *v.*, tied, joined
kno: *v.*, know; knois, knoist: knows; knone: *p.p.*, known

lade, *ST* 45, 53, 74, 75, 90, *W* 371, 379: *n.*, lady
lade, *W* 872: *v.*, taught, led
lafte; *see* leyve (*v.*)
lange, *W* 103: *n.*, language
large, *W* 931: *adv.*, freely
larn, *W* 886: *v.*, teach; larnyd, *W* 995: learned
larnyng, *W* 15, 194, *Wa* 15: *vbl.n .*, learning
las, *ST* 664: *adj.*, less
law, lawe, *W* 409, 935, 953: *n.*, law; lawis, *W* 290, 1144: *pl.*, laws
lawdacion, *ST* 248: *n.*, praise

lawde, *W* 54, 527: *v.,* praise; lawdyng, *W* 255: *pr.p.,* praising
lede, *ST* 734: *n.,* the land, country
leyche, *ST* 93: *n.,* physician, healer
leyde, *ST* 93, 176, *W* 483, 764, 770, 1140: *v.,* lead, maintain, teach
leyd, *W* 1008: *n.,* lead
leyde, *ST* 299, *W* 955: *v.,* laid
leygence; *see* aleygence
leygis, *ST* 168: *n., pl.,* leagues
leyuer, *W* 347, 568: *adv.,* rather
leyve, leve: *v.,* leave; lafte, lafft, *W* 823, *Wa* 53: *p.p.,* left
leyve, leve, *ST* 620, 707: *n.,* leave
Leyve, *W* 84: Levi
lenage, *ST* 75, 355, 360, *W* 89: *n.,* lineage, ancestry
lend, *ST* 180: *v.,* remain
lenger, *ST* 38, *W* 301, 333: *adj.,* longer
lengur, *ST* 839, *W* 515, 1167: *adv.,* longer
lent, *W* 878: *v.,* granted
lere, lern *W* 866, 894, 936, 992: *v.,* learn
lett, *W* 956: *v.,* forbear; let, *W* 930: *p.p.,* refrained
letter, *W* 29, *Wa* 30: *n.,* text
leve, *ST* 151: *v.,* live; levid, *W* 671, 1078: lived; levyng, *W* 1148: *pr.p.,* living
lybarte, *Wb* 58: *n.,* liberty
lyff, *ST* 657, *W* 60, 206, 213, 230, 566: *n.,* life; lyvis, *W* 1096: *n., pl.,* lives; lyvis, *W* 254: *gen.,* life's
lyggyd aloo, *W* 435: laid low
lyght, *W* 911: *v.,* entered, alighted
lyght, *ST* 571, *W* 1025: *adj.,* happy
lyghtar, *W* 315: *adj.,* happier
lyis, *ST* 30, 521: *v.,* lies (posture); lyist, *ST* 647: lies
lymys, *W* 729: *n., pl.,* limbs
lyne, *ST* 290, 359, 363, 377: *n.,* line, lineage
lysence, *W* 1101: *n.,* permission
lystun, *W* 850: *v.,* listen
lyttul, lyttull, *W* 127, 550, 652: *adj.,* little
loggyn, *ST* 299: *n.,* lodging, abode
lokid, *W* 250, 679: *v.,* looked
lolle, *ST* 776: *v.,* sooth with sounds
loyve, *W* 233: *n.,* love
loyuer; *see* louer

lond, londe, *ST* 147, 517: *n.,* land
loo, *ST* 146, *W* 79: *adj.,* low
loo: lo (*interjection*)
loo, looe, *ST* 201, 205, 218: *n.,* mound, hill
looly, *ST* 93: *adv.,* lowly, humbly
loovid, *ST* 242: *v.,* praised
losyngere, *ST* 805: *n.,* flattering liar, deceiver
louer, loyuer, *W* 226, 231: *n.,* loved one, lover
loute, *1-Mar* 135: *v.,* bow
loving, *W* 928: *pr.p.,* praising
lowe, *W* 336, 477, 596, 652, 847: *n.,* love
lufly, *1-Mar* 97: *adj.,* praiseworthy
lulla, lully, *ST* Song II: be quiet, hush
lust, *W* 459, 596, 847: *n.,* desire, pleasure

ma: *v.,* may
made, mayde, *ST* 24, 239, 513: *n.,* maid
maydinhod, *ST* 26: *n.,* maidenhead, virginity
mayre, meyre, meire, *ST* (colophon), *W* (colophon), *1-Mar* 158, 160, *2-Ed* 3: *n.,* mayor
make, *ST* 553: *v.,* intend
males, *ST* 447: *n.,* malice
mancion, *ST* 322, *W* 130, 714: *n.,* mansion, dwelling place
manyffecence, maugnefecens, maugnyffecens, *ST* 261, 637, 650 (cf. magneffecens, *W* 340): *n.,* magnificence, liberality, sumptuousness
marce: *n.,* mercy
m*ar*cefull, *ST* 39: *adj.,* merciful
mard, *ST* 727: *v.,* marred
Mare: (Virgin) Mary
mareage, *W* 646: *n.,* marriage
markis, *ST* 474: *n., pl.,* marks, monetary units of 160 pence each
marle, *W* 431: *adj.,* marl, a kind of loam
mast, *ST* 566, 830: *v.,* may
mayne; *see* myght nor mayne
meddis, *ST* 458: *n.,* middle
mede, *ST* 736: *n.,* reward, *probably in the sense of a* bribe; *W* 438: deserving, merit

medyll, *W* 1005: *v.,* interfere
meydin, meydyn, meydyn*n*, *ST* 29, 50, 137, 235, 286, *W* 367, 682: *n.,* maiden
meymorre, *W* 442: *n.,* memory
meyne, *ST* 693: *v.,* speak; *W* 941: signify
meyne, *W* 368: *adj.,* mean, musical term meaning middle part
meyre, meire; *see* mayre
meynes, *ST* 351: *n.,* means
meyte, *ST* 229 *s.d.*, 463: *n.,* food
mell, *W* 1032: *v.,* mix, mingle, have to do with
mellyflue, *1-Mar* 16: *adj.,* sweet
ment, *ST* 541: *v.,* bound, intending (to go); *ST* 523: *v.,* intended, foretold
merrettis, *W* 602: *v.,* merits
mesere, mezere, *ST* 4, 344, *Wb* 29: *n.,* misery
Messe, *ST* 378, *Wb* 50: Messiah
mete, *W* 629, 634 *s.d.*: *v.,* meet, encounter
meve, *ST* 37: *v.,* move, discuss
myche: much
myddis, *ST* 196, 241: *n.,* midst
might, *ST* 220: *n.,* power, ability
myght *ST* 466: *adj.,* mighty
myght nor mayne, *W* 936; myght and mayne, *W* 1075: strength, determination
mynde, *W* 444: *v.,* pay attention to, remember
myr, myre, *ST* 655, *W* 136: *n.,* myrrh
myrre, *ST* 33, 251, *W* 1116: *adj.,* merry
myrrele, myrrely, *W* 621, 633: *adv.,* merrily
mys, *W* 715: *n.,* imperfection, sin
mys, myse, *W* 402, 1125: *v.,* miss, lose; myst, *W* 1089: missed, lost
mysname, *ST* 150: *v.,* incorrectly identify
mystecawlly, *W* 916: *adv.,* mystically, as from the Godhead
mystere, *W* 76, 86, 887: *n.,* mystery, hidden aspects; mystereis, *W* 957: *pl.* mysteries
myte, *W* 652: *n.,* small thing, *here* a small child
moo, *W* 757, *3-Ar* 26: *adj.,* more
moche: much
mode, *ST* 727: *n.,* mood, state of feelings
moder, modur, modr: *n.,* mother
moght, mote, mot: *v.,* might, may

molde, *ST* 573: *n.,* earth, soil
mon, mon*n*, *ST* 33, 270, 342, *W* 791, 1187: *n.,* man, one
mone, *W* 179: *n.,* moon
mone, *W* 505: *v.,* moan
monyssion, *W* 1180: *n.,* summons
montens, *ST* 531: *n., pl.,* mountains
Mosees, *W* 990: Moses
mote, mot; *see* moght
mothe, *ST* 272: *n.,* mouth; mothis, *W* 926: *pl.,* mouths
move, *Wa* 32: *v.,* put forward; movid, *W* 139: moved, impelled
mowe, *1-Mar* 51, 122, *2-Ed* 16: *v.,* may
mvndall, *W* 186, *Wb* 6: *n.,* world

nar, *ST* 390, 641, *W* 550: *adj.,* nearer
narmys, *ST* 275, 777: *n., pl.,* arms
natevete, *ST* 320, 382, *W* 22, 282: *n.,* nativity, birth
naye, *ST* 237: *n.,* denial
nede, *ST* 374: *n.,* necessity; nedis, *W* 1134: *pl.,* necessities
nede: *v.,* need, require; nedith, *W* 893: require
nedis, nedys, *ST* 663, 770, 786, 832, *W* 449, 453, 553, 564, 799, 1134: *adv.,* necessarily
nedefully, *ST* 752: *adv.,* of necessity
nedly, nedely, *ST* 704, *W* 379, 419: *adv.,* necessarily
neybur, *W* 962: *n.,* neighbor; neyburis, *W* 983, 989: *gen.,* neighbor's
neowell, *ST* 424: *n.,* Noël, Christmas; *unconnected to* novellis (news)
neuerthelas, *ST* 331: *adv.,* nevertheless
nev, *W* 85, 447, 967: *adj.,* new
nevis, *ST* 267, 535, 604, *W* 4, 143, 323, 405, *Wa* 4: *n.,* news
nevly, *ST* 849 (collophon), *W* 1186 (collophon): *adv.,* newly
ny, *ST* 169, 240: *adv.,* nearly
nyll, *W* 565, 1086: *v.,* will not
nynee; *see* iee
nodur; *see* nothur
noght, *ST* 588, 790: *adj.,* not
noght, *ST* 646, 835: *n.,* nothing
noise, noyse, *ST* 264, *W* 590: *n.,* music
noyse, *ST* 444, *W* 298: *n.,* sound
nold, *W* 209: *adj.,* old
non, *W* 127: *pron.,* none

none, noone, *ST* 75, 745, 772, 837, *W* 677: *adj.,* own
no nothur, *ST* 342, *W* 1147: none other
nothur, nodur, *ST* 102, 405, 407, 799, *W* 964, 936, 1041, 1088, 1147: *adj.,* neither
novellis, *ST* 313, 315: *n., pl.,* tidings, news
nowelte, *ST* 384: *n.,* novelty, innovation

obeydentt, *W* 626: *adj.,* obedient
obles, *2-Ed* 44: *n., pl.,* unconsecrated hosts
obskevre, *ST* 328: *adj.,* hidden, not openly revealed, obscure
oddur, *W* 360: *n.,* odor, scent
odir, *Wb* 1: *adj.,* other
of, *W* 477: *adv.,* off
off: *prep.,* of
offece, *ST* 651: *n.,* official position
offece, offes, *W* 355, 608: *n.,* office, prayer service
offeryng, offerynge, *ST* 703, *W* 376, 411, 420, 537: *pr.p.,* offering, oblation
offur, *ST* 528, 652, 736, *W* 419, 636: *v.,* offer (gift); offurd, offurde, *ST* 710, *W* 133, 307, 712: made offering
olyue, *1-Mar* 130: *adj.,* ?alive
omage, *ST* 271, *W* 134: *n.,* homage
on, *ST* 370: *adj.,* one
ondefyld, *ST* 327: *adj.,* undefiled, pure
ondowtid, *ST* 357: *adv.,* surely, undoubtedly; ondowtedle, *Wb* 62: undoubtedly
one, *ST* 85, 338, 344, 369, 614, 624, *W* 178: *adj.,* own
onpossibull, *ST* 81, 346: *n.,* impossible
ons, *3-Ar* 10: *adv.,* once
onsundr, *ST* 441: *adv.,* asunder, apart
onwysely, *ST* 626: *adv.,* unwisely, injudiciously
onwyttely, *ST* 626: *adv.,* against good judgment, ignorantly
oone, *W* 653: *adj.,* own
oonowre; *see* honowre
oopun, *W* 140: *adv.,* openly, not in secret
oopunly, ooponnly *W* 142, 855, 877: *adv.,* openly, not in secret
or, *W* 459, 1090: *prep.,* ere, before
ordur, *W* 1026: *n.,* protocol
Orent, oreient, orrent, *ST* 452, *W* 3, *Wa* 3: *n.,* Orient, the East
othys, *W* 986: *n., pl.,* oaths

oure, owre, *W* 330, 599, 665, 689, 820: *n.,* hour
ovncion*n*, *W* 202: *n.,* healing medicine
ownowre; *see* honoure
owre: *adj.,* our

page, *W* 731: *n.,* boy
pales, *W* 185: *n.,* palace
pacence, *W* 150: *n.,* patience
paynym, *1-Mar* 118: *n.,* pagan
parence, *W* 183, *Wb* 3: *n., pl.,* parents
parrage, *ST* 357: *n.,* parentage, lineage, descent, rank
parties, *ST* 676: *n., pl.,* parts, regions
pase, *W* 755: *v.,* pass
paseporte, *ST* 615: *n.,* passport, *in modern terms, a* visa
pay, paye, *ST* 668, *W* 616: *n.,* satisfaction
pece, *1-Mar* 118: *n.,* peace
peysable, *W* 276: *adv.,* peaceably
peytission, *Wb* 43: petition
perdy, *W* 825: *interjection,* indeed
perdyssion, *ST* 340: *n.,* perdition, damnation
perell, peryll, *W* 852, 1028, 1035, 1165: *n.,* danger
perfett, *ST* 2: *adj.,* perfect, free from flaw
perfettly, perfettly: *ST* 345, *W* 302: *adv.,* perfectly
peryng, *ST* 536: *pr.p.,* appearing
pes, *ST* 613, *W* 203, 237, 600, 879, *Wb* 24: *n.,* peace
pyctore, *W* 225: *n.,* image
pyght, pyth, *W* 160, 318: *v.,* arranged, placed
pyle, *ST* 403: *n.,* small castle
pyne, *1-Mar* 87, 118: *n.,* pain, severe discomfort
pyrie, *ST* 213: *n.,* gust (of wind)
pytt, *ST* 307: *v.,* put
pytte, *ST* 795: *n.,* pity
place: *n.,* location; placis, *W* 903: *pl.,* locations
platt, *W* 940: *adv.,* plainly, bluntly
plece, *1-Mar* 44, 51, 122: *v.,* satisfy, please
pleysid, *ST* 191: *v.,* pleased; i.e., assisted
plyght, *W* 1172: *v.,* pledge, promise
plesaunce, *2-Ed* 7–8: *n.,* pleasure
polatike, *W* 863: *adj.,* judicious, sagacious
pra, p*r*ae, p*ra*ee, pray, praye, prey: *v.,* pray

preych, *W* 912: *v.*, preach, proclaim (the truth)
prese, *W* 1000: *v.*, praise; presid, *Wa* 55: praised; presyng, *ST* 401: *pr.p.*, praising
presseos, pressiose, *ST* 501, 548, *W* 225: *adj.*, precious, holy
presseoosely, *W* 318: *adv.*, preciously
pressession, *W* 634 *s.d.*: *n.*, procession
preve, *ST* 39, *W* 57, 386, 749, *Wa* 58: *v.*, prove
preve, *W* 386 *adj.*, privy, secret
prevy, *W* 140: *adv.*, secretly
prestheod, *ST* 651: *n.*, priesthood
prist, *W* 136: *n.*, priest; pristis, *W* 83, 136: *pl.*, priests
probacion, *ST* 352: *n.*, test
probate, *W* 109: *n.*, proof
produstacion, *W* 93: *n.*, protestation
profece, profeci, profisse, *ST* 377, 410, 730, *W* 5, 37, 51, *Wa* 5: *n.*, prophecy; profeciys, *ST* 236: *pl.* prophecies
profet, profeta, profett: prophet; profettis: *n.*, *pl.*, prophets
pronostefide, *W* 39: *v.*, predicted; pronostefying, *W* 17, *Wa* 17: *pr.p.*, predicting
provysssion, *ST* 660: *n.*, preparation
pwynt, *W* 1062: *n.*, point; pwyntis, *W* 891, 965: *n.*, *pl.*, points

quere, *ST* 251: *n.*, choir
quyke, *W* 1012: *adj.*, alive
quyte, quyt, *W* 438, 544: *v.*, repay

rage, *ST* 101: *v.*, engage in wanton behavior, have sexual intercourse (in this context)
rayvisschid, *W* 808: *p.p.*, carried away by force
rappis, *ST* 442: *n.*, *pl.*, blows
rawe, *ST* 726: *v.*, rave, cry out
rawe, *W* 890: *adj.*, not yet mature, unprepared
red, redde, *ST* 731, 768, 1006: *n.*, counsel, advice
redde, red, rede, *ST* 372, *W* 951, 957–59, 995: *v.*, read, recite, interpret
redde, *ST* 568, 612, *W* 607, 619, 631, 741, 778: *adj.*, ready
recownfort; *see* reycomforde
refeccion, *1-Mar* 120: *n.*, refreshment
refrayne, *W* 938: *v.*, hold back
regallete, *ST* 336: *n.*, royalty, kingship

reybukyng, *ST* 818: *pr. p.*, rebuking
reych, *W* 908: *v.*, reach
reycomforde, recom*m*ford, recownfort, *W* 280, 1077, *W Song II* 11: *v.*, give strength to, console; recomfordyng, *W* 67: *pr.p.*, consoling
reycompence, *W* 88: *n.*, recompense, reward
reyconid, *W* 728: *v.*, reckoned, calculated
reycownt, *ST* 450: *v.*, tell, narrate at length
reydemcion, *ST* 379, *W* 201, 644: *n.*, redemption
reydeme, *ST* 31, *W* 171: *v.*, redeem, re-purchase; reydemyd, *ST* 340: redeemed
reydowndid, *ST* 468: *adj.*, famous, honored
reydres, *ST* 660: *v.*, correct, bring to a right course
reygardid, *W* 1036: *p.p.*, looked upon
reygeon, *ST* 12: *n.*, region; regeons, reygeons, *ST* 465, 482: *pl.*, regions; reygend ryall, *ST* 322: region royal, i.e., heaven
reygur, *W* 978: *n.*, harshness, severity
reyhers, *W* 20: *v.*, repeat; reyherssid, *ST* 681: rehearsed, repeated
reyjoyse, *W* 300, 592: *v.*, rejoice
reyjurnyd, *W* 1175: *v.*, adjourned, postponed
reylacion, *W* 95: *n.*, relation, telling
reyles, reles, releysche, *ST* 6, *W* 201, 601, *Wb* 30: *v.*, release
reyleue, *Wb* 38: *v.*, give relief for
reymayne, *W* 188, 859: *v.*, remain
reymedy, remede, *ST* 23, *W* 450, 451, 481, 1045, *W* 1045: *n.*, remedy, solution
reymemburance, *W* 220: *n.*, memory
reymeve, *W* 347: *v.*, remove, take away
reyn, *1-Mar* 84: *n.*, reign
reyned, *1-Mar* 109: *v.*, reigned; reynynge, *3-Ar* 36: *pr.p.*, reigning
reynowne, *ST* 676: *n.*, distinction, fame
reypaste, *ST* 289: *n.*, repast, food and drink, meal
reypeyre; *see* repeyre
reypriff, *ST* 349: *n.*, reproof
reyquere, *W* 229: *v.*, require, need to
reyquest, *W* 275: *n.*, request
reysemelyng, *ST* 466: *pr.p.*, resembling, in the likeness of
reyseyve, *W* 311, 335, 584, 587, 600, 623, 654: *v.*, receive
reysid, *Wa* 44: *v.*, raised
reysoning, *ST* 353, *W* 891: *pr.p.*, reasoning, drawing of conclusions

reyspecte, *W* 3: *n.*, to give heed, observation
reystore, *W* 65, 683: *v.*, restore, bring back
reysun, *W* 285, 580, 593, 677, 888: *n.*, reason; reysons, reysunis, resonis, *W* 871, 908, 956: *n., pl.*, reasons
reyvelid, *Wb* 51: *v.*, revealed
reyuerence, *ST* 498, *W* 147: *n.*, reverence, devotion
reyuerent, *ST* 53, *W* 371: *adj.*, worthy of deep respect
reywarde, *ST* 661: *v.*, reward; reywardid, *ST* 421: rewarded
reme, *ST* 617, 819, *1-Mar* 15, 34, 55, 111, 116, *2-Ed* 64: *n.*, realm, kingdom
rent, *ST* 726: *v.*, rend, tear, pull things into pieces
repast, *ST* 226: *v.*, partake (of food)
repeyre, reypeyre, *ST* 415, 773, *W* 848: *v.*, go
repute, *W* 350: *v.*, value with regard to reputation
resite, *W* 59: *v.*, speak, recite
ryall, riall, *ST* 481, *W* 82, *1-Mar* 6, 49, 85: *adj.*, royal
rially, *1-Mar* 109: *adv.*, royally
right, *W* 222: *adj.*, true
rightwesenes, rightwessenes, *W* 74, 77, 80, 243: *n.*, righteousness
rysyng, *ST* 745–46: *n.*, rebellion
rote, *ST* 9, 495, *1-Mar* 17: *n.*, root

Sabatt dey, *W* 972: the Sabbath
sade, *W* 844: *adj.*, unhappy, depressed
saff, *ST* 775: *adv.*, safely
salme, *W* 923: *n.*, psalm
saluer, *W* 949: *n.*, healer
sapence, *W* 1103: *n.*, wisdom
sarpent, *ST* 5: *n.*, serpent, Satan
sarten, *ST* 140: *adv.*, certainly
sarve, *ST* 569: *v.*, serve
sarwand; *see* serwand
Saueower, Saweowre, *W* 335, 660: *n.*, Savior
saw, sawe, *ST* 40, 141, 193, 496, *W* 499: *v.*, save
schado, *ST* 67: *v.*, shadow, enwrap
schal: *v.*, shall
schamyde, *W* 1040: *p.p.*, shamed
schapp, *ST* 686: *n.*, shape, proportion
scharmen, *ST* 847: *n., pl.*, shearmen
sche, schee: *pron.*, she

schede, *ST* 375: *v.,* spill, shed
schent, *ST* 99: *v.,* dishonored, disgraced
schynith, *ST* 230: *v.,* shines; schone, *W* 124: shone
scho, schoo, *ST* 157, 317, 383, 598, *W* 110: *v.,* show; schode, *ST* 558, *W* 703: showed; schoide, *W* 968: *p.p.,* showed
schortun, *W* 819: *v.,* shorten
sclayne, slayne *ST* 756, 784, 831, *W* 856: *v.,* slain, killed
Sebbellam, *W* 196: Sibyl; Sebbellis, *Wb* 16: *pl.,* Sibyls
sede seylesteall, *ST* 323: throne of God
see, *W* 81, 178: *n.,* seat, throne
seed; make seed, *W* 69: *v.,* plant
sey, *ST* 833: *v.,* see
sey: *v.,* say; seyth: says; seyd, seyde: said
seyde, *W* 199: *adj.,* aforesaid
seylesteall; *see* selesteall
seycretly, *ST* 396: *adv.,* secretly, covertly
seycrette, *ST* 1: *n.,* secret, hidden thing; seycrettis, *W* 160: *pl.,* secrets
seying, *ST* 669: *vbl. n.,* saying, statement
seylesteall; *see* selesteall
seyne, *ST* 113, 414, *W* 216, 611, 810, 815, 944: *p.p.,* seen
seyse, *ST* 7, *W* 202, 241: *v.,* cease
seyth, *ST* 94 *s.d.*, *W* 365 *s.d.*: saith, says; seying, seyinge, seyng: *pr.p.,* saying
seithe, *ST* 1: *v.,* sees
Seythe, *ST* 21: Seth, son of Adam
seke, *W* 506, 1059: *v.,* search for, seek; sekyng, *W* 1006 *s.d.*: *pr.p.,* looking for, seeking
selesteall, seylesteall, *ST* 323, *W* 174, 176, 369: *adj.,* celestial
semys, semyth: *v.,* seems
semly, *ST* 408: *adv.,* seemly, pleasant
sendyght, *W* 292: *v.,* sent forth
sensyng, *2-Ed* 43, *3-Ar* 40: *pr.p.,* censing (using thuribles)
sertefy, *ST* 594: *v.,* verify
serten, sarten, *W* 812, 831, 897, 906: *adv.,* certainly
sertes, *W* 828: *adv.,* in truth
serveture, *W* 128: *n.,* servitor, one who provides assistance, attendant
serves, *W* 802: *n.,* service, rite

servis, serves, *W* 742, 780: *v.,* serves, attends upon
serwand, sarwande, *W* 227, 694, 973: *n.,* servant; sarvandis, *W* 670: *pl.,* servants
seth, *1-Mar* 147: *conj.,* since
sett, *W* 905: *v.,* sit; *W* 954, 1157: sitting; settys, *W* 291 *s.d.: sits; settyth, W* 907 *s.d.*: places; sett forward, *W* 581: set out; sett on side: *W* 1164: put aside
syence, *W* 193, 863: *n.,* knowledge
syn, *ST* 118, 123: *n.,* sin
syn, *ST* 596: *prep.* since
singnefis, *Wa* 28: *v.,* signifies; syngnefyith, singnefith, *ST* 257, *W* 27, *Wa* 22: signifies; syngnefyid, *W* 22: signified
syngnefocacion, *ST* 246: *n.,* sign, implying great significance
sircumstanse, *W* 289: *n.,* circumstance
systur, *W* 252, 622: *n.,* close female friend, not necessarily a blood relative
sith, syth, sythe: since
sytte, *W* 794, 837, 845: *n.,* city
skwyar, *ST* 803: *n.,* squire
sley, *ST* 790: *v.,* slay, kill; sleyis, *ST* 801: slays
sloo, *ST* 797, 842: *v.,* slay; slowe *1-Mar* 92, 110: slew
soche: such
socheonon, sochun, *W* 499, 928: such a one
sofferent, sufferent, suffrent, *W* 217, 259, 634, 660, *Wb* 45: *adj.,* supreme
sofferent, sufferent, *ST* 1, *W* 303: *n.,* sovereign, God, or one in charge; sufferen*n*tis, *ST* 28: *pl.,* persons of superior rank
solas, *W* 389: *n.,* solace, comfort
solam, solame, *W* 216, 294, 298, 303, 323, 590, 810, 815, *Wb* 44: *adj.,* sacred, associated with religious ceremony
solamyst, *W* 610: *adj.,* most sacred
solemnete, *ST* 265, *W* 217: *n.,* solemnity, *suggesting* ceremony
soll, *ST* 67: *n.,* soul; sollis, solis, *ST* 40, *Wb* 35: *pl.,* souls
sollamle, *W* 802: *adv.,* solemnly, *here referring to* ritual
solyssionys, *W* 1152: *n., pl.,* solutions
sond, sonde, *ST* 103, 490, *W* 708, 792, *2-Ed* 40: *n.,* message, messenger (from God)
sone, *ST* 223, 769, *W* 384, 827, 828: *adv.,* in the near future
sone beme, *1-Mar* 134: sun's beams
song, *ST* 399: *v.,* sang; *W* 803: sung

songe, *ST* 424: *n.,* song
soore, *W* 915, 943: *adv.,* with distress, seriously
sore, *W* 949: *n.,* wound or infection, here a metaphor signifying sin
sothe, *ST* 108, *W* 132: *n.,* truth
sownde, *ST* 669: *adj.,* safe, free from disease or injury
spede, *W* 309: *v.,* prosper
speyke, *ST* 579, 583, 799, *W* 416, 471, 1099: *v.,* speak; spekyth, *ST* 490 *s.d.*: speaks
spesschally, spesschalli, speschalle, *W* 12, 77, 138, *Wa* 12: *adv.,* especially, in particular
spere, *ST* 326, 394: *n.,* sphere
spreyd, *ST* 178: *v.,* spread
sprete, spret, *W* 51, *Wa* 23: *n.,* spirit
spretis, *ST* 48, *W* 300, 324, 808: *n., pl.,* spirits, which sustain life
spring, springe, spryng, *W* 26, 43, 60, 71, 687, *Wa* 27: *v.,* rise up
spy, *W* 417, 493: *v.,* see
stall, *W* 82: *n.,* place (in a position of rank)
stare, *ST* 536, *W* 125, 128: *n.,* star; staris, *W* 179: *pl.,* stars
stede, styde, *ST* 796, *W* 1010: *n.,* place
steyle, *W* 982: *v.,* steal; steyleth, *W* 808 *s.d.*: slips (away) unnoticed
steyre, *ST* 814: *v.,* stare, take notice of
styde; *see* stede
stynt, *W* 573: *v.,* stop
stond, *ST* 209, *W* 515: *v.,* stand
strangis, *W* 4, 48, *Wa* 4: *n., pl.,* novelties
streymis, *W* 98: *n., pl.,* streams
streyte, *W* 860: *adj.,* restrictive
stryff, strywe, *W* 568, 573: *n.,* strife, commotion
subscrybe, *W* 52, 594: *v.,* write; subscribyd, *W* 873, 953: written
subscryve, *ST* 360: *v.,* ascribe, concede, acknowledge
sufferent; *see* sofferent
suld, *ST* 110: *v.,* should
sun: *n.,* Son (of God)
sure, *W* 40: *adv.,* certainly
sureness, *W* 73, 236: *n.,* security
surs, suris, *ST* 588, *W* 333, 620, 893, 917, 919, 950: sirs
sute, *W* 349: *n.,* pleading
sweyre, *ST* 755: *v.,* swear; *W* 987: curse
swete, swette: *adj.,* sweet

tabulis, *W* 859: *n., pl.,* tables (of the Law)
tale, *W* 1046: *n.,* story; talis, *ST* 823, *W* 829, 884, 1063: *pl.,* matters, stories
tane, *W* 855: *p.p.,* taken, arrested
tarre, *W* 526, 557, 1081: *v.,* wait
tast, *ST* 845: *v.,* have experience of, explore
teyche, *ST* 612, *W* 910, 914: *v.,* teach
teyre, *W* 516: *v.,* tear
teyris, *W* 191, 1054: *n., pl.,* tears, weeping
tempull warde, *W* 850 *s.d.*: (into the) temple place
tent, *W* 884: *v.,* attend to
the, *W* 553: *v.,* thrive
the, þe: *pron.,* thee; *also* they
then, *W* 345, 397: *conj.,* than; Than all we, *W* 996: Than all of us
þer, there: *gen. pron.,* their
thyddur, theddur, *ST* 218, 287, *W* 383, 387, 1042: thither
thryd, *W* 137, 970: *n.,* third
throg, *ST* 473: *prep.,* through
tyde, *ST* 96, 177, 224: *n.,* space of time
till, tyll, *W* 121, 1079: *prep.,* to, unto
tyme, *Wb* 62: *n.,* time; tymis, *W* 153, 1137: *pl.,* times
tirrant, *3-Ar* 13: *n.,* tyrant
to, *W* 670, 968: *n.,* two
to, *W* 401, 418, 520, 528, 965: *adj.,* two
to, *W* 375, 886: *adv.,* too
tocun, *ST* 774: *n.,* sign; toccuns, *ST* 507: *pl.,* signs, landmarks
tocunyng, tokynyng, *ST* 649, *W* 137: *pr.p.,* signifying
togedr, togedur, togydr, togeddur, togethur: *adv.,* together
tong, tonge, *W* 593, 632, 895: *n.,* tongue
towchis, *W* 981: *v.,* has connection with; towchyng, *W* 29: *pr.p.,* referring to
towris, *ST* 407: *n.,* towers, fortified buildings
trayne, *ST* 138: *n.,* trickery, entrapment
trawthe, trewth, trowthe, trothe, *W* 472, 939, *W Song II* 12: *n.,* truth; trawthis, *ST* 352, *W* 997: *pl.,* truths
trawth, trawthe, *W* 452, 743: *n.,* loyalty
tre, *W* 171: *n.,* tree, cross
Trenete: Trinity (Father, Son, Holy Spirit)
tret, *ST* 106: *v.,* treat
trewth; *see* trawthe

trybus, *W* 107: *n.,* tribes
tryomfande, *ST* 464: *adj.,* triumphant, victorious
tryomfe, *ST* 605: *v.,* triumph, to engage in pomp, celebrate
trist, *1-Mar* 157: *v.,* trust
tro, troo, *ST* 99, 535, 829, *W* 506, 551, 948, 1099: *v.,* trust, believe
trone, *ST* 35, 58: *n.,* throne
truage, *ST* 474: *n.,* customs duties, tribute
truse, trusse, *ST* 122, *W* 574: *v.,* bind up, *possibly* pack up; *figurative* ?become shrunken (in status); *see also Commentary for note on* ST *122*
turtill, *ST* 69: turtle dove (term of endearment)
turtyll, *W* 418: *n.,* turtle dove; turtuls, turtullis, turtulis, *W* 374, 401, 419, 504: *pl.,* turtle doves
twynke, *ST* 456: *n.,* wink
tyraneos, *ST* 454: *adj.,* tyrannical

vmayne, *W* 180: *adj.,* human
vmanyte, vmanete, *ST* 339, *W* 166: *n.,* humanity
vmblee, *ST* 545: *adv.,* humbly
umellete, vmelete, vmelyte, vmyllete, *ST* 504, *W* 212, 311, *Wb* 33, 40, 45: *n.,* humility
ungcion, *Wb* 23: *n.,* uncion, medication
vpsoght, *ST* 754: *v.,* sought out
vthe, *W* 747, 787, 1150: *n.,* youth

vast, *W* 429: *v.,* lay waste
velany, *ST* 780: *n.,* villainy
velen, *ST* 727, 747: *adj.,* villainous
v*er*abull, *ST* 356: *adj.,* veritable, true, genuine
vere, verre, *ST* 446, 594, 597, *W* 550, 648, 892, 1171: *adj.,* very, actual
veyis, *ST* 530: *n., pl.,* ways
viage, *W* 440: *n.,* journey
viallis, *ST* 488: *n., pl.,* viols, bowed string instruments
vysedome, *ST* 323: *n.,* ?wisdom
voise, woise, *ST* 208, *W* 103: *n.,* voice

wace, *1-Mar* 154: *v.,* was

wache, *W* 115: *n.,* watch
wache, *W* 116: *v.,* watch; wachid, *ST* 231: watched; wachyng, *ST* 387: watching
waynis, *ST* 828: *n., pl.,* wains, wagons
wayte, *W* 338: *v.,* wait (on a person of superior status)
wale, *W* 186: *n.,* valley
Walys, *2-Ed* 2: Wales
warke, *ST* 328, 347: *n.,* work; warkis, *ST* 130, *W* 289: *pl.,* works, deeds
wasse, *W* 917: *v.,* existed
wast, *W* 1099: *adj.,* useless, a waste
wat, *ST* 665: *pron.,* what
waxith, *ST* 273, *W* 729: *v.,* grows more and more; waxun*n*, *W* 508: grown
weddur, *ST* 303, *W* 485, 1120: *n.,* weather
weddur; *see* whydder
wede, *ST* 713: *n.,* clothing
wedurs, *ST* 197: *n., pl.,* clouds
weykist, *W* 445: *adj.,* weakest
weyle, *W* 779: *n.,* sorrow
weyre, *W* 697, 1118: *v.,* were
weldith, *ST* 611: *v.,* controls, commands
wele, *1-Mar* 26: *n.,* welfare
wele, *ST* 115: *v.,* wail
well, *W* 1062: *n.,* in a satisfactory condition, happiness
wende, wynd, *ST* 182, 188, 312: *v.,* go
wene, *W* 463, 812: *v.,* think
wengance, *ST* 822: *n.,* vengeance
were, *ST* 219, *W* 575, 701, 797: *adj.* weary, tired
were, werre, werie, *W* 108, 510, 787: *adj.,* very
werely, *ST* 171: *adj.,* weary
wey: *n.,* way; weyis, *W* 998, 1136: *pl.,* ways
wheddur, whedar, *ST* 815, *W* 140, 487, 557, 565: *conj.,* whether
whydder, whyddur, *W* 217, 786: *adv.,* whither
wholle, whole, *ST* 167, *W* 38, 52, 68, 199, 205, 246, 253, 408, 639, *W* 857, *Wa* 39, 53: *adj.,* holy; wholle off wholleis, *W* 246: holy of holies
wholl, wholle, *W* 287, 408, 707, 901, 966: *adj.,* whole, intact
wholly, *W* 29: *adv.,* entirely
Wholle Gost, *ST* 66, 187, 677, *W* 911: Holy Spirit

wholIenes, wholines, *ST* 10, *W* 205, *Wb* 26: *n.,* holiness
whom, whome, *ST* 134, 603, 663, 674, 721, *W* 378, 557, 697, 806, 1029: *n.,* home
whomly, *W* 443: *adv.,* homely
whomwarde, *W* 816, 839: *adv.,* homeward
wyddurde, *ST* 785: *adj.,* withered, physically shrunken
wyde, *ST* 689: *adj.,* far apart, at such a distance (from each other)
wyde in worde, *W* 946: widely in the world
wyff: *n.,* wife; wyvis, *ST* 790, *W* 1137: *pl.,* wives
wyle, *W* 833: *v.,* allure
wynd; *see* wende
wynd, *W* 512: *n.,* breath
wyrke, *ST* 561, 761, 798: *v.,* work; wyrkyng, *ST* 348, *W* 159: *pr.p.,* working
wys, *ST* 282: *v.,* know; wyst, *ST* 217, *W* 53, 1090: knew
wyse; on this same wyse, *W* 59: in this same way
wysse; *see* be noo wysse
wytt, *ST* 65: *n.,* wit, intelligence
wodkoce, *W* 430: *n.,* woodcock
wode, *ST* 726, 812: *adj.,* mad, insane
woise; *see* voise
wol, woll: *v.,* would; wold, woldist: would, wouldest
wolde, *ST* 386: *n.,* hill
won, *ST* 302, 354, 359, 449, 456, *W* 207, 352, 379, 605, 767, 1174: one
wone, *W* 1114: *v.,* dwell
wonly, *W* 64: *adj.,* only; *W* 858: *adv.,* only
wonde, *ST* 5: *n.,* wound
wondurs, *ST* 837, *W* 907, 919: *n.,* wonders, miracles
wondurs, *ST* 105, *W* 1155: *adj.,* wondrous
wondursly, *ST* 776: *adv.,* wondrously, marvellously
wonys, wonis, wons, wonse, *ST* 790, *W* 435, 1091, *Wb* 20: once
woo, *W* 463, 779, 809, 813, 843, 1013, 1062, 1068, 1074: *n.,* sorrow
worethe, worthe, *ST* 130, 696, *W* 76, 224, 1043: *adj.,* worthy
worthist, *ST* 713: *adj.,* worthiest
wott, *ST* 159, *W* 1037: *v.,* know
wreyche, *ST* 821: *n.,* despicable thing, vile event
wreychis, wrychis, *ST* 628, 747, *W* 55: *n., pl.,* wretches, miserable persons, hapless individuals

wroght, wroghte, *ST* 480, 748, 752, 837: *v.*, carried out; *W* 584, 702, 784, 904: brought into being
wrothe, *ST* 705: *adj.*, angry, perverse
ws, *1-Mar* 51: *pron.*, us

yarthe, yorthe; *see* yerth
yate, ȝate, *1-Mar* 20, *2-Ed* 9, *3-Ar* 6: *n.*, gate
yeeis, *W* 283: *n.*, *pl.*, eyes
yevyng, *2-Ed* 6: *pr.p.*, giving
yeyre; *see* eyre
yend, yende, *W* 189, 254, 348, 501, 502, 1169, *1-Mar* 20, *3-Ar* 90: *n.*, end
yendide, *W* (collophon): *v.*, concluded
yerth, yerthe, yarthe, yorthe, *ST* 249, 446, *W* 79, 179: *n.*, earth
yewe, *Ar-3* 18, 35, 49, 81, 86: *pron.*, you
yong, yonge, *W* 464, 790, 886, 897, 924, 929, 944, 1156, 1161: *adj.*, young
yonglyng, *W* 892: *n.*, child, youngster